Teachers
of
Young
Children

Robert D. Hess
Stanford University

Doreen J. Croft
De Anza College

With the assistance of Anne Kirby

HOUGHTON MIFFLIN COMPANY • BOSTON

Atlanta • Dallas • Geneva, Illinois
Hopewell, New Jersey • Palo Alto • London

Teachers

of

Young

Children

Second Edition

Printed in the U.S.A.
Library of Congress Catalog Card Number: 74-11954
ISBN: 0-395-18711-7

To Karen and Colleen Croft

Jared, Alyssa, Devin, and Bradley Hess

Preface

This book is for and about teachers. The first edition was intended to serve their special needs; this one goes even further in its attempt to respond to the external reality and the inner life of a teacher who interacts with young children.

With the apparent diffusion of the family as the dominant and persuasive group in the world of the young child, the teacher's place expands in scope and importance. His and her significance to the total society is thus enhanced. The hand that rocks the cradle and rules the nation is now more often found in day care centers, nursery schools, and other places where teachers have been asked to help with nurturing and maternal roles.

We are more convinced than ever that the teacher is the focus of early education and day care as a societal activity—so much so that the new sections to this volume are predominantly oriented toward the problems and potential of teachers. Our remarks in the preface to the first edition still seem to the point —so much that we repeat them below.

The spotlight in early education is shifting from the child to the teacher. During the past decade of rapid change, children—especially those from low-income families—have held the center of the stage. This concentration upon the need to prepare children cognitively for school has produced a wealth of research results, new materials, innovative programs and new teaching techniques. There has probably been no period in the history of early education that has produced such an outpouring of new resources.

These new ideas and materials are effective only to the extent that they are properly used. The teacher is obviously the key person in the process. Without the teacher's touch and skill, the most sophisticated curriculum will be limp and boring. It is the philosophy and technique of the teacher that makes the difference.

This book is thus oriented toward the teacher. The complexity of early education demands more professionalism than ever before. The days of the nursery school teacher as a "glorified baby sitter" (if indeed they ever existed) have disappeared.

Working directly in classrooms with young children is only one of many roles to be played. There are other audiences which must be considered if a teacher's work with children is to be most effective: these include colleagues organized to exert influence upon the field through local, state and national associations, parents of the children in classes, and a community which wants to have a part in making decisions about the education of its children.

The teacher is often observed by researchers and evaluators, who with their reports and lectures, are often in a position to influence policy and availability of public funds. The nursery school teacher must know the competition—the corporation nursery schools, franchises, child development centers, "drop in" schools run by colleges, and mobile units which cover wide rural areas—and also keep up with the new programs and techniques recommended and implemented by colleagues and others.

Through it all the teacher's career must be considered. What are the implications of the new laws on gaining credentials, what's happening to salary levels, what new courses are being offered and how are the course credits needed for advancement made available?

And, always, there is the ultimate question—how can the teacher do a more effective job with the children in a class?

Although we refer to the teacher most often with the feminine pronoun, this is in no way intended to suggest that early childhood education cannot be an immensely rewarding profession for both sexes. The teacher entering the field of early education can look forward to an exciting and successful career if he or she is willing to take the time and get the training needed to become a real "pro." We hope this book will help with the first big step.

RDH
DJC

Palo Alto, California

Acknowledgments

This second version of the ideas we wanted to discuss with teachers is, like the first, a blending of the perspectives and contributions of many people. Because it draws from and builds on the earlier edition, many of the acknowledgments offered then are still relevant.

In the first edition, Anne Kirby helped work out ideas and gave much support and assistance with the original drafts of many chapters. Her phrases and her skill in presenting ideas to the reader in lively style still echo in this revision and although she was not directly involved, her influence and her warmth are still present and felt. Her husband, Robert Van Valkenburgh, continues to give advice and support. We acknowledge the help and encouragement of these two generous people.

Several people continue to give comments and to offer specific suggestions. Richard Mansfield, attorney-at-law in Palo Alto, and Dr. Birt Harvey, clinical professor of pediatrics at Stanford University, critiqued the appropriate sections in the chapter about crisis, and added technical information about law and health. Pam Sharpe, a graduate student at Stanford University, reviewed the chapter on the arts and offered useful comments and suggestions. Lillian Quirke and Deanna Bartels also reviewed the chapter on the arts and offered their perspectives. Some program descriptions on parent education were adapted by Louise Manning from a paper in press prepared by Barbara Goodson.

Romayne Ponleithner compiled the index and gave counsel on details of manuscript preparation and proofreading. The typing of revised material was done efficiently and promptly by Nora Koblos, often on short notice and always with good cheer. Fran O'Connell helped assemble chapters, send for permissions, and in other ways assisted in the manuscript preparation and correspondence.

Many others helped us orient our writing toward the perspectives of colleagues in early education. Directors of other programs and of nursery schools offered comments and told us how their staff responded to the materials we had prepared. Parents gave permission for the use of photographs of their children.

The photos, in part, represent the skill of Bob Overstreet and Mel Malinowski.

We are also in debt to Dorothy Hamlin, Director of the nursery school at De Anza College, and Ann Smith and Helen Pillsbury, staff members at Greenmeadow Nursery School, who continued to support our efforts, and the students in our classes, who responded (not always with applause) to some of the ideas and material in the new chapters. We were especially helped by the second-year students in the De Anza nursery school training program who made detailed comments about the material on self evaluation.

All of these people have made the book better than it would otherwise have been. This is to let them know that we will not forget their contributions.

Contents

Teachers of Young Children

Chapter 1 Early Education as a Career

The Motivation to Teach Young Children

Assume for a moment that you have recently been hired as a teacher of young children. It's your first day on the job. Although you don't know yet which of the children is LeRoy, David, Cordelia or Mary, you recall most of their names from a list given you. You're a bit anxious but nonetheless you feel prepared.

While the children enter the room you spend the first moments helping them take off and hang up their coats and sweaters and showing them where to get a drink, and where to wash their hands and go to the bathroom—in general, getting them used to their new surroundings. When the head teacher is called to the office you are left alone with the children. During the time she's gone:

Two boys begin to fight over a truck.
A thumb sucker stands rubbing his genitals.
One child starts crying, "Mama, Maamaa, Mamamamam, aaAAaa . . ." her sobs turning into gigantic hiccups.
The block builders create a dangerously high structure.
Arms outstretched, a boy zooms around the room with appropriate sound effects.

1

Two children sit passively on small chairs.
What will you do? First? Next?
Why?

There are many responses to these situations, some of them effective and constructive, some less useful and less likely to help you cope with the nursery school scene depicted above. Although a teacher is not often called upon to deal with so many minor crises all at once, he or she is frequently in the midst of situations that demand immediate action. The preschool classroom is a constantly changing, challenging scene.

As a teacher in such a classroom, you will have two major resources to draw on in dealing with incidents and in providing conditions in which young children can learn. One of these is your training—what you've been taught about the behavior of children, your knowledge about research and new developments in the field, and your mastery of techniques and procedures of the daily curriculum, including ways to stimulate enthusiasm, cool a fight, soothe hurt feelings, or get children to listen to a song, story, or lesson. The other resource is what you as an individual bring to your work. Although your training may be identical to that of another teacher, each of you will function quite differently because of dissimilarities in background, values, and attitudes. The unique way that you combine your personal experiences and your training will emerge, especially under stress. There will be times, perhaps more often than you expect, when the pressures of the situation will be such that you won't have time to recall what the textbook said or what a teaching supervisor did. You'll be on your own!

Why are you thinking of going into the field of early education? Your motivations reflect your experience and personality, and affect both your training and future success. Your reasons for wanting to become a teacher reveal something of the image you have of what being a teacher will mean and of the rewards and gratifications you will get from working with young children. What are your reasons? What will they mean on the job?

Perhaps you've been told, "You're certainly good with kids!" Or, you realize you enjoy children and are much more comfortable with them than with adults. Maybe you've read a news account similar to the one shown in Figure 1-1 and agree with the veteran's reasoning. However, there will be many days on the job when love for little children or idealism will not be enough. Your ingenuity and talents will be taxed to the utmost and nothing will seem to work; or the children may present no dif-

Figure 1-1

Vietnam Vet Chooses Career as Nursery School Teacher

Donald Ryerson, recently returned from two years in Vietnam, is the only male in a class of 31 students taking Education #110-A at Northern State College.

"Being with so many gals is really great," Ryerson conceded, "but it's not why I took the course." Then he explained that he had had a lot of time to think of the world situation while in Vietnam.

"It seemed to me that mankind's only salvation lies in young children," he said, "and I want to have something to do with them."

Ryerson estimated that it will take two to four years to complete his work for a standard teaching credential with specialization in early childhood education.

"It will be worth it," he said, "if it means I can help bring peace for the next generation."

ficulties, but the demands of teachers, parents, and administrators will be frustrating.

You may think of yourself as a teacher because you want to help children from low-income or minority groups get a better start in life. Perhaps you believe that what they need is the tender loving care and personal attention that you assume they haven't had. You may be surprised and hurt to discover that they are not as grateful as you had hoped, and that they don't all want to be like you and your friends. They and their families may have ideas that are quite different from yours about what to expect from school and from life, and you find you can't help.

Perhaps you are a housewife ready to extend your career beyond home and family by capitalizing on the experience you have had with your own children. You may find, however, that during years of child-rearing you have developed a unique style for dealing with children and that the varied demands of a preschool group call for a more flexible approach. Your style may be difficult to change—you may need to relearn rather than rely on familiar ways of handling children.

The expectations that brought you to this class are important and it is useful to try to recognize and examine them. They have provided the initial motivation for your training. They will be a source of satisfaction and occasionally of disappointment. This is the initial phase of your preparation, however, and with growing experience you may find that your ideas about early education will change and your motivations will be somewhat different than those you brought to this class.

The knowledge now available about children and about techniques of education make it possible to develop good, basic teaching skills. This does not mean that there is only one cluster of talents that make for effective teaching. Competence with young children involves a dynamic set of processes which go far beyond the question of whether your personal characteristics match a set of criteria on some "ideal teacher" list. Good teachers are successful in their own unique ways, combining ingenuity and experience with professional training.

Success in a program of early education is no more accidental than success in any field. Just as it is possible to learn to perform delicate surgery, or to defend clients in court, it is possible to learn skills and strategies that will help you deal effectively with young children. You will be competing in an increasingly complicated field. New programs, alternative methods of teaching, and knowledge about early education and growth and development of children have increased enormously because of the research and experience of the past few years. It will take hard work and serious study to become an effective professional, and a continuing effort is necessary to keep up with the field.

A real professional in early education is not merely a "glorified baby sitter." There is a body of knowledge and concepts and a range of skills to be mastered. The more professional you become, the more you can contribute to the field, and the more gratification you will get from your work. While it is important that you want to work with young children and feel a genuine warmth and attraction for them, this is not enough. The thing that counts most is willingness to learn both about yourself and your profession.

Social Relevance of Early Education
The Teacher's Impact Upon Society

The teacher of young children has a special place in our society which goes beyond that of the school or classroom. She has other audiences, and needs to recognize that her influence extends beyond her own class and school to the community and to the larger society. She also carries a responsibility to these more, sometimes unseen, distant audiences.

In a complex society with great diversity of tasks and roles, relatively few workers are trained and selected to represent the values and traditions of their communities to the young. Those who hold this role have a special place and their influence reaches far into the future. The teacher of young children is obviously in this group. Whether she wants to or not, she is part of an *influence system*—part of the socializing network of parents and parent substitutes.

As one who transmits values and skills to the young, the teacher is a key person in the maintenance of society. Political systems and other institutions of a nation are no more stable or reliable than socialization makes them. Unless young people have internalized the values, attitudes and beliefs of the dominant sector of adults in the society, it is unlikely that they will maintain the stability of the social community. Although in the past the responsibility for inculcation of values was the prerogative of the family, the teacher of young children now shares this responsibility whether she enjoys it or not.

Education During Times of Social Change

There are severe social cleavages in this country which raise new questions about the role of education. These lines of conflict and division are: *first,* between racial and ethnic groups, especially between whites and the third-world members of the society: *second,* between the poor and the middle-class groups; and *third,* between a generation which was encouraged to value achievement, growth, industrial development and expansion and a younger generation which, threatened by the consequences of war, overpopulation, pollution, and waste of natural resources, is reconsidering those values. In the midst of such profound conflict and change, it seems hardly appropriate to perpetuate patterns of behavior that have created these national crises. In such times the value of education to society lies in its capability to help prepare the young for the task of dealing with these new and emerging issues.

Today the teacher of young children has a social responsibility not presented to school or home in the past. She helps prepare children for life in a world of technology where rapid change is a common feature. She is asked to help even very young children select, interpret, and evaluate information from media virtually unknown to their fathers and mothers, grandfathers and grandmothers. Television, radio, movies, and pictorial journalism constantly bombard children with enormous amounts of information and stimuli. Children need to know how to select and deal with what they are seeing and hearing from these sources. What is real and what is unreal? Is the funeral of a King or a Kennedy the same or different from a funeral in a cartoon or movie? How is the killing and maiming witnessed in some of our more lurid gangster programs better or worse than historical documentaries of the everyday life of our soldiers in Vietnam, Korea, or World War II? If it's commendatory for a man to walk on the moon, what's wrong with a boy exploring a nearby creek or quarry?

The need to teach children to relate to the new technological features of their world, without suffering loss of their own humanity is only one of many important new areas of learning in a changing society. Perhaps even more critical is the need to teach children attitudes and techniques that will help them protect an environment from the consequences of an excessive number of people. In a sense, the education of the young now must include attitudes and skills for survival. While much of the learning about the functional relation of people to their environment comes during and after formal schooling, it is possible to begin to instill as early as preschool an awareness of the importance of protecting the environment from humanity.

Early Education as Social Opportunity

One area in which changes are taking place is the improved educational opportunities for the poor and the minority groups in the United States. Institutions involved in early education are assuming more of this responsibility than in the past. This has come about in part through a recognition that there is a need for educational improvement at all levels, and a conviction that schooling in early years will be particularly effective in increasing later opportunities for children from low-income homes. In effect, though not usually intentionally, this also implies a dissatisfaction with the family as the agent for early education of poor children. Some programs are designed to change parental behavior toward their children (see chapter 5). This seems to support the assumption that the family as a socializing agent, especially in poor communities, has not done as well as was expected, and a number of writers place the blame of early failure in school on the family.

There is a great deal of dissatisfaction and disagreement with this accusation, however, especially among ethnic groups who feel that such an attitude denigrates the cultural contributions that the family makes. Consequently, attempts are underway to develop programs that will recognize and utilize the resources of the various cultural backgrounds from which children come.

The widespread growth of compensatory educational programs represents a change in the responsibilities for socializing young children, and professionals in early educational settings are often involved. While the need for improving educational experience is evident, it should also be recognized that the school is taking on a role that is different in several basic ways from its traditional function.

Education as Intervention

Education, whether carried on by the family, the school, or some other agency, is intervention. It changes the lives of individuals. It is an attempt to help the child (no matter what his social stratum) to become a competent adult. Traditionally the school has supported the family in this molding process and their joint venture is intended to prepare the child to maintain the values of the society.

The process is much more complex than this, however, especially in eras of social change. Conditions have so altered educational needs that they have forced adults responsible for the training of young children to modify their values so that they are more suited to contemporary circumstances. Children are now being socialized for change. This means that the school no longer only supports the family's values and patterns of behavior. It also introduces new ideas and attitudes.

When a teacher attempts to teach traditional values, children are encouraged to develop into adults very much like their parents. When the teacher seeks to promote behavior different from that of the parents, society is faced with some profound implications.

Under these conditions, children will grow to be *unlike* their parents. They will acquire values and patterns of behavior not patterned after those of their own immediate communities.

One of the more obvious consequences is a competition that is created between family and school. Actually there is potential competition whenever someone other than the family works with preschool children. Because the teacher is responsible for working with quite young children, some barely out of infancy, she necessarily fulfills the role of mother as well as teacher. Helping a child with clothing, attending to toilet needs, providing comfort as well as band-aids and ointment when a child is physically hurt—these and many other highly personal attentions are now part of the teacher's daily relationship with the children, to whom she is also teaching cognitive and learning skills.

In many communities the goals of the teacher and those of the families she serves are likely to be compatible, especially when the teacher comes from a socio-economic background similar to that of the community. In some other situations, however, the teacher may have quite different views from those of the surrounding social environment. This may happen if she is from a different ethnic or social context, or if she feels that her ideas are superior to those of the children's families. In such instances, she may try to "unteach" certain patterns learned at home—social, linguistic, political—and provide experiences for the children which she believes they are not likely to get in their homes.

When she engages in such activities she assumes still another role—that of an "expert" who knows better than the parent what to do. Until quite recently, parents would not permit this, at least not insofar as teachers of young children were concerned. Personality development and morality training were primarily the responsibility of the family with, in some cases, an assist from the church. But rarely if ever were they left up to the school or the teacher. Even though this responsibility is seemingly relinquished when a child enters first grade, schools are still expected to support the basic values established by the family, while taking care not to tamper with them.

However, in any early education program the teacher necessarily will be transmitting values and attitudes at a highly critical time in the life of children. From this standpoint she may actually be in direct competition with the family. This will be especially true if there is a difference between what the family teaches and what she advocates. Even if the difference is not very marked, the teacher takes over a large part of the parent's role. In a federal or state program, she is, in effect, an agent of the government with the additional authority that this implies.

A program that places the parent in a subordinate position is likely to encourage either dependence on and compliance with the teacher and school or frustration and even rebellion. In a middle-class community parents often feel that they, too, are experts and if they disagree with the teacher, they can confront her. If they can't out-talk her, they can deal with the situation in other ways.

But parents in low-income areas, on the lowest rung of the socio-economic ladder, find it difficult to match the teacher's expertise and advantage in education, experience, and language. In a dozen ways, even without meaning to, the teacher can put them down. The impact of what the teacher does in her contact with the family can be significant.

The Teacher as
Community Adviser

Viewing the trend to educate children at ever younger ages, some people have voiced concern that the process is being turned over to the educational system in its present form. These people are not satisfied with what the schools are doing now at elementary and secondary levels. They dislike the idea of giving an educational system which they consider to have failed a chance to extend its influence by setting up a preschool program.

As more and more women join the work force, industry as well as government is becoming concerned with child care. Who will make administrative decisions? What programs will be offered? How will they be selected and tried out?

Schools are receiving large amounts of money and great authority to spend their own funds. Because early education is a new addition to many public schools, they will need assistance in making judgments in these areas. As a teacher you will have an important role in both the lives of young children and in the community.

Career Opportunities

Let us assume that you are strongly motivated to work with young children and are convinced you can develop the competence to be a positive influence on the children in the communities in which you may work. You have made the decision to teach. What are the opportunities for a career in this field?

Public Commitment to
Early Education

Within the last two decades a great deal of attention has been given the impact that early experience has upon the development of young children. As long ago as 1950, the White House Conference on Children approved of early education in the form of kindergarten and nursery schools as a "desirable supplement to home life," a recommendation repeated and expanded by the conference of 1970. But parents and school districts were relatively slow to translate these recommendations into schools, and job opportunities were scarce.

By 1960 the Educational Policies Commission of the National Education Association recommended that all children aged four or over have the opportunity to go to school at public expense. This recommendation has been slow in being realized. A decade and a half later, however, it is much closer to reality.

Perhaps the beginning of widespread governmental support for Head Start in 1965 was the landmark of change in early education. This national program, which was inspired by earlier efforts by private foundations, widened the base of preschool participation to low-income families, many of which had available only custodial child care arrangements, often of low quality because of lack of financial resources. The support of the federal government provided new personnel, new facilities, new materials and programs, and a dramatic increase in interest in early education in both poor and affluent communities.

The period following 1965 was one of rapid growth and change for the field of early education, with a dramatic increase in career opportunities as a result of the expansion of both research and innovative programs. Early learning and education acquired a degree of attraction, visibility, and salience for educators and behavioral scientists that had been unknown before.

This rise in interest was undoubtedly a consequence of the commitment at the national level to early education and especially to early education as a route to greater opportunity for children from poor and minority families. Large increases in federal funds for both experimental and operational purposes also intensified interest.

Rise in Preschool Enrollment

In 1972, there were more than 20 million children under six years of age in the United States. This is the group that represents the need and the potential demand for early educational and child care programs. Let's examine them more closely.

Q. Is this group growing in numbers?

A. Yes. By 1979 there will be roughly 30 percent more, or about 27 million children under six years of age.

Q. How many of these 27 million children are enrolled in preprimary programs?

A. In 1971 about 40 percent of the 3's, 4's, and 5's were in some kind of preprimary school program. The 3 to 5 group numbered about 10½ million; over 4 million of them enrolled in school.

Q. In what kinds of schools were they enrolled?

A. Most of them—about three-fourths—were in kindergarten. About 80 percent of 5's were in kindergarten or primary grades. One child in eight of 4-year olds was in kindergarten. About a million, mostly 3's and 4's, were in non-kindergarten schools.

Q. Does this include children in day care or custodial care arrangements?

A. No. These figures apply only to organized educational programs.

Q. How many additional children were in non-educational (child care and custodial) programs?

A. Including both licensed centers and unlicensed family daycare homes, there were about 1,400,000 more children in child care settings in 1970.

Q. Are there enough child care and early educational programs to meet the needs?

A. No. Almost a third of children under six (5.6 million in 1970) have mothers who work. A Westinghouse study (1970) estimates that less than 11 percent of the preschool children of working mothers are enrolled in child care centers. Most of the others are cared for in the child's own home by relatives. Five percent of all children under age 6 (about a million children) have no special arrangements for their care. Some are latch-key children; others stay where one of their parents, usually their mother, works.

Q. Why do mothers of young children work?

A. Mainly for financial reasons. Many are single. In 1971, about one-half of all working mothers with children under 6 were heads of households or had husbands with incomes below $7,000.

Table 1-1 *Kinds of schools using personnel trained in early childhood education*

Facility	Ages Served	Description
Day Care Center	2–16	Eligibility generally based on economic need. Hours usually from 7 a.m. to 6 p.m. Full time and part time staff. Older children provided "home base" when not in school.
Home Day Care	1–6	Program operated by women or men in their own homes, serving 1–5 children of pre-school age or after school care for older children. Licensed, must meet health and safety standards, financed by public and by private funds. A cluster of homes may be supervised by coordinator trained in early education.
Compensatory Programs	4–6	Summer and year-round programs supported by federal, state, and/or local funds. Provide schooling for children considered educationally disadvantaged. Half-day sessions with hot meals. Trained staff and aides who are usually from local area, volunteers and parent assistants.
Kindergarten	5–6	Program geared to needs of children prior to entering first grade. Some public, others private. Generally headed by credentialled teacher with assistants.
Laboratory/Demonstration School	2–5	Primarily intended to train teachers and used as a facility for research. Commonly located on a school campus. Student teachers from sponsoring institution of higher learning work under supervision of teachers from school faculty.
Nursery School	2½–5	Usually half-day sessions though many schools have programs both mornings and afternoons. Most often privately owned or financed as a cooperative. Some under adult education program for local school district. Head teacher usually credentialled and has assistants, aides and volunteers to help.
Parent Cooperative	2½–5	Formed by parents to provide program for children and instruction for themselves. Parents participate regularly along with trained teachers. Some night meetings with fathers and mothers.
Play School	2–6	Private facilities in homes, churches, and other locations where owners are licensed (in some states) to take children for supervised play in small groups. Can be half or whole day.

The Range of Early Educational Programs

The number and variety of programs for preschoolers are increasing. This means, of course, broader opportunities for employment. A brief description of some of the programs and a summary of their staff needs are given in Table 1-1.

In addition to those facilities provided for preschoolers, some communities provide centers with special facilities for children with specific physical or learning disabilities such as blindness, deafness, crippling, retardation, aphasia, and autism. Such centers are staffed by trained personnel although some also use volunteers and aides. These centers are both publicly and privately sponsored.

More and more child care facilities are being established by industry to serve the needs of their employees, especially by organizations that hire large numbers of women. They find that women who are relieved of the worry of providing adequate care for their children tend to be more reliable employees. At present, the care is often safekeeping and playtime interspersed with meals and rest periods. Gradually, perhaps, management will also become interested in offering educational experiences for young children.

Institutions such as hospitals and universities are beginning to provide care or facilities for children of both their professional and their service staffs. Their responsibility frequently extends from early infancy beyond preschool ages. Directors of these programs, like industrial leaders, are seeking help in designing environments and programs that are best for children. Such new and emerging institutions are particularly in need of professional advice and information.

In recent years the federal government has set up parent-child centers in various areas of the United States. Several states have established child care and early educational programs for preprimary children. Many of these programs require that parents be involved in the management of the center and also make it mandatory for supervisors and teachers to be trained in child growth and development.

Where Will You Work?

Where you decide to work may well be determined by the opportunities made available through funding and legislation. As more facilities are provided for young children, and as the need for trained personnel increases, you will want to examine the advantages and constraints of the program in which you choose to work. The information you will need is generally available from local boards of education, departments of social welfare, newspaper ads, and visits to schools and early education associations. If certification is required (as it most certainly will be if you decide to work within a public school system that has made provision for educating children at kindergarten and earlier), this information is available from hiring agencies and the school districts themselves.

You may gain some perspective on the importance of salary if you stop to answer these questions:

What am I likely to be doing ten years from now?
What do I *want* to be doing ten years from now?

Considered in these terms, a comparatively low-paying job for a year or two may provide just the experience needed for the kind of work you really want later on. Also, many jobs in-

1 Early Education as a Career

volving education of young children are especially satisfying in that they offer opportunities to serve society and bring about change. Most important, working with young children may be a start toward the realization of many of the hopes you have for a better world.

SUMMARY

Chapter I examines some of the motives people have for wanting to teach young children. Because of the increasing complexity of early education, the teacher must be a real "pro." The role of the teacher in today's complex society has far-reaching effects. She is faced with diverse challenges to prepare young children for life in a world where rapid change is a dominant feature. Schools now have more responsibility for providing opportunities to poor and minority groups. Children are being socialized for change, which may mean the teacher no longer supports only existing family values, but introduces ideas and attitudes that are new and different. The consequence is competition between family and school. The teacher needs to understand the various roles she is expected to play in the complex task of early education.

SOME POINTS
TO REMEMBER

1. The purpose of this book is to help a teacher become a competent professional.
2. Training helps, but the teacher's values and viewpoints may be more important.
3. Understanding your motivation for wanting to be a teacher is a good place to start.
4. Teachers are in the business of changing the lives of children.
5. The teacher is part of a large societal effort to train the young.
6. A teacher is one of the influencing factors in a child's life, along with ministers, community leaders, and his parents.
7. A teacher not only transmits values and ideas, but also may alter the flow of culture from parents to their children.
8. Different parts of the society have different values, skills, and mores; each part of the society (ethnic, regional, religious, etc.) wants its children to adopt the adult values.
9. Teachers are sometimes caught in the middle.
10. If the teacher introduces too many alien ideas she may come into conflict with parents and the community.

11. The responsibility of the teacher is to the community as well as to herself and the children.
12. Social change around her forces her to think about what the children will need in the future as well as what present values should be maintained.
13. Career opportunities for teachers are expanding.
14. Women are seeking more out-of-home care for children and seem likely to continue to do so.
15. Many women need child care for economic reasons.
16. The range and type of child care and early educational programs are wide and growing.

REFERENCES

U.S. Office of Education, National Center for Educational Statistics. *Preprimary enrollment: October 1971.* By L. A. Barker. Department of Health, Education and Welfare, Publication No. (OE) 72-197, Washington, D.C.: Government Printing Office, 1972.

U.S. Department of Labor, Employment Standards Administration, Women's Bureau. *Who are the working mothers?* Washington, D.C. U.S. Government Printing Office, 1972.

Chapter 2 Can Early Education Make a Difference?

The Importance of Early Experience

Since it takes a great deal of time and effort to become a competent professional in early education, it is important to consider whether you and other teachers will be able to have a significant effect upon young children. This is an ancient question and one on which evidence is still accumulating. Early education is the concern of a broad spectrum of educators, sociologists, psychologists, philosophers, physiologists, biologists—in short, of men and women of many professions. It is a field that has been expanded by the contributions of scholars of many disciplines.

As long ago as the third century B.C., Plato argued that children be removed from their parents at an early age and transferred to institutional care and training. Leading thinkers of the seventeenth, eighteenth, and nineteenth centuries maintained that serious social problems could be avoided if education were begun early (Figure 2-1).

Concern about early learning and development is reflected in studies and programs involving thousands of children all over the world. Much of the inquiry and discussion in the field of early education is concentrated in the following questions:

Does heredity or experience have more influence on behavior?

What conditions make for optimal growth and development?

Do early educational programs boost later school achievement?

Frederick Froebel (1782–1852), German educator who devised a system of educational games for children and founded the kindergarten.

Jean Jacques Rousseau (1712–1778), French philosopher who believed education should start at birth and continue through 25th year.

Johann H. Pestalozzi (1746–1827), Swiss educational reformer who emphasized use of objects at early age to develop powers of observation and reasoning.

Figure 2-1

Subjects for these studies have included both humans and animals. Children have been observed in institutions, laboratory circumstances, cooperative nurseries, and in programs such as Head Start and Follow Through. The significance of studies on animals is limited, of course, by the fact that we are not certain that humans would react in similar ways. Nonetheless, these studies provide a body of knowledge that helps to shape new research questions and to reach more sophisticated theories about the relationships between behavior and environment.

One of the significant conclusions of these studies is that what is learned first stays longest and is the most difficult to eradicate. Studies of language show that first learnings serve as a filter through which subsequent experiences are understood and interpreted. Because they are novel experiences, whatever is learned first is likely to make the greatest impression. Also, once something is learned and a pattern of behavior is established it is more difficult to learn to do the same thing in another way.

Does Heredity or Experience Have More Influence on Behavior?

The extent to which behavior is determined by genetic endowment—that is, through heredity—and how much it is shaped by environmental influences is still being debated.

One recent analysis (Jencks, et al., 1972) describes the contributions of experience and genetics as three distinctly different components. The first is the biological base that is not affected

2 Can Early Education Make a Difference?

Robert Owen (1771–1858), Welsh socialist who believed that character is determined by environment.

John Amos Comenius (1592–1670), Czech educator who wrote first text using pictures for teaching children.

John Locke (1632–1704), English philosopher who theorized that understanding is derived from one's own experience of the external and social world.

by experience; the second is experience; the third is the result of interaction between the two—the effects of experience upon the genetic endowment. This reflects the notion, which is supported by research, that experiences can alter and modify the physical basis of behavior, changing the genetic resources. The estimates of the relative importance of these three components are: genetic, 45 percent; experience, 35 percent; genetic and experience interacting together, 20 percent (Jencks, p. 315). Thus the growth of an organism is dependent both on its innate capabilities and on the modification of these factors through interaction with its environment. Therefore, it is useful to go beyond the question of which of the two factors contributes the most to a particular behavior. In the search for an explanation of anything so complex as human intelligence, it is also helpful to question *in what manner* genetic and environmental factors contribute to the specific behavior under observation. It is true that both influences are constantly present, but the amount of influence of each varies with the characteristic.

Physical features such as the color of skin and eyes, the quality of nails and hair, are almost wholly products of genetic endowment and are changed little if any by environment. A study of Hopi children made by Dennis and Dennis (1940) presents an instance of the predominance of a genetic factor over environment. They observed that children who are swaddled and carried on their mothers' backs learn to walk at about the same ages as children whose arms and legs are free. Genetic factors also influence behavior often thought to be social in nature. Twins reared from birth in separate environments show first social smiling at nearly identical times (Freedman, 1965). This suggests the primacy of genetic influence over situational factors for this particular behavior.

In addition to affecting specific human behaviors, environmental elements also influence general features and behaviors such as physical growth and social development. At one time it was thought that the final shape and height of body structure was set genetically at birth. Children were destined to be tall or short, fat or thin by virtue of the general characteristics of the families into which they were born. However, the overall increase in height and weight during the last several decades for the average populations of several countries, including the United States, shows strong influence of environmental factors on human growth.

There is evidence that experience not only changes behavior but actually modifies biological structure itself. Rosenzweig and his associates (1962) found in their work with rats that enrichment of the environment produced chemical and anatomical changes in the brain. In addition, they found noticeable improvement in the ability to solve certain problems. Krech (1966) took the opposite course by depriving rats of the stimulation of an enriched environment. His results mirrored those of Lindsley who found that isolation produced underdeveloped, restless organisms. Casler's studies (1961) concluded that poor physical growth and reduced mental growth result when sensory exploration is not encouraged.

Studies by Kugelmass, Poull, and Samuel (1944) of undernourished children over two years of age show that restoration of proper diet was accompanied by IQ gains of as much as 18 points. The physical development of young children who have recovered from chronic malnutrition is apparently less than that of children of the same age and race who have not been nutritionally deprived.

Available evidence indicates that malnutrition also interferes with the central nervous system. Another consequence of malnutrition in young children is apathy. Malnourished children show much less response to stimulation than well-nourished children. David Glass (1968, p. 49) notes:

Apathy can provoke apathy and contribute to a cumulative pattern of reduced adult-child interaction. This has consequences for learning, for maturation, for interpersonal relations, and so on—the end result being significant risk of backwardness in more complex learning.

Psychological factors of the environment may affect physical growth. Widdowson (1951) worked with children of four to fourteen years of age in two German orphanages. He noticed that although the kinds and amounts of food given to the children were equal, the average gain in weight of one group was very nearly three times that of the other over a six-month period. However, switching supervisors of the two institutions reversed the trend. By the end of the next six months, the children who had gained the most weight now lost their lead even though they were given amounts of food greater than the other group. Since the most obvious difference between the two situations was the harsh tactics used by the supervisor of the institution in which the children lost weight, Widdowson concluded that the children's fear made the difference in growth.

There have been remarkable recent discoveries about the role that genetic factors play in producing behavior. These include studies of genetic material and "mapping" of specific parts of genes that are related to distinct physical growth. It seems possible, even likely, that within the next few years there will be information available that will make possible the production of specific types of behavior in offspring by manipulation of genetic material. The legal and ethical implications of such experiments are now being seriously debated. One of the outcomes, however, will be an expanded knowledge of the relationship between genetic resources and daily behavior. One of the implications of these findings for teachers is that we may soon know much more about which types of behavior are most susceptible to change through experience and teaching and those that we are not likely to be able to modify.

What Conditions Allow Optimal Growth and Development?

What sort of an environment do children need in order to thrive? We know that children may be affected by trauma, deprivation, and mistreatment. We also know that there are general conditions that appear to stimulate and support development. Obviously, children acquire different kinds of behavior in different cultures—social rituals (such as deference to adults), language, display of aggressive behavior, and the like—but these are signs of normal development and growth. No matter what the cultural context, however, there are a number of basic needs that all children have in order to thrive physically and emotionally. In addition to adequate physical care they include physical contact and emotional interaction (dependency) with an adult, some predictable experiences and familiar structural routines, opportunities to learn what is expected by the adults in the environment, care or love as expressed through communication, and opportunities to explore and to interact with a stimulating physical environment.

Although our information is not precise, studies have revealed that certain environments appear to impair seriously the normal developmental processes.

One such pseudo-experimental situation exists in orphanages or similar institutions. Children who grow up in such circumstances have often been compared with children from family settings.

In a comparison of the development of infants raised in a nursing home with children brought up in an orphanage, Spitz (1945) noted that those in the orphanage were dull, fearful, had impaired physical growth and skills, and showed little initiative. Both groups of children had had comparable medical care, food, and housing facilities. Genetic factors apparently did not account for the differences in behavior. It was observed, however, that the children in the nursing home had received both direct and indirect human contact; those in the orphanage had undergone marked social and sensory deprivation during the same period. Thus, at a time of relatively rapid growth, that is, during a critical period, one group was exposed and vulnerable to positive influences on development, the other to negative influences. The subsequent desirable and undesirable results appeared to be the outcome of these different treatments.

Some of the most striking evidence of the influence of environmental factors on the total development of human organisms can be found in two studies by Harold Skeels (1966). His original work, which took place in the early 1930s, was followed up thirty years later with startling results. Initially an experimental group of thirteen children, all under three years of age and all considered unsuited for adoption, were transferred from an orphanage to become "house guests" in an institution for mentally retarded girls and women between the ages of eighteen and fifty. Tests showed that the ten girls and three boys had no gross physical handicaps but that their development was seriously retarded. IQ's ranged from 35 to 89.

No special program or training was planned for the experimental group in their new environment other than fitting into the routines of the inmates. One, or at most two, children were placed in each ward. From the first, the attendants and older girls became fond of the children, gave them gifts, and saw that they had privileges and outside experiences as well as constant attention and stimulation.

As they grew old enough, the children attended the institution's regular kindergarten, spent time with orphanage children their own age on the playground, went to movies, and had opportunities to participate in school programs, group singing, and chapel services. Each child had an older girl or adult who figuratively "adopted" him or her, thus setting up a close one-to-one relationship. The personal interest shown the younger child and his activities and achievements was a unique feature of the experimental setting.

Once the data had been analyzed, a contrast group of matching composition (except slightly higher in intelligence scores) was observed and tested on the same factors over a similar period of time. This group, however, remained in the original cottage environment of the regular orphanage.

The thirteen children of the experimental group were observed from six months to four and one-half years. Final tests for mental development showed an IQ change of anywhere from +7 to +58 points. Each child showed some gain. The contrast group, however, in an experimental period of not quite two to three and one-half years, showed only one child with a gain in IQ (2 points) and negative change ranging from −8 to −45 points. In his original report Skeels (1966, p. 17) stated:

The contrast between the richly stimulating, individually oriented experience of the children in the experimental group and the depersonalizing, mass handling, and affectionless existence in the children's home can hardly be emphasized enough.

In a follow-up study of adult achievement, Skeels (1966) sought to determine what happened to the two groups of children when they became adults. By extraordinary effort he succeeded in locating all subjects from both the experimental and contrast groups. A summary of his findings appears in Table 2-1.

Skeels (1966, p. 56) pointed out that his was a pioneering study, involving only a few subjects, and that it would therefore "be presumptuous to attempt to identify the specific influences that produced the changes observed." However, this contrast in outcome between the children who were in a deprived, unresponsive environment and those who experienced enriched environmental opportunities is one of the most significant studies of the effect of early environmental experience.

The highly complex traits that make up human intelligence result from the interaction of vast numbers of gene combinations and environmental conditions. Behavior of this type is not eas-

Table 2-1 *Adult status of Skeels' research groups*

Data	Experimental Group	Contrast Group
Survival	All 13 reached adulthood, 11 in adoptive homes.	One subject died in the institution age 15. None had been adopted.
Occupational Level	All self-supportive; none were wards of any institution or exhibited delinquent behavior, economic dependency, or need for psychiatric or agency support.	4 were institutionalized and without occupation. Others worked as dishwashers, part-time cafeteria help, or gardeners. One became a typesetter.
Marital Status	8 of 10 girls married, 1 boy. Nine had children. 1 divorce. None of the children showed any sign of abnormality or organic pathology. As a group they were considered well developed and attractive.	1 married, 1 divorced—latter had a child that tested mentally retarded. Married man, however, had 4 normal, fine children.
Education	Mean grade completed: 12.8. One male had B.A. degree—4 others up to 2½ years of college—these figures compare favorably with 1960 census for similar aged adults in U.S. as whole.	Only one educated beyond 8th grade—he had one semester of college. Median: 3rd grade.

Adapted from H. M. Skeels, "Adult status of children with contrasting early life experiences," *Monographs of the society for research in child development 31*, No. 3, Serial No. 105 (1966): 32, 39, and 40.

ily related to particular contributory elements. Nonetheless, one of the factors that seemed to be critical in the development of the children in Skeels' study was the close emotional relationship they had with older girls and women.

Do Early Education Programs Boost Later Achievement?

Researchers have been concerned with the effects of formal and more diffuse educational programs on young children. Since there seem to be optimum times for learning, and evidence shows that these are most likely to occur in early life, the questions of what, how, and by whom young children should be taught become increasingly significant.

Acquisition of motor and intellectual skills is linked to the levels of maturation of an organism. Children cannot be taught to talk before a certain stage of motor development, nor taught to reason logically without first reaching the necessary level of maturation. They are not simply miniature adults but have their own patterns of physical and mental growth. In recent years the work of behavioral scientists and technologists has demonstrated that very young children can be taught a variety of specific skills. For example, they can learn to read, to spell by punching keys on a typewriter, and to memorize more complex poems earlier than had been thought possible for children of their age. Sometimes, however, there is little enduring advantage; such skills are eventually acquired by other children and apparent gains level off.

Many persons feel that formal instruction implies an academic pressure which emphasizes only right answers, and correct ways. They believe that such an instructional environment can only result in harm to young children who need to explore and find out for themselves what the world has to offer and what it demands. However, the work of both Benjamin Bloom (1964) and J. McV. Hunt (1961) supports the view that early education of *some kind* is desirable since children's ability to learn and their actual achievement are both influenced by early experience.

Some Research Evidence

One example of the effects of early intervention is the early training project conducted by Susan Gray and her associates (Klaus and Gray, 1968). Their program involved preschoolers, with subsequent follow-up through the primary grades. Their subjects were sixty-two children of disadvantaged parents who lived in a small Tennessee town, and a control group in a similar town some distance away. The experimental group of preschoolers was given classroom instruction for ten weeks during each of two (or three) successive summers. The children and their families received home visits and instruction between the summer sessions.

The program provided specific experiences designed to "develop attitudes conducive to school achievement . . . and to enhance certain intellectual abilities" (p. 1). Short-term IQ gains were significant, but testing at the end of first grade showed little difference in IQ gains between the experimental and control groups. Subsequent implementation of the program, however, and testing in reading readiness, language, and personality characteristics favored the experimental children, although once again not all gains held more than two years.

In addition to the changes effected in the program's subjects, Klaus and Gray found evidence that benefits accrued to both the families and the total community of the experimental group. These findings appear especially significant when it is realized that program contacts represented only about 2 percent of the average waking hours of a child from birth to six years. Their research suggests that the question is not whether programs of early intervention should be used, but how such programs can be made as effective as possible.

One of the most informative experimental efforts of the decade is a cluster of studies by David Weikart and his staff in Ypsilanti, Michigan (Weikart, 1973). Beginning in 1962, with one of the first Head Start types of intervention in the United States, he and his staff have followed with interviews and tests the progress of the children with whom the intervention studies were begun. He has also initiated several subsequent projects. Two of these touch on important questions: Does intervention improve the cognitive performance of children from low-income backgrounds? How substantial are the effects? How long do they last? Do they affect the non-cognitive behavior of children?

Weikart's first study, the Perry Preschool Project, began in 1962 with a selection of twenty-eight children from low-income backgrounds whose intelligence test scores at the age of three suggested that they might need some remedial course work later during the elementary grades. (A comparable group was selected in each of four subsequent years, for a total sample of 123—58 experimental and 65 control children.) An intervention program was organized and maintained with each group for a period of two years. Half of the children were assigned to a comparison group who were not in the educational part of the program. In order to determine whether the program had any benefit from the experimental group, the comparison group was tested but no intervention was done.

The curriculum for the Perry Preschool Project had several aspects. It included weekly visits to the home, during which the staff members worked with the mother and child. As one of the initial efforts in the country, the curriculum of this project was not geared to any single philosophy but offered a variety of cognitive, social, and affective experiences. Weikart's goal was to give these children sufficient advantage so that they might be able to complete the elementary and high school work in the local district satisfactorily and without failure.

Some of the initial and long-term results of the program show that impressive gains in IQ (from 79.6 to 94.9) were made by children in the experimental classes. These gains began to fade after the program was terminated. Slight gains were also made by children in the comparison group but not as significant as those in the experimental group. When the experimental group entered the first grade, they became part of the regular school population and received no special treatment. The IQ gains of the experimental group gradually declined; it now appears that the two groups will be at virtually identical levels (about 85) by the time all the children complete the eighth grade.

These figures, however, do not tell the whole story. There were gains by the experimental group that were not revealed on the scores of the children on standard tests. The children in the program had less difficulty in school than the comparison group. During the elementary school years, 12 percent of the experimental group needed special educational classes, while 29 percent of the comparison group in the same district needed special help. Since these children initially had been identified as those who might need special classes, this result is obviously a significant achievement for the program and for the children. Weikart's staff is continuing to test all the children each year and there is reason to believe that they will find that there are social benefits as well as educational benefits to be gained as the experimental group moves into its adolescent years.

In an attempt to ascertain if there are different effects from different kinds of programs, Weikart, in another study, compared the results of three distinct curricula.

One of these was a highly structured program of a type devised by Bereiter and Englemann in the mid-sixties. The second was a program oriented toward the theories of Piaget, developed by Weikart and his group at Ypsilanti, Michigan, called the Cognitive Curriculum. The third was designed to be a more traditionally child-centered approach to preschool education. Children were assigned to one of the three projects on a random basis so that no accidental advantage would accrue to any of the programs. In each case there were visits by the staff members to the homes of the children involved. It should be noted that home visits were not part of the original Bereiter and Englemann type of program. In this sense, Weikart's structured program goes beyond those that were devised by other professionals.

Each program was monitored by a supervisor who asked teachers in each curriculum to describe, each week, the things that had gone well with the program and those that had not. Each teacher could then work out techniques for improving the program and for diagnosing and dealing with individual children. This was a constant monitoring, feedback, and assessment of the effectiveness of the teacher's work. It continued throughout the two years that each of the programs was in progress.

The interim results of this study are now available and there will be continual follow-ups at least through the second grade year so that longer range results can be assessed. The initial conclusion, however, is that all three programs' results produce roughly the same level of gain and that these benefits are similar to those which were apparent in the earlier preschool projects.

Other effects that differentiate the programs may appear when the children have been in elementary school for a period of time, but these are not indicated by the data collected by Weikart at the end of the project. It should be noted that, in both this project and the Perry Preschool Project, the gains made by the children do not bring them up to national norms even though they do show a substantial increase and achievement in the early phases of the program and for a short time afterwards.

One of the important results of this study is that even the children in the traditional program showed gains. This is the sort of benefit not found in the Westinghouse evaluation of Head Start nor in evaluations of other traditional programs. In discussing the unusual results of his study, Weikart has expressed the opinion that the way in which the programs were implemented rather than the specific curricula themselves was responsible for the gains made by the children. In other words, it was the care that the teachers took in assessing their methods of implementing the curriculum, the morale of the staff, and the constant attention they showed to the program and the children that may have been responsible for the results. This suggests that most experimental programs have one important advantage—a sense of expectation and faith on the part of the staff that leads to careful monitoring and more attention to the day-to-day interaction with children. This sense of expectation is most likely communicated by the staff to the mothers and the children in subtle ways.

It may also be that working with the mothers in the home on a weekly basis had an indirect effect on the performance of the children in the program. The important point, however, is that different philosophies of preschool learning do not necessarily produce different results. Weikart's finding of no difference in the effects of apparently dissimilar programs is supported by some other studies but not by all. (See Miller, et al., 1971, 1972; Karnes, 1969; Gordon, 1973 for other findings). This will be discussed further in Chapter 5.

It has been shown, thus, that significant short-term effects result from early intervention programs at the preschool level. Some generalized effects on later achievement in school have also been noted, especially where parents have been involved. However, much remains to be learned and research scholars are cautious about stating results until more can be determined about long-term effects.

There are a number of reports indicating that an initial acceleration in the rate of development does not continue after the first year of formal schooling, whether that year is kindergarten or first grade. Those who were not in the program often caught up with those who were. Despite the many explanations offered for this situation (usually the suggestion that the quality of the preschool training is not maintained in the public schools), none fully accounts for the leveling off that takes place. Nor has there been a definitive statement on what kinds of programs of early education offer the most lasting effects upon achievement.

As Director of the National Laboratory on Early Childhood Education, James O. Miller (1969, p. 6) proposed these generalizations about short-term intervention:

1. Where limited intervention objectives in the psychomotor and cognitive areas are clearly delineated and intervention techniques are specifically designed to accomplish those objectives, significant gains can be obtained over a short intervention period.
2. Such gains can be obtained over the chronological age range from neonate through early school years.
3. Little evidence is available concerning the longevity of obtained effects or the effect of specific gains on more complex skills.

Continuing research is needed to assess adequately both the immediate and long-range effects of early education and of the relative impact of different types of curricula. A national evaluation of several different kinds of programs in Head Start and Follow Through is now under way. Results soon will be available through the U.S. Office of Education. These reports should offer the most definitive conclusions reached to date on the overall impact of programs of intervention directed at low income and minority children. In addition, they should indicate whether certain types of programs are more effective in producing academic gains and social-affective behaviors than others.

A number of reviews of evaluations of smaller projects are soon to appear. Those available now are consistent with Miller's conclusions, which were based on early and incomplete evidence (Stearns, 1972; Bereiter, 1972). One of the most thorough of these reviews of evaluations of early educational programs is by Bronfenbrenner (1974). He examined research reports of both school-based and home-based experimental programs, which had been underway long enough to indicate if gains were produced and whether these gains might extend for a significant time beyond the termination of the program. Included in his review are programs that were assessed by use of standard achievement tests. Bronfenbrenner's conclusions are that early intervention can be effective, especially, indeed perhaps only, if the family is involved in the program in a significant way.

If it is unlikely that dramatic cognitive gains are produced by programs of early intervention, what about the effects of such programs upon the social and affective behavior of children and upon others, especially parents, for whom the programs were designed?

The evidence of these non-academic and supplementary benefits is not very good, but it seems to be consistent. The conclusions that can be drawn are general but they indicate that early intervention has a positive effect on children from low income backgrounds. Children who have been through these special programs tend to be more positive about school, more outgoing and verbally assertive with one another and with adults, more able to work independently, and more comfortable in school situations (Stallings and Kaskowitz, 1974).

Parents of children who attend programs such as Head Start and Follow Through report that their children like the program. These parents are positive and favorable about the changes they see in their children, more interested in and informed about school, and more likely to interact with the teacher and participate in the school program (Westinghouse Learning Corporation, 1969).

What Does This Mean for the Teacher?

Research results in education have a way of being provocative but frustrating. It is difficult to find final answers. Why, then, is it important for the teacher to know something about research evidence on topics not yet settled?

There are several important reasons. First, in order to keep up with the field and understand new findings, the teacher needs to have a sense of the history of the issues and controversies that affect her. Some of these disputes and problems will be clarified, hopefully, by new data. For example, knowing that short-term gains are produced from early educational programs but that these gains are often not maintained, will help a teacher interpret reports that show that under certain conditions these gains are not so transitory. Second, such knowledge will develop resistance to "oversell" and help a teacher avoid the danger of being overly impressed by a program that seemed to have lasting effects but which, in reality, produced only short-term results. Third, teachers are often called upon to make choices of programs and materials. A sense of the efforts that have been made by others to evaluate such materials and programs will give her a perspective on the claims made by producers of new programs. Fourth, information about the issues and literature in the field gives the teacher a resource to use in finding out more about topics that may be of particular interest. For example, knowledge of a national evaluation of different kinds of programs may help in the discovery of related studies and additional follow-up assessments, which might offer evidence about a particular approach or program. These research perspectives help the teacher interpret the new data that she reads and provide a base of knowledge for making decisions about programs.

SUMMARY

Chapter 2 reviews some of the evidence that early experience is important in shaping the development of the young. Experience not only affects behavior, but appears to alter biological structures as well. Heredity and environment interact to create a combined effect. One current research problem is to determine just what specific experiences influence young children and how the most beneficial of these may be included in programs of early education. Experimental programs seem to have short-term effects on the development of mental abilities but long-term gains are more difficult to create unless school and home work together.

SOME POINTS
TO REMEMBER

1. Research on early development shows that experiences have a significant effect on the young.
2. Experiences can also affect the biological resources of the child.
3. Behavior is not the simple addition of genetic resources and experience; they also modify one another.
4. Early educational programs appear to affect later social and school performance of children.
5. Early educational programs produce changes in cognitive performance.
6. These changes often fade if the program is not continued.
7. Different kinds of programs produce similar gains.
8. It is not clear what elements of a program are most effective in promoting school-related growth.
9. Early educational programs also promote social behavior rewarded in school.

10. Early educational intervention seems to be most effective if the family is involved in the program.
11. Teachers can gain a sense of the history of their field by keeping up with research findings.
12. Knowledge about the history of early education helps protect teachers from naivete and gullibility for flashy innovations.
13. Research information helps a teacher apply more rigorous standards to her program and curriculum.

REFERENCES

Bereiter, C. An academic pre-school for disadvantaged children: conclusions from evaluation studies. In *Preschool programs for the disadvantaged,* edited by J. C. Stanley. Baltimore: The Johns Hopkins University Press, 1972.

Bloom, B. S. *Stability and change in human characteristics.* New York: John Wiley and Sons, Inc., 1964.

Bronfenbrenner, U., *Is early intervention effective?* Office of Child Development, U.S. Department of Health, Education and Welfare, Washington, D.C. 1974.

Casler, L. Maternal deprivation: a critical review of the literature. *Monographs of the Society for Research in Child Development* 26, No. 2, Serial No. 80(1961).

Dennis, W., and Dennis, M. G. The effect of cradling practices upon the onset of walking in Hopi children. *Journal of Genetic Psychology* 56 (1940): 77–86.

Freedman, D. An ethological approach to the genetical study of human behavior. In *Methods and goals in human behavior genetics,* edited by S. G. Vandenberg, New York: Academic Press, 1965, pp. 141–161.

Glass, D. C., ed. *Environmental influences.* Proceedings of a conference under the auspices of Russell Sage Foundation and Rockefeller University. New York: Rockefeller University Press, 1968.

Gordon, I. J. *The Florida parent education early intervention projects: a longitudinal look.* Progress Reports. Institute for Development of Human Resources. College of Education, University of Florida, Gainesville, 1973.

Hunt, J. McV. *Intelligence and experience.* New York: Ronald Press Co., 1961.

Jencks, C. et al. *Inequality: a reassessment of the effect of family and schooling in America.* New York: Basic Books, 1972.

Jensen, A. R. "How much can we boost IQ and scholastic achievement?" *Harvard Educational Review* 39, No. 1 (1969): 1–123.

Karnes, M. B. *Research and development program on preschool disadvantaged children: final report.* Washington, D.C.: U.S. Office of Education, 1969.

Klaus, R. A., and Gray, S. W. The early training project for disadvantaged children: a report after five years. *Monographs of the society for research in child development* 33, No. 4, Serial No. 120 (1968).

Krech, D., Rosenzweig, M. R., and Bennet, E. L. Environmental impoverishment, social isolation and changes in brain chemistry and anatomy. *Physiology and Behavior 1* (1966): 99–104.

Kugelmass, I. M., Poull, L. E., and Samuel, E. L. Nutritional improvement of child mentality. *American Journal of the Medical Sciences* 208 (1944): 631–33.

Miller, J. O. *Review of selected intervention research with young children.* Urbana, Ill.: ERIC Clearinghouse on Early Childhood Education, College of Education, University of Illinois, 1969.

Miller, L. B. *Four preschool programs: their dimensions and effects.* Progress Report No. 10. Public Health Service, Psychology Department, University of Louisville, Louisville, Kentucky, 1972.

Miller, L. B. *Experimental variation of Head Start curricula: a comparison of current approaches.* Progress Report No. 9, Office of Economic Opportunity, 1971.

Rosenzweig, M. R. et al. Effects of environmental complexity and training on brain chemistry and anatomy: a replication and extension. *Journal of comparative physiological psychology* 55, No. 4 (1962): 429–437.

Skeels, H. M. Adult status of children with contrasting early life experiences. *Monographs of the society for research in child development* 31, No. 3, Serial No. 105 (1966).

Spitz, R. A. Hospitalism: an inquiry into the genesis of psychiatric conditions in early childhood. In *The psychoanalytic study of the child,* 1. 3rd ed., pp. 53–74. New York: International University Press, 1945.

Stallings, J. and Kaskowitz, D. H., *Follow Through program classroom observation evaluation,* 1972–73. Division of Elementary and Secondary Education, U.S. Office of Education, Department of Health, Education and Welfare, Washington, D.C. August, 1974. Stanford Research Institute, Menlo Park, California.

Stearns, M. *Report on preschool programs: the effects of preschool programs on disadvantaged children and their family.* U.S. Department of Health, Education and Welfare, Office of Child Development, Final Report, HEW OS71-16, 1971.

U.S., Department of Health, Education, and Welfare, Office of Education, National Center for Educational Statistics. *Preprimary enrollment: October 1971,* by L. A. Barker. Publication No. (OE) 72-197. Washington, D.C.: Government Printing Office, 1972.

U.S., Department of Labor, Employment Standards Administration, Women's Bureau. *Who are the working mothers?* Washington, D.C.: Government Printing Office, 1972.

Weikart, D. P. "Development of effective preschool programs: A report on the results of the High/Scope-4 Ypsilanti preschool projects." Paper presented at High/Scope Educational Research Foundation Conference, May 1973, Ann Arbor, Michigan.

Westinghouse Learning Corporation. *The impact of Head Start: an evaluation of the effects of Head Start experience on children's cognitive and affective development.* Athens, Ohio: Westinghouse Learning Corporation, Ohio University, 1969.

White, S. H., Day, M. C., Freeman, P. K., Hantman, S. A., Messenger, K. P. *Federal programs for young children: review and recommendations.* Cambridge, Mass.: The Huron Institute, Contract Number HEW-OS-71-170, Publication Number (OS) 74-103, 1973.

Widdowson, E. M. Mental contentment and physical growth. *The Lancet* 1 (1951): 1316–1318.

Chapter 3 # Schools and Systems of Early Education

The Structure of Responsibility

Successful teachers understand the structure of their school, are able to adjust to or change the social organization in which they work, and have a capacity to develop their own zone of influence and effectiveness.

Every complex human social organization has two structures–one visible and explicit, the other unseen and implicit. Even in relatively simple organizations, such as a preschool with half a dozen staff members, there is a complex arrangement of formal expectations and informal understandings that help people relate to one another.

The formal expectations of how people in an organization carry out preassigned tasks is the more obvious and more easily learned part of the network of human interaction. The informal system, unstated but equally important, includes more subtle relationships resulting from the ways people work with and regard one another. Both formal and informal structures are crucial in the operation of an organization, and both must be understood for effective performance.

A new teacher may be given a list of prescribed duties such as the following.

8:30 a.m.	Mix paints and prepare art materials for the day
9:00 a.m.	Greet children at the door
9:20 a.m.	Supervise indoor play areas
10:00 a.m.	Serve juice
10:20 a.m.	Read stories

Since so many spontaneous factors go into teaching, the many ways her tasks could be carried out are not entirely specified. If it *were* possible to anticipate how each teacher might follow formal expectations, the instructions would possibly contain these or similar additions:

8:30 a.m.	Mix paints
	Compare notes on staff impressions of a particularly difficult child
9:00 a.m.	Greet children
	As children are brought to school chat with some of the mothers, especially Colleen's
9:20 a.m.	Supervise indoor play areas
	When Franco's mother comes to help, ask about the sister who's in junior high
10:00 a.m.	Serve juice . . .

However casual such extensions of a formal role may seem, they can increase the value of a teacher's contribution to the school. For example, when greeting children at the door, a teacher recalled that just the day before Colleen F.'s mother had been surprisingly abrupt. She wondered whether the behavior indicated dissatisfaction with the school or its staff. Therefore she made it a point to engage Mrs. F. in conversation. She complimented her on her dress and they talked about the details of how it was made. The mother seemed friendly and glad to talk. Nothing was said about Colleen, but the teacher felt that by taking time for conversation at this level, she was making it possible to have more direct discussions later. Also, when the conversation ended she felt that Mrs. F.'s abruptness had not been caused by anything at school.

The informal structure of a school system is not openly defined and can be learned only by participating in the system itself. The use of titles, the right to rearrange the chairs and tables in a room, the deference paid supervisors and visitors, the shared understandings of unspecified behaviors, many of which depend solely on the personalities of the people involved—all of these go to make up the informal structure of an organization. Although designated as "informal," the expectations are not necessarily friendly and flexible. On the contrary, they can be quite harsh and even rigid, as many a teacher realizes when she finds herself subtly ostracized because of something she did. The reactions of others in the organization may be as binding as any written rule.

Both formal and informal aspects of the matrix of roles and duties affect all members of an organization. A sensitive person utilizes this knowledge to express some of her own views about the organization. For example, the director of a school made it a point to share the assigned duties of all her staff members. She helped an aide change the children who had dirtied their clothes; she occasionally took over cleaning the easels; sometimes she read stories and supervised group activities. In this way she was communicating that she understood what it was like to be in the position of her teachers. Without any verbal statement she was letting them know she would not permit her formal role to interfere with sharing human qualities, and that as far as she was concerned, recognizing feelings was as important as stressing roles.

As with any organization composed of human beings, the way a school functions is a matter of how well people understand and carry out their roles. Even though tasks may be well-defined, not everyone sees them from the same perspective.

Conflict among staff involved in early education or child care can often be seen as a disagreement about the expectations they have of the roles they are to play. We tend to impose our own role definitions upon others and feel disappointed if they do not live up to our own notions about how they should perform their assignments. A parent, for example, who wants the teacher to uphold his or her own standards of discipline, tidiness, or modesty may feel that the teacher is inadequate or incompetent if she lets the child do things at school that are contrary to what the parent tries to teach at home. The parents may also feel that the teacher is not carrying out her role if she does not give advice on how they can help stop temper tantrums, thumb-sucking, or other behavior which they wish to change or discourage. Understanding viewpoints other than your own can help you see how your role complements and supports those that others play.

Table 3-1 presents a summary of the duties and responsibilities associated with some of the roles in a preschool program. The larger and more complex the school, the more specialized each of the roles becomes. Conversely, the smaller the organization, the more one person tends to assume the duties and responsibilities of several roles. For example, child care for a group of children in a private home may be handled by the owner who is also director, teacher, nurse, treasurer, and in charge of maintenance.

How do those involved in preschool education think of themselves and their roles? Examples of what people have to say about themselves and their work follow. Although each person speaks as a unique individual, he also expresses a perception of the school as a system, which comes from the particular place he occupies in it.

An Assistant Teacher's Concerns

Today was Monday—the first day in another week of kids and school at the Oak Street Community Center. Barbara D. walked briskly along, thinking about the day ahead. After two years of being a teacher—well, assistant teacher—but why did the teacher always have to introduce her as "our assistant teacher"?—it seemed that on many days she did as much teaching as Mrs. J. In fact, it seemed to Barbara that more and more Mrs. J. was being called to the office to talk to a parent or to see somebody about fixing something. Thank goodness Barbara could be with the kids most of the time—they were really great. Sometime it might be nice to talk more with parents, though. She'd certainly like to see what kind of mother prissy Eleanor had. Did that woman go around putting everything in its place all the time, too? But today was Monday and that meant having to think about all the materials that needed readying for the week's art projects and science projects and cooking projects and whatever good old Mrs. J. had decided they were going to do. Did all teachers insist on having materials arranged a week ahead? Not that anything ever went wrong—Mrs. J. was just great that way—she really kept things moving. And she was getting a lot better about letting people make suggestions, though Barbara wished she wouldn't interfere with discipline so much . . . like the time last Friday when Mrs. J. found Johnny sitting at a table and suggested he go outside even though the aide had told him to stay right where he was until she called him. But Barbara had to admit she probably wouldn't be able to do as well when she got to be a head teacher.

She knew that no matter how much work she had to face today, at least she hadn't called in sick as she had done twice last year. She still

Table 3-1 *Summary of duties and responsibilities within a preschool program*

Owner/Board	Director	Teacher	Assistant Teacher
Overall legal responsibility and financial management	Hires, trains, directs staff	In charge of and responsible for smooth running of daily program	Teaches and works directly with children under supervision of teacher
Selects site and/or buildings	Confers with parents and leads discussion groups	Sets atmosphere of school and classroom	Assists teacher in preparation of materials—often prepares all materials for a special project
Sets policy for school as a whole	Coordinates work of school with community agencies	Determines duties and responsibilities of other teachers	Helps plan daily activities
Chooses director	Has charge of public relations and publicity	Maintains discipline of staff and students	Contributes to observation and evaluation of children
Decides on enrollment, staff size, salary scale, fees, and school year	Responsible for record keeping—health, employment, personal data, testing	Usually determines schedule and curriculum	Supervises and works with aides and often with volunteers
Provides for maintenance of buildings, grounds, and equipment	Selects and purchases most equipment and material	Assists with parent meetings and conferences	Fills in for teacher upon request
	May or may not teach	Responsible for seeing that materials are on hand and ready as needed	May relieve teacher of responsibility for specific activities of daily schedule or special activities such as field trips
	May or may not direct research	Teaches and works directly with children	
		Serves as model for on-job training	
		Has charge of teacher evaluation	

felt guilty every time she thought about that. She had known she wasn't really sick. The first time it was because she felt so ashamed for slapping Maxie when he spit at her. The worst part was that no one had said a word to criticize her. It was almost as though they had known exactly how she felt and that it would never happen again. She hadn't had nerve enough to bring it up herself and Maxie did get better about following group rules. The other time was only four or five weeks later. By then she was getting along pretty well with the kids but finding herself angrier and angrier because she always seemed to be the one who had to clean up the paint jars. It was such a small thing she didn't want to mention it to Mrs. J.—well, actually there had never been a chance because everyone was too busy to have meetings for anything but announcements or planning for a special project. And besides, they were so nice to each other—it was just that you never could be really sure how they felt about you. Barbara still considered that the paint job should be taken care of by the aide. Wasn't that what aides were for? Facing her feelings again she knew the same answer. She'd just been jealous because the aide was so popular with the kids . . . this year it was better, though. Besides, it was a different aide, one that was much more helpful and didn't always have to be told what to do. Barbara hated supervising anyone else, even though she knew that she was expected to work with aides and volunteers who came to help with the regular program.

Then she remembered. This week, in fact this morning, a new volunteer was coming—a man. She knew his name was Tom and that he was going to be at school for two or three weeks. It was her job to see he had a chance to be with the children as much as possible, especially outdoors. Did that mean no chores? What was so special about him besides the fact he was a man? Why shouldn't he take his turn with everything? Barbara knew these answers, too. She could still hear Mrs. J. explaining, "We need volunteers, especially men. And we want Tom to enjoy his work and to know how important we think it is to give children a chance to interact with him. I know you'll do your best to see they are together as much as possible."

Barbara knew she'd follow Mrs. J.'s instructions. But wouldn't it be great if Tom turned out to be someone with whom she too could interact?

What is expected of an assistant teacher depends in large measure, of course, on the kind of school in which she works. It also depends on how long she's worked there. In some programs she will assume most of the tasks and duties of the teacher but without ultimate responsibility or authority. Many are in charge of a group of children, supervise the work of aides and volunteers, often deal with parents, and generally make choices and decisions on their own.

Even though a teacher may direct the overall program, once a general notion of what needs to be done has been established, an assistant often functions relatively independently. Others in this role serve as assistants. They work within sight of the teacher, are held responsible for most of the housekeeping chores such as mixing paint, seeing that children are properly clothed, and getting out and putting away supplies. As far as direct contact with children is concerned, they usually work with small groups for a short period of time at the suggestion of the teacher.

Whether assistant teachers are on their own or under constant supervision, their concerns about themselves and their work are

Announcement of Opening / Martin Luther King Children's Center

Position: *Teacher* 6 hours per day; flexible scheduling.

Job Description The teacher works under the supervision of the director in carrying out the curriculum with young children, other staff members, parents, and volunteers.

Duties The teacher is responsible for

1. planning and conducting orientation conferences with families enrolled at the center.
2. curriculum planning and implementation with the director and staff members.
3. spending the major portion of the day teaching and interacting with the children.
4. coordinating and utilizing services of parents, volunteers, and others working in the center.
5. keeping classroom records.
6. participating in parent education meetings.
7. conducting parent-teacher conferences as needed.
8. participating in regular staff meetings.
9. performing other appropriate duties as needed or assigned by the director.

Qualifications

Education At least 12 semester units or the equivalent in child development or related field including at least one course in Home, School, and Community.

Experience At least 180 hours of experience with preschool children. Experience in working with parents and volunteers desired.

Credential Must be eligible for a Children's Center Permit as required by State Dept. of Education within six months from date of employment.

Salary $475 per month

---

surprisingly similar. They wonder if they **are** doing a good job, they wonder what the staff and parents and children think about them, and they wonder whether they might find greater opportunity and satisfaction in another school.

A Teacher's Perspective

Mrs. E. is a teacher in a large private nursery school. She is a tall, vivacious woman in her mid-forties who has been teaching nearly a dozen years. The school employs four other women like her, each with an assistant and a helper (aide). She has twenty-four children as her direct responsibility.

Except for hiring (and firing), which is done by the school's owner largely on her recommendation, she works as autonomously as a teacher in a smaller school. She plans her own curriculum and day-to-day procedures. Once a week she and the three other teachers meet with the director and with the owner of the school to go over mutual concerns. The following dialogue tells something about how Mrs. E. views her role as a teacher:

Q. Mrs. E., how would you define your role as a teacher?

A. That isn't easy to answer. I guess I see myself mostly as someone who plans for individual children and then sees that the plans are carried out.

Q. How do you do this?

A. Well, I know pretty well how the owner and director feel about the children and it's up to me to work out a program that satisfies what they want to achieve. Of course I agree with their philosophy or I would never have taken employment with them.

Q. Do you work directly with children?

A. Oh, yes, indeed. Every day. All of the staff shares equally in teaching and observing the children. Perhaps I don't have as many of the housekeeping chores, but I'm responsible, and during school hours I'm with the children as much as anyone.

Q. You say, "During school hours." Does this mean you have school-related work at other times?

A. Well, I spend a good many hours keeping up reports and records,[1] talking with parents formally and informally, and . . .

Q. Are you the only person who has contact with parents?

A. Yes, I guess I am. Of course, if a parent is visiting we don't expect the assistant or any member of the staff to be rude or to ignore our visitor. But I am the only one who discusses the children's work with them.

Q. Who purchases equipment and supplies?

A. I do—or at least I make up lists of things I feel are needed and throughout the year I can draw on a general fund up to any amount that has been budgeted. If I'm lucky I'll have an assistant with an eye for inexpensive or junk materials and she'll make suggestions or bring things in. But purchases are up to me.

Q. How does your staff know what you expect them to do?

A. Do you mean do we have lists of duties, staff training sessions, and that kind of thing?

Q. Something like that.

A. Well, first of all, the owner rarely hires anyone who hasn't some experience and training. But training goes on all the time—especially with new staff. Once they are hired and we talk over the general purposes of the school and perhaps discuss the few specific rules such

---

[1] Table 3-2 describes some of the kinds of information Mrs. E. and many teachers keep on file. Such records make readily available both background and experiential information.

as "No running with juice," "No throwing sand," and so on, they are pretty much on their own. But they are expected to watch how things are done and to ask questions. And all of us feel free to offer suggestions to one another. If I see a situation being handled improperly, we stay a few minutes after school and go over it. Of course I would never speak critically to an assistant or helper in front of the children!

Q. What do you consider your most important function?

A. As far as staff is concerned, or the children?

Q. Both, or either.

A. Well, as far as staff is concerned, I think it's important to see that they know whether they are doing a good job or not and to help them realize how important they are in the lives of the children. As far as the children are concerned, I think I try hardest to provide a responsible environment for all their needs. By this I mean I want every child to develop both skills and concepts.

Q. One more question. Suppose at the end of a year you were to say to yourself, "This has been a good year." What would you mean?

A. Now, that's easier to answer. It's a good year when the children have made progress. That is, when their curiosity has grown, they're interested in many activities and are eager to go on.

The Viewpoint of an Aide

Private schools, such as the one for which Mrs. E. works, frequently hire aides. Those who fill this role are often high school students fond of children, housewives who want to work part-time, young men and women interested in careers in social service or recreational work, and students seeking experience in the field of preschool education. They tie shoes, take children to the toilet, mop up spilled juice, and do a variety of other essential tasks. Many also spend time helping teach and are given responsibility for specific activities such as rhythms, dramatic play, and supervising the use of equipment. Their close relationship with the children can be an important source of feed-

Table 3-2 *Examples of the type of records judged "most useful" by nursery school teachers*

Health History	Family and Social History	Identification and Emergency
Immunizations, by kind and date	Marital status of parents	Names, addresses and home and business phones of parents
Allergies, especially in regard to food	Names and relationship of other members in the household	Whom to call in case of emergency if parent can't be reached
Physical conditions requiring special attention at school	Where is child cared for and by whom when not in school?	Names of persons authorized to take child from the nursery school

Job Opening / Campus Child Care Center

Position: Teacher's aide, part-time—4 hours per day beginning September 10 and ending June 15.

Requirements   At least 6 units or the equivalent in field of child development.
Some experience working with young children.
Three references for use by the hiring committee to screen selected candidates for oral interviews.

Duties   The teacher's aide works directly under the supervision of the head teacher in implementing the curriculum. Most of the time will be spent in direct interaction with the children in the program.

Salary $2.50 per hour

back for teachers working out activities to meet individual needs.

Compensatory programs use aides in much the same way but often with an important difference. Under guidelines set by state and federal agencies, these aides often must be hired from applicants who already live in the target area and know the families and children whom the program serves. Their familiarity with the neighborhood and the people make them a valuable liaison resource.

Glancing up from the stack of applications which lay on the desk before her, the program coordinator called "Marlena, Marlena García?"

Hearing her name, a slender, dark-haired teenage girl hesitantly crossed the room with a small boy at her side. As she reached the desk she pulled him slightly behind her and waited quietly.

The woman spoke again. "Are you Marlena García?"

"Sí, señora." The child stepped forward and answered, too. "Me llamo José." Then proudly added, "José Castillo."

The coordinator, busy with her papers, took no notice. "You applied for work as an aide in the Community Day Center?" she asked.

"Sí, señora, I need work bad." Marlena waited, unconsciously stroking the child's black hair while the woman returned to the application form she held.

"How far do you live from here?"

"¿Perdón?"

Not sure whether the girl hadn't heard or hadn't understood, the coordinator spoke louder. "Do you live near here?"

"Aaahh. Sí. Sí. Vivo en la calle Bonita. It is near. Two blocks—three."

"Good. Can you work full time?"

Again Marlena stood in doubt. "¿Perdón—what you mean please?"

```
APPLICATION FORM

Name    Marlena Garcia

Address  160 Bonita Street    Phone  no

Age  18  Citizenship Mexican-American Married  yes

Education  1½ years high school  Children 1 dead

Experience   none
_____
_____
```

The coordinator drew a breath and sought to explain in Spanish "¿Puedo—puedes trajabor todos—todo día?"

"Oh, sí, sí, señora." Eyes aglow Marlena pulled the boy closer daring to hug him delightedly. Then she turned to answer the coordinator. "Puedo trabajar las horas que tú quieres, señora." At ease now in her own language and with hands and eyes explaining and emphasizing, Marlena told the woman that she could work many hours "anytime they wanted her," that she was a good worker and loved "los ninos" very, very much. Hugging José, who returned her affection with a warm smile, she explained that she needed work because her husband was laid off his job and . . .

She was interrupted. "How long have you lived . . ." Remembering, the coordinator tried again. "¿Cuanto tiempo tienes . . . viviendo . . . en la calle Bonita?"

Marlena hesitated. Did it really matter how long? Truthfully she replied, "Maybe a year en la calle Bonita, señora."

The coordinator considered. Here was a girl eager to work. One who could certainly help with the children, one who knew the neighborhood and was sufficiently bilingual to serve as interpreter. But would she be able to get the parents to listen to her? Had she lived in the area long enough to know the families she would be asked to deal with?

José began shifting from foot to foot, tugging at Marlena's skirt. "Vámonos, Marlena, estoy cansado."

This time the coordinator noticed him. "Is he yours?" she asked.

"Oh, no, señora. Es mi hermano."

"You have other brothers and sisters? They live here?"

"Sí, señora. Two brother. Four sister." Marlene smiled proudly. "Todo mi familia. I live with them until I marry and go to calle Bonita."

Now the coordinator was smiling, too. "Can you come to work tomorrow?" she asked. "We really need your help."

"Sí, señora."

Volunteers: An Important Resource

Just as aides are an important resource in many preschool programs, so too are volunteers. Those with special interests or talents often enrich a preschool program by visiting briefly and sharing what they know or do best. Others are involved as aides; they contribute their time and abilities on a day-to-day basis. One such volunteer is Karen, a tall blond girl in her late twenties who works in a day care center.

During convalescence from a serious accident, Karen had looked for work that she felt she could handle on a part-time basis. "I love children," she explains, "and though I had never had any experience or training, I decided helping out two or three days a week would be just about right for me."

The first few days were difficult because it took her a while to become accustomed to the continuous activity and high noise level of the children. By watching the teacher and her assistant closely, however, and by listening to their explanations, she soon began to feel a more efficient part of the school and is now working the same schedule as the teacher and assistant—five mornings a week.

At first the teacher would find moments to tell Karen specifically what she wanted her to do and how to go about the various tasks assigned her. "The assistant teacher was very helpful, too," Karen recalls. "I always felt they expected me to ask about anything I didn't know."

Every morning when she first comes to school Karen looks at the schedule the teacher has posted for the day. "That way I know what special things are planned," she says. "Some days I'm at the clay table, or maybe I help with a holiday craft. But since the assistant comes an hour early and puts all the materials out, all I do is look them over so I know what they are."

She remembers an occasion when one of the mothers volunteered to come in and sing for the children and then to teach them a new song. "Of course we told her how much we appreciated her coming, and talked with the children about how nice it was for people to volunteer to help. . . ." In recounting the experience she laughed. "By the time the mother came I had become so involved with the children that I found it impossible to remember I was a volunteer too, and I don't think they did. At least no one mentioned it."

Because she has become so interested in preschool education, after the year's work is up she plans to take courses and perhaps get a degree in nursery education. According to Karen, that will be time enough for her to make some of the changes she's thought about.

"I'd have the children out more on field trips, for instance," she suggests. But she doesn't think it important enough to mention yet. Her satisfaction comes from seeing a child accomplish something they've worked on together. "The day five-year-old Silvano wrote his name and realized he could do so again and again," Karen said, "I don't know who was proudest!"

Like many volunteers, Karen finds gratification in working with children. Her lack of training in a particular field has not meant she is not effective. Through her willingness to learn and her efforts to interact with children and staff, she has found she can contribute a great deal to what she considers proper education for children.

Unlike Karen, but like the mother who sang for the children and then taught them a new song, many volunteers come only occasionally for special purposes. Some are highly skilled, such as doctors and dentists and artists; others bring knowledge of different cultures and languages; many are willing to share job skills or hobbies. Some come into the classroom and interact with the children; a few prefer to help by building or repairing equipment.

Like many busy people, a children's dentist in the San Francisco Bay area looks forward to the annual invitation he receives to visit a cooperative nursery. He puts on a bright Hawaiian shirt, brings a huge set of teeth, an oversize toothbrush, some free samples of tooth paste, and sugarless gum. His simple, clear explanations about healthy teeth keep a large group of three- to-five-year-olds and their parents entranced. He obviously enjoys having the children tell him what they eat, and he tells them that if they eat the same foods that a rabbit does, they will have good, strong, healthy teeth.

He demonstrates how and when to brush teeth. The children swarm around him to touch the things he has brought and they respond with exclamations of joy when he hands out the sugarless gum. Parents have many questions to ask and he seems pleased to be able to talk with them about their children's health. He is a very busy man yet he willingly spends two hours or more at the school whenever he is invited. Preparing his presentation, ordering the samples, and adjusting appointments takes additional time, but he puts aside work that pays him in money for the feeling he has of contributing to his community. Mostly he likes *being appreciated,* and the poster the children made for him is prominently displayed in his waiting room.

Many potential volunteers will never let a teacher know they have a special interest or talent; it will be up to the teacher and her staff to find out what resources of this kind are available. In whatever capacity volunteers serve, they need to be relied on and appreciated as individuals.

Administrators:
The Supporting Roles

Teachers, assistant teachers, aides, and volunteers in a pre-school program are generally in direct contact with children. Important roles are also filled by people who may rarely inter-act with preschoolers. This is not because they prefer isolation, but rather because their duties and responsibilities often keep them too busy to be in the classroom.

Mrs. C., director of an all-day program involving some eighty-five children and half a dozen teachers backed up by assistants, aides, and volunteers, is one such person.

"I spend so much time on the phone finding staff and then interviewing and scheduling them that I have little time for much else," she says in a tone of regret. "I'd like it much better if I could just pop into a classroom when I have a minute or two. But if I go out, that always seems to be the time when I'm needed right here."

The program she administers involves a great deal of record

Employment Opportunity / Parent Cooperative Nursery School

Position   Director/Instructor

Qualifications

Education At least a bachelor of arts degree in an area related to early childhood education.

Credential Must be eligible for appropriate adult education credential.

Experience At least two years teaching experience with 3- to 5-year-old children and their parents. The candidate should have a demonstrable level of professional competence and leadership in the early childhood education field, including parent education. He or she must have proven ability in administration coupled with a high degree of initiative and an ability to work constructively with parents, preschool children, community agencies, boards, administrative staffs, and professional colleagues. A thorough professional knowledge of both the current practices and literature in the field of early childhood education is necessary.

Duties   The director/instructor is expected to perform three clusters of interrelated duties: (1) directing duties, encompassing supervision of staff instructors and parent volunteers; curriculum planning, fiscal planning, and reporting; staff development. (2) teaching duties, which involve the children, parents of the children, and meetings with the staff members. (3) community and public relations duties, including maintenance of liaison with licensing and funding agencies, colleges and universities, and individuals and groups having a special interest in early childhood education.

Salary $800 per month plus benefits provided with placement on a regular certificated salary schedule.

---

keeping, frequent budget crises, and many parent conferences. She says she's lucky to get to see the teachers, much less the children. "We can't seem to find a time when it's convenient for us to get together," she explains. "But my door is always open to the staff members, literally as well as figuratively, and they know it."

Mrs. S., Chairwoman of the Board of Directors of a parent co-op, feels more fortunate. "I'd probably never get over to the school except, thank goodness, I'm a parent, too. That means I'm obligated to help with the children one morning a week."

In her role as Board Chairwoman she feels her concerns are not only those of a director but also those of an owner. With one exception. "I'll bet I get more phone calls from people wanting to know why the grass is cut so short, or which fathers were supposed to repair the tree house," she explains. "That's because in a parent co-op *everyone* feels he's running the whole show!"

Like most directors and owners, Mrs. S. keeps in close touch with the person in charge of the school program itself. "I'll miss those phone calls when I'm no longer chairwoman," she admits. "I've had a good relationship with our teacher and with the parents, just as I hoped I would when I joined the group. I've made many real friends."

However much their individual programs may differ in general, owners and boards of directors have the following functions in common:

Legal responsibility
Financial control
Responsibility for director
Site selection and maintenance

Either individually or as a group, they secure the license for the school if one is required, prepare whatever financial reports are necessary, raise and disburse funds, and generally conduct the business affairs of their programs. They select the person who runs the school, and he or she is directly accountable to them. In choosing a site they see that the property meets the various health, safety, and building code standards set by the licensing agency or other regulatory body. If qualified professionally, owners frequently serve as directors and/or teachers of their schools. When this is the case, they naturally assume the duties, responsibilities, and privileges that accompany these roles, too.

Perhaps these comments by the kinds of people you will be

working with extend your understanding of a preschool program and your place in it. It takes time to learn techniques for working with staff members and children and to be sensitive to their needs. Knowing something of the roles they play, however, may help you become the kind of teacher you want to be.

Population statistics as shown in Table 3-3 indicate the estimated number of children likely to be living in the United States at the end of this decade. If present trends continue, public kindergarten may become compulsory, voluntary programs will be provided for three- and four-year-olds at public expense, and the number of day care facilities will be expanded.

Table 3-3 *Children under 5 in the United States*

1970	17 million
By 1975	19 million
By 1980	21 million

From U.S. Department of Commerce, Social and Economic Statistics Administration, Bureau of the Census. *Current population reports. Population estimates and projections. Demographic projections for the United States,* 1972. Page 5.

This will mean an increase in school enrollment of five million children aged three to five by 1980. Day care, even if it can be found, will not be enough. During 1968 American colleges and universities graduated only 1200 teachers trained specifically to work at the preschool level. Helping young children develop their potential during the formative years from three to five requires more than concern for physical safety. Special training is needed to meet the demands of rapid change in a human organism with special patterns of learning.

Trained and experienced specialists are needed not only as directors and head teachers of nursery schools, day centers, and other early education programs, but also for college teaching, agency supervision, and community consulting. In addition, highly qualified men and women are needed as assistant teachers. Others with varying degrees of training and experience must be found to serve as aides and volunteers.

Programs of Training

In talks with prospective teachers, certain concerns come sharply into focus over and over again. Students want to know whether the training they are getting will really prepare them for the work ahead. Will they be able to do their part to the satisfaction not only of themselves, but of professionals already in the field? Are they learning enough to be able to hold a job in a good school? Young teachers want to know about salaries and the possibilities of advancement and opportunity, of course, but the most central question is whether they will have the qualifications to establish themselves as professionals. What kind of training did other teachers have that qualified them for the work they're doing? An overall view of a typical structure of the training qualifying persons for the various professional steps in the field of early education is given in Figure 3-1.

There is a continual assessment of the particular abilities needed by teachers of young children, and curricula are being developed and revised accordingly. Each state and school with programs has its own regulations concerning such matters as degree requirements, unit hours of work, and transfer of credits.

At present only a few institutions of higher learning in the United States grant baccalaureate or graduate degrees in Early Childhood Education. Such programs are offered through several different kinds of departments and schools—psychology, education, home economics, arts and sciences—and where

Figure 3-1 *Personnel training levels in early childhood education*

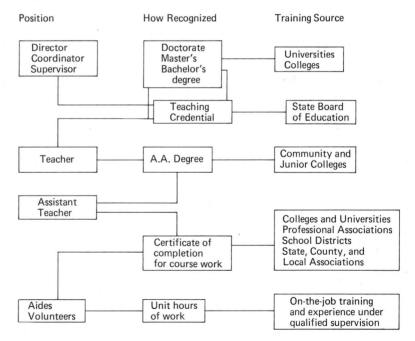

formal degree programs are not offered, courses are often available in a number of related areas, such as the following:

> Child Development or Psychology
> Language Development
> Child, Family, and Community
> Nursery School Theory and Practice
> Developmental Psychology
> Early Learning
> Children's Speech Arts
> Children's Literature
> Educational Psychology
> Observation of Preschool Children
> Fundamentals of Testing
> Personality Development
> Supervision and Administration

Two-year programs for training in nursery school or preschool teaching are offered by many community and junior colleges. Credit is given for courses that satisfy the requirements of an Associate in Arts (A.A.) degree. The course content of these programs overlaps to some extent with programs in four-year colleges and universities.

Colleges and extension divisions of many universities offer night school and home study courses leading to professional upgrading. Workshops and a variety of special weekend and summer programs offered by professional associations and school districts also make continuing education possible. Such training usually includes a certificate of completion.

Certification and Licensing Requirements

Degrees or certificates do not automatically qualify one for employment as a teacher. Work in public school kindergartens and in many of the supervisory positions in preschool programs also require credentials. Through separate boards of education, the various states issue teaching credentials based on a variety of requirements. Two of the prerequisites usually required are: (1) a degree from an accredited institution and (2) certain combinations of major and minor course work. Some states further require that without a fifth year in education at upper division or graduate level, plus practice teaching, only a provisional credential will be issued for a limited period of time.

Private and public nursery schools and other early education programs are often licensed to operate under the supervision of a

Table 3-4 *Requirements for teachers in early childhood education programs*

Directors and/or Head Teachers	Teachers and Assistant Teachers
At least 21 years of age	At least 18 years of age
University or college degree with emphasis on course work in field of early childhood education	At least 12 semester units of course work in early childhood education
From 1 to 4 years teaching experience in early education programs	At least 3 hours experience per day for 100 days in a calendar year under qualified supervision
Either 3 semester units or the equivalent in administration and/or staff relations	

state or other controlling agency. It is usually not necessary to hold teaching credentials to be hired as a teacher or assistant teacher in these programs. However, persons seeking positions will necessarily have to meet educational and experience standards set by one or any combination of the following groups:

> State licensing agency
> County licensing agency
> City licensing agency
> Business licensing agency
> School district
> Individual owner

Typical educational and experience requirements for teachers in early childhood education programs are given in Table 3-4. Nursery school programs are not usually part of public educational systems. Public schools have their own teacher qualification standards. Kindergartens frequently are an integral part of the schools, and teachers at this level must meet the same professional requirements as elementary school teachers if they wish to work in public school programs.

In many states, there is more than one way to qualify as a nursery school teacher or assistant teacher. In addition to approved university and college programs, recognition may be awarded for demonstrated on-the-job competence whether or not accompanied by course work or degrees. Such credit is often given with the requirement that in order to maintain a teaching position, the teacher must take course work and special training as they become available.

Even after students in early childhood education programs get a background of course work, observation, and laboratory school or student teaching experience, they may wonder whether they are ready to handle a full time job. They are if they recognize that their education does not cease with a degree or certificate; their competence will grow with experience on the job.

The directors and teachers in well-run schools are aware of the value of training through experience for all personnel. They instruct assistant teachers and aides, especially in the details and procedures of their particular organization. Much of this instruction is quite informal, given along with the assignment of a specific task. It ranges from the details of routine rules, which can be picked up readily, to more complex problems of teaching and interpersonal competence. A supervising teacher may say, "I'd like you to be sure that the children use smocks or aprons for water play as well as painting," or "Try to get the children to put away the equipment—they need help in developing a sense of responsibility." This casual way of imparting information, along with the teacher's own example, is one of the most frequent kinds of training. In addition, throughout the day, teachers spend many moments discussing behavior of the children and techniques for dealing with especially significant examples. The head teacher may take time just before or after school to mention various procedures or methods she wants the staff to follow. Even routine tasks offer opportunities for learning-by-doing. Much training for beginning teachers comes both from participating in activities and from evaluation of their performance.

New teachers often express a need and appreciation for curriculum ideas that other, more experienced teachers have found useful. Some examples of what to do and how to do it, such as the tasks presented in the companion handbook to this volume (Croft and Hess, 1975), can be a useful resource for teachers, parents, and aides.

As part of staff meetings, it is not uncommon for the person in charge of training to present specialists in various subjects, other speakers, or films. Time may also be set aside for sharing new songs, finger-plays, crafts, and supplies with the entire group. Some employers offer released time (with pay) for staff members to attend community workshops or local and regional conferences. Often partial or full payment of fees is extended as well. Directors sometimes encourage their teachers to go back to college and work for higher degrees, helping them adjust their work hours to make this possible.

The teacher who wants to keep up with what is going on in

her field and develop her own competence can do so in several ways. She can continue to learn through her own experience, from her fellow staff members, and from a variety of sources outside the school. These include meetings of local preschool or early education associations, regional conferences, and workshops or extension courses offered by universities. Resources are also offered by several major professional associations, such as the National Association for the Education of Young Children, which publishes a journal called *Young Children;* Association for Childhood Education International, which publishes *Childhood Education;* The Child Study Association of America, with its publication, *Child Quarterly;* The Child Welfare League of America, and its monthly journal *Child Welfare;* and the Society for Research in Child Development, and its publications *Child Development* and *Monographs.* In addition, the Office of Child Development, under the Secretary of the U.S. Department of Health, Education, and Welfare, produces and distributes materials dealing with many aspects of child care, development, and education.

Some nursery schools subscribe to journals that provide the staff with information about their work and new developments in their field. In addition, many teachers belong to one or more organizations, attend conferences, workshops, and meetings. In a rapidly growing field such as early childhood education, continuous self-education is part of the job.

Features That Differentiate Schools

Few communities are without some program of early education. The wide variety of existing preschools is apparent in the listings in the telephone directory of most large cities. Programs operate under many different names, a sampling of which is given in Table 3-5.

Advertisements accompanying the listings frequently emphasize the "courteous" trained and/or certificated staff; the provision of snacks and hot meals; availability of private transportation; half-day or full-day sessions both summer and winter; academic, social, artistic, physical, and character development as well as expert supervision and guidance; "structured programs" and "non-permissive progressive programs." A few of the schools promise language training (usually French, German or Spanish). Also mentioned are phonics and field trips. When the facilities themselves are described, it is in terms such as "separate buildings," "shaded," and "well-equipped play yard." Groups that have full-day programs frequently make a special appeal to "working mothers."

Table 3-5 *Types of early childhood education programs*

Nursery	Day nursery	Adult Education Preschool
Nursery Home	Cooperative Nursery School	Parish School
Nursery Kindergarten	Real Life Nursery School	Preschool Learning Center
Nursery and Kindergarten	Infant Nursery	Neighborhood Center
Nursery and Preschool	School	Children's Center
Nursery School	Day School	Education Center
Church Nursery School	Community Center School	Child Care Center
Church Co-op Nursery School	Play School	U.S. Govt. Navy Dept. Child Care Center
Temple Nursery	Preschool and Kindergarten	Parent-Child Group
Archdiocesan Opportunity Program	Church Preschool	Head Start Program
Parent's Community Co-op Nursery School	Preschool Training	Infants Day Care Home
Community Association Nursery School	Christian School	Day Home for Infants

In general, the programs differ in such areas as organizational structure, the roles teachers are asked to fill, and whether or not parents are directly involved. There are several distinctions that may help a teacher understand what to expect and whether her interests will be served by a particular school.

Differences Based on Purpose

Perhaps the most fundamental consideration is the school's *purpose*. From this viewpoint, nursery schools fall roughly into the following categories:

1. *Educational and compensatory* These are schools that have as their goal the improvement of the child's readiness for formal schooling. In compensatory programs they concentrate on helping him catch up in pre-academic skills or in developing his abilities still further.
2. *Child care* These schools provide a substitute home for children whose parents cannot be home because of work schedules, illness, or other circumstance.
3. *Commercial or franchise* The purpose of these schools is generally determined by the owner-investor or corporation which grants the franchise. The program is often organized around a curriculum which promises early attainment of cognitive skills.
4. *Social-developmental* Schools of this type give children an opportunity to develop social, emotional and intellectual capabilities in an out-of-home setting. They provide the child another context in which to pursue his natural growth, to learn to deal with other children—perhaps with those from different social and ethnic backgrounds.

5. *Training and research* Schools established for research and training purposes including teaching experience for students enrolled in colleges and universities.

Differences Based on Sponsorship Schools differ with respect to their *sponsorship.* In many instances, the corporate or individual owner is responsible for the school, but it is possible for an agency to sponsor a program without ownership. Table 3-6 summarizes a number of ways in which preschools differ in sponsorship.

The sponsors of schools generally establish the enrollment policy. Most agency programs, including all federally supported compensatory groups, are primarily limited to children of families designated "poor." Many local agencies also use this criterion but perhaps not as rigidly. Church groups may or may not be restricted to children of families who are members of the church; many are available to any child in the community. Private schools and parent co-ops are selective by virtue of the fees they charge and, in the case of co-ops, the requirement that parents actively participate in the program on a regular basis.

Table 3-6 *Different forms of sponsorship*

Sponsor (Owner)	Distinguishing Features
PUBLIC	
Federal or state agency such as Office of Economic Opportunity; Department of Health, Education and Welfare; State Department of Welfare; or State Department of Education	Funds allocated by Congress or state legislatures. Program developers and supervisors may be quite remote from schools themselves. May be experimental programs on a year-to-year basis. Programs exceedingly varied, including those of compensatory education
Local agency such as a neighborhood council, community service organization, or welfare agency	Primarily day care centers in low-income areas. May also include schools providing services to special groups such as retarded, handicapped, etc.
PRIVATE	
Individual or group	A small school operated by a single owner or a large enterprise with absentee owners who leave running of the school to a professional director and a staff
Religious group	May use church personnel for staffing and have secular emphasis, or may simply permit use of church facilities
Parents' cooperative	Parents hire professional director and then serve as assistants on a rotating basis with regularly scheduled meetings for families

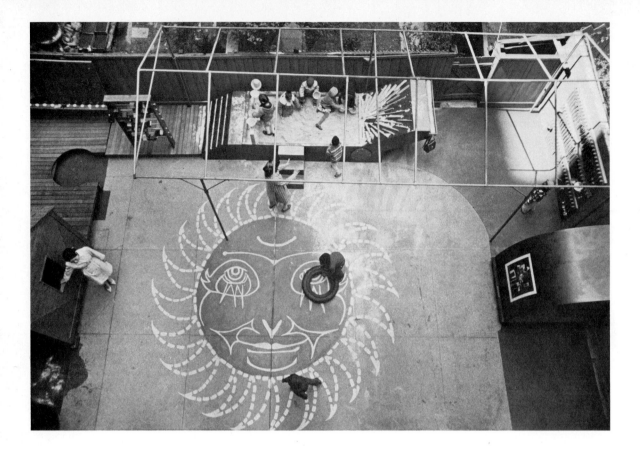

Other Elements of Differentiation

When considering differences among preschools, it is also useful to take into account the following factors: *physical setting, facilities, licensing, staff competence and training,* and *funding.*

Preschools differ as a consequence of *physical setting,* which includes location, climate, and the socio-ethnic backgrounds of the available population. The owners of a school in Alaska would have quite different factors to consider from those who run a school in Florida. So, too, would owners of schools in desert country as contrasted with those whose schools are in or near a waterfront community. An inner-city complex has an economic and social make-up different from that of a suburban locale. The information in Table 3-7 indicates that teaching in a school located in Aztec, New Mexico, for example, is likely to be quite different from teaching in one in Fargo, North Dakota, or Birmingham, Alabama.

Differences in *facilities* are especially significant since those used by preschool programs conform to no single type. Some exist wherever suitable space can be found; others are an in-

Table 3-7 *Population in selected states*

	Alabama	New Hampshire	North Dakota	New Mexico
TOTAL	**3,266,740**	**606,921**	**632,446**	**951,023**
Am. Indian	1,276	135	11,726	340,000
Chinese	288	152	100	362
Japanese	500	207	127	930
Mexican-American				95,102
Negro	980,271	1,903	777	17,063
Puerto Rican	663	212	68	433

Adapted from *Statistical abstract of U.S.*, 93rd ed. U.S. Bureau of Census (Washington, D.C.: Government Printing Office, 1972, 29f).

tegral part of the planning for a university community center. Young children attend school in many structures from downtown gymnasiums and vacant stores, to church-school rooms. Some preschool groups occupy a series of buildings; others are crowded into a single room of a private residence, a converted garage, or the basement of an office building. A few use rooftops or nearby parks for their outdoor play area; most have fenced-in yards of one kind or another. Anyone touring nursery school facilities soon realizes that for all their variety they are usually geared to the needs of children in a particular program. As long as they meet these needs, uniformity is not only unimportant, it is highly impractical.

Schools sometimes advertise that their facilities are *licensed.* This indicates that they comply with certain health and safety requirements, staff ratios, and other state and/or local agency standards considered minimum for running a preschool program. Not all states require licensing. While it is true that even without licensing some schools may meet appropriate criteria, it is important to inquire whether schools are operating within established state or local standards.

An increasing number of states require a license in order to legally establish and operate a group day care program. In 1940, only three states required licensing; in the mid 1960's nearly thirty states had licensing regulations. In general, licensing is handled through a state department of public welfare. Of concern are requirements covering such factors as staff qualifications, amount of indoor and outdoor space per child, health and safety features, record keeping, financial accountability, and ages of the children. Owners must also meet local regulations such as those covering zoning, building codes, and parking areas. Typical of these regulations covering staff-child ratios are those listed in Table 3-8.

Table 3-8 *Suggested staff-child ratios in preschool programs*

Ages	Minimum Staff Required
3	For each 12 children a trained head teacher and an assistant
4	For each 16 children a trained head teacher and an assistant
5	For each 20 children a trained head teacher and an assistant

The Head Start standard for 4's and 5's is 15 children and a trained teacher plus an assistant and community area volunteers.

A school reflects the preparation and philosophical orientation of its personnel. The level of *staff competence* and the type of *training* are two of the most important criteria of differentiation.

Staff competence reflects the selection policies of the school both by attention to individual qualifications and personal attributes of teachers, and by the amount of training they have received. The philosophical orientation of the school creates a permissive, child-centered atmosphere or a more structured and predetermined program according to the preferences of the director and staff. Expectations for the teacher are obviously quite different in a school modeled after the relaxed pattern of an English Infant School, than that of a classroom with teaching schedules emphasizing specific pre-academic skills.

Another important element of difference in nursery schools regards their *funding*. Operating budgets and per-pupil costs vary widely depending on the type of program and the source of funds. Some private owners and groups raise or borrow money to begin a school and then continue to operate by collecting tuition fees sufficient to make a profit. Many parent co-ops and other group programs depend primarily on tuition, but also raise money through school fairs, raffles, auctions, cake sales, donations, and the like. In such schools teachers may or may not be expected to participate in fund-raising activities. Church programs are usually part of the overall operation of a local group, and their support is budgeted and voted upon at annual meetings.

Government programs are, of course, tax supported and usually funded on a year-to-year basis. Public school programs (sponsored, for example, by an adult education department) depend largely on state and county tax money allocated by the legislature on the basis of average daily attendance (ADA). Under this arrangement they are provided a certain amount of money per pupil depending on the number of students in school on a given day.

Knowledge of the variety of nursery schools, and some of the ways they are differentiated gives the teacher a basis for judging in what sort of school he or she is likely to do the best work.

Some Considerations in Making a Job Decision

Suppose you are applying for a teaching position and you acquire the following charts showing the administrative organization of three different schools. How can this information be helpful in your decision on a job? What are some of the implications of these organizational structures for your role and success as a teacher?

Opportunities to Influence Policy

One of the things you may be interested in knowing is how much you will be able to influence policies of the school such as the curriculum plan, choice of equipment, admission criteria, teacher role and responsibilities, and procedures for interacting with parents.

In owner-operated schools the teacher is in direct contact with the person who decides how the program will operate. In larger

Figure 3-2 *Organizational structure of three different types of early education units*

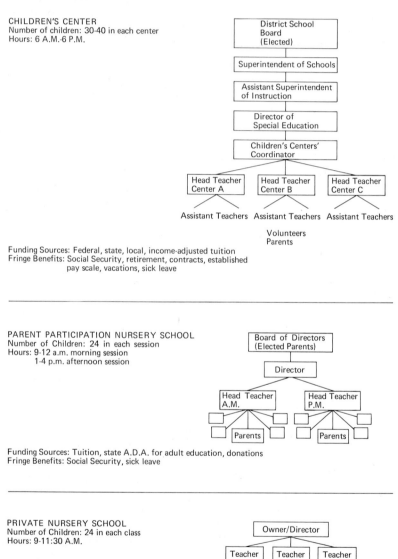

CHILDREN'S CENTER
Number of children: 30-40 in each center
Hours: 6 A.M.-6 P.M.

Funding Sources: Federal, state, local, income-adjusted tuition
Fringe Benefits: Social Security, retirement, contracts, established
pay scale, vacations, sick leave

PARENT PARTICIPATION NURSERY SCHOOL
Number of Children: 24 in each session
Hours: 9-12 a.m. morning session
1-4 p.m. afternoon session

Funding Sources: Tuition, state A.D.A. for adult education, donations
Fringe Benefits: Social Security, sick leave

PRIVATE NURSERY SCHOOL
Number of Children: 24 in each class
Hours: 9-11:30 A.M.

Funding Sources: Tuition
Fringe Benefits: Social Security

3 Schools and Systems of Education

organizations, the teacher generally is farther removed from those who make policies. For example, in large children's centers policies are likely to be established in part by remote groups, not excluding the school board or the state legislature. A number of different kinds of persons and professional groups—teachers' unions, legislative committees, and the like—may participate in these decisions and they may have economic and political implications not always obvious to persons unfamiliar with the local political and educational scene. Such decisions, once made, are particularly difficult to change.

Both professionals and non-professionals may be involved in formulating policy. The influence of professionals in relation to laypersons varies from one type of organization to another. Professionals usually are much more actively involved in decisions made for large organizations by school boards and state legislatures and nonprofessionals are more likely to participate in smaller units. In a parent participation program, for example, the policies are often made by non-professionals and the preferences of individual parents may be urged upon the teaching staff. One aspect of this situation is that the teacher's role is likely to be subjected to more frequent redefinition in parent-oriented programs. In short, there will be more people watching you and trying to tell you what to do.

Job Benefits and Opportunity for Advancement

There are likely to be different salary levels in organizations of varying size and structure. Schools supported by public funds, for example, will probably be able to offer better salaries. In centers operating within public boards of education, the salary structure will be similar from center to center and sometimes higher than a private school can afford to pay. In addition, fringe benefits—insurance, retirement, sick leave, vacations with pay, etc.,—will sometimes be better in the larger organization. Some schools, both private and public, may also pay tuition for teachers who want to take course work or workshops, which give both inservice training and course credit.

Opportunities for advancement may be better in larger systems. A teacher working as an assistant to an owner-director of a small private school has no promotion possibilities. A related concern is the job protection that may be offered by different schools. A teacher in a small private school is more vulnerable to dismissal, in some instances, than one employed by a school district. Personnel policies of larger systems may make it difficult for a teacher to be fired. However, it may also mean that less competent teachers may be kept on in larger systems because of the relatively greater difficulty involved in establishing grounds for dismissal.

In small organizations employing a small number of people, the tasks of the different teachers will probably be more varied from day to day and less circumscribed. The teacher will be responsible for a wider range of activities and probably for more children, and he or she will have fewer colleagues to call on for help. In a more complex organizational structure, the teacher's task will often be more specific. He or she may also have less flexibility in planning activities, need to share responsibility, and do more team planning and teaching. The teacher in a small organization will exercise more autonomy and possibly be responsible for making more decisions alone. The team teacher will share responsibility for decisions.

How does a teacher make the best choice? The opportunity to study information about the structure of a school and determine the advantages and disadvantages of each position helps a teacher to evaluate more realistically the chances for success and satisfaction. A decision based on such knowledge will reduce the risks that are inherent to committing oneself to a job. Satisfaction in a job will depend to a great degree on two factors: the people with whom you work and the structure and organization of the school. As you volunteer in or visit schools where you are likely to work, try to determine the sorts of satisfactions that the staff derive from the different aspects of their roles. How much of their feelings of discontent or of satisfaction is due to how well they work with their colleagues? How is this accomplished within the structure? In what ways can you see yourself fitting into such a role? Perhaps sharing responsibility and trying to please many "bosses," as in a parent participation program, feels less comfortable and efficient to you than making the decisions on your own.

You may prefer to work in a situation in which you are subordinate to a group that spells out exactly what is expected of you. Or, you may find that you are happiest when you can be flexible and operate in a less clearly defined structure.

Whatever your preference, it is important that you think about different roles in relation to yourself whenever you have the opportunity to talk with teachers or to work in different kinds of settings. What were the ingredients operating in each situation that you could identify as contributing to a satisfactory experience? What didn't you like and why? If you become more aware of the separate sources of satisfaction, you will not only be better able to decide where you would like to work, but you will also be more effective in dealing with problems on the job and increasing your feelings of competence and satisfaction.

The Impact of the Physical Environment

Interaction with the physical environment is an important part of the learning context for young children. A great deal of what three-to-five-year-olds learn in a nursery school program comes from direct interaction with their environment. They explore and discover with their bodies and senses the excitement of high places, the fascination of tunnels, the motion of swings and rope ladders, the texture and shape of a multitude of objects and materials. Their senses continuously bring both general and specific knowledge of all that surrounds them. In creating their own world they use what is in the environment to build and tear down and then to build all over again. From dealing with their surroundings they learn firsthand to choose and judge—they find out which objects and situations they can control and which they cannot. Teachers who are aware of their influence plan and use the facilities of a nursery school to provide a constructive as well as pleasant learning environment.

Effect on the Goals of a Program

Thinking of the space that children occupy in a school in terms of how many square feet per child will most nearly assure meeting the goals of the school. Children need room to run and jump, to wheel buggies and ride trikes, to move about freely without jostling and bumping into one another or the teachers. They need quiet corners and out-of-the-way nooks as "escape hatches," and a chance to be alone. They need areas for eating and cleanup and toileting, for activity and rest.

How space is filled has a great deal to do with whether or not a nursery school meets the needs of the children it serves. Well-planned attractive arrangements invite exploration and minimize staff work. When related interest areas are grouped with a thought to traffic patterns and the relationship of noisy and quiet activities, they virtually draw children to them. Arranging and rearranging movable furnishings such as shelves and bins and tables so as to create centers for "house" play, dressing up, block building, puzzles, craft projects, science, reading, and art, contribute to a natural flow of activity. Flexible organization of this kind stimulates free choice and varied interests.

Needs differ widely in different kinds of programs. All-day

care, for example, involves space for meals and naps not needed by half-day session schools. City schools are often more limited in outdoor area than suburban schools. In general, however, desirable ranges are as follows:

| Indoor | 50 to 100 sq. ft. per child |
| Outdoor | 75 to 200 sq. ft. per child |

These figures refer to space to be used by the children, not that occupied by storage units, trees, or other relatively permanent items.

Child-height tables and chairs and shelves, together with child-size tools and equipment, invite children to imitate adult activities and to try out ideas of their own. Ample bulletin boards and display areas at children's eye level encourage them to mount their own work and to notice what others have made.

The way a room is arranged determines in part the kind and amount of supervision required. If all or most children can be seen from one or two vantage points, less patrolling and check-up is needed. This in turn means that teachers have more time for constructive, individual attention. For planning structured group projects—story hours, films, snacks, music, etc.—space should be provided that requires a minimum of arranging either before or after each activity. Less supervision is needed when toilet areas are located so they can be directly entered from indoor and outdoor play areas. Also when boys and girls share toilet facilities an opportunity is provided for learning about the opposite sex.

School affairs are likely to run more smoothly for everyone concerned if the staff has some space of its own. An adjacent tastefully appointed combination office and teacher room which can also be used for parent conferences, staff training, or an isolation room is an asset to a nursery school program.

Well-planned and well-equipped outdoor areas have as great an impact on the goals of a program as their indoor counterparts. Ideally, one is simply a modified extension of the other. Smooth transition between the two can be achieved by using wide, easily opened doors and windows low enough to extend a child's vision to resources both inside and out. A wide overhang, shaded as well as sunlit spaces, and areas sheltered from the wind, make it more pleasant for children to be outdoors in all but the coldest or most stormy weather.

In such surroundings there is no reason why many activities traditionally thought of as taking place indoors cannot be enjoyed outdoors. Butcher paper tacked along a fence soon becomes a gay mural or garden decoration at the hands of eager artists; juice and crackers under a shade tree turns snack time into a picnic; in mild weather records and musical instruments can be heard as well outdoors as in. Activities in a new setting often tempt children who originally bypassed them.

Traffic patterns are as important in the play yard as they are indoors. Children's tendency to speed on wheel toys, and to run without constraint can be minimized by providing relatively short expanses of unrestricted space. A cement walk that rings a grassy mound allows for distance riding with no sharp corners and therefore fewer spills.

Children develop judgment along with physical skills if the outdoor areas contain a variety of facilities for climbing, crawling, sliding, jumping, balancing and hanging. Low-limbed trees often make better climbing devices than many jungle gyms because they force children into choices not needed when hand-holds all have identical size, and mounting rungs are evenly spaced.

Children should be allowed to discover for themselves the properties and delight of a variety of surfaces and textures. Paper, wood, wire, canvas, cement, grass, sand, tanbark, gravel, hardtop, metal—all have something to impart to the child acquiring knowledge about himself and his relationship to the physical world.

Children are stimulated by their physical surroundings, and nursery school facilities planned with their needs in mind provide a safe environment in which they can explore, create and learn in ways that prepare them for adult life.

Influence on the Emotional Climate

Spacious rooms filled with light, color, warmth, and order appeal to children as well as adults. They make them feel comfortable and welcome. Play yards enriched by a variety of sturdy, multi-use equipment and different levels and surfaces are not places where children wander aimlessly with nothing to do.

Two factors that influence the emotional climate of a nursery school are light and noise. Natural light coming through doors and windows without glare, yet adequate to brighten the farthest corner of a room, makes for a cheerful atmosphere. When artificial light provides soft, even, overhead illumination, eye strain and fatigue are lessened. The scraping, pounding and clicking, the humming and laughter—all the noises that accompany active children can often be muted to keep from setting nerves on edge or fraying tempers. For example, a nearly square room is a better noise absorber than a long, narrow one, especially when its walls and ceiling are made of sound-absorbing material. Floors should have a surface that can be readily scrubbed yet will not set up reverberations from every running step or pushed-back chair. Occasional rugs and mats help minimize noise. So does a quiet-voiced teacher.

Independence is encouraged when storage areas are within reach of children and they are free to use them. Cubbyholes for boots and hooks for coats and sweaters; individual compartments for personal belongings; special shelves for books and puzzles and paper; food adjacent to animal cages; water easily accessible—all these help cut down work time and encourage freer use of equipment.

Having enough—but not too much—equipment and materials for children to use fosters sharing and taking turns; having too little of popular kinds of equipment may lead to competition, frustration, and feelings of jealousy.

No listing of physical facilities and equipment can be made that insures a "perfect" setting for carrying out a nursery school program that meets individual needs. Not only do choices depend on particular circumstances, but even the most favorable selection and arrangement will only be as effective as the imagination and flexibility of good teaching make them. Keeping the purposes of a program in mind will make choices a great deal easier, however, and bring about the results you want.

The illustrations that follow represent pictorially many of the specifics that go into planning the environment of a nursery school in order to achieve maximum benefit from the physical facilities.

SUMMARY This chapter helps the teacher look at his or her job in a school as part of a social organization in which each person has a crucial role in the total operation. Vignettes give typical viewpoints of the various staff members in a number of programs of early education. There is a discussion of training programs, licensing and certification and different kinds of schools. The reader can consider making a job decision based on charts showing the administrative organization of three different schools. Other considerations include job benefits, opportunities to influence policy, clarity of the teacher's role. The last section deals with physical planning and impact of the environment on the learning of young children.

1. You work in a social system of approval-disapproval, power-weakness, autonomy-constraints, and this system helps determine your behavior and effectiveness.
2. The more you understand it, other things being equal, the better you can deal with it.
3. The system is both formal, with stated rules and expectations, and informal, with implicit, unmentioned expectations and taboos.
4. Conflict occurs when individuals in the system do not agree on the implicit and explicit rules.
5. Each member of a staff has a personal, unique role, and a public, defined role which is different from the roles of others in the group.
6. Different kinds of schools have roles which express their own purposes and organizations.
7. Knowing something about different kinds of schools informs you about what the expectations probably will be.
8. The demand for child care and early education is likely to increase.
9. Professionals in early childhood and child care are trained at many different levels of colleges and universities.
10. State credentials or licensing are often prerequisites to employment in child care agencies.
11. Certification requirements vary from one state to another.
12. Once basic formal training is completed, professional experience becomes the lifelong training program.
13. Differences among schools are often related to sponsorship, purpose, physical setting and facilities, licensing, funding, staff competence, and ideology.
14. Decisions about jobs can follow several criteria: opportunities to influence policy, job benefits, opportunities for advancement and the clarity and specificity of the teacher's role in the staff.
15. The physical environment can be arranged to affect the activity levels, mood and safety of the children.

REFERENCES

Aaron, D. and Winawer, B. P. *Child's play, a creative approach to play-spaces for today's children.* New York: Harper & Row, 1965.

Bengtsson, A. *Environmental planning for children's play.* New York: Frederick A. Praeger, Inc., 1970.

Croft, D. J. and Hess, R. D. *An activities handbook for teachers of young children.* 2nd ed. Boston, Mass.: Houghton Mifflin Company, 1975.

Dattner, Richard. *Design for play.* New York: Van Nostrand Reinhold Company, 1969.

Hurtwood, Lady Allen of. *Planning for play.* Cambridge, Mass.: MIT Press, 1968.

Kritchevsky, Sybil and Prescott, Elizabeth with Walling, Lee. *Planning environments for young children: physical space.* Washington, D.C.: National Association for the Education of Young Children, 1969.

Ledermann, A. and Trachsel, A. *Creative playgrounds and recreation centers.* New York: Praeger Publishers, Inc., 1968.

Stone, J. G. and Rudolph, N. *Play and playgrounds.* Washington, D.C.: NAEYC Publications Department, 1970.

U.S., Bureau of the Census, *Statistical abstract of the United States* (93rd ed.). Washington, D.C.: Government Printing Office, 1972, 29f.

U.S., Office of Economic Opportunity, Project Head Start. *Designing the child development center,* by R. W. Haase in consultation with D. Gardner. Washington, D.C.: Government Printing Office, 1968.

Equipment should be safe, long-wearing, easily maintained, and adaptable to a variety of uses.

A variety of textures underfoot.

Swings with no boards or handles . . .

*Equipment should encourage independence
and imagination.*

Trees and bushes and plenty of grass invite learning about heights, distances, depth perception, and how it feels to be tall.

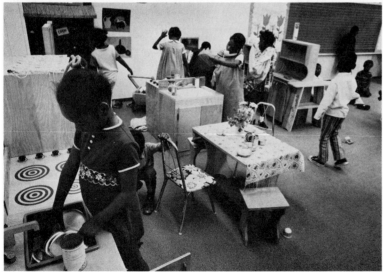

Materials should encourage creativity and the expression of feelings.

Equipment should lend itself to a variety of uses, be sturdy, safe and durable . . .

aid in exploring, discovering, learning . . .

. . . encourage imagination and open new worlds.

Chapter 4 School and Family: Partners or Competitors?

Relating to Parents as a Group

As she went through the mechanical steps of setting up the large coffee pot and counting out enough measures to make thirty-six cups of coffee for the evening meeting, Mrs. B.'s mind was projected to an imaginary scene which could very likely be taking place in the next hour:

Mrs. W. (president of the parent co-op group): "At our last meeting we decided to settle a difference of opinion on curriculum once and for all by taking a confidential poll. Tonight, I'm pleased to distribute the following results, which we just tabulated."

Mrs. B. can imagine a slight smile on Mrs. W.'s face as she hands the results of the poll to her.

Responses of Eighty-four Families and Ten Teachers of Citywide Children's Center Listed According to Order of Priority:

PARENTS	TEACHERS
1. Learning school-related skills	1. Strong self concept
2. Good manners	2. Self-reliance
3. Getting along with other children	3. Getting along with other children
4. Strong self concept	4. Learning school-related skills
5. Self-reliance	5. Good manners

With each monthly meeting Mrs. B. felt more and more that her judgment was being challenged by the group of parents. The results of the survey (recommended by Mrs. W.) would probably turn out to be close to what she had imagined. What then? Tonight she would have to defend her priorities or let Mrs. W. have her way. Maybe she would have to resign her job as director. "Life would be so much easier if I didn't have to deal with parents!" she thought. "I wonder if other teachers have these same problems?"

Mrs. B.'s situation is not an unusual one. Although she knows Mrs. W. personally as a parent and interacts easily with her on a one-to-one basis, tonight Mrs. W. is more than a parent; she is a member of a community of parents who approach the school as an institution they would like to influence. Mrs. B. and Mrs. W. now represent an institution and the community. It might be useful for Mrs. B. to think about her situation in these terms.

Teachers in early education centers have relationships with parents as both individuals and as groups. Even though the same people are involved, the skills needed by the teacher to deal with the parents in these different roles are not quite the same; groups of parents may approach the school and the teacher with expectations and demands that are only vaguely related to their communication on a personal level.

The school as an institution, represented by Mrs. B., serves the community, and if public funds are used to support the school, it is, in a sense, obligated to carry out the community's purposes. The relationship between a school and the parents of a community is dynamic and changing.

Parents respond to the school partly from their knowledge of the school staff and its image in the community, and partly from their desire to see the school carry out a program that serves the needs of their children. In this interaction, the community and school have different roles and responsibilities. The extent to which parents as a group can exercise control over the school varies greatly from one community to another. A strong parent group one year may be replaced by a passive group the next. Although many factors enter into the relationship, the teacher contributes a great deal to determining the kind of relationship it is at any given time.

The interaction between Mrs. B. and Mrs. W. is a typical example of a natural separation between the two major socializing agencies in the life of a small child—the family and the school. This separation contains an inherent stress that comes from potential disagreement over the way the school carries out its task. If the school becomes too far removed from the values and needs of the community, there will be some kind of corrective response, protest, or objection. Whatever the source or form of schooling, in our society the responsibility for educational decisions ultimately rests with the community.

Community involvement and control is, of course, not a new concept. Schools were traditionally under political and social control in rural areas and small towns in this country. Over the past fifty years, however, the size and complexity of school systems have increased. A wide tax base was needed to help support schools in low-income areas, and education itself needed to become more professional.

With the growth of professional training in education, there is a tendency for teachers and administrators to regard themselves as the educational experts and decision-makers and the parents as clients or customers. This view of education as the business of educators may create a gap of communication between community and school and lead to a school system that is divorced from the needs and values of the community it presumably serves. This happens even more easily in large systems which have centralized administrative functions and control. In recent years such separation has led to demands by parents for community control of the school. At the preschool level such concern applies especially to publicly-funded programs but may also include private nursery schools.

The school board may be composed of parents from the community who exercise direct control over such matters as the type of program to be adopted and the hiring of teachers. The involvement of parents as advisory groups that participate in decisions made by the school will very likely continue and perhaps increase.

Some school professionals have been distressed at this development. They argue that parent groups are difficult to work with and that groups of protesting parents tend to want fundamental changes in the school system itself. It is worth noting that in recent years the most urgent demands for control have come from large cities and minority communities where the schools have separated themselves too much from the community life and the needs of the people which they serve.

This has led to a kind of revolt in which parents are demanding a voice in the decisions concerning the educating of their children (Hess et al., 1971). This reassertion of parental rights to have control of the schools and to help decide what children should learn, is of great significance. The teacher who understands this will be able to engage parents in policy and decision making that will help use the resources of the community effectively and avoid open conflict.

The disagreement between Mrs. B. and Mrs. W. over the curriculum might result in a compromise acceptable to both sides, but the issue is one of whose priorities will prevail. Parents resent the fact that someone else is asked to define the priorities of the school when they are not consulted about their own views.

The disagreement over priorities may be only a symptom. Sometimes the feelings of being ignored and brushed aside become so great that the overwhelming motivation of parents in the community is to assert their own ideas and to take control of the school. These efforts may have ideological or educational elements but they are also struggles for power.

Conflicts between community groups and a school vary tremendously in their intensity. Usually they will involve the director of the school, members of the board and others centrally associated with the school. Such conflicts are less likely to develop where the communication between parents and the school staff is open and positive. Almost inevitably, there will be early signs of dissatisfaction which the teacher will recognize in time to begin conversations with both individual parents and groups of parents about their views, goals, and objections. The chance of getting things resolved is much better if problems are discussed as they arise rather than letting things accumulate and intensify until there is a showdown. Communication with members of the community will tell most teachers what the basic problems are and whether there is hope of resolution. The

4   School and Family—Partners or Competitors?

teacher will often be able to decide in advance of group meetings what the possible approaches are and what outcomes will be acceptable or unacceptable.

There has been a great deal of emphasis upon parental involvement in early education in the past few years, especially as a part of programs designed to increase educational resources and opportunities for children from low-income areas. Although there may be benefits to the children whose parents take an active part and to those schools that have the support and assistance of parents, the case for parental participation goes beyond these particular gains. Involvement is not an optional luxury, it is a right and obligation of the adult community.

Many teachers who are accustomed to traditional authority and administrative structures of schools may underestimate the potential influence of community groups. As they are often oriented to the school administration, teachers may not be aware of the extent to which the potential authority over the school may reside in several sources, rather than only in the director and board.

There are many forces that contribute to the involvement of groups of parents. These are expressed in both federal and state legislation that give parents specific types of control over the planning and implementation of early educational programs. The school, especially in urban areas, is much less insulated and isolated from the community than it was even a few years ago. As a profession, we are still gaining experience and understanding about the issues and problems involved in community participation in education and child care.

The Different Roles That Parents Play in the Life of a Teacher

During training, a teacher will be exposed to the many advantages of parent participation. Generally these interactions are friendly and supportive. It is useful, however, for the teacher to think about the various ways she and parents relate—whether they irritate or support one another, communicate or withdraw, agree or disagree. Rather than dwell on isolated incidents, the teacher may find it more helpful to fit these into a more comprehensive perspective, to think about parent-teacher interactions in general terms, and to consider their implications for the operation of the school.

There are at least four broad patterns of interaction between parents and the staff of a school.

Peer and Friendship Roles

For many teachers, probably the most frequent kind of parent interaction is with adults as parents of the children in the school. In this kind of situation the parents and teachers have a joint concern about the welfare and growth of the children and are responsible in different ways for their development. Parents do not surrender their rights as parents when they enroll their child in a school; at the same time, teachers have responsibilities to the school to carry out official policies and practices. There is obviously a zone of teaching behavior in which the rights and obligations of parents and the rights and responsibilities of teachers are unclear or in apparent conflict. Some type of communication between parents and teachers is needed to identify and keep clear these issues of joint responsibility. The teacher must take the initiative in clarifying the roles that she and the mother play in the school setting, making it clear to the mother that she has her own style and her own ways of relating to the children under her care. But both parent and teacher need to recognize that the welfare of the child is a common concern and both share in the responsibility for achieving their goals.

As colleagues, in a sense, parents are supportive in various ways—reinforcing the teacher and her methods, assisting with tasks in the classroom, helping to take children on field trips, raising money for new equipment, maintenance of the school, and other activities. Much of the day-to-day interaction falls into this category.

The Boss and Employee Roles

One type of parent involvement takes the form of parent groups that are formed to make policy for the schools, to oversee hiring and firing of staff, and to help formulate programs. These community groups may contain persons who themselves have no children in the school. They hold a political relationship to the school and its staff. Some publicly-funded children's centers, for example, extend to community groups considerable authority over the school. In some states, legislation requires council or advisory groups of parents and gives these groups a formal role to help plan and govern the early education or child care programs.

Parents as Staff Members— Assistant Teachers and Aides

Another form of involvement is participation of parents in the day-to-day activities of the schools. This differs from the pattern described above in that it calls for regular (usually volunteer) help in the classroom and in routine activities of the school.

4 School and Family—Partners or Competitors?

Roles That Parents Play in the Life of a Teacher

Some schools are set up to provide for reduction in tuition for families who volunteer in this way; other arrangements call for hiring of aides on a regularly paid basis. In all these cases, however, the parent is assisting the teacher in carrying out her role in the school.

Parents as Home-based Teachers

One form of parent involvement, which has been expanding rapidly since the beginning of Head Start, is designed to prepare the mother to teach the child at home. The underlying purpose of this form of involvement is to help the child prepare for formal schooling, but it also often is intended to give the mother advice and information about her role as parent. This form of involvement typically puts the teacher in the role of educational authority on what it is that the child should learn and on techniques the parent should use in teaching the child. It is a contrast to the type of parental involvement described above, which puts the control of the school and of its policies in the hands of the community.

There are a number of issues inherent in these different forms of parent participation, and most are discussed in Chapter 5.

Exchanges between teachers and parents of the children in their schools do not always fall neatly into these general categories. Some encounters may involve more than one dimension within the space of a few minutes. Within a single conversation, the roles of the parent and those of the teacher may change. A parent may switch from speaking as a member of a school advisory board to speaking as a parent virtually from one sentence to the next. Or he or she may play the part of an aide or assistant, then shift suddenly to the part of a parent of one of the children in the group.

One useful way to think of these interactions is in terms of the different authority positions they represent. That is, the relative authority of the teacher and parent may quickly change. For example, when the teacher is employee, her authority and power are much less than those of the parent. However, when the parent volunteers to help the teacher carry out her activities, the parent has assumed a subordinate role to the teacher for that particular period of time and activity. If a parent drives children on a field trip sponsored by the school, the school and teacher are responsible and thus both are in charge. If the parents ask for help in teaching their child, the teacher again is in an authoritative position in the relationship. In the peer-friendship interaction, they are equals, with different roles and responsibilities.

The Teacher as a Part of the Parent-Child System

Interacting with groups of parents and interacting with parents as individuals are quite different activities. They call for different approaches and offer their own unique satisfactions. Sometimes this type of interaction is called "involving parents" but in our view it is not a question of *whether* parents of the children in your school are involved but in *how* they are related to you and the school. When a child is enrolled in your school, you are connected to the parent through your joint responsibility and care for the child. You are hooked into an existing system as soon as you accept the child and make a commitment to the parents to perform certain services for them and the child. They, in turn, are related to you through the fact that they have accepted a commitment to bring the child to school (or see that he or she gets there) and to carry out their own responsibilities in relation to the school's program.

One way to think about this is to see the parents and child as a social and emotional system into which you have entered. The mother-father-child tie is the central one, based on the complexities of love, neglect, guidance, resentment, frustration, discipline, and attachment that make up the different kinds of primary ties between parents and child. No matter how important you become to the child, you are a supplemental and tangential part of the system. But you are, nonetheless, a real and significant part.

How this basic and sometimes powerful system of parent-child-teacher deals with the things that tie them together is one of the most perplexing aspects of a teacher's life. It is also one of the most rewarding.

In certain ways, each individual family system* brings a unique unit to the school and the teacher relates to them in a unique way. In this sense, parent involvement is a cluster of individual systems of interaction with each family—a sort of telephone switchboard with the teacher interacting with each family individually. The parents' groups and public meetings sometimes are more like communicating through a loudspeaker to a group; the individual parent-child-teacher system is more like a three-way telephone conversation.

The demands and opportunities of each of these systems are different from all others. Each presents its own problems; each calls for its own solutions. The teacher will gain in experience

---

* Although each family unit may consist of father, mother, grandparents, siblings, the reference is generally to "parent-child" because the most common unit interacting with the school is the mother-child.

and sensitivity as she learns to deal with the uniqueness of each system and she or he will learn that it is impossible to have pat answers or formulas for responding to the problems they present. The most sensible route will be to understand the unique aspects of each system and use this as a basis for applying your own good sense and experience. The answers and responses you think useful for one family may not be helpful for another; the answers you call on early in your teaching career are probably somewhat changed as you gain in experience and judgment.

A fairly typical comment like "I told Janey that you don't like children who won't eat all their breakfast," shows how a teacher can innocently become tied into a system in which the parent uses the teacher to blame or punish the child.

A teacher plays many roles in parent-child systems. For example, the following is one in which she sides with the child against the parent:

"These paintings are so wet," complained Mario's mother. "I don't want them in our car." "No! I want to take my paintings home today!" protests Mario. "You know," the teacher interjects, "Children are proud of what they make and it helps their self-esteem by being appreciative."

Sometimes one parent will enlist the support of the teacher to strengthen his or her position in the system: "My husband spends so much time on his work that he doesn't have time for his family. Would you talk with him about the importance of fathers in the sex development of young children?"

At times both parents will be aligned against the child and will attempt to convince the teacher to reinforce the existing dynamics of their system: "Sheryl is always doing something naughty on purpose just to get attention. The other night the whole family got dressed up for a dinner party. We had some very important guests coming and just as the doorbell rang, Sheryl deliberately wet her pants so the whole family was forced to pay attention to her!"

The teacher-parent-child system can be a powerful, positive contribution to the child's development, especially if the goals are clear and if the child is involved in setting the goals. It is particularly important for each member of the system to recognize how much they can do for one another by supporting and strengthening the unit.

In all these patterns of interaction, it is clear that the parents play a decisive role. They know the child best, are in a position of responsibility and authority. The teacher can play a facilitating role and sometimes provide a model which the parents can observe and decide whether they want to imitate. The teacher isn't likely to change the basic parent-child tie—certainly not by giving advice or lecturing. She can help, sometimes, by supporting the parents and contributing to their confidence or by reflecting or interpreting behavior. Natural, unselfconscious parental interaction with a child is in itself a great resource. It is no contribution to parents to tell them what they are doing is wrong if the consequence is to make them feel less capable and more guilty over their behavior toward their child.

Sometimes a teacher must ask himself or herself just how much he should intrude into the parent-child system. Some situations are best left alone; others are best referred to a counsellor or family service agency. It is not always easy to decide what the teacher's most useful role should be.

As a facilitator and transient member of a family system, it is important to assess continually your value in strengthening the basic family unit. You are only a temporary influence. The family still remains the most constant teacher in the life of a young child.

Some of the issues inherent in school-parent interactions can be seen most clearly through examples of situations that arise frequently. These examples make it possible to evaluate the consequences of different kinds of action on the part of the teacher and the parent. Following are a range of situations which call for quite varied responses on the part of teachers. Consider each of them in terms of the issues that are involved and how you think they should be handled. By identifying the issues, you may be able to develop a personal policy which will be useful as you gain additional experience.

Possibly no part of a teacher's role is more sensitive and potentially more bruising and perplexing than the teaching of basic values about sex, religion, political attitudes, and the like. Here are some instances of what can (and do) happen: "My husband stayed to visit for a few minutes at school this morning, and he's very upset about your program." It was George's mother on the phone reporting an unexpected impression. "Why, I spoke with him about how well George was doing and he appeared pleased," said the director. "He gave no indications whatsoever of being unhappy with us." "Well, my husband saw George ironing in the dress-up corner and he's very much concerned. You know, George is very quiet and much shyer than our other children and he seems to prefer 'girl-type' activities to playing with the boys."

A conference was set up for both parents and the director and Miss S., the teacher. The father expressed his discomfort at being outnumbered: "I know you women don't think it's anything to be concerned about, and you may be right, but I have to say how I feel about this. I rarely come into the school and the one time I show up, what do I see, but my child playing with girls and ironing!"

"It's unfortunate that you saw only a small sample of his daily activities," volunteered Miss S., "because he does play outdoors and works at the carpentry table."

"George is a quiet child who seems more comfortable in small, well-defined areas indoors, like the art and housekeeping corners," reported the director. "However, our observations indicate that he interacts with boys as much as girls, and he seems to enjoy the traditional boy-type activities like playing ball, carpentry, and climbing."

"Well, what's wrong with boys ironing?" interjected Miss S. "I think we make too much of the sex roles. I object to sex differentiated activities and to teacher and parents imposing these culturally stereotyped masculine and feminine roles on children! I'm tired of sexism in the preschool curriculum!"

"I told him he was worrying about nothing," added George's mother.

Looking dejected and sounding somewhat distant, George's father commented, "I knew I'd be outnumbered today. I didn't expect you women to understand what I'm trying to say." Then with a note of anger to his voice, "You say you want to involve the fathers more in your program, but you women always have to run the show with your set ideas about what's good for my kid!"

"I think you are partly right, Mr. B." agreed the director. "Teachers often do not hear the concerns of parents because of their own biases or values, but I would disagree that it is us women against you, the man. I think it would be much more useful if we could talk about another issue at stake here. Your concern about George and our program brings up the question of how much we, as teachers, should impose our own personal views on the children, especially if they are in disagreement with the parents."

"What do you think, Miss S.? As George's teacher, do you think you will encourage him to iron, even though you know his dad doesn't want him to?"

Obviously, there are many ways to deal with the above situation. Some of them have dramatically different outcomes and consequences for the child and for the teacher-parent relationship. As the teacher, you may turn off and alienate this father if you refuse to accept his feelings as genuine and legitimate. But if you attempt to follow a plan which carries out the father's wishes and actively try to keep George from the ironing board and similar female sex-typed activities, you may create more distress for him. He may be working out some very sensitive feelings of his own about being a boy and interacting in different ways with boys and with girls. Ignoring the father's problem while appearing to accept what he says seems insincere and possibly unethical. The father has a right to be involved in the education of his child. Also, you have your own feelings and opinions about sex typing and the teaching of sex roles to young children. These may or may not coincide with those of George's father. In short, whatever you do will have consequences and will not satisfy everyone in the scene.

You will probably never experience an encounter exactly like the one just described. Each situation carries its own set of considerations which change in some way the kind of response you would give. Perhaps it is more important to develop ways to consider and evaluate these situations than to try to figure out the right answer to any one of them.

What are the most important aspects of such parent-teacher confrontations?

Five Ways to Evaluate
Parent-Teacher Interaction

Exchanges, especially if they are confrontations between teachers and parents, usually raise matters of substance as well as of personal feelings. To deal with feelings is essential but it is not enough. Actions of some sort will always result from such encounters, even if the action on the part of the teacher is to be evasive or ambiguous or perpetuate the friction by keeping the matter unresolved.

Certain aspects of encounters may be presented in the form of five questions, which may help the teacher to get a perspective on the problem. The answers to these questions should help her formulate an appropriate solution.

1. Does the problem involve the rights of parents to teach their children basic values about such things as religious beliefs, morality, ethnic, and cultural customs?
2. Are there legal or ethical constraints involved in the problem?
3. Does the situation involve professional standards and the expertise of the teacher? This includes professional knowledge that is related to the welfare and progress of the child or the instructional practices of the program.
4. Does the situation raise a question about the right of the school to set administrative policy for the sake of efficiency or convenience?
5. To what extent are the rights and welfare of the child involved?

Think of the encounter with George's father in these terms. Does a family have the right to decide what attitudes about sex roles will be taught? Probably so. At least they have primary responsibility.

Is there a legal or ethical problem? Probably not, although there might be if teachers tried to change children's ideas about sex roles without informing the parents.

Is professional expertise involved in this decision? It seems unlikely that there is sufficient knowledge on the effects of sex-typed activities on development of young children to offer a definite answer.

Is a school policy involved and does the parent's request set a precedent for changing school policy to meet the needs or desires of an individual family? Perhaps so. To exclude or include children in school activities on the basis of sex of the child would be difficult to implement and would put an additional administrative burden on the staff.

Will the decision affect the growth and development of social, emotional, or physical capabilities in the child? Possibly the child's preference for ironing means something important about his social development. It may indicate some discomfort in interacting with other boys and competing with them in games and physical activities.

These questions are not designed to provide you with answers but with some guidelines to help develop a rationale on which to act. You may change your answers as you gain more experience and your perspectives will change with each situation, but the answers you supply will provide a clearer picture so you will at least know why you are doing what you are doing.

Some additional examples will give you an opportunity to apply these questions. See whether they help suggest solutions to the conflict or problem presented.

Mrs. W. is the kind of person no one can ignore. In her early 40s, she is the mother of Jeff, one of the five-year-old boys in the children's center. Teachers complain that they hate to come to work on Mrs. W.'s day to volunteer. She is humorless, bossy, loud, and obviously interested only in Jeff's activities in school. She often neglects the area assigned to her supervision in order to keep an eye on Jeff. Whenever there is a dispute over a favorite toy or trike, all Jeff has to do is run and tell his mother. "It's impossible to work with Jeff when his mother is around, so we have learned to leave them alone," reports one of the teachers. "Actually, it's to Jeff's disadvantage because he's getting a lot of inconsistent treatment. He behaves very differently on the days his mother does not work; he's reasonable and receptive to our suggestions and our methods of discipline." Should the teacher confront Jeff's mother? Why?

Few parents who help as temporary staff members are like Jeff's mother, but there are some who, because of differences in background and training, will disagree with the teachers on effective child rearing methods. Often, teachers are not prepared to handle such differences, especially if the parents are resistive to new or different ways of discipline. It is important for both the teacher and parent to recognize that the child suffers from lack of agreement between school and family.

Jenny is a four-year-old, born out of wedlock. She is one of many children from one-parent families served by the Neighborhood Child Development Center.

Her twenty-one year old mother, a high school dropout at sixteen, has been picked up twice for possession of hard drugs. The mother's employment record is erratic—two months on an assembly line at a local electronics firm, six weeks as a waitress in a short order restaurant, two other short-term jobs.

Jenny's attendance reflects the instability of her home life. She is often late or absent, and seems to be uninvolved, listless, irritable, and difficult to reach. Teachers report that Jenny has suspicious looking bruises on her back and thighs. "Involving disinterested, uneducated parents seems simple compared with Jenny's mother," remarks one concerned teacher. "That poor woman is so vulnerable to all kinds of disaster that I feel guilty asking her to do anything that would require another ounce of her physical or emotional energy." "Maybe the best thing we can do is keep Jenny out of her hair while she seeks help for herself," commented another teacher.

This mother obviously needs support and help in various ways, but the primary concern of the teacher at this point is how the mother's problems affect the child. Perhaps this situation is one that justifies extreme measures, despite the teacher's reluctance to add to the mother's burdens. No matter how much the teacher sympathizes with the mother's situation and her helplessness, she may be compelled to intervene for the sake of the child. In fact, in many states, the teacher is required by law to report child abuse.* If she does not, she may be legally guilty of contributory negligence.

Mrs. F. rushed to the block corner too late to prevent David from punching Jimmy in the face. This was most unusual be-

---

* Two worries teachers may have about reporting possible child abuse are whether the parent will be told who submitted the report and whether suit can be brought against the teacher. The local policy and the state laws vary on these points. In some states, no action can be brought against a person filing or submitting a report. In some local instances, persons who report are not required to give their names in order for some investigation to be initiated by local authorities. You should find out about local policy and state laws in whatever location you will be working.

havior; the two boys were friends. "Why are you fighting?" asked Mrs. F. Jimmy was too angry to answer. Mrs. F. looked at David. "He said my mommy's wrong." "About what?" "No," shouted Jimmy, rubbing away his tears. "He said that when I die I'll go to heaven and be an angel."

"That's what my mommy told me," interrupted David. Then looking questioningly at Mrs. F. "My mommy's right, isn't she, Mrs. F.?"

A teacher may have difficulty maintaining integrity with her own beliefs while treating with respect the ideas of the children and their parents. What if she is a person with strong religious convictions? Should she side with David? If she believes David's mother is wrong, does she side with Jimmy? She can, of course, cop out by dealing only with the argument between the boys and ignoring the question of who was right about their beliefs in heaven.

How might she have reacted if the question had been about Santa Claus? Or about the stork bringing a baby brother or sister? What is the teacher's responsibility?

Scene in the teachers' coffee room:

Mrs. C. I can't stand the way Julie's mother treats her! It's all I can do to be civil when she comes to pick Julie up after school.

Miss F. I feel the same way! She's such a creep. We spend all day helping Julie to develop some self esteem and she comes along and in the space of 3 minutes, she undoes everything we've been working on all day. Yesterday she scolded Julie for getting dirty and made some crack about her being a pest.

Mrs. C. She never acknowledges Julie's attempts to share her happy feelings with her. I have never seen her hug or kiss Julie, even though Julie tries to get close to her mother. She just ignores her physically and verbally.

Miss F. I see by her folder that she has lots of personal problems but what can we do for Julie, especially since we agree that the mother's treatment of Julie is wrong?

Up to this point, in applying the five questions to the situations described above, we have concentrated upon criteria that speak to the nature of the conflict, and not to the tact and understanding with which these sensitive situations are handled. The teacher's attitudes and approach to the discussion are critical to a resolution of a confrontation. For any solution, the approach of the teacher can be abrasive or it can be sensitive and considerate. Even on questions of the legal rights of the child, the teacher can still handle the communications with warmth and understanding. Or, she can make matters worse by acting in a punishing, guilt-creating manner. If the parent is right, the teacher can either react with defensiveness and resentment, or respond with acceptance and dignity.

These affective dimensions of the interaction are a matter of the teacher's personal style and interpersonal ability. They do not themselves provide the answer to the problem. A teacher's answer may be so persuasive and gentle that the parent is convinced that the teacher is correct, even though she may not have taken the parent's rights into proper account. There can be a vast difference between the nature of a solution and the way it is carried out.

Sometimes the most important outcome of an encounter is the feelings on the part of the parents that the teacher is perceptive, warm, sensitive and that she has tried to understand their viewpoint. The teacher's first response, perhaps, is to accept that parent's complaints and feelings and then try to move to a discussion of the underlying issues.

Probably any solution is bad if it leads to unresolved anger and alienation of the family from the school or to a feeling on the part of the teacher that she has been put down by a parent. One consideration, then, is *the feelings of the people involved about the confrontation itself.*

Gains and Losses in School-Community Interaction

Because the school and family have joint responsibility and both are oriented to the same children in different ways, there are stresses that seem to be natural, that is, unavoidable, features of family-school interaction. At the community level, these appear as issues of community control vs. the right of educational experts and professionals to direct a program. There is also tension, however, in the direct exchange between a specific family and a teacher.

Competition Between Mother and Teacher

One potential source of tension is a subtle competition between mother and teacher for the child. For some mothers, nursery school is the first occasion for separation from their young children, and while the problem of separation is usually seen as a problem for the child, there is a complementary stress for the mother. The child, who as a baby and infant has been almost completely dependent on her, now is dependent upon someone else. Both teacher and mother share responsibility for his care and both expect loyalty and dependence.

In this situation, the parent may view the teacher as a competitor for the child's attention. What, for example, will the mother's feelings and attitudes be if the child becomes more at-

tached to the teacher than to her? Or if the school becomes a more appealing and desirable place than the home in the judgment of the young child? While the question is almost never

4 School and Family—Partners or Competitors?

stated in such bold terms, it arises in some parent-teacher relationships and can complicate interaction between parent and school.

Parents also occasionally see teachers as potential evaluators and critics. For some mothers, participating in a school program will be their first opportunity to observe their children's behavior in comparison to groups of other children of approximately the same age. ("Behavior" here is used in the full developmental sense, not simply in reference to discipline.) Whether or not they express their doubt, many mothers may fear in the back of their minds that the teacher may find something about their child that indicates parental failure to do an adequate job. No matter how tactful a teacher may be, her expertise carries a potential threat.

Parental Concern Over the Child's Development

Some parents may worry about how normal the developmental skills of their children are compared with those of their peers. The parent's belief about whether the child is less bright, as bright as, or brighter than others may have great impact on the future of her child. What she decides from her observation, and through interaction with the teacher, often determines how much she encourages her children to achieve what she hopes for them and what she will push them to do.

There is also the possibility of difficulty between teacher and mother if the teacher feels that the mother has been neglecting or mistreating the child in some way or is uninterested in the child's progress. The evaluation may be accurate or it may simply be a reflection of the teacher's tendency to feel possessive about her class. For example, a teacher sees the effort a child puts into creating a picture. Hearing the mother comment that she wishes her child would ". . . paint something I can show his father instead of always making such a mess" can upset a teacher and lead her to feel that the mother is unappreciative. In such circumstances, it is understandable why she might characterize the mother as one who does not give proper support to the child and to the efforts of the teacher.

The question of the extent to which the family and the school share similar goals and expectations, and agree on patterns of achievement is particularly relevant for schools that work with children from low-income families. Because there is often a disparity of cultural background, education, and socioeconomic level between the mother and the teacher, there is potential for problems of communication in their relationship. Some of the elements for misunderstanding and conflict that exist in parent-teacher situations have already been described—i.e., the challenge the teacher represents to the mother's competence, the worry that separation can bring, the competition for the affection of the child, the feeling that the teacher disapproves. These are heightened when the mother comes from a background which the teacher does not understand or where opportunities were meager in comparison with those of the school staff.

In some instances, teachers have the attitude that mothers from economic and social levels less advantageous than their own lack interest in their children's education. This is a myth (Hess and Shipman, 1968). On the contrary, women with few resources often see the school as the beginning of advantage for their children. If the teacher's attitudes about the parents of her students are stereotyped and biased, they obviously interfere with the communication between school and home.

The Teacher as Confidant

Many relationships between parents and teachers are gratifying to both. For some mothers, a warm, understanding teacher may come to be a maternal figure for them as well as their child. The teacher is often the one to whom the mother turns for advice and encouragement with any number of personal problems. Teachers spend many hours in the role of sympathetic friend and counselor. Not only do they want to help, but they may understandably feel flattered to be trusted with confidences of a personal nature.

However, this relationship of confidante presents a number of hazards for both teacher and mother. The teacher's assuming the role of adviser or amateur therapist may change or even destroy the professional teacher-parent relationship. Too often it encourages dependence on the part of the mother, forming an alliance which is essentially outside the function of the school. In addition, the teacher loses the objectivity needed for effective interaction with the total family to the best interest of the child. In being a sympathetic listener to the mother, the teacher typically only hears one side of a situation and thus is not in a position to make valid judgments. Where the confidences are about the husband's behavior as father or mate, the father is often reluctant to come for a conference, not because he lacks concern for the child, but because he may feel the mother-teacher relationship has already excluded him. Perhaps when advice is sought on matters outside the needs of the child, the teacher's most professional and sensible response would be to suggest other resources that are available.

The nursery school gives parents a chance to examine, and in a sense to validate, their own behavior as well as to observe their children. By watching their children in a school environment, they can see whether their own techniques and attitudes are as influential as are those of others. Thus, they gain a sense of whether their problems and ways of dealing with them are different or the same as others, and what methods are the most effective. The nursery school affords an important source of information for parents who want to become as adequate and competent as possible in dealing with their young children.

In some instances a mother may need help in handling her preschooler and yet be unaware that she has a problem. She feels, perhaps, that Teddy is going through a stage and he will eventually grow out of whatever she finds objectionable. Meanwhile, she'll just keep extra close watch on him. Having a chance to compare Teddy's behavior with that of other children his age, and talking over her observations and experiences with the teacher and with other parents, may be all this mother needs to bring about better results with her son. Or a mother may know she has a problem and yet be too proud, or, for some other reason, unwilling, to ask for help. Close parent-teacher relationships make it possible to share problems of this kind and to work them out together for the benefit of the child.

The School as a Community Resource

Where there is effective community participation, schools may also serve as centers where parents can obtain information not only about their children but about themselves and ways to improve their individual lives. This expresses a more general plan to use the schools as educational institutions for communities and families.

Programs have been set up that provide, in effect, training centers for the family as well as nursery school experiences for young children. Such centers make it possible for mothers to watch a skilled staff interact with their children and to work as assistant teachers. This kind of model introduces mothers to alternative ways of dealing with their children and may help them develop more effective techniques of their own. Other specific kinds of information which can be made available to families at these training centers are:

How to shop
How to save money
How to prepare balanced meals
Birth control advice
Medical advice
Retraining and career opportunities
Self awareness and fulfillment
Consumer information
Legal advice

The benefits that accrue to the family from interaction with the school are part of the rationale for parent involvement. These benefits may come directly through conferences with the teacher, attendance at parents' meetings, and informal discussions with other mothers. Or they may arise indirectly as a parent develops greater understanding of her relationship with her child through classroom observation. Seeing how other children and parents interact gives her a better perspective on her own behavior. In addition, the mutual respect and friendship that grow between parents whose children attend the same nursery school program not only help to satisfy them as individuals, but frequently lead to a realization that as a group they can achieve ends not otherwise possible.

The Contribution of Parents to the Program

Parent involvement often makes possible the expansion and enrichment of a preschool program. Special talents and resources are found among people of all social and economic backgrounds. As mentioned in Chapter 3, the teacher may need to seek out the mother or father who can play a musical instrument, speak a foreign language, take school pictures, or in other ways add to the school program. But the effort is rewarding. Fathers who appear in their roles as firemen, milkmen, auto mechanics, doctors, sports figures, or whatever the composition of the class offers, add interest and substance to any day's schedule. Mothers frequently provide the extra help needed for field trips, library visits, and special projects of all kinds. Parents can also be a valuable resource to teachers in providing and maintaining equipment. Slides, sandboxes, stoves, and workbenches are often built by parents; tables, chairs, dolls, and swings have been kept usable through parent's skills.

When interaction that is built on mutual interest and common goals takes place between family and school, the resulting sense of support and harmony can give the child a feeling of security and continuity. His life is less fragmented; he is more free to talk about his experiences at home and at school. There is, in short, less need for him to separate in his mind the things that are separated by distance. On the other hand, home and school may be teaching quite different attitudes and patterns of behavior and this may create problems if the differences are not understood or accepted. But the differences need not always create problems. If close contact is maintained between home and school, teachers are less likely to violate the cultural and personal standards of the family by what they teach children to do and say at school. They can also reduce the possibility of conflict by helping parents understand the school's goals for the growth and development of the child.

SOME POINTS TO REMEMBER

1. In interaction with parents, teachers discover that a given individual may act in one situation as a parent but in another as a member of a community group. Their behavior in these two situations may be quite different—personal in one, formal and challenging in the other.
2. Both family and school have a vested interest in caring for the child. This may sometimes bring them into disagreement.
3. The ultimate responsibility for educational decisions rests with the community.
4. The professional training of the teacher and school staff tend to make them regard themselves as more expert in educating or caring for the child than the child's parents.
5. Parent involvement is of several different types, from control over hiring the faculty and drawing up the budget, to assisting the teacher, to inquiring about their child's art products at school.
6. Conflict between school staff and community persons will be signaled by subtle indications of disagreement or resistance.
7. Parent involvement and sharing in school control is now being mandated in many states by legislation.

8. Parents play different types of roles—peer and friendship, employer, assistant teachers, teachers of the child in the home.

9. One parent may play different roles at different times.

10. The teacher, child, and parent are part of a single system of interaction. The major question is not whether parents are involved but *how* they are involved.

11. The teacher-parent-child system has many forms, one of which is that two of the three may align in some way against the third.

12. Another form the system can take is for all three to agree on goals for the child and to support the child in working toward them.

13. Conflict between teacher and parent may arise when they have different values they would like the child to adopt. This presents a most difficult professional problem for the teacher.

14. There are guidelines which help resolve such conflicts, involving the rights of parents, legal or ethical constraints, professional standards of school or teacher, administrative policies of the school, the rights and welfare of the child. The resolution of a particular situation, however, is a judgment call.

15. Perhaps the most important aspect of conflict is not what decision is made but the spirit of cooperation with which it is discussed.

16. Parents sometimes worry about the teacher as a critic of a parent's handling of the child, or an assessment of the child stating that he is less than average in performance.

17. Mothers from low income, low education backgrounds typically have high aspirations and goals for their children.

18. A teacher who becomes the confidante of a mother may find professional interaction threatened or a tendency to pull the teacher into an alignment with the mother.

19. Observing at a nursery school or child care center gives parents opportunities to learn from other parents and to see their children in a more objective perspective.

20. A sense of support and agreement in goals between school and family is essential to the maximum growth of the child.

SUMMARY

The natural separation between family and school contains inherent stress. The teacher plays an important role in recognizing the needs and values of the larger community. A section of this chapter identifies the different roles parents play (peer-friendship, boss-employee, etc.) A useful way for the teacher to think about his or her involvement is that of tying in to an existing parent-child system. Each "system" is a family unit to which the teacher relates, recognizing the uniqueness of each unit. Some examples provide ways to recognize and think about the dynamics of teacher-family relationships. Five ways to evaluate parent-teacher interactions are suggested with some examples of typical problems in the classroom. The last section deals with gains and losses in school-community interaction.

REFERENCES   Auerbach, A. B. *Parents learn through group discussion: principles and practices of parent group education.* New York: John Wiley and Sons, Inc., 1968.

Davies, D. *Citizen participation in education: an annotated bibliography.* New Haven, Conn.: Institute for Responsive Education, 1974.

Giesy, R. (ed.) *A guide for home visitors.* Nashville, Tennessee: CARCEE, Peabody College, 1970.

Hess, R. D. and Shipman, V. C. Maternal attitudes toward the school and the role of pupil: some social class comparisons. In A. H. Passow (ed.), *Developing programs for the educationally disadvantaged.* New York: Teachers College Press, 1968, pp. 109–129.

Lillie, D. I. (ed.) *Parent programs in child development centers.* First Chance for Children, Vol. 1. Technical Assistance Development System, University of North Carolina, Chapel Hill, 1972.

Lundberg, C. M. and Miller, V. M. *Parent involvement staff handbook: a manual for child development programs.* Mississippi Head Start Training Coordinating Council, P.O. Box 22591, Jackson, Mississippi, 1972.

Project Head Start. *Parent Involvement—a workbook of training tips for Head Start staff.* Washington, D.C. U.S. Department of Health, Education, and Welfare, 1968.

Rood, L. A. *Parents and teachers together: a training manual for parent involvement in Head Start centers.* Washington, D.C.: Gryphen House, 1971.

Stanford Research Institute. *Parent Involvement in Compensatory Education Programs.* Prepared for Office of Planning, Budgeting and Evaluation. U.S. Office of Education, Washington, D.C., August 1931.

State Education Agencies and Parent Involvement: A National Survey of State Legislation and the Policies and Perspectives of State Department of Education, Center for the Study of Parent Involvement, Berkeley, California, February 1974.

Chapter 5 Parents and Teachers as Collaborators

Increasing Interaction with Parents and the Community

Although teachers are connected with parents and necessarily interact with them, they can often affect the nature and extent of the interaction that takes place. The tempo and frequency of interaction is usually determined by the teacher because of a natural barrier to communication between them.

It is easy to isolate parents or to become isolated from them. When the child is brought to school on the first day, contacts are such that the parents are urged to leave the child as soon as possible, sometimes even before the child stops crying. The teacher wants, quite appropriately, to get the child accustomed to his new social world and to the routine and to other children. It is a mark of the teacher's success that the parent can easily and quickly leave the child at the school or center. Parents are usually persuaded to accept this mode of behavior and the parents' absence thus becomes a success for teacher, child, and parent. In this way the objectives of the school staff actively isolate the parent and set a pattern of non-participation. Once this separation is achieved, it is less easy or comfortable to bring the parent back into the activities of the school, except in groups on parents' night or some such ritualistic occasion. The teacher may, herself, feel more comfortable interacting with the child than with the parent. She can put the child's name tag on, introduce him to other children, show her the work table or sandbox and do other things that she sees as part of her job. Besides, she probably assumes that the parent wants to leave as soon as possible.

It is also more convenient and efficient for teachers to do their jobs without the necessity of relating to parents in an intensive fashion. Parents complicate the life of a teacher. If they are brought into deliberations, they slow down the process of arriving at decisions and they obviously add an element of risk. Suppose the teacher cannot persuade them that her own policies and procedures are the best. She must then face a possible conflict or encounter or she must give in to a plan which is not her preferred pattern. Parents also have other demands upon them that make their participation as assistants less reliable than the teacher would like. A sick child, or other important demands lead to a greater absence rate among volunteers, generally, including parents. The presence of a parent sometimes stimulates a child to be more dependent or more active or in some cases, parents take advantage of their role as assistants in the classroom to protect their own children, or discipline them, in ways that are disruptive and not in keeping with the routines of the school. Parents are not only easy to isolate from the activities of the school—it's sometimes more comfortable for the teacher when they're not around.

Some social changes in the society are also creating conditions which limit the amount of time that parents have to interact with the school. In one-parent families, especially, the full burden of responsibility for child care and economic resources fall upon one adult. This leaves little time or energy for interaction with the teacher unless there is an obvious reason for doing so. The rise in employment rates among married women means that mothers are unavailable during the day, even if they are part of a complete family. They may easily see the school and teacher as resources that help them keep their jobs and they may feel that it is the responsibility of the center to care for the child during working hours. In short, many parents are less available.

Mothers who do not work but who send their children to nursery school for two and a half to three hours a day may have their own personal and family schedules to meet. They may count on the time the child is at school to run errands, do the shopping, visit friends, contribute time to a civic or charitable group. They want or need this time to follow their own interests. One mother puts it: "If I get into the wrong line at the market, I'm in trouble."

Encouraging Parent Participation in the Goals of the School

What can a teacher do to include parents more actively in the school program? How does she let them know that their participation in the life of the school is both desired and expected? It is the responsibility of the teacher to take the initiative, especially in working with families from low-income areas. She should not expect the parent to make the overture but should herself be the one to reach out to let parents know what kind of person she is and what she expects. The program in which she works may have procedures to follow that will help her establish a cooperative, professional relationship with parents, but the responsibility is ultimately hers.

Creating an atmosphere that shows that the school is a place where there is someone to talk to and where parents are welcome requires a minimum of effort on the part of the teacher. Some useful techniques and strategies for involving parents include:

> Greet parents by name and engage in casual, friendly conversation when child is brought to school and picked up.
> Send notes and samples of child's work home.
> Make phone calls inviting parents to school programs and suggesting home visits.
> Provide a place for parents to have coffee.
> Plan, or have parents plan, more formal meetings.
> Seek help with special projects.
> Schedule conferences on a regular basis, not just when child has a "problem."

Suggestions such as "Greet parents by name and engage in friendly conversation" may seem obvious and unnecessary, but not all teachers make it a point to engage in day-to-day contacts of this kind, and some fail to realize that techniques like these build positive learning situations. Simple procedures can go a long way to make parents feel they are welcome and that the teacher is interested in them and in their child. Commenting favorably on the work of the child also tells the parent that she and the child are important in the program.

```
Dear Parent:

    We are planning to have 3 meetings at school this year.
Which of these things would make you want to attend?
                                                    Check
        Slides or movies of my child               _____
        Free baby sitting at the school            _____
        Informal discussion about
                    child development              _____
                    discipline                     _____
                    mental growth                  _____
        Guest speaker                              _____
        Refreshments                               _____
```

An occasional spontaneous note pinned to a child's jacket when he's ready to go home stimulates interaction between teacher and parent. Criticism of the child, or a report on his lack of achievement should never be handled in this way, however. This kind of discussion, if needed at all, should be reserved for personal conferences.

The model of teacher-parent interaction that we are suggesting here is a mutual, reciprocal one in which there is a contribution from both sides. For example, if you are planning two or three group sessions, why not send a note to parents asking them what they would like to have happen on these evenings. Make some suggestions of your own to let them know what some possibilities are, but remain open and responsive to the preferences and needs they express.

Formal parent conferences can be scheduled with the convenience of the parents in mind. This may require after-school or evening hours, perhaps even a visit to the child's home. Whatever the setting, a formal meeting should be unhurried and directed toward the particular reason for its being held.

Often the most meaningful and helpful conversations will take place informally and spontaneously at the school entrance or over a cup of coffee during a parent's visit. When the teacher or director is available and receptive, parents will often share an immediate concern in an impromptu fashion. Sometimes minor problems, which seem too unimportant for a conference, build into crisis proportions if no opportunity exists to air them.

Meetings with groups of parents take many forms. Three of the most common are:

    Informal meetings
    Open house meetings
    Workshop meetings

Some parents find it interesting and helpful to see a film or hear what the teacher or outside person has to say about topics such as When Brothers and Sisters Fight or Discipline and Self-Control.

A meeting on how children learn might present some of Piaget's ideas in an interesting and easily understood format by showing parents some slide pictures and playing a tape recording of some of the children in the school.

TAPE RECORDING	DESCRIPTION OF SLIDE PICTURE
1. **Child** I want to play with these buttons. **Teacher** Okay. Put them into piles for me.	Teacher and child examining a cigar box filled with buttons.
2. **Child** Can I make any piles I want? **Teacher** Yes. (other chatter and conversation)	Child selecting buttons.
3. **Teacher** Good! You sorted these buttons into how many piles? **Child** One, two, three.	Child with three piles of buttons.
4. **Teacher** Why did you put these buttons in this pile? **Child** 'Cause they're red. **Teacher** Yes, now why did you sort these buttons into this pile? **Child** 'Cause they're big. **Teacher** And these? **Child** Um-m, let's see, I don't know. Oh, wait, I know. Because, see . . . this has two holes and this one has two holes and this, and all of them have two holes.	Teacher and child pointing to a pile of buttons.
5. **Teacher** That's good, Lonnie. You sorted the buttons three different ways. I like what you did. **Child** Let's do some more. **Teacher** Okay. Let's think of some other ways we might sort them.	Picture of teacher hugging child. Both smiling.

Activities in Which Parents Can Become Involved Directly or Indirectly:

Supervise kitchen activities on "cooking" days
Repair books
Teach school-related skills
Transcribe tape recordings
Supervise pasting of pictures for scrapbooks and displays
Cut out art materials
Help prepare and plant school garden
Address and stuff envelopes for mailings
Print children's names on book covers

After the visual demonstration, a guest speaker tells how children tend to learn and retain more if they are given an opportunity to interact physically with the materials, "Show them and let them do it, rather than lecture to them or tell them." The parents also hear some theories and ideas about reinforcing the positive things that a child does and rewarding him for good behavior rather than punishing him for incorrect behavior.

After the speaker's presentation, the teacher leads a discussion with the parents, asking how they might have sorted the buttons. She points out the importance of letting the child sort the buttons his own way, rather than suggesting how he should do it. Many of the parents will become intrigued with the different possibilities, remarking that it had never occurred to them that children's minds could be so unique. They are excited about the meeting and eager to try out some of the ideas on their children. They acquire some useful information which they can immediately adapt to their own needs.

Open house meetings, especially those that are informal and include the entire family, are an effective means for involving parents. The following description by the director of a cooperative nursery describes an especially successful open house at her school:

We took examples of the children's art work such as paintings, collages, crayon and felt pen drawings and had each child "dictate a story" about his creation, which we then typed. We mounted these stories and pictures next to a snapshot of each child and displayed them at the children's eye level. Then we invited the entire family to an early potluck supper at school where the proud youngsters were able to show their work to the visitors.

5 Parents and Teachers as Collaborators

The teachers and children also demonstrated how they used some of the materials and equipment at school, such as listening individually through earphones to a recorded lesson about right and left hands while following along with corresponding pictures in a book. One teacher had prepared a tape recording of the children's responses to questions about a story and placed the recording alongside the appropriate books so the children could turn the tape recorder on and play it for their parents.

Some parents welcome an opportunity to attend workshop meetings where they find out what the children are learning and can thus reinforce the same behavior at home. This might include math concepts such as teaching the child to count, to give someone two or four or whatever number of something he is asked for, to choose the third or fifth (or any other such as the middle, last, or fourth), and to know how many of something he will have if he adds one more.

Some parents comment that their children expect them to know the words to songs and finger plays learned at school. The teachers can demonstrate some popular activities and have the parents participate. Parents often repeat the songs and finger plays with apparent delight, asking for copies of the words to take home.

Many adults have never had experiences with easels or finger paints, mobiles, collages, tie-dying, or many of the other activities through which nursery schools encourage creative expression. The chance to learn about these often leads to a willingness to be involved in other aspects of the program.[1]

Some teachers rely heavily on telephone calls to keep them in close touch with parents, especially those who live some distance from the school or who work during school hours. Rather than waiting for a problem to develop before getting in touch with a parent, the teacher phones to introduce herself and subsequently to report progress or seek information. This makes it possible for her to interact with the parents in the child's education even though she may or may not meet them during the entire school year.

Another technique for involving parents, which is used widely in grade schools, is the system of "room mothers." This entails more than asking parents to furnish empty juice cans, old magazines, egg cartons, or supplies needed for various projects; it may involve a request for the parents to come to school and help with activities requiring teaching skills.

With little extra effort teachers find it possible and rewarding to involve most parents both directly and indirectly in the nursery school program.

Involving Different Kinds of Families

The expectations of families from various socio-economic and ethnic backgrounds may be quite different, and the teacher should learn to adapt his methods of relating to families to be responsive. The differences are not differences in interest or in regard for the teacher and the school so much as they are variations in experience and in cultural definitions of the relative roles of parents and teacher. Some families may come from cultures that hold the teacher in very high regard and expect the parent to give full authority to the school. The teacher may represent a person of considerable status and inspire more respect and deference in such homes than he or she will in others where teachers are seen as neighbors who happen to have teaching as their occupation.

For fathers and mothers for whom the teacher is a more formidable figure, the teacher needs to respect their perceptions and feelings and not violate them by hasty, overly informal

---

[1] See Croft, D. and Hess, R. *An Activities Handbook for Teachers of Young Children* 2nd ed. (Boston, Mass.: Houghton Mifflin, 1975).

approaches. The task of a teacher in encouraging participation of parents is first to find out where the parents are and meet them on a mutually comfortable ground. If they are reluctant, through shyness, the teacher must be more clear about her desire that they participate. If they have had unfortunate personal experiences in schools as students, she may help them see schools and teachers in a more positive way. Adults in the presence of teachers may often feel mild echoes of their own past and may even begin to adopt the role of pupil because that is the only role that many adults have had in the classroom.

Parents whose children are in programs that give partial scholarships or economic considerations for welfare and other low-income families are in a particularly sensitive position. The program itself reminds them of their economic problems and even though they do not want to accept welfare, there may be a period during which, for various reasons, they cannot manage without some outside help. Families who have accepted funds from state or federal programs realize that some agencies may be overzealous in enforcing their regulations. The families may be quizzed, visited on quasi inspections and in other ways made to feel that they are under special examination and suspicion. The teacher may be seen as a representative of governmental agencies and should take special care to make her role clear and to let the parents know that she is interested primarily

in working with them for the benefit of the child. You can assume that any parent—whether from high-, middle- or low-income origins, a highly educated background or one of limited schooling—is interested in helping his child in school.

Sometimes circumstances in the home make mothers and fathers sensitive and reluctant to have the teacher visit. One mother with a low income and head of her household reported that she was worried about the teacher's visit because she didn't even have a coffee pot and her cups were cracked and chipped. But she naturally hoped the teacher would think that she was indeed a good mother. To her, being able to serve coffee in the finest of china was associated with being a good mother. An upper middle class mother reported that she, too, was tense and nervous about the teacher's visit. Though she was able to serve coffee in china cups, she was anxious about making a good impression as a mother. Successful involvement of parents is stimulated by teachers who are aware of the feelings all parents have in common.

The home visit serves many useful purposes, but needn't be the only avenue for home-school interaction. Many successful teachers report that they prefer to identify a common ground on which families can begin to share some mutual interests. Often that place may be the school room. However, mothers and fathers from single-parent families may prefer to meet with the teacher in their homes because of babysitting problems; or the school may need to make some child care services available for other children when the families come to the school. Sometimes a visit to the home is one way a teacher can convince a parent that she cares. In any event, the teacher should be flexible in arranging to meet with parents.

A student teacher reports:

After my visit to Lou Ellen's house, I began to feel I knew her better because I had met her family and knew what her home was like. At school Lou Ellen had been shy but afterwards she was eager to have me talk to her about my visit. She reminded me on several occasions that she remembered my coming and used this to start a conversation with me.

Visiting a child's home often helps the teacher understand something of the reasons behind the child's behavior and his patterns of activity in the class. She is likely to understand better the kind of person he is and the problems he and his parents have to face. Because of her increased understanding, she can often give more individualized attention to particular children.

A teacher in a child-care center reports

Seventy-five percent of our children come from one-parent families. If I relied on the old-fashioned, come-to-school parent conference, I'd never see most of the parents. Just the other day I took my car into a service station which was two miles out of my way so I could meet Jimmy's father. I took along some of Jimmy's art work and carpentry so I could chat with him while he serviced my car. I also shop frequently at a grocery store where Evelyn's mother is the checker. These parents really look forward to my informal visits and to me these are some of my most valuable parent involvement experiences. Besides, I get extra good service!

Building rapport with individual parents has many gratifications. One of them is that it makes it possible for the teacher to enlist their support in strengthening the program of the school. If fathers and mothers are convinced that their involvement will really enhance the program and thus benefit their own children, they are more likely to make the sacrifices necessary to participate.

Once a sense of confidence and ease has been established between the teacher and individual families, the teacher will find it easier to get a group of parents together to work with her. One strategy for such meetings that is probably overrated, however, is to plan discussions of child development. In their personal lives, families tend to deal with fairly specific and concrete things. To move from direct, practical matters to abstract principles of child-rearing may make the session seem irrelevant. The Let's-talk-about-our-program-and-our-problems approach so common to middle-class teacher groups does not always work well. Parents might be persuaded to talk about the school and its needs, or about community needs, but these subjects should be handled with care to keep the discussion on the kinds of problems that directly concern the people in the group.

One teacher tells of meeting with a dozen mothers and using all the techniques she'd been taught during training—chairs in a circle, paper and pencil available for note taking, name cards that all could see and read, formal recognition from the chair for each speaker, and everything kept business-like. Her subject was "Individual Children and Child Development."

She admits the meeting was anything but a success. Afterward one of the mothers told her if she wanted to have a good meeting, one that would really do some good, she ought to bring food, have soft music, and let the children, no matter what their age, come with their parents. The teacher followed this mother's advice. According to her standards the session was unusual, but the parents came and participated. They talked about what mattered to them even though their concern was not by any means child development. But they talked and they wanted to meet again.

Another teacher faced the reluctance of a group of Chinese mothers to let their preschoolers go on a field trip to a city park. They worried about the bus being in an accident, about the children going so far from home, and about what the children would eat and wear. The teacher invited them to go along. She also asked that they bring fruit for a salad. At the park, while the children explored nearby under a teacher's supervision, the mothers made a salad and prepared other food which had been provided by the school. With something to do, and their children within sight and hearing, the mothers felt at ease. During lunch they talked freely with one another and with the teacher. In the following weeks the teacher was able to carry out several more formal meetings at the school based on what she had learned at the park of the ways and concerns of the mothers in regard to their children.

Involving Fathers

There is a good deal of confusion as to how much fathers participate and should participate in preschool programs. Perhaps some of the reasons for the controversy over this issue is that the father's presence or nonpresence at school has often been equated in the teacher's mind with his degree of interest in his child. Obviously, a father is involved with his child in many ways other than putting in an appearance at school, and he does not necessarily see his physical presence there as a measure of his concern. Discussion about father involvement also tends to pair his role with that of the mother when it might be helpful to see their relationships to the school as separate and different.

Fathers may contribute to the education of their young children in many ways. In the home, support of their children's interest in learning, and reinforcement of school achievement, shows the child that his father cares. By going to school and participating in a program, a father would acknowledge his support of the mother's interest and involvement, but this might or might not influence his child's performance. Also, his attendance at various ritualistic events such as Parents' Night and Clean-Up Day would encourage the teacher to feel that he cares about what she is doing in the school program. Yet it is an obvious truth that many fathers do not come to school meetings, do not visit the classroom, and are not especially eager to know what the school is doing. This does not mean that they are not concerned with their children.

Perhaps it is useful for teachers to consider their own motives for wanting fathers involved, and what kinds of activities would meet the interests of the fathers. Before setting up any kind of program, however, it might be well to consider why fathers haven't participated in school affairs more often.

Traditionally the father has been asked to play a role that is often awkward and even embarrassing to him. In his visits to school, his abilities or preferences are not really differentiated from those of the mother and the teacher. That is, many fathers walk around the classroom looking at drawings in which they have little interest except to find a name so they can later say to their child, "I saw the picture you drew." While there is some point to be served in their attempt to be cooperative, their effort is frequently motivated by a sense of obligation and they are made to feel guilty if they don't participate. Their expression of interest is often the result of external pressures rather than an indication of their own concern about the school and the child's activities in it.

This is not to suggest that fathers are not interested in schools. They are. But they should be offered appropriate ways in which to express their true interest. Many seem not to be interested because they are asked to do things which, from their point of view, may be silly or childish.

Of course, many men do not become involved simply because they have no free time that coincides with the hours of a nursery school program. The employed father quite naturally puts the demands of his job ahead of those of a school program. The unemployed father is either too busy looking for work or too involved in dealing with his own concerns to participate in school affairs.

A factor which keeps many men with limited education away from school (and which in some instances applies to mothers as well) is that they fear the teacher will ask them for information or help they are unable or unwilling to give. Understandably, they are reluctant to expose themselves to the sophistication and expertise of a trained teacher or of other parents. But fathers can and should be involved in school affairs in ways that reflect their real interest and abilities.

Perhaps one of the most effective beginning strategies is to ask for help in specific types of jobs—such as construction, moving of equipment, and maintenance—that are commonly considered to be "men's work." However, it must be remembered that not all men are competent in these areas and may be quite unwilling to display their ineptness. Once fathers come to school, they often see for themselves what needs to be done to help the children. One teacher recalls such an instance:

This father was a somewhat older man and you could sense that he didn't particularly feel part of the group of men who had come to help one Saturday morning. But he noticed that the children had no way of hanging up their coats or sweaters, that these garments were folded and placed at the bottom of small lockers. He offered to install hooks and from then on took an active interest in the program of the school.

It sometimes helps to make fathers aware that other men are making a contribution of time and talent to the school. Men who know that others participate in and contribute to a pre-school program, especially that of their own child, feel better about making an effort themselves. Seeing clippings and news items concerning the importance of preschool education, and hearing about fathers who have come to school and demonstrated their special skills as hair cutters, fishermen, and kite-makers, or who have simply served the ice cream cones at an all-school party, helps other men understand how they might be involved in a way they consider worthwhile.

Initial contacts with fathers can sometimes be made by scheduling a home visit at a time when both parents are likely to be there and by including the father in whatever conversation takes place. A teacher tells of the following experience:

The father was at home; in fact he was the one who opened the door and invited me in. He did most of the talking because the mother spoke very little English. The visit wasn't going very well until I happened to notice some flowers he had planted. I admired them and with that he went into a long explanation about varieties and told me a great many details about their care. He cut some for me and insisted that I take them back with me. When I finally left, we still hadn't talked about his son and the boy never came into the room. But several days later, Mr. Y. brought some flowers to school for a holiday celebration. We talked to him and he returned the following week to show the children how to plant a garden. I was able to tell him how much we appreciated what he was doing for the children and he promised he would come again.

As in all human relationships, appreciation goes a long way with fathers, too. Those who are made to feel that their efforts count and that their interests and opinions are important obviously will tend toward involvement far more than those who feel unwelcome, unwanted, or merely supportive of the mother and teacher. One of the most rewarding aspects of fathers' involvement is the chance it gives children who are without fathers in their homes to identify with a male figure—especially one who is interested in children and wants to help with their education.

Perhaps the most effective way for a teacher to involve fathers is to take time to let them know the educational goals of the program and the role she wants them to play. If she wants them in the role of lending moral support to the school—that is, nodding and smiling as they walk around the classroom—then she invites them to a Parents' Night. If she wants them to help teach their children skills that will prepare the children for formal schooling, then she makes sure they know what the curriculum is and how they can reinforce her teaching and help their children learn. A sensitive teacher will find many ways to convey to the father that she does not have a predefined role she expects him to fill. His "maleness" may indeed be traditionally expressed in "helping types" of activities, but if she allows it, it will also be expressed in more effective kinds of interaction with children such as soothing, sympathizing, reassuring.

Getting fathers to participate in school activities is often difficult. Their time is limited and their preoccupation is generally with their own work; many feel that the care of the young child is primarily the responsibility of the mother. But these are circumstances that can be overcome. Certainly it is in the interest of the child to do so.

Parents and Teachers as Partners in Developing Educability

Much of the contact between parents and teachers centers around administrative activities. There is another important area, however, in which they also interact. They are both committed to fostering the child's growth and development. In this they have separate responsibilities, but they may also work together to provide a more effective environment for the child than either of them could offer separately. Their collaboration is especially important in preparing the child for school experience.

Parents are Important, Too

Parents influence the educability and educational achievement of their children in many ways. This is one of the most important reasons for collaboration between school and home and for involving parents in the early schooling and care of their children. We can think of the preschool years as a time when the child develops *educability,* i.e., a readiness and capability to learn in a formal institution such as the school.
Educability has three components:

1. *Cognitive skills* Ability to recognize and label objects, to count, to name letters of the alphabet, to pick out colors, to talk and ask questions, to see relationships, to generalize, etc.
2. *Motivation to succeed in school* Acceptance of school as a reasonable place to commit energy and effort; development of a desire to learn and to succeed in the sorts of things the school experience represents.
3. *Acceptance of the role of pupil* Recognition of one's relationship to the school and its rules, to the teacher, and to learning; tendency to adopt an initiating, assertive approach to the world of information, to attend to tasks and persist in them.

A child can learn skills and attitudes that will prepare him to perform successfully in school. Children tend to develop these in homes where the family has a high regard for education, where parents themselves read and also read to their children; where

youngsters have their own books and are encouraged to ask questions; where their questions are respected and answered.

Parents provide children with an orientation toward the school. Those parents who feel rejected by the school are likely to give their children attitudes that will negatively affect their acceptance of the school and the ability to benefit from its teachings. The mother who believes she is respected and wanted by the school and who is made to realize she is assisting in education that will benefit her child is more likely to give the child positive and useful attitudes toward both the school and the teacher, as well as all that this implies for future success in school (Hess and Shipman, 1968).

We usually think of the beginning of public school as the time for formal learning, but the preparation for school experience begins long before the actual school term starts. Attitudes toward the school and toward teachers are picked up from older brothers and sisters, from playmates, from parents. Even the design of a house and its furnishing shows the interests and priorities of a family. These give the child familiarity with the resources and materials which his parents prize and examples or models of a way of life that emphasizes some styles and rejects others. The ways in which parents arrange and organize the experiences of the small child begin to orient him toward schools and schooling or away from achievement in the classroom.

The young child is also shaped by more immediate interaction with his parents. A number of studies show that parental behavior in these areas of interaction may be related to school achievement. They identify behavior that falls roughly into three categories.

Interaction about
Intellectual Activities Some parents express directly to the child their demands or expectations for high achievement. A mother may say in response to a drawing the child has made, "That's fine, dear, but I'm sure you can do even better." She may also take time to participate with the child in school-related games and skills, playing word games, challenging the child with small problems to solve. She may also talk a great deal to the child, using language as a way to develop the child's ability to speak clearly, to master the meanings of new words, and to express ideas.

Some mothers use more or less formal teaching techniques, buying books and toys that are designed to teach the alphabet, colors, numbers, shapes, and the like. Or the mother may encourage her child to watch television programs like Sesame Street that are designed to teach basic preschool skills.

Several studies have shown that the child who is given opportunities and praise for engaging in conversation with adults and who participates in experiences that tend to enlarge his vocabulary is likely to show more advanced achievement in school. Apparently, even for a young child these opportunities can be tied to school performance. They include the parent's correcting the child's use of a word, persuading him to talk in sentences and asking him questions which stimulate verbal response.

Perhaps the most important type of behavior, from the standpoint of future school success, is the parent's tendency to become engaged with the young child's mental and cognitive activity— to gear into his ideas and responses and to monitor his performance. This kind of behavior is indicated by the parent's knowledge of what the child is doing in school, her concern and interest in the child's activities at school and at home, and her desire to contribute to his efforts. This behavior is applicable not only to definite tasks at school, but also to the interests and games that small children get involved in at home.

The parent's interaction with the child and her sensitivity to him are effective.

The parent's ability to teach her child in ways that help him define and master tasks also influences cognitive growth and achievement in school. This may include giving the child specific instructions and providing him with feedback on how well he has done. It presents another person's point of view and encourages the child to talk and ask questions about the task in which he's engaged. In these activities, the parent acts as a model and as a specific source of information.

Affective Relationships

A second important group of parental behaviors related to academic achievement derives from the affective relationship between parents and the child. Parental behavior of this type can be divided into two general categories: establishment of a warm, emotional relationship with the child and expressions of positive self-esteem. There is evidence that a parent's support and affection for her child as shown in her physical and verbal responses to him, and her positive regard for herself and her child, seem to have a good influence on his level of achievement. These supportive attitudes release the child's ability to concentrate on mastery of the task at hand and to increase in a diffuse way his sense of competence and willingness to explore and test his ability. Children who are worried about their relationship to their parents or family may be distracted and fail to complete whatever they are doing. It is not entirely clear just how maternal and paternal affection influences school achievement, but it seems likely one of the significant effects is that it may free the child to turn psychic energy to the tasks of the school. It may also give him a sense of a supporting and rewarding audience at home, which cares about his school experience.

Patterns of Regulation
and Control

A third area of parental behavior affecting school achievement includes patterns of interaction between the mother and the child. Parents encourage self-reliance by teaching children to dress and feed themselves, by making them responsible for their own belongings, and by seeing that they have a chance to solve many of their own problems. Three-year-old Mark's mother used the latter technique the day he rode his tricycle into a corner and fussed because he couldn't get it out. She made no attempt to come to his aid but suggested that he could work it out himself. When he accepted the fact that he was on his own, he stopped fussing and considered his alternatives. After a

moment he climbed down, shoved the trike through a 180° turn, remounted, and rode off.

There are large differences between parents in the pressure they put on young children to be independent and acquire specific types of behavior. Some mothers expect even very young children to fix themselves something to eat in the morning. Others let young children select their own television shows, answer the phone, play out on the street, etc., at much earlier ages than others. Expectations for developing social courtesies, as in certain forms of "Thank you" or "Please" or addressing adults by a title or last name vary tremendously from family to family in the United States.

The exact relationship between these early expectations and later school achievement is not entirely clear, but it appears that parents who help children develop control over their own activities and who give them reasons for the expectations they impose also orient them toward achievement in school and toward accepting the goals and standards of the teacher.

The family and the school have the joint goal of promoting the intellectual, social, and physical development of the young child, and the success of their efforts is enhanced if they can support and reinforce one another. This is one area in which competition between home and school can have disastrous consequences for the child. If the objectives for the child are shared and if they are consistently sought by both parent and teacher, the child is more secure and is able to progress more quickly.

If the child sees the school and the home as offering conflicting demands and rewarding different and inconsistent behavior, he or she is much less likely to adopt either the attitudes and behavior of the school or the home. He is also more likely to follow some other direction later. In short, the chances are that he will internalize patterns of behavior that are rewarded by both family and school than those rewarded only by school or by the home. If you want to affect the behavior of a child, you will be more successful if you get the parent on your side and you work with the parent in setting the goals the child is encouraged to reach.

The child is part of both the school world and the home world. Collaboration between family and school is thus a two-way street. The parents can be brought into a closer contact with the goals and activities of the school and their values and wishes respected and supported. The goals of the school can be supported by the home, through both interest and positive attitudes and through participation by the parent in preparing the child for later school experience and accomplishment.

Collaboration Between Family and School in Home-based Programs

Recognition of the impact of the family upon school achievement has heightened our awareness of how important it is for parents to support and extend the child's preparation for school through the activities they carry out in the home. This not only helps develop specific skills for the child, but also shows the parents' interest in the child's progress. The parents' participation in school-related activities can take several forms.

The importance of the family as an educational resource is recognized even more now than it was when Head Start and other large pre-kindergarten programs were planned. It is easier to influence the educational performance of children through programs if these programs are conducted with the cooperation and support of the family. The families who had positive attitudes toward the importance of learning and of education were those who sought out ways to give their children better educational experiences both at home and through involvement in the school process.

The most extensive of the various programs to help parents give their children positive and strong momentum in early learning is Home Start. This program was originated by the Office of Child Development of the Department of Health, Education and Welfare in Washington, D.C. It echoes the philosophy of Head Start, as is obvious from its title, but the approach it takes is to see the home as the place where the head start can begin. The founders of the program were encouraged by the apparent success of more experimental programs that had been in operation, in some cases, for several years. The Home Start program was developed to take advantage of these earlier efforts and also to give the local school system and parent groups a significant part in the development of their own programs.

These home-based programs are very different from one another in some essential ways. Some use toys as a base for interaction between mother and child; others utilize a more formal instructional approach. Some were developed by sponsors of Head Start and Follow Through programs, such as Ira Gordon's efforts in the southeastern part of the United States, and the programs of David Weikart in Michigan. Weikart's curriculum and program for working with mothers and children in the home was the first major program of its kind in the United States.

There are probably more than a hundred home-based programs in this country. Many of these are local efforts, which, although they may be very effective, have not reached national attention, usually because they have no funds to disseminate the procedures and results of their activities. Many have received attention, however, and can be examined for their usefulness and interest. There is not space here to describe many of these programs, but the brief descriptions that follow may offer an overview of some of the purposes, procedures, and successes of selected examples. These were chosen because they illustrate differences in approach and because they had sufficient time to develop programs based on rather extensive experience. Following these brief descriptions are some suggestions about how information in more detailed form may be obtained.

Although many of the programs that have been developed in connection with Head Start, Follow Through, Home Start, and other programs for low-income communities, the impact of the family and home are as critical in middle-income areas as in any other part of the community. Mothers in middle class areas vary enormously in their tendencies to assist their children in school-oriented learning. Some get books that show numbers, letters of the alphabet, and other concepts and specific bits of information to read to the child even before he can talk. They may encourage him to watch Sesame Street or other television programs that have features oriented toward reading, counting, and other school-related activities. Some make a point of having the child repeat numbers or letters of the alphabet and may use part of reading time to give mini-lessons in colors and shapes. They may also buy construction toys which include things the child will see in school—chalkboards, crayons, paper with lines for printing, and the like. And, perhaps most importantly, they show the child their interest in his learning and their confidence that he will easily acquire these preschool skills.

Other mothers from the middle class may take an attitude of "Let it happen when he's ready. If not sooner, he will learn these things at school. Other things are more important anyway." They may also believe that the child is the one to decide how much effort he will put into school work and whether he should drop out to do something else before completing high school. These attitudes, as well as the specific activities, set the stage for the child's orientation toward school, toward learning and toward himself as a person who enjoys learning and sees it as part of his daily life, not merely as an assignment at school.

These programs, then, represent one approach to the total important area of family involvement in the education of the child. They may be of particular usefulness to parents with limited time and resources.

Early Childhood Stimulation through Parent Education Project

Director: Ira Gordon

Since its beginning in 1966/67, this rural Florida program has been training low-income women to be "Parent Educators" and to help low-income mothers in providing a stimulating environment for their children in their own homes. The age of the children on entering the program has ranged from three to twelve months, and most of the families involved have been black. Participation has varied from nine months to three years.

The goals of the program have been to prepare children for a successful school experience by enhancing their potential for development through stimulation at a young age. The program also aims to teach parents new skills of playing and interacting with their children, as well as helping them to develop positive attitudes about school, their children, and themselves.

Among the basic assumptions of the program's directors are that the early years are the most important in the development of a child's personality and that a child's educational potential is related to the amount and type of stimulation he receives in his home. Home relationships are assumed to be crucial in the development of a child's motivation for achievement.

How Does It Work?

The Parent Educators, chosen from backgrounds similar to those of program participants, receive intensive training before working with the mothers in their homes. Once a week home visits are made during which the mothers are introduced to a sequenced series of stimulation exercises, primarily sensory-motor activities. No toys or other special materials are used. The exercise tasks are sequenced developmentally to correspond to the child's stage of growth. The Parent Educator visits the home to demonstrate a specific task, help the mother understand its purpose, and encourage the use of the exercise during the week. The teaching techniques used are role-playing and modeling, although some direct instruction has been necessary. The visitors are trained to let the mother be primarily responsible in working with the child.

In 1968 another learning situation, the Home Learning Center, was added to the program. Children who have participated in the home-based activities for two years are introduced to a group-learning session for two-hour periods twice a week in the backyard of one of the program mothers. There are five children in each group. The Parent Educators continue to have weekly meetings with the families in their homes.

What Are the Special Features?

This program was designed so that mothers would have the main responsibility for carrying out the stimulation activities with their children, and for that reason the teaching techniques used centered on active participation. Special features of this program have been the training of low-income women as Parent Educators, the use of concrete, sequenced tasks, and assignments to be completed.

How Successful Is It?

The children who were involved in the program performed better than other children not only on a test based on the stimulation activities, but also on standardized tests. The program staff felt that it was particularly significant that children with the training were more readily able to perform new, unfamiliar motor activities. Long-range studies have shown that these children retain their gains up to three years after leaving the program.

Several evaluations of this program, comparing children who received the training throughout the three years with those who received it for a shorter period of time, indicate that it is not necessarily true that the earlier a child receives such specialized attention, the higher will be his achievement. All indications have been that the crucial factors are the mother-child interaction and the concrete, specific tasks and activities that provide a guided, structured involvement for the parents. The parents themselves reported that they were spending longer periods of time playing with their children and that they had higher expectations for their children's school achievements.

Mothers' Training Program | Director: Merle Karnes
Institute for Research on Exceptional Children
College of Education, University of Illinois

This program for training mothers to be tutors of their own children was instituted in Illinois in 1967. Its purpose is to promote a stimulating home environment and to offer basic preschool skills. During its first year the program involved the mothers of three- and four-year-olds and lasted for 12 weeks. Later, however, the mothers of younger children (aged one and two years) participated for a two-year period. All of the families in the program have been low-income and most have been black.

The goals are to increase the children's general and verbal intelligence and prepare them for school by furthering their motivation to learn, their attention span, and their work habits. At the same time the mothers would become conscious teachers of their own children, especially by increasing verbal interaction and acquiring specific knowledge about child development. A basic assumption of Merle Karnes and her associates is that language patterns and cognitive style are particularly crucial to a child's subsequent development and that learning problems in these areas can be avoided by special attention at the preschool age. They also assume that for the learning process to be most effective parents should be actively involved.

How Does It Work? | The program centers entirely on parent/teacher interaction. Once a week mothers attend a two-hour group meeting where experienced teachers direct both mother-centered and child-centered activities. Group discussions directed at child-rearing problems are designed not only to increase the mothers' sense of involvement with their families and communities but also to develop a working relationship between parents and school personnel.

The child-centered activities, however, are the most important part of the group meetings. Highly trained, skilled professionals present the mothers with educational toys (such as nested boxes, stringing beads, and wooden in-lay puzzles), some of which the mothers construct themselves in the group, and then demonstrate ways in which these toys can be used to encourage verbal interaction. The toys are introduced in a developmental order. The teaching principles stressed are (1) developing a good working relationship with the child, based on respect; (2) offering praise rather than criticism; (3) dividing new tasks into separate steps; (4) thinking of learning as fun.

The program staff feel that group meetings rather than individual parent/teacher sessions have certain advantages in that they bring the mothers together in a supportive, self-evaluating, and reinforcing atmosphere.

During the week between meetings the mothers work with their children using the provided materials and make note of their childrens' progress. The staff members visit the families' homes twice a month to observe mothers interacting with their children, to offer support, and to make suggestions.

What Are the Special Features?

An essential consideration of this program is that mothers are the primary teachers of their own children, a concept which includes recognizing them as members of a team along with professional teachers. Another major emphasis is on active parental involvement in the training, rather than a passive, lecture-oriented situation. It is also important that the mothers construct some of the toys themselves; this gives special meaning to the materials as they are being used in the home. In addition, this program combines group training of mothers with individual home visits.

How Successful Is It?

Several evaluations of the Mothers' Training Program have indicated significant improvement in cognitive performance and language growth in children whose mothers were involved in the special training program. One evaluation involved a comparison group of older brothers and sisters of the program children; since the same mothers were involved, the fact that the younger children showed more improvement could more readily be attributed to training effects.

The changes observed in the children affected by the Mothers' Training Program were taken as evidence of changes in the attitudes and practices of the mothers themselves. According to program reports, many of the mothers who participated in the training made changes in their own lives, reflected in such things are increased involvement in community activities.

Another separate program directed by Merle Karnes that combined mother's training with a structured preschool program had much less emphasis on parental responsibility, and the results showed control groups actually to have done better than the children who received the preschool training. This is another indication of the importance of active parent participation in childrens' learning experiences.

The Mother-Child Home Program	Director: Phyllis Levenstein

Director: Phyllis Levenstein
Mother-Child Home Program of Family Service Association of Nassau County, Inc.
5 Broadway, Freeport, New York 11520

Begun in 1967 on Long Island, New York, this preschool cognitive program was designed to be conducted entirely in the home. Low-income mothers are offered two years of home-visit training emphasizing verbal interaction with their children that might be especially pertinent to school-related skills. Participation in the program begins when the child is two or three years old. The participants are from both black and white families.

The program operates under the assumption that an emphasis on verbal interaction with children along with introducing cognitive enrichment in home relationships will contribute to the child's later success in school. The specific goals are to develop the child's ability to use language symbolically and to train mothers to initiate their own verbal interaction with their children in the home.

How Does It Work?   Twice a week for seven months of each year visits are made to the homes of the participating families by trained "Toy Demonstrators." Each visit lasts for about half an hour. The first visit each week is for the purpose of introducing the books and educational toys to the mother and child and demonstrating with them various verbal interaction techniques to be used along with the materials. Hammer and pegs, block carts, jigsaw puzzles, and puppets are some of the toys used. At the second visit, the techniques are reviewed and the Demonstrator answers the mother's questions. The children are allowed to keep the books and toys brought by the demonstrator. The teaching methods used with the mothers are (1) demonstration by the staff visitor (modeling); (2) practice by the mother under supervision of the Demonstrator (role-playing); and (3) verbal encouragement (positive reinforcement).

What Are the Special Features?

The most important aspects of the Mother-Child Home Program are the concentration on the mother/child relationship and the fact that all training takes place in the home, involving both mother and child. The mothers are considered to be the primary teachers with Demonstrators playing the role of a partner or colleague, although in the early stages of the relationship the Demonstrator is necessarily more of a teacher. As the visits continue, the mother hopefully assumes the more active position. Another special feature is the use of structured home assignments.

How Successful Is It?

All evaluations of the program have confirmed a rise in both the general and verbal intelligence of the children involved. Mothers' comments were for the most part supportive, and many of them indicated improvement in family verbal interactions. In general children with two years in the program retained their IQ gains into first grade. Comparison children who had not received the training were scored consistently below experimental children in psychosocial behavior by their teachers. The follow-up results suggest that full, active parental involvement in a child's development may be especially significant in retaining gains made in more formal preschool programs.

As of late 1972, roughly twenty organizations were successfully instituting the Mother-Child Home Program in other locations. The evaluation methods make the results trustworthy: a large number of children have been involved; control groups have been maintained; a number of standardized tests were applied; and follow-up studies have been carried out. It is obviously a successful program, perhaps the most successful of any well-known parent-oriented program for low-income children.

The Preschool Program

Sponsor: Oakland, California, Public Schools

A large number of 3- and 4-year-olds from low-income families have participated in this kindergarten-readiness program since it began in 1966. Most of the families involved have been black.

The children attend one of the Oakland public schools for classroom instruction. Parents are involved through parent education meetings, volunteer classroom work, and personal contact with the teachers.

The main goal of the program is to increase the children's potential for success in a school situation through progress in mathematical and language skills, physical development, social-emotional adjustment, and communication. The secondary goals are concerned with improving parent-school relationships and furthering parental interest in the children's education.

How Does It Work?

The children attend preschool classes for half days during the school year. The theoretical basis for the curriculum and amount of structure varies among the school sites involved. The major classroom activities have consisted of manipulative play, dramatic play, science experiences, language experiences, and community excursions. The primary purpose of all activities has been to enrich the children's experience and thereby expand their knowledge as well as stimulate their curiosity.

Although the emphasis of the program has been on the children themselves, the improvement of parent-school understanding has been seen as an important aspect. Four different ways of involving parents have been used. Daily parent-teacher contact at the school has been encouraged by asking the parents to pick up their own children after class. The parents have also been requested to volunteer to work as aides in the classroom for two days each month. In addition, monthly group parent meetings were organized where information on the program and its progress was shared, workshops on nutrition and child development were held, and educational films were shown. The meetings combined a lecture situation with teacher-led parent discussions. The fourth method of parent involvement was a parent advisory council, which made suggestions for the program, both in objectives and ways to further interest the children's families.

What Are the Special Features?

Because the program's main goal has been to increase the children's school readiness, the major effort has been toward the classroom aspects. Many avenues of parent participation are planned, but parent involvement, in any form, is not highly structured. The parent involvement is considered important in building a more supportive learning environment for the child; parents are not trained as teachers or to change their home interactions. Emphasis is on changes in attitudes and knowledge, not behavior. Parents have functioned as aides to the teachers and as students. Contact between parents and teachers has always taken place in the school.

The evaluations of the Oakland Preschool Program indicate quite simple and therefore reveal only a limited amount of information on the program's success. It does seem that the participating children have made IQ gains, but that the effects of their learning experiences and IQ scores began to decrease shortly after the classes end. Some of the children from the Preschool Program went on to participate in a Follow Through intervention program. Children who had been in the preschool showed higher reading and math scores than children who had only the Preschool or the Follow Through experience. The level of participation has been high and the parents have been favorable to the program.

The Ypsilanti-Perry Preschool Project

Director: David Weikart

This Michigan program supplemented a structured preschool situation with weekly home visits to the children and their parents. The participants during the five years of the program (1962–1967) were predominantly black three- and four-year-olds from low-income families. Each child attended the preschool for two years five half-days a week from October to May.

The program's goals centered on increasing the children's general intellectual growth in preparation for greater academic success in school. The primary emphasis was on furthering the children's symbolic representation through work with motor skills, number concepts, and language development. The program directors also hoped to improve the parents' relationship with the school and with teachers, so that they would be likely to take an active part in their children's education.

It was assumed that children's early environment and experiences are crucial in their development of cognitive functioning and that it is important for them to have diverse and varied experiences through interaction with their environment.

How Does It Work? The preschool program was structured, with a learning situation specially designed for each child at his or her own stage of development. The children were gradually transferred from direct physical manipulation of materials to more symbolic manipulation, through language.

Teachers devoted equal amounts of time to classroom teaching and home tutoring. One purpose of the home visits was to further individualize the learning activities for the child. The teacher's concern was to augment and extend the school experiences on a one-to-one basis with the child.

It was also felt that by watching the teacher working with her child the mother would become engaged in the education process and would learn to restructure her interactions with her child so as to offer more stimulating home learning activities. The role of the mother could range from passive observer to active participant as partner to the teacher, depending on the individual mother and on the kind of information being communicated. Parent participation was encouraged but not required. Teachers took the initiative in the home teaching. There was also some discussion of child-rearing methods and problems, but this was always informal and secondary to the teacher's work with the child. The visits lasted about an hour and a half.

What Are the Special Features?

The program was developmental and structured. The combination of the structured, developmental preschool classes plus home visits offered the children individualized instruction. Parents were primarily involved through home visits, even though visits aimed at teacher tutoring and parent training. Parents were involved as students, aides, and partners to the teachers. The parent's primary responsibility as teacher was not emphasized.

How Successful Is It?

There have been a number of evaluations of the success of the Ypsilanti-Perry Preschool Project, most of which have indicated that the children did benefit from their participation. All of the tests, however, have been on two groups, those who participated and those who did not, so that it has been difficult to evaluate exactly what factors of the program have been effective and under what conditions.

The program group's mean IQ scores were consistently higher than mean scores for the nonprogram group at every testing time through the third grade, although sharp differences after immediate participation in the program gradually diminished. On achievement tests, as well, the program children consistently made higher scores, and they seemed to do better in general on socio-emotional ratings. Program children were much more likely to be working at their expected grade level.

The program sponsors felt that the results were highly favorable and that both immediate and long-term positive impact had been demonstrated. The pattern of results indicated that the children's experience had not greatly changed their measured intellectual level but had provided a foundation for improved academic achievement and emotional adjustment in school.

Using Programs as a Source

The local experimental programs described here are sometimes supported by grants from federal or state agencies and will not last indefinitely. They may be sources of information about these programs, however, and provide additional information as well. Information about Home Start can be obtained by writing to the Office of Child Development, Department of Health, Education, and Welfare, Washington, D.C.

State departments of education also may have information about local programs. The National Association for the Education of Young Children has a list of publications that may include information about home-based programs and descriptions of projects that have gained some recognition.

These programs are a part of the total effort to disseminate information to adults, both professionals in early education and parents who want to work with children in the pre-school years. The parents are the most informed resource for their children's welfare and have primary responsibility for their care and schooling. The teacher who is aware of the many ways in which she can facilitate the efforts of parents and other adults who work with young children can obviously extend her usefulness and effectiveness.

SUMMARY

Some typical examples are given to show how easily parents can become isolated from the school. This chapter specifies some useful techniques and strategies for involving parents. Sections about different kinds of families and about involving fathers are included. A rationale stressing the importance for encouraging closer collaboration between family and school is given. Recognizing the importance of the family as an educational resource, the Office of Child Development has sponsored Home-Start Programs. Several of these are described at the end of the chapter.

SOME POINTS TO REMEMBER

1. The organization and purpose of the school for the child makes it natural and easy for parents to become unintentionally isolated.
2. One tendency toward isolating parents is that teachers often seem more comfortable when parents are not around.
3. Parents are sometimes restrained from interacting with the teacher because of the demands of their jobs or their feelings that it is the teacher's task to care for the child when he is at school.

4. It is the responsibility of the teacher to take the initiative to increase the involvement of parents in the school activities.
5. Techniques for involving parents are more likely to be simple, day-to-day procedures—such as an occasional note pinned to a jacket—than dramatic major involvement programs.
6. If interaction is seen as a mutual, reciprocal relationship, the parent can make substantial contributions to the program and the planning of the school.
7. Open House meetings are one of the most effective occasions for involving parents.
8. During Open House, parents may be shown the materials and equipment, introduced to the concepts which the children are taught, become acquainted with the goals and purpose of the school and learn how to support and encourage the teacher's activities.
9. The system of "room mothers" or "room fathers" is an effective way to share responsibility with parents for the operation of the program.
10. Families from different cultural and socio-economic backgrounds expect different things from the teacher and the school, though they all tend to see the teacher in a positive way.
11. The childhood experiences of parents when they were in school help determine their attitudes and expectations toward teachers of their children.
12. Parents in welfare programs are especially sensitive to the possibility that the teacher may represent an agency which has some influence over their income.
13. Home visits, while often effective, may make parents uncomfortable unless the teacher is reasonably certain she is welcome.
14. Discussions with parents may easily be too abstract or loaded with professional jargon which is of little interest to the parents.
15. The familiar advice to "start where the child is" applies to parents too, and they should be encouraged to talk about what they would like from the school. This gives the teacher a perspective on their concerns and expectations.
16. Fathers may relate to the school and teacher either in formal and indirect ways, even when they are intensely interested, or show their interest in the school and their child's progress in quite different ways than do mothers. Their reactions should not be evaluated in the same terms as the mothers.'

17. Centers often do not give fathers opportunities to participate in ways that fit their skills and interests; they may try to be active because they are made to feel guilty if they don't.

18. Families help prepare their children for school experience by developing attitudes toward learning, the teacher, and the school as an institution.

19. Families who emphasize interaction around intellectual or school-related activities, such as reading, are more likely to prepare their children for successful performance in school.

20. Parents may contribute to the child's school achievement by providing experiences that tend to enlarge vocabulary and by showing interest in the child's school related tasks and accomplishments.

21. Parental warmth and emotional support for the child contribute to the child's later school achievement.

22. There are large differences among families in the way they prepare their children for the school experience, both in the cognitive experiences they provide and in the attitudes toward rules and discipline they develop.

23. If the child sees the school and home as offering conflicting demands and rewarding different behaviors, he is less likely to adopt the behavior of either.

24. Home based programs in which parents teach their children school related skills and attitudes are apparently successful; they are growing in popularity and number.

REFERENCES

Badger, E. *Mothers' training program: the group process.* Urbana, Ill.: ERIC Clearinghouse, 1970.

Croft, D. J. and Hess, R. D. *An activities handbook for teachers of young children,* 2nd ed. Boston, Mass.: Houghton Mifflin, 1975.

Gordon, I. J. and Lally, R. *Intellectual stimulation for infants and toddlers.* Gainesville, Fla.: Institute for the Development of Human Resources, College of Education, University of Florida, 1969.

Hess, R. D. and Shipman, V. C. Maternal attitudes toward the school and the role of pupil: some social class comparisons. In A. H. Passow (ed.), *Developing programs for the educationally disadvantaged.* New York: Teachers College Press, 1968.

The Home Start Demonstration Program: An Overview. Office of Child Development, U.S. Department of Health, Education and Welfare, P.O. Box 1182, Washington, D.C., February 1973.

Noward, Norma K. *Mother-child home learning programs: an abstract bibliography.* (Compiler). Urbana, Ill.: ERIC Clearinghouse in Early Childhood Education, April 1972.

Pickarts, E. and Fargo, J. *Parent education: toward professional competence.* New York: Appleton-Century-Crofts, 1971.

Chapter 6 Social Opportunity and Educational Achievement

The Nature of the Problem

In any group, children differ from one another because of the individual circumstances of genetic endowment, age, sex, and the unique aspects of their personal experiences. There are other influences upon behavior, however, that operate in less apparent, though very powerful ways. These affect the child through the social, cultural, and racial backgrounds from which he comes.

Influence of Socio-cultural Factors on Behavior

Such influences create differences not only between individual children but between *groups* of children. In great part they arise as a consequence of the way our society treats individuals from cultural, social, and racial backgrounds that differ from those of the majority. Because they often come from outside the child and his family group, they may be beyond his power to change. For children from such backgrounds, educational experience has a particular significance because of its potential for helping the individual deal with his own circumstances and for helping change the attitudes and opportunity structure of society.

The problems of children from low-income and "minority" groups are obviously important to the teacher of young children. She needs to know how they follow from the child's social and cultural experiences so she may understand him and help him get as much from school as possible. She also needs an understanding of these social processes in order to evaluate the usefulness of programs of intervention that may be urged upon her from various sources.

In working with a child whose socio-cultural background has placed him at a disadvantage, the teacher has a major problem. She must support him as an individual, respecting his background and social heritage, and at the same time give him skills that will make him more likely to succeed in the larger society. To help make the decisions involved in offering an educational experience, she needs to understand how the social system works and the ways it has affected the child and his family. This chapter deals with the social structure of society and its consequences for the child in an educational setting. To describe how group differences arise and how they are perpetuated by the social structure is not to suggest that they are desirable or inevitable. Rather it is to provide information that will permit a teacher to understand better the families with whom she works.

Poverty in the
United States

For all its wealth, the United States has 24 million people who are living in poverty, a population of poor that equals or exceeds the total population of most of the countries in the world. Poverty in the United States is officially measured by a fixed standard of real income based upon the cost of a minimal human diet. Any household is officially defined as "poor" by the Social Security Administration if its annual money income is less than three times the cost (in current prices) of a minimal diet for the persons in that household.

Figures change somewhat from survey to survey, but the relationships between racial groups shown in Table 6-1 have remained relatively constant over the last two decades. There has been a dramatic change, however, in the proportion and number of families below poverty levels that are headed by women. Since 1959, the number of low-income families headed by males has decreased by more than fifty percent while the number of low-income families headed by women has increased by 13 percent. Of all low-income families, those headed by women changed from 23 percent in 1959 to 43 percent in 1972.

In a broader sense, poverty is not only having too little money;

Table 6-1 *The official view of poverty*

Poverty in 1972	
Poverty-level income for a 4-person family	$4,275
Total population designated as poor	24,460,000
White (1 out of 11)	16,203,000
Nonwhite (1 out of 3)	8,257,000
Percentage of all U.S. citizens in poverty (1972)	11.9
Percentage of poor living in metropolitan area	58.0

Adapted from *Consumer income: characteristics of the low-income population 1972*. U.S. Department of Commerce, Series P-60, No. 88, June 1973.

it is a matter of how much opportunity one has to get more. Many institutional arrangements in our society, presumably designed to furnish assistance, in actuality may reinforce dependency and a sense of failure and defeat. Welfare regulations may penalize initiative (such as part-time jobs). Our economic institutions exploit the ignorance of the poor by charging them prices for housing, food, goods and services that are higher than in middle-income areas. These institutions perpetuate poverty by omitting low-income people from social insurance plans, measuring welfare services in quantity rather than quality, and by providing poor quality schools and often the least qualified teachers.

The pictures and descriptions on the following pages show some of the conditions of poverty under which millions of young children live in the United States.

Speaking at the First Texas Conference for Mexican-Americans, Congressman Henry B. Gonzales (1967, pp. 112, 113) expressed the meaning of poverty in these words:

If one is hungry, hope itself is a distant thing; if one is defeated, promises of things to come ring empty. If one's world is limited by dirt floors and tin roofs, tomorrow holds no promises, as the greatest ambition is to live through today.

Society as a whole has never cared much about the poor because they have always been there, and because there has never been much reason to believe that poverty would, or even should, be eradicated. We decided somehow that a poor man is poor only because of his own failure, and we have too often said that a poor man deserves to be poor and should get no help. In recent years, however, there has been a change in attitude among us. We have realized that the great American dream is not open to everyone; and we are now able to understand that poverty is a symbol of waste and that it can be ended. We have come to understand that some men are poor because society has denied them a chance to be anything else; and the poor should not and need not be despised or forgotten. . . . One thing we have been doing is to make an effort, for the first time, to understand why people are poor and what can be done about it.

Traditionally one of the principal routes out of poverty and discrimination in the United States has been through education. Oscar Ornati (1966, p. 67), in a report to the directors of the Twentieth Century Fund, summarizes the importance of this avenue for upward mobility.

There was a time when it could generally be assumed that individual effort matters, that human beings could control their future. It is no longer clear that this can happen if individual efforts are not crowned by a diploma. It is also clear that many of the poor, possibly believing that this means growing up absurd, are not getting and will not get their diplomas. That if they do not get their diplomas they will stay poor is certain.

Many young people who do not finish high school still maintain faith in education as a means of equalizing opportunity. They assume that education prepares the young for higher paying, more prestigious jobs in the economy. National and local government planning reflects this assumption; the introduction of multicultural programs in public schools and colleges illustrates one effort to offer more effective education. The society is also turning to programs of early education as a way to give children from all socio-economic and cultural backgrounds a more nearly equal opportunity to receive quality education. The consequences of intervention through education in socio-economic and cultural disadvantages are not always predictable.

Table 6-2 *Family size and poverty*

Number of children in family 18 years and under	Percent of families who were poor
0	7.2
1	9.3
2	8.9
3	12.5
4	17.6
5	26.2
6 or more	35.7

Adapted from *Consumer income: characteristics of the low-income population 1971.* U.S. Department of Commerce, Series P-60, No. 86, December 1972.

Poor children often have few suitable places to play . . .

they are inadequately housed . . .

they are often hungry . . .

. . . and lonely.

The Nature of the Problem

The Sources of Inequality

Poverty is one extreme indication of inequalities in a social and economic system. In this country, it is often the consequence of two conditions: first, *socio-economic inequalities* related to industrialization and competition, and second, *discrimination* against groups on the basis of racial or cultural characteristics. Poverty and other social disadvantages are rooted to a great degree in these sources. Both socio-economic influences and racial-cultural prejudice limit opportunity and resources for large numbers of people, creating conditions that affect the educational and occupational achievement of both young and adult.

Socio-economic and ethnic discrimination create inequalities in the availability and kind of education, housing, job opportunities, income, political power, tax assessment, economic resources, and civil rights within the system. These inequalities often determine how children are treated and how well they are respected as people—factors that in turn greatly influence behavior.

Evidence of differences based on socio-economic factors and ethnic discrimination appears in many forms. That there is inequality implies, of course, that someone has more of something than someone else. If the differences are great, some members of a society will be quite rich, others very poor. Affluence and poverty are not absolute, of course, only relative, and a man's subjective sense of poverty depends somewhat on his frame of reference and on his own particular biases. Conditions that seem inadequate in one society may be considered quite satisfactory in another.

The people in a society who occupy a socio-economically dependent or a culturally subordinate status, and who do not share opportunities to obtain the rewards of that society, are disadvantaged. Poverty and lack of opportunity separate them from the mainstream.

Socio-economic Basis of Inequality

Societies, especially modern, complex, industrialized societies (of which the United States is but a single example), are highly stratified. They have a hierarchy along which privileges, wealth, and power are distributed. In some societies, even today, these different strata take the form of castes—that is, hereditary social categories sanctioned and rigidly enforced by custom, law, or religion. In a caste system, members find it virtually impossible to escape the social position they enter at birth.

Distinctions of this kind are not so rigid in the United States. We speak of lower class and middle class, but our use of such

No person except a natural born citizen or a citizen of the United States at the time of the adoption of this Constitution, shall be eligible to the office of president; neither shall any person be eligible to that office who shall not have attained to the age of thirty-five years and been fourteen years a resident within the United States.

From the Constitution of the United States. Article II, Section I, Clause 4.

terms is diffuse and vague. In the face of social and economic hierarchies we cling to an ideology of equality; we claim that anyone has a chance to be president if he or she meets the basic qualifications specified by the Constitution. The Horatio Alger myth that a youngster starting at the bottom and working hard can rise to financial success and all attendant rewards has not disappeared from our national values or social reality—approximately one-fifth of our population still tends to rise substantially along the socio-economic scale.

The unequal distribution of privileges and resources in the United States today results in part from the differentiation of roles, functions, and tasks upon which an industrial complex depends. Within a factory, for example, or in a school or a business corporation, there are different types of tasks to be done. Such specialization means that some people will be policy makers and some will be delegated to carry out policies. Except in very small companies or organizations, the people who work with ideas are not usually those who deal with personnel, and the personnel staff isn't likely to be involved in procurement or manufacture, record keeping or maintenance.

Different parts of the system create different demands. The skills needed to assemble a watch are not at all the same as those needed to sell the finished product. A TV repairman would scarcely be trained to tune pianos; waitresses are not expected to prepare the food they serve.

Because all but the least skilled jobs in a socio-economic hierarchy require some degree of training, the rewards and privileges accruing to the job are generally related to how long the needed training takes, how specialized it is, and how many people are qualified to perform the same task. Most work requires cooperation among persons who perform a wide variety of tasks. Each role has rewards in terms of prestige, income, security, working conditions, or personal satisfaction. Those who fill roles at the top levels—roles requiring the most skill and training and involving the greatest responsibility—expect and usually receive the highest return for their efforts. People at each level compete for prestige, power, and opportunity for themselves and their children to acquire material wealth, education, and a high standard of living.

Although it appears to be inevitable that complex organizations require specialization of tasks and thus create differentiation and a hierarchy, this does not indicate the extent to which these differences will result in unequal rewards, such as salary, privileges, and prestige. These are distributed in part on the basis of the values of the group and the power that sub-groups can exert to improve their share of the benefits. The change in prestige and income of workers in certain industries in this country over the past 30 years is an example of how the relative advantage of levels within the system can be altered.

Racial and Ethnic Discrimination

A second major source of poverty and disadvantage in the United States is racial and ethnic prejudice. It is ironic that this should be so, since the history of this country is the history of various ethnic groups that, despite their differences, eventually achieved a national identity. The need to establish a sense of national belonging and loyalty and to minimize ethnic distinctions gave rise to the insistence that new arrivals learn to speak the same language and to identify with traditions and heroes of this country rather than (or at least in addition to) those of their native origins.

Thus the notion of the United States as a vast melting pot of different peoples was created. In this tradition change was possible for many and schools were the principal instrument for change. Although often facing discrimination, members of most ethnic minorities were relatively free to move from one socio-economic stratum to another and thus become integrated into the dominant element. Public schools and social centers offered opportunities to acquire the language, training, and culture needed for better jobs and upward mobility. In turn, steady employment furnished the means to move to more attractive neighborhoods; and marriage made social mobility possible. In addition, some ethnic origins could be disguised by a change of name and adoption of different ways and values. Thus, acceptance into the mainstream of society was within the reach of many who availed themselves of the opportunity.

But the American melting pot has not been effective for everyone, including citizens who have been here for generations. Many of those who are ethnically identifiable, such as the Negro, the Mexican-American, the Puerto-Rican, the Chinese-

or Japanese-American, or the American Indian, have encountered prejudice and discrimination so pervasive that regardless of education, skill, talent, or background, they have been kept in an inferior status.

Concepts of the inferiority of certain ethnic groups, which have sometimes been used to justify the reprehensible social, economic, and psychological treatment afforded some minority groups, have been overwhelmingly discredited. In general, social scientists hold the view that the cornerstone of ethnic prejudice is ignorance and fear. David Tyack (1969, p. 8) makes a crucial point about the meaning of equality:

Even if it could be scientifically demonstrated that certain groups had different innate capacities, [as] one anthropologist has recently asked, would that alter their constitutional rights or their need for equality of opportunity? If, for example, Chinese-Americans on the average had larger brains than Caucasians, would that mean that they should be a dominant caste?

Figure 6-1 *Typical administrative organization of a large city school system*

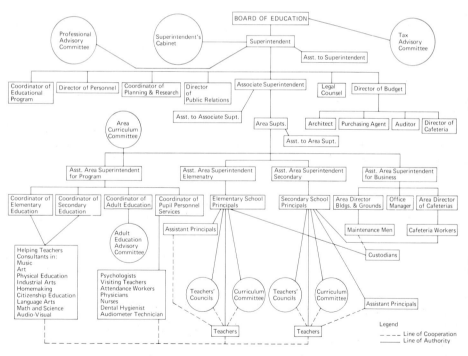

From Griffiths, Clark, and Wynn, *Organizing schools for effective education* (Danville, Illinois: Interstate Printers and Publishers, 1962), p. 14.

Although many of the laws restricting identifiable minorities have been declared unconstitutional (for example, the laws calling for segregated public facilities such as schools, transportation, rest rooms and theaters), the conditions that created them have been only partially eradicated and some such laws remain.

In recent years job opportunities have increasingly opened up to minority group members. Selection procedures sometimes still have a subtle or hidden bias, however. The use of forms or tests alien to a nonwhite frame of reference may jeopardize the chances of some applicant for equal consideration. Differences in the quality of education received by applicants may eliminate some who would otherwise be qualified. To discover whether discrimination based on ethnic prejudice exists in your community and in this country consider the following questions.

1. Can an educated, regularly employed, ethnically identifiable resident of your community
   a. Buy or rent any available house or apartment?
   b. Register for a room in any motel or hotel?
   c. Become a member of the same churches, social organizations, country clubs, and civic groups as whites?
   d. Enroll his children in all schools including dancing classes, horseback riding academies, and swim groups?
   e. Get appointments with doctors, dentists, attorneys, bankers, or in barber and beauty shops on the same basis as whites?
   f. Enter the nearest hospital as a patient?
   g. Be buried in the nearest cemetery?
   h. Buy property, secure building permits and business licenses, or get loans on an equal basis with whites?
   i. Join a trade union?
   j. Realistically hope to become president of the company or director of the organization for which he works?

2. What is the ethnic or racial origin and sex of the following
   people?
   > President of the United States
   > Chairman of the Board of General Motors Corporation
   > National Director of the American Red Cross
   > Archbishop of New York
   > National Commissioner of Baseball
   > President of the American Medical Association
   > Chairman of the Joint Chiefs of Staff
   > National President of the P.T.A.

Being ethnically identifiable obviously subjects people to stereotyped labelling without reference to individual merit. Additionally, since many of the members of some ethnically identifiable groups have low incomes, relatively little education, and live in slums and ghettos, all are presumed to share these circumstances. However, just as a society has various strata along which rewards are distributed, so does each ethnic group within that society. The black community in America, for example, has doctors, lawyers, politicians, scientists, businessmen, factory managers, teachers, shopkeepers, and artisans as well as unskilled laborers and unemployed people. This does not prevent prejudice, however, even where some of the economic inequalities have been ameliorated. Numerous Mexican-Americans have made names for themselves as legislators, writers, attorneys, teachers, priests, athletes, and musicians. Many Americans of Chinese and Japanese ancestry in this country own their own businesses and are involved in professional services and careers. They, too, are vulnerable to prejudice.

Although some individuals from groups that have been discriminated against have found recognition and acceptance in the mainstream of society, prejudice is still persistent. It can be found in discriminatory employment, education, housing, and social practices. Educated, skilled, and well-qualified persons repeatedly come up against the barrier of discrimination that exists in this country. Prejudice applies to members of all ethnically visible minorities, but perhaps the plight of blacks has received the widest publicity.

While there are many individual examples of the insults of racial discrimination, the total impact is perhaps best documented by the effects upon the crucial area of income. The annual earnings of nonwhites are dramatically lower than those of whites, *at every level of education* and for both men and women. Discrimination applies to middle- as well as working-class levels of our society (Tables 6-3* and 6-4.)

The basic principles of equality of opportunity and equality before the law are compatible with all that is known about human biology. All races possess the abilities needed to participate fully in the democratic way of life in modern technological civilization.

David Tyack, *Nobody knows: black Americans in the twentieth century* (New York: Macmillan Co., 1969), p. 8.

Although recent social, economic, and political developments have improved the status of nonwhite women workers, there still are substantial differences in the employment patterns of nonwhite and white women. Department of Labor statistics on women workers reveal that a higher percentage of nonwhite than white women are in the labor force, are working wives, and are working mothers. In general, nonwhite women have higher unemployment rates, lower income, and less schooling than white women. In addition more of them are concentrated in low-skill, low-wage occupations.

The Disadvantaged Experience

In a society that increasingly depends on technology and science for its well-being, unequal distribution of resources means poverty for many who lack the opportunity to acquire the skills needed to compete. In a country where prejudice may be directed against appearance regardless of accomplishment, ethnic group members who are visibly different face unequal opportunity. Separately, poverty or discrimination signify disadvantage; in combination they ensure despair.

Features Common to Disadvantaged Groups

However dissimilar disadvantaged individuals may be from each other or however different one ethnic minority may be from another, they share various experiences. Unlike members in the mainstream of society they fill places in two worlds—their own and that of the dominant majority. In their environment they may hold roles of leadership and trust, yet they are often

* The Bureau of the Census reported in July, 1974 that the median family income for blacks has fallen from 61 percent of the white median in 1969 to 58 percent for 1973. Median family incomes in 1973 were $7,269 for blacks and $12,595 for whites. When adjusted for inflation, the median for blacks did not increase from 1969 to 1973; the median for whites went up 6.1 percent even after taking inflation into account. (U.S. Department of Commerce, Bureau of the Census, Consumer income: money income in 1973 of families and persons in the United States, Series P-60, No. 93, July 1974.)

Table 6-3 *Full-time earnings in 1969 for women in the U.S., 25 to 64 years of age, in relation to formal education*

Years of school	White Median	Black Median	Spanish-speaking Median
Elementary 0–8	4023	2569	3717
High school 1–3	4445	3580	4269
High school 4	5106	4565	4911
College 1–3	5766	5595	5667
College 4	7255	7118	6366
College 5+	8894	8787	7258

Adapted from *Subject reports, earnings by occupation and education: 1970 census of population.* Bureau of the Census, PC(2)-8B. Tables 7 and 8.

subjected to stereotyped attitudes and treatment by those outside, who may consider them unambitious, disinterested in planning for the future, lazy, or shiftless. There is little overlap between the majority population and the disadvantaged. Young children of the poor are more frequently seen by the comfortable majority in documentary films or as part of advertisements for camp and club donations than on the streets where they play. However, by means of television, radio, billboards, newspapers, and magazines, the poor are in contact with a culture and standard of living unlike their own. They see what resources and material comforts are available. In addition, they work in the same factories, buy many of the same kinds of food and clothing as those better off than they, but in direct contact with the middle class the poor are usually in subordinate roles and unseen by the people they serve. Whether or not these circumstances can appropriately be called a culture of poverty (Lewis, 1959), lower-class life differs dramatically from that of the middle class, especially where it is also influenced by ethnic culture. Gordon Parks (1966, p. 48), writer and film-maker, recalls this one-sided view.

Table 6-4 *Full time earnings in 1969 for men in the U.S., 25 to 64 years of age, in relation to formal education*

Years of school	White median	Black median	Spanish-speaking median
Elementary 0–8	7160	5043	5880
High school 1–3	8488	6176	7321
High school 4	9187	7041	8080
College 1–3	10,398	7918	8838
College 4	13,228	8952	10,349
College 5+	14,313	11,373	11,927

Adapted from *Subject reports, earnings by occupation and education: 1970 census of population.* Bureau of the Census, PC(2)-8B. Tables 7 and 8.

The world inside the M. Club was one of spacious rooms . . . of thick carpeting, of master and servant, of expensive wines and liquors, of elegant table settings and epicurean tastes. Influential men . . . sat about smoking long cigars and ornate pipes . . . and I, in a suit of blue tails, white tie, and striped red vest, would stand near them discreetly listening to their confidential talk of financial deals, court decisions . . . families . . . and weather. To most of them I was invisible and unhearing, a sort of dark ectoplasm that only materialized when their fingers snapped for service.

As a whole, the disadvantaged poor have little to say about what will or will not be done on their behalf. No one stops to ask, "What do you think should be done?" Decisions of this kind are made for them. They are subject to economic control by a variety of government agencies: medical services from public health and welfare groups, and education based on decisions made by remote boards of education. In many instances their lack of education handicaps them in knowing where or how to get information and even how to take advantage of the information that may be available to them.

Knowledge about what they might do to improve their situation is often not available and may be deliberately withheld from them. This results in ignorance which makes them susceptible to exploitation by members of their own social community and by con men, unscrupulous repairmen and women, loan agencies, and other individuals, agencies and groups. Thus lotteries and other long-shot ventures hold great attraction.

The life circumstances of the poor restrict their range of alternatives of action. Lack of economic resources, power, education, and prestige drastically reduce physical mobility and the availa-

---

One of the sorest points of our system of justice until recently was the difference in treatment for the rich and the poor. A person who could pay his fine in a criminal case was set free. A person unable to pay the fine often was kept in prison to work off his fine.

Early in July 1970, the United States Supreme Court, in an 8–0 decision, ruled this procedure as unconstitutional. The case involved a convicted thief who remained in jail a year, then was ordered to remain another 101 days to work off a $500 fine.

A new federal law benefited the poor at about the same time that another new law, Title III of Truth-in-Lending, came into force. It prevents a creditor from garnishment of all of a worker's wages. Anyone making $48 a week or less could not have any of his wages seized by a creditor.

---

bility of different options for residence, housing, employment, and other areas of their lives.

As a group they are dependent upon the policies and resources of the federal, state, and local public health and welfare agencies who supply them with services. The range of medical services open to them is severely restricted and their bodies are likely to be exploited for medical education and research as a contingency of medical services at low cost. A low level of literacy and education and lack of experience about how to obtain information make it difficult to discover and take advantage of those alternatives that may be available.

The disadvantaged are frequently more subject to arrest and detention with little regard for their rights. Coretta Scott King, wife of the Nobel Peace Prize winner, Martin Luther King, Jr., recalls an incident of this kind that occurred several years after the Montgomery bus strike had been won (King, 1969, p. 163). She and her husband were standing quietly outside a courtroom with a friend who was to testify in a private case. A policeman ordered them to move on. When Dr. King stood his ground, courteously explaining that he was waiting to see his attorney, the policeman threatened him and together with another officer grabbed him, twisted his arms behind him, and pushed Dr. King down the stairs.

. . . I ran to get our friends, and when I came back into City Hall Martin had disappeared. He was kicked and roughed up, and then, when they discovered who he was, he was charged with disobeying an officer and released on his own recognizance.

Not only are the civil rights of the disadvantaged often ignored, but the services they are provided, from emergency care in hospitals to visits by welfare agency workers, are often inferior and made with little consideration for human dignity or concern about the invasion of privacy.

Poverty and its consequent powerlessness leaves people overly vulnerable to disaster. Many disadvantaged people are in the ranks of unskilled and semi-skilled labor and therefore are usually the first to be laid off when work is slack and last to be hired when work picks up. The poor typically are not only without financial reserves of their own, but are most likely to be given little advance notice when laid off from work. Because of their record of intermittent employment and lack of property or financial reserves, the disadvantaged possess little credit or borrowing power and are unlikely to have friends who can help them (Cloward and Elman, 1966a; 1966b). If a crisis develops in their lives, recovery is more difficult and requires more time for them than for people with some resources (Koos, 1950). The poor live on the edge of tragedy which they are powerless to avert.

Consequences of
Disadvantage

These conditions of poverty—*powerlessness, low status, lack of alternatives,* and *little access to experience or information* inevitably bring their own consequences. Individual differences in ability to cope with adverse circumstances cannot be overlooked, of course, for some men and women manage somehow to rise above severe socio-economic and cultural handicaps. Nevertheless, certain consequences result for the majority of people who lack opportunity and face discrimination.

Because powerlessness is at the core of their condition, their own relationships are often oriented to power, coercion, and force. Physical punishment is a common form of discipline in families. In verbal interaction, mothers govern children largely by phrasing their comments and instructions as imperatives; fathers may see their children's respect for them as expressed in their obedience to commands. Because adults have little power outside the family, they frequently blame those who are in control for the problems and misfortunes that daily beset them.

Self-esteem is low among the disadvantaged largely because of an accumulated sense of ineffectiveness. Their response to this frustration is often apathy and resignation. It is not that parents *teach* their children to be passive; rather the unpredictability of their lives and the lack of order and stability in their experience with their environment bring a realistic sense of caution and apathy.

On the whole, disadvantaged people tend to embrace familiar experiences and routines rather than attempt novel or unfamiliar circumstances. In general, a disadvantaged person has little opportunity to make the kind or number of decisions he would if he were in a middle-class environment. For example, he cannot be concerned whether an apartment is of a certain size or on a certain floor, when there is a question whether he will have an apartment at all or be able to meet the rent payments. People who know they are going to have to live in a hovel are not as likely to worry about how far it is from the bus stop.

Also, the life circumstances of the poor orient them to practical action. Their participation in their jobs has not typically been that of policy making. The world of abstract ideas has less place in the practical realities that must be dealt with day after day. Since the disadvantaged do not participate in policy making or any long-range planning either for themselves or others, it is essential to deal with the immediate present.

The impact of poverty upon families is expressed in many ways. One particularly significant manifestation of the process by which social circumstances are translated into behavior is in the way mothers prepare their children for entry into school. The orientation a child receives and the attitudes he develops toward teachers, toward learning, and toward his own role as a student in the classroom may affect his subsequent school achievement as well as his self-esteem in areas of scholastic performance.

In a study conducted by Hess and Shipman in Chicago (1965), it was found that mothers from different socio-economic backgrounds in the black community prepare their children in different ways for their first school experience. To obtain the mothers' definitions and perceptions of school, 163 black mothers from four SES (Socio-economic Status) groupings (Table 6-5) were asked to imagine that it was the first day of school and then to respond to the question:

Your child is going to school for the first time—what will you do, what will you tell him?

The responses showed that mothers in low-income levels tend to conceive the problems that the child will have at school essentially as getting along with the teacher and dealing with the school as an institution. Accordingly, they tend to teach their children to comply, to "be good," to "mind what the teacher says," and to stay out of trouble. Mothers from professional homes are more likely to talk to their children about the teacher and to present her in a more favorable light. They describe the school situation as one in which the child will learn and, in general, enjoy learning. Her attitudes are related also to her place in the society and the way she and her family have been treated by its institutions.

Table 6-5 *SES groupings for Hess and Shipman study*

Group A	Group B	Group C	Group D
College education, professional, executive and managerial occupations	Skilled blue-collar occupations, not more than high school education	Unskilled or semi-skilled occupations, predominantly elementary school education	Same occupational and educational level as Group C, but fathers absent from home and families supported by public assistance

As discussed earlier in this chapter, each mother sees the social world from her own point of advantage or disadvantage, and her attitudes and responses reflect the nature of the society in which she lives. The child who comes from a low-income home is oriented more towards questions of discipline and authority and whether or not he will conform to the rules, than he is toward the school as a place in which he can and will be expected to learn. This conception of school and of the school situation reflects, in part, the differences in the control strategies and techniques that the mothers use. Mothers from low-income homes are more likely to be concerned with external appearances and behavior and less oriented towards subjective experiences with which the child will be involved.

The images that mothers transmit to young children are particularly relevant to early education and the children's success in school. The mothers' attitudes in the Hess and Shipman study indicate that the problem is not due to a lack of respect for the school, lack of interest, or to the belief that it is ineffective. The low-income mothers regard the school as a distant, formidable institution with which they have very little interaction and over which they exercise little control. Thus the initial relationship between many children and the teacher is posed in terms of authority rather than interaction; as a matter of rules and obedience rather than inquiry and exploration. These patterns arise in response to the circumstances of their own lives.

Many of the programs developed in the past ten years, especially for children from poor families, adopted the concept of *deficit* as their central theme for program design. That is, they were based on the assumption that the child has come to school lacking in experience, concepts, language development, social abilities, and the like. From this simplistic (and incorrect) diagnosis of the educational problem, programs of cultural enrichment were created. The school became responsible for seeing that children had experiences which would overcome the deficit they faced.

Gradually it has been recognized that children come to school with a wide range of skills, adaptations, and coping strategies. The problem is that many from low-income areas come with behaviors which are not readily applicable to the tasks expected by the school or oriented to middle-class values and expectations. Some mutual accommodation is needed; the child must be helped to develop attitudes and behavior necessary for success in a school setting; the school must revise its program to respond to the particular needs, talents, and experiences of the child from a low-income community.

Differences in Educational Achievement
Performance Related to Socio-economic Level

Children share the consequences of disadvantage and the effects are evident in many areas of behavior. Of particular concern to teachers of young children are the effects of disadvantage upon capabilities and attitudes that are instrumental in performance in school, and that ultimately determine the skills and abilities needed to work and live effectively in a complex social community.

Children from families with unskilled and semi-skilled occupational backgrounds tend to be less successful in school than children from families with professional, managerial, and executive occupations. These differences have been evident for many years and appear in most types of school achievement and test scores. These discrepancies in performance between children from low-income level and high-income level families appear early in the child's educational career; the traditional school has not been very successful in improving the relative achievement of many children from low-income homes.

To recognize the scope of the problems involved in dealing with inequalities of educational opportunity, it may be useful to review the differences among socio-economic and ethnic groups on tests. In the early years of this century the French psychologist Alfred Binet devised a test to detect children who were likely to have serious academic problems. The individual intelligence test which he worked out, and which was later revised, is still one of the classic and most-used measuring instruments in the field. In early uses of this test in Europe it was discovered that children from so-called working-class backgrounds scored at a lower level than those from middle-class homes. This finding has been repeated many times, not only on the Binet test and its revisions, but with other measuring instruments as well.

The size of the difference varies with the test used and to some extent with the population to which it is administered. Children from middle-class homes show a clear advantage; generally the discrepancy is on the order of 10–15 IQ points.

There are a number of theories as to why these differences exist. Most of them present explanations about the effect of environment upon the development of mental capabilities, although some claim that achievement differences between socio-economic groups are based on genetic factors. As was indicated in Chapter 2, this is a very complex problem. To think of it in terms of genetic factors seems unproductive and somewhat futile; such an approach discourages attempts to improve the child's educational experience. Rather, one needs to consider the kinds of learning contexts that can be provided in the child's environment so that no matter what his native or biological talent he may develop his abilities to their fullest extent.

One of the common criticisms of intelligence tests is that the items were constructed by middle-class, academic persons with knowledge obtained from their middle-class, philosophy-oriented language, objects, and experiences. Many of the test items contain a bias, however unintentional, which favors children from middle-class homes (Davis, 1948). This criticism of the application of intelligence tests to children from quite different backgrounds holds that many of the activities, skills, and adaptations needed for successful performance are acquired only within the context of middle-class community and school situations.

Children from city slums and rural communities develop aptitudes that are not always readily assessed by middle-class, academically oriented testing devices. Children from dissimilar socio-economic and ethnic communities even within the United States have vastly divergent experiences, and the initial and most urgent efforts of education should be to assess the effects of environments and examine differences in achievement in these terms before surrendering to the genetic arguments with their easy answers of inevitability and despair. The first place to look for explanations, though not the only one, is in differences of opportunity and experience.

Discrepancies that appear on IQ scores have a parallel in other levels of educational attainment, in dropout rates, in college attendance, and in aspirations and expectations for achievement. This is not surprising since the so-called general intelligence tests are strongly weighted in the direction of reading ability and school-related information. The differences in level of achievement in reading, arithmetic and other academic subjects have shown up in the early grades and were maintained as the child progressed through elementary and high school.

Although achievement of middle-class children compared with that of children from unskilled and semi-skilled occupational levels might seem to be higher on items that have to do with verbal performance, this may not generally be the case. Rather, the art of test-taking itself appears to influence a fairly wide range of item types.

A survey conducted in a large metropolitan center in the midwestern United States illustrates the extent of difference in educational attainment between such groups. In this survey twenty-one school districts were ranked by criteria consisting of a composite of median level of income and median level of education of the adults in the school districts. These were compared with a crude index comprised of the combined scores of two reading tests and two tests in arithmetic at the fifth grade level. In those districts that were in the top third of the socio-economic scale, student performance ranged from achievement at grade level to achievement roughly one grade or one full year above the norms for the city. Students from all districts that were on the bottom level of the income scale performed about one year below expected grade level. Similar patterns were apparent in reading readiness scores for first grade children where only 40 percent of the districts that fell in the bottom third of the socio-economic ladder were up to national average in this crucial set of skills.

In another survey, a comparison of the performance of children in twenty-six schools in California showed that differences among the schools varied considerably according to subject matter. The greatest disparities appeared in science where the percentiles ranged from approximately 83 for the highest socio-economic level schools to a percentile of 14 for the lowest—where the schools had been categorized into four socio-economic levels. The smallest differences were in writing where the highest socio-economic group was at the 76 percentile and the lowest at 37.

Another index of difference in educational attainment between middle-income and low-income children has to do with the tendency of young people to drop out of school. The number and proportion from low-income areas who leave before high school graduation is disproportionately high especially when combined with ethnic group information. It is also significant that young people who have the ability to go on to college tend less often to do so if they come from poor backgrounds or backgrounds where the education of the parents seems to be low (Table 6-6).

Table 6-6 *College enrollment from different socio-economic levels, 1967*

Family income	Percent of high school graduates entering college
Under $3000	19.8
$3000 to 3,999	32.3
$4000 to 5,999	36.9
$6000 to 7,999	41.1
$8000 to 9,999	51.0
$10,000 to 14,999	61.3
$15,000 and over	86.7

From U.S. Department of Commerce, *Current population reports,* Series P-20, No. 185, July 11, 1969 (Washington, D.C.: Government Printing Office, 1969), p. 6.

The varieties of behavior shown by individuals from dissimilar cultural and ethnic groups is a fascinating topic of study in human activities. In the United States variations in cultural and ethnic (including racial) patterns of living and working have always been part of our national life. These ethnic differences appear in academic performance as well as in other areas of daily life. They are not fully understood but they reflect to some degree an inequality of educational opportunity. Not all ethnic groups have been allowed to realize their intellectual and scholarly potential, even in a society that presumably is concerned with developing the ability of all children.

One of the most comprehensive surveys showing ethnic differences in elementary and secondary school achievement was made by Coleman (1966). This was a national study of the academic performance of children from low-income communities and racial minority backgrounds. The study revealed discrepancies in the performance of children from the different ethnic groups tested. These discrepancies were apparent in grades one and persisted through grade twelve.

Lesser and his associates (1965) designed a project to study the relative effects of social class differences and ethnic-racial variations on intellectual performance of young children in New York City. They selected or constructed tests and developed conditions that were intended to minimize cultural and social bias. The tests covered four mental abilities—verbal ability, reasoning, number facility, and space conceptualization—and were administered to 320 children in the first grade (ages 6 years 2 months through 7 years 5 months) from four different ethnic groups. These groups—Chinese, Jewish, black, and Puerto Rican—were themselves subdivided into middle- and working-class. These SES categories were not comparable from

Table 6-7   *Rank of mental abilities within cultural groups*

Ability	Chinese	Jewish	Black	Puerto Rican
Verbal	4	1	1	4
Reasoning	3	3	2	3
Numerical	2	2	4	2
Spatial	1	4	3	1

Adapted from Lesser, Fifer and Clark, "Mental abilities of children from different social class and cultural groups." *Monographs of the Society for Research in Child Development 30,* No. 4, Serial No. 102 (1965): 82.

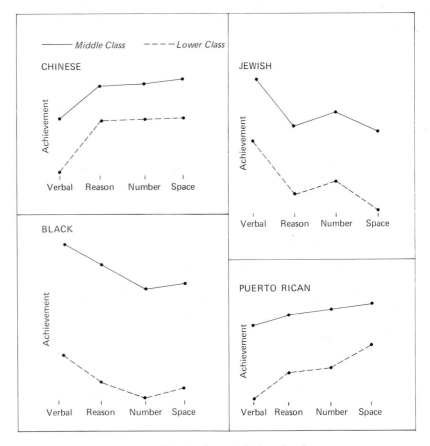

Figure 6-2 *Patterns of ability by social-class level*

Adapted from Lesser, Fifer, and Clark, "Mental Abilities of Children from Different Social Class and Cultural Groups." *Monographs of the Society for Research in Child Development 30,* No. 4, Serial No. 102, (1965): 65–68.

one ethnic group to another, however. The "low" SES Jewish group was probably closer to the "middle" than to the "low" SES black group.

The study, which was replicated in Boston, confirmed that both socio-economic status and cultural background exert strong influences upon mental ability. These influences, however, act in quite different ways. Cultural background affects the *pattern* of mental ability regardless of social class background; social class background affects the *level of achievement* in the different abilities tested. This is apparent in the data presented in Table 6-7 and Figure 6-2.

The essential points of the Lesser findings are first, there are different *patterns* of ability among children from different cultural backgrounds. Second, within each group there are different *levels* of performance based perhaps on unequal opportunity, presumably, for broad educational experience.

Implications for the Classroom

A careful examination of socio-economic and cultural differences in the United States and of the extent of racial discrimination reveals the seriousness of these problems and of the complexity of any effective solution. It becomes clear that the problems of poverty and discrimination are related to a total life pattern and that any simple or single solution cannot be sufficient. This means, of course, that attempts to produce educational gains and advantages will be effective only if they are accompanied by changes in other areas of life—employment, housing, health, physical safety, and security. These interrelationships are recognized by the government and programs such as the 4 C's (Community Coordinated Child Care) are established to coordinate child care services.

The desire or the decision to intervene in the life of a young child or his family and the attempt to change his style of life, cultural pattern, or socio-economic level is a critical decision and raises ethical problems (Gray, 1971). The teacher will often find herself torn by the inconsistencies that arise between her own values and those of the child's home.

How much should she try to alter the cultural and social patterns that the child brings to school? Why? Assuming that she could be effective in her efforts, the teacher needs to be aware of the impact of attempts to change the values of a child or family. However, part of the opportunity that school can offer is the chance for educational routes out of poverty and disadvantage. To develop a child's potential to read and to succeed in school is to increase his alternatives. The teacher can help give the child more alternatives than he would otherwise have and help his family see that there are more options and possibilities that they may not have realized were available. This will not happen in dramatic ways with every child, of course, but it will happen often enough to justify the teacher's efforts.

It is important, also, that we not promise more than our programs can achieve. In the early days of compensatory education, the impression was conveyed (through titles like Upward Bound, Higher Horizons, Head Start, etc.) that these new efforts held a special sort of immediate promise for many children. They were often less effective than the publicity might have led parents and community leaders to believe and the resulting disappointment added to the mistrust of the system.

In a real sense, these are philosophical and political problems as well as educational ones. The ethnic communities in this country are increasingly insistent upon participating in the decisions that affect their children, and schools are becoming responsive and sensitive to these community pressures. This is a familiar pattern in American education. Schools are instruments of the community and are supposed to carry out the community's educational plans. In the past, many who set the curriculum for low-income and ethnic groups were not from the communities themselves but from a part of society far removed from the realities of the low-income groups and ethnic families. This trend toward community participation in setting goals for children who have been disadvantaged is in line with a historic educational tradition in this country.

The teacher thus needs an understanding of the kind of behavior he or she may expect from the children with whom she works She also needs a sense of how she may best assist each child to achieve the goals his family and community set for him. Perhaps the most difficult and important task the teacher has is to give the child a versatility and competence to succeed in both his own world and others he may encounter and wish to enter.

SUMMARY The nature of socio-economic and ethnic influences on behavior and the origins of inequality in poverty and ethnic discrimination are described. The subjective meaning of disadvantage as personal experience is illustrated. These experiences lead to several different kinds of response and behavior toward the larger social group. Disadvantage affects the school performance of children in part through its own impact upon individual esteem and capability and through the inability of the schools to adapt to the special needs of children from poverty areas. The different ways ethnic background and socio-economic inequality affect test performance are shown in research findings.

SOME POINTS TO REMEMBER

1. Head Start, begun in 1965, was the first national program of early education.
2. Head Start was oriented toward improving educational opportunities for children from low-income backgrounds.
3. More than 20 million people in the U.S. are living in poverty.
4. The number of poverty level families headed by males has

decreased since 1959; the number headed by females has increased.

5. Poverty is not only the lack of money; it is the lack of opportunity to get more.

6. The twin inequalities in this country are based on socio-economic differences and discrimination against ethnic groups.

7. Complex societies, which are highly stratified and call for many different types of roles, tend to produce inequality in economic resources and social prestige.

8. The traditional melting pot concept of the early development of the U.S. is not nearly as viable as our idealistic history presents.

9. The effects of ethnic discrimination are most apparent in income and job opportunities.

10. The poor of a society usually know more about the affluent than the affluent know about the poor.

11. The features of being disadvantaged, economically or socially, are powerlessness, low status, lack of alternatives, and little access to experience or information.

12. Families from different socio-economic backgrounds prepare their children for school in different ways.

13. Children from low-income backgrounds tend, on the average, to do less well in school than children from middle class families.

14. One criticism of intelligence tests is that the items are oriented toward children from middle class backgrounds.

15. Experience with tests and test taking seems to influence performance on many items.

16. Both ethnic and socio-economic backgrounds influence performance on tests, but in different ways. Ethnicity influences the pattern of abilities; socio-economic status affects the level of performance.

17. The problems of discrimination and low income are so complex that no single approach will do much to solve them; a massive coordinated effort is needed.

REFERENCES

Bureau of the Census, U.S. Department of Commerce. *Current population reports.* Series P-20, No. 185, Washington, D.C.: Government Printing Office, July 11, 1969, p. 6.

California Elementary School Administrators Association. *The neighborhood and the school: a study of socio-economic status and school achievement.* Burlingame, Ca., 1962.

Cloward, R. A. and Elman, R. M. Poverty, injustice and the welfare state. An ombudsman for the poor? Part 1. *Nation* 202, No. 9, 28 February 1966, pp. 230–235.

Cloward, R. A. and Elman, R. M. Poverty, injustice and the welfare state. How rights can be secured. Part 2, *Nation* 202, No. 10, March 1966, pp. 264–268.

Coleman, J. S. et al. *Equality of educational opportunity.* Washington, D.C.: Government Printing Office, 1966.

Davis, A. *Social class influences upon learning.* The Inglis Lecture. Cambridge, Mass.: Harvard University Press, 1948.

Downs, A. *Who are the urban poor?* Supplementary Paper No. 26, rev. ed. New York: Committee for Economic Development, September 1970.

Fantini, M. D. and Weinstein, G. *The disadvantaged: challenge to education.* New York: Harper & Row, 1968.

Gonzales, H. B. The hope and the promise. In *Improving educational opportunities of the Mexican American, Proceedings of the first Texas conference for Mexican Americans,* edited by D. Estes and D. Darling. Austin, Texas: Southwest Educational Development Laboratory, 1967.

Gray, S. W. Ethical issues in research in early childhood intervention. *Children.* Washington, D.C.: U.S. Department of Health, Education, and Welfare, Office of Child Development, May–June 1971, Vol. 18, No. 3, 83–89.

Griffiths, D. E. et al. *Organizing schools for effective education.* Danville, Ill.: The Interstate Printers and Publishers, 1962.

Hesburgh, T. M. Foreword to *Prejudice, U.S.A.,* edited by C. Y. Glock and E. Siegelman. New York: Frederick A. Praeger, 1969.

Hess, R. D. and Shipman, V. C. Early experience and the socialization of cognitive modes in children. *Child Development* 36, No. 4 (1965), 869–886.

King, C. S. *My life with Martin Luther King, Jr.* New York: Holt, Rinehart and Winston, 1969.

Koos, E. L. Class differences in family reactions to crisis. *Marriage and family living* 12 (1950): 77–78.

Lesser, G. S., Fifer, G., and Clark, D. H. Mental abilities of children from different social class and cultural groups. *Monographs of the Society for Research in Child Development* 30, No. 4, Serial No. 102 (1965).

Lewis, O. *Five families.* New York: Basic Books, Inc., 1959.

Ornati, O. *Poverty amid affluence.* New York: The Twentieth Century Fund, 1966.

Parks, G. *A choice of weapons.* New York: Harper & Row, 1966.

Tyack, D. *Nobody knows: black Americans in the twentieth century.* New York: The Macmillan Company, 1969.

U.S. Department of Commerce, *Consumer income: characteristics of the low-income population 1972,* Series P-60, No. 88, June 1973.

U.S. Department of Commerce, *Consumer income: characteristics of the low-income population 1971,* Series P-60, No. 86, December 1972.

U.S. Department of Commerce, Bureau of the Census, *Subject reports, earnings by occupation and education,* 1970 Census of Population, PC(2)-8B.

Chapter 7 A New Era for Early Education

Head Start Expresses a New Priority

National Concern About Equality in Education

Shortly after 9 p.m., January 4, 1965, reading slowly and pausing often to emphasize his points, President of the United States Lyndon Johnson called for legislation that was to lead to far reaching changes for early education in this country. He spoke from the rostrum of the House of Representatives, not only to a packed chamber and gallery of those attending the opening sessions of the 89th Congress, but also to a vast radio and television audience. It was only the second time in the history of the United States that a State of the Union message had been delivered at night. During his speech, the president said:

I propose we begin a program in education to ensure every American child the fullest development of his mind and skills. . . . Every child must have the best education our nation can provide. . . . In addition to our existing programs, I will recommend a new program for schools and students. . . .

    For the preschool years we will help needy children become aware of the excitement of learning.

    Never before had education at the preschool level been singled out for this kind of attention. Eight days later the President sent a message to Congress devoted entirely to his plans for all levels of education. His recommendations regarding preschool education, although brief, showed an awareness of the lack of school achievement of children from backgrounds of poverty, and a belief in the importance of early education in the lives of all children. He called for an initial expenditure of $150 million for preschool programs.

Education must begin with the very young. The child from the urban or rural slum frequently misses his chance even before he begins school. . . . Action on a wide front will begin this summer through a special "head start" program for children who are scheduled to begin school next fall.

And so Operation Head Start was launched. A number of trends and events brought about this response at the national level to the educational needs of poor children. Perhaps the most significant was the growing concern over the inequality of educational opportunity for black children in the United States and the more general concern for economic, legal, social, and civil rights of minorities.

The work of a few social scientists in scattered parts of the country was another important influence. These men and women had been conducting research on the educational development of poor children and constructing experimental programs intended to raise the children's school achievement. Most of these programs were sponsored by universities and funded by private foundations. Before these efforts, there had been a few formal programs of instruction, particularly of the sort represented by Montessori (1870–1952), who began her work with poor children in Rome. But on the whole, prior to the mid-1960s, little systematic effort had gone into devising effective preschool programs based on learning theory and research. The concern expressed by the President led to increased interest in early education and a wide variety of programs for intervention. Each of the publicly financed programs was different from the others, but all sought to help children avoid educational failure.

The concept of Head Start and the availability of funds from private and government sources evoked a great deal of professional response. Intense efforts were begun to develop theories and construct programs of early education. The activities of these professionals were concentrated on experimental programs and on research that would increase the effectiveness of methods of instruction in the classroom and other settings.

As ideas were put into practice, their proponents argued the merits of alternative programs. Competition among programs stimulated a process of evaluation that still continues. The relative value of different programs is a major controversy; the advantages of investing in curriculum as opposed to investing in teacher training or other aspects of early education (use of aides from low-income communities, for example) are issues still under consideration. The impact of Head Start and its attendant experimental and research efforts has been enormous, however; early education has gone through an irreversible transformation.

Support for these programs of educational intervention came largely from concern over the effects of poverty and discrimination on the cognitive growth of children. It was inevitable, therefore, that the programs that emerged would be based on theories about the problems of children from slum areas. Considerable attention was also given to the study of learning processes and the knowledge gained from these efforts has had an effect on preschool education for all children, advantaged as well as disadvantaged.

Different experimental programs and points of view have stimulated the evolution of a number of distinct philosophies and teaching techniques for early education. Although ideally a teacher selects and adapts programs to fit her own teaching style or the child's needs, there is a tendency for her to align herself with a particular philosophy, sometimes rejecting programs as too unstructured, mechanical, academic, or traditional, or because she intuitively doesn't like them.

Programs do indeed reflect different theories and techniques, but they are not necessarily competitive; they can be seen as providing the teacher with a variety of tools and resources. Although a teacher will probably prefer one type of approach, she need not reject other techniques and ideas, if they can contribute to her program. It might be useful for a teacher occasionally to vary her methods if only to see more clearly how her own ideas and practices contrast with those of others. Obviously, a teacher can select more effectively the methods and techniques she needs if she is familiar with contemporary and historical points of view about the educational process.

Assumptions About the Impact of Poverty and Discrimination

Many of the recently developed programs were designed for use with children from low-income backgrounds and are thus oriented toward the needs of children from underprivileged areas. These new programs and their related reports have offered various explanations as to why some children from poor families (and especially those who also face ethnic discrimination) don't do well in school.

The center of the problem is seen by some to be within the child. Others direct attention to family relationships and community influences. Sometimes the school system, and the interaction between teacher and child, is considered a principal cause of children's failure to achieve the cognitive development needed for school success. A fourth explanation focuses on the structure of society itself, and how this structure creates disadvantages that affect children's learning and educational performance. Each viewpoint has its proponents. Learning something of the assumptions helps explain the programs that evolved from them.

The child as the locus of the problem: The deficit model

One of the first and most popular explanations of why certain groups of children fail to achieve in school is that they suffer a deficiency of school-related experiences. Such children, in this view, have not been adequately exposed to the beneficial stimulation and care that build the basis for academic achievement in our school system. Indeed, one of the most widely read books on education of low-income children in the early 1960s expressed this view in its title, *The Culturally Deprived Child.* This sort of terminology persisted for many years and is still found in some writings about low-income children. The analogy that comes to mind is to compare a physically undernourished child who has never been given enough vitamins, proteins, or other body-building nutrients to establish and maintain good health, with a picture of the socio-economically and culturally "malnourished" child who lacks the skills and experiences most needed for success in school.

This view of the role of early experience is an echo of the writing of John Amos Comenius (1592–1670), who wrote of the School of the Mother's Knee where, during the first six years of life, the child was taught by the mother so that when he reached school age he possessed simple facts and skills that prepared him for school. It also borrows from the ideas of John Locke (1632–1704), who described the mind of the young child as a *tabula rasa,* a blank tablet, on which experiences were to be impressed and transcribed. In this view, the disadvantaged child was an empty vessel, lacking and insufficient.

From this viewpoint, in terms of program planning, the locus of the problem is in the child himself who comes to school with an educational and cognitive deficit. Writers holding this view elaborate this notion in the following ways:

Lack of Stimulation. This perspective suggests that the poor have not been sufficiently exposed to beneficial stimuli at home or in their neighborhoods to provide adequate background for school experiences. In this sense beneficial means exposure to middle-class language patterns, social experience, and achievement training. Stimulus deprivation, in this view, also includes lack of exposure to the geographically wider community, books and libraries, magazines, concerts, art galleries, and other of the "educational and cultural" experiences which presumably prepare children for school. A writer in the mid-sixties (Lyford, 1970, pp. 49, 51) described a child's life in Harlem.

It is the crowds of children most of all who contribute to the neighborhood atmosphere. According to my census there are about three dozen of them, mostly Negroes. Some belong to the Methodist Church Sunday School and sell Girl Scout Cookies. All of them spend the summer racing up and down the block looking for something to do. Since they do not have any equipment for the usual games, they invent their own, which is a misfortune for the city because the major emphasis—in spite of Sunday School—is on breaking bottles, setting fire to trash, opening hydrants, and sending in false alarms. But with all their rushing about and daredeviling, the children regard the four corners of the block as the outermost limits of the universe. Whatever travels they take are imaginary ones in the hulk of an abandoned car that periodically turns up along the curb. Very few of the children leave the block even to climb the big rocks that loom up on the edge of Central Park a few hundred feet to the east.[1]

This view of the lives of poor children who lack the parties, vacations, experiences with pets, trips to beaches and jaunts at amusement parks that are often a part of the lives of middle-class children, is a familiar one, especially in the early literature of Head Start.

Another related but distinct view is that there is a *lack of pattern in experience* in poor neighborhoods. One may distinguish between random experience and stimulation and the ordering of experience into patterns of meaning. As young children explore the world around them, they learn that their actions elicit response. Adults approve of or respond to certain behaviors and

---

[1] From "In My Neighborhood An Adult Is a Dead Child." Reprinted, by permission, from the November 1970 issue of *The Center Magazine,* Vol. III, No. 6, a publication of the Center for the Study of Democratic Institutions, Santa Barbara, California.

disapprove of or ignore others. Some people pay attention to them, others appear not to notice their presence. The consequences of their actions may vary according to the occasion. Through their experiences children build an array of patterns and association linking what they do to the consequences, and these make it possible for them to understand their world. If the responses they receive are random and therefore not predictable, they have no way of knowing where they stand. Unless the stimuli to which children are exposed are presented in a pattern that permits them to generalize and cope with future situations, they won't be able to make sense of their world. A deficit of this sort results not from an absence of stimuli, but from the absence of a *pattern* to the stimuli presented. According to this interpretation of the effects of poverty upon early cognitive development, children who are not accustomed to seeing patterns of cause and effect and who have lived with inconsistency, are likely to reach school less able to cope academically with what is expected of them.

Another facet of the deficit approach emphasizes *the substandard conditions of the poor* and the consequences of this economic fact upon their lives. Unable to purchase necessities in the form of goods and services of various kinds, they lack a balanced diet and nutritional problems become severe. The National Nutrition Survey begun in 1968 suggests that multiple deficiencies of specific nutrients occur in higher than expected proportions among poor people (Read, 1969, p. 11).

Those who have worked with undernourished or hungry children know that they exhibit behavioral alterations. These include apathy, lethargy, inability to pay attention, and perhaps overconcern about food to such a degree that responses to classroom stimuli do not occur.

The notion that the disadvantaged child is deficient in the learning he brings to the classroom was the basis of the first major wave of programs for intervention. The programs often included what were considered culturally enriching trips: to museums, zoos, parks, stores, gardens, factories or wherever children might gain needed experience. Some youngsters visited overnight in suburban homes. Others received special attention in language training. Underlying this approach was the general philosophy that children who lacked advantages should be exposed to the world of those who had them, thus making up the deficit.

The misfit between cultures: the cultural disparity model

Sociologists, linguists, and anthropologists interpret the difference in school performance between poor children and middle-class children from the *viewpoint of cultural differences*. According to this theory, the ghetto child, rather than suffering from a deficit in learning, faces a conflict in values and goals because of the difference between what he has learned at home and what he needs to know in order to succeed in school. This approach, which places the locus of the problem within the family and community, takes several forms.

Cultural Pluralism. Family ways and values differ from culture to culture as well as along a socio-economic hierarchy. Differences in food preparation, religious beliefs, and holiday customs do not usually affect school performance, but some cultural patterns and customs do cause difficulties in the classroom. For example, many Puerto Rican and Mexican-American children are taught to show respect for their elders by turning their eyes downward when they are spoken to. If the teacher's reaction is that shown in Figure 7-1, this is obviously a problem in communication. For some tribes, American Indian life traditionally centered around sunrise and sunset; time was relative and unimportant. Even today it is frequently difficult for Indian children and their parents to adapt to the ways of a school program that is regulated by clock time, yet they are judged by school norms of punctuality.

Perhaps one of the most significant aspects of cultural pluralism concerns language usage in the home and in school. Many poor children speak either a dialect of English or an entirely different language. In either case, however well they communicate at home, their speech is often not that approved for classroom use. Although these children may daily hear standard English on television, they often have little occasion to use the forms themselves and so come to school linguistically different, only to find that they are expected to speak, read, and comprehend standard English.

The educational and occupational opportunities of disadvantaged minority children and their families are limited not only

by discrimination, but also by lack of accurate information. They often have few contacts with levels of society other than their own, and their knowledge of the economic and occupational aspects of the larger world is based mainly on hearsay rather than personal experience.

The cultural patterns of poor children, especially those who also face racial or ethnic discrimination, may conflict with those the child is expected to follow at school. If they do, he has to make choices. This may be difficult, for he does not come to school ready to change what he already knows and embrace a new set of values. If he does not succeed in school, he becomes more isolated. From five to fifteen he learns to know his own culture even more perfectly, the school culture less and less. Therefore many children explicitly reject the school and its values long before high school graduation; others choose to hide the conflict from view.

Acquisition of Behavior Not Rewarded at School. The child who lives in a ghetto or impoverished rural community learns to deal with and adapt to the environment in which she lives, no matter how poor, dangerous, or unrewarding it may be. She learns to cope with the threats of exploitation and of physical danger from fire, rats, traffic, etc., to deal with harassment from police, and to hold her own physically with peers and older children. She learns not only to protect herself in an often hostile environment, but to extract from it some of the things she wants or needs. The inner-city ghetto is not always a friendly or happy place. Its inhabitants are painfully aware of the contrasts between the wealthier, more powerful, established dominant culture and their own situation. It is a way of life that demands special resources and coping abilities but these are not of a type likely to bring success in the classroom. This analysis does not hold that the inner-city child has failed to learn during her preschool years, but that she has learned the wrong things, from the school's point of view.

Schools as the locus of the problem: the miseducation model

The following statement from a report to the United States Commissioner of Education (Panel on Educational Research and Development, 1964, p. 30) is typical of some assessments of the quality of education in the slums:

By all known criteria, the majority of urban and rural slum schools are failures. Across the country in neighborhood after neighborhood, more than half of each age group fails to complete high school and 5 percent or fewer go on to some form of higher education.

In the face of this kind of evidence, the schools themselves have come under attack. In effect, those who blame the schools for low achievement of poor children are saying, "We spend money on schools, buy books, provide equipment, pay good salaries. Why aren't the schools doing their job?" They see children's failure to be one of teaching, not learning. Therefore they also ask, "Why haven't teachers been better trained? Why are so many unable to understand children from backgrounds other than their own?"

To these critics, the teacher's inability to comprehend the circumstances of the poor and minority groups represents a lack of sympathy for the child and his problems. They see it as the teacher's ineptness in communicating with children and general failure to help them learn about and relate to the larger society. They grant the possibility that some children from low-income families have learning problems, are poorly disciplined, and have had little practice with abstraction. But to them this does not explain why many teachers are ignorant of the needs of these children, perceive poorly the abilities the children do bring to school, and have not acquired the skills needed to teach them.

The picture books, texts, stories, and songs used in the early grades show a life and a people far removed from the world experienced by children who live in slums, on sharecropper farms, or in migrant work camps. Poor children's imaginations encompass giants and fairies, talking animals, and tug boats, but fail to respond to a life for boys and girls that is shown to consist of:

. . . happy neat, wealthy white people whose intact and loving families live only in clean, grassy suburbs. . . . and the most serious crises they have to face are the loss of the family pet or who in the household will have the use of the car (Fantini and Weinstein, 1968, p. 133).

Discontent with teaching has led to demands for schools oriented to ethnic and ghetto cultures, new ways of teaching, and better teacher training. Those who blame the schools sometimes give the impression that the best solution is to do away with the entire system and start anew. Their reform movement is less formal and less coordinated, perhaps, than some of the others, but the voices of their representatives are clearly heard.

Society as the locus of the problem: the destructive system model

Disadvantage is inherent in a highly differentiated social system such as that in the United States. In turn, the disadvantages incurred affect individual cognitive activity and achievement. Those who view the social structure as being responsible for the many school failures among poor children see socio-economic disadvantage, combined with discrimination, placing individuals in situations that permit little latitude for choice or comparison. For example, children are expected to comply with rules without explanation, just as parents themselves must comply with seemingly arbitrary decisions made for them by institutions on which they are dependent—the housing authority, medical service, or school board. Alternatives and reasons are not given or thought necessary, and decisions are often based simply on expediency or availability.

Since the parents have few chances to evaluate or choose among alternatives in their own lives, they are not likely to provide situations in which children are encouraged to compare, to select or to think for themselves. As a consequence, the cognitive operations (ability to plan, categorize, select, order, etc.) needed for success in public school are less often stimulated in children of the poor.

A graphic expression of this viewpoint appears in Lyford's article (1970, p. 53).

One of the tidal facts that has impressed me most is the continual waste and loss of human life that is taking place in our city. I am not talking about the murders or assaults that have terrified most of the people I know—poor people, middle-class people, well-to-do people. I am talking about the destruction of children. Of the enormous number of crimes that take place in the city, the largest amount and the most terrible are committed against children. Only a small portion of these crimes have to do with outright physical abuse. From the time tens of thousands of newborn infants are removed from the hospital, they become subjected to what I call "the process." That is, they are introduced to a style of existence that eventually cripples or destroys huge numbers of them, and occasionally other people with whom they have come in contact. . . . The children who do survive this tempering process become adults, but in my neighborhood an adult is a dead child.

And again, on page 55:

What has happened is that we are in the middle of a system that makes the "process" inevitable; that requires more and more human beings in various parts of our country—Appalachia, Selma, Watts—to grow up to be dead children, or, as some people put it, welfare babies. The system I am talking about is turning more and more of our resources away from the nurture of human life and into the destruction of it.

If the structure of modern American society contributes to school failure, so also does discrimination against minorities.

Discrimination affects learning and cognition by creating a sense of incompetence and low efficacy and, consequently, an unwillingness to be assertive in the environment.

President Johnson's public acknowledgment of the already known discrepancy in school achievement between middle-class children and those from low-income families stimulated broader interest and public funding to deal with this problem. Although all of the above assumptions have some validity, planners who began to develop programs often preferred one to the exclusion of others. Obviously, decisions as to whether the root of the problem lies in the child, the family, the school, society, or in some combination, determined the types of programs of intervention chosen.

One of the features of programs developed in response to the educational needs of low-income and minority children is that they were more focused to the needs of a particular part of the population than had generally been true in the past. Different conceptions of the problem, however, gave rise to a variety of approaches. Some of these are instructional programs in the usual sense; others are more general strategies for changing the environment in various ways or attacking the educational problem in a supposedly more effective way.

Strategies of educational intervention tend to fall into the following broad categories:

1. Enriching the cultural and educational environment
2. Engineering an instructional program
3. Involving parents in the educational process
4. Giving communities greater control over the school
5. Beginning instruction at earlier ages

Enriching the Cultural and Educational Environment

Perhaps the most popular and extensive educational effort has been in response to the concept of cumulative deficit. The idea that children's cognitive experiences can be incomplete—that children need exposure to the elements of a wider (middle-class) society to help raise their performance in school—excited the imagination of many educators. In an enrichment program, therefore, children engage in numerous cultural and social activities and the classroom environment provides an opportunity for the development of language and cognitive skills. These efforts are based on a philosophy that there are natural benefits to the child that come from an exposure to new cultural experiences.

Engineering an Instructional Program

Another early response was to create a highly engineered environment. Research had shown that even before disadvantaged children reach school age, they are behind in a number of the verbal and cognitive skills needed for school success. Selecting specific and significant educational objectives and gearing the teaching effort explicitly to their attainment seemed to some to offer the hope that inequality might be overcome. Accordingly, instead of permitting children in nursery school to engage in whatever catches their interest, they are taught systematically, in an engineered program. The exact behavior desired and the sequences for achieving the objectives are defined and structured, whether the task is to identify a color, name a letter, describe a space relationship or respond, "I don't know." Project directors set up an environment to elicit the desired behavior and work out a reinforcement schedule. Teachers are then trained to teach according to techniques specified in the program.

This approach to intervention proceeds from a belief that children who are behind the norm in school-related learning need to be given more than the opportunity to learn. In effect, they need a kind of forced feeding of the skills and concepts which will best serve them in the school experience and enable them to begin formal schooling with an ability equal to that of middle-class children. From this point of view have come a number of engineered programs as well as considerable controversy.

Involving Parents in the Educational Process

Involving parents was discussed in Chapter 3 and no attempt will be made here to develop further the ramifications of this subject. However, one point regarding parent involvement as an approach to intervention needs emphasis.

Research shows maternal behavior to be influential in children's early cognitive and academic development. The ways mothers talk to their children and develop their language skills, the ways they attend to and interact with children's activities,

---

Introducing "I Don't Know" Statements

These are valuable because they help the children articulate what they know and what they do not know about an object. The "I don't know" statement sets the stage for deductive processes that require more than a single step.

Show the children two juice cans, both at room temperature. Hold one up and ask, "Is this can cold?" If a child offers an answer, explain; "You are guessing. You don't know that this can is cold. How can you tell? You have to touch it."

Let the children feel the can and determine that it is not cold. The second can is introduced unopened, and the procedure is repeated.

The children are likely to assume that this one must be cold. "You are guessing. Do you know? Did you touch it? . . . No. You don't know. Say, 'I don't know.' Say it."

From C. Bereiter and S. Engelmann, *Teaching disadvantaged children in the preschool* (Englewood Cliffs, N.J.: Prentice-Hall, Inc., 1966), p. 149.

---

the expectations they have for their children, and the control techniques they exercise have a bearing on school achievement. This suggests that success in public school depends on far more than the few hours a day spent in a nursery school regardless of the level of teaching, the ratio of teachers to children, or the kind of program offered. If it is to be lasting, cognitive development seems to require reinforcement beyond that which the school can give. Family support that results in consistency between what goes on at home and in the classroom is essential. Such a relationship not only improves the child's orientation toward school, but also helps the parents see their importance as educators.

On the whole, parents are interested in the education of their children. When this interest is translated into active support of the school, it reinforces the goals of the school by helping children develop positive attitudes toward themselves and toward learning. In family-oriented programs, decisions as to what is to be done for the child and how to do it remain the responsibility of the school, even though the impact on the child is made primarily in the home by the parents.

Giving Communities Greater Control over the School

Those who conclude that the core of the educational problem is in the failure of the schools and the dominant members of society believe that it is not sufficient to concentrate on reforming instructional programs and the curriculum. Their conviction leads to quite different approaches to educational intervention— approaches that are aimed not only at the child and his learning but also at the social and institutional context in which he learns. Accordingly, there have been vigorous attempts recently to involve parents as power groups and to shift responsibility for the school directly to the local community.

This feeling is especially intense in ethnic communities. Many members of ethnic groups feel, with considerable justification, that they have been ignored in the formulation of educational policy. Many of today's minority groups not only see their cultural ways as right for their children, they also resent the omission in the curriculum of the contributions made by ethnic leaders to the development and well-being of the country. It may be appropriate for many children to read in their social studies text, "Our forefathers came to this country to find freedom." But this is not the sort of history that has meaning for many ethnic children whose parents were brought as slaves or imported for the purpose of providing cheap labor on the railroads and in the mines and factories. When the schools fail to take into account the important values of children from different backgrounds and fail to offer programs relevant to their cultures, the families and community leaders quite naturally blame the schools for their children's failure to succeed.[2]

In recent years, therefore, a general strategy of shifting responsibility and power for decision making from the schools to organizations within the community has been gaining strength. A community-oriented program sees the community as exercising specific influence and control in decisions concerning the hiring and firing of school personnel, the choice of curriculum, and the setting of policy as to how the school shall be run.

This approach to education can bring about many changes:

1. People called upon to make decisions about hiring and firing soon develop a sense of effectiveness.
2. People responsible for deciding what children are to learn and the means to be used develop a sense of control.
3. People in charge of anything as complex and important as a school acquire status in their own eyes and in the eyes of the community.

In addition, children recognize and respond to their parents' positive orientation to the school with a greater commitment to education. Although the goals of various approaches to education may be alike—that is, the socialization and welfare of children—the political and social consequences of community control are unique to each community.

Beginning Instruction at Earlier Ages

Because one of the most obvious measures of school failure in ghetto and poverty areas is the high rate of dropout in secondary school, some of the first efforts at educational intervention involved work with adolescents. This proved relatively ineffective, however, and attentions was turned to programs for children in the elementary grades. Success in these measures was not spectacular, and many scholars became convinced that effort was needed at even earlier levels. Head Start, involving four- and five-year-olds, was a recognition of the importance of learning during the preschool years.

More recently, emphasis is being placed on infancy as the prime time to establish a base for later learning in specific skills and concepts. In addition, Parent-Child Centers—federally

---

[2] See specific example regarding test bias, Chapter 13, p. 377.

funded programs established for children from infancy on focus on specific instruction under the supervision of personnel trained in early childhood education. This is in contrast to the more traditional day care center where the emphasis is on caretaking during the time the parent is at work. The approaches described above are seldom if ever represented in any single curriculum or program and it is thus difficult to tell whether one approach is more effective than another. The experience of many program directors is that no single effort or unique approach will solve the complex and intertangled problems that contribute to diminished educational opportunity and achievement. There are no magic techniques, no secret formulas, no shortcuts. Effective programs are a combination of resources and methods; the route to equality in education and opportunity is neither simple nor smooth.

Some Consequences of Head Start

We have had roughly ten years of experience with Head Start and other programs of intervention developed to meet the need for more equal educational opportunity. What has happened to these programs? What have we learned about designing effective intervention? Where is the field of early education headed?

It is clear that education will never again return to the pre-Head Start stage. Changes have occurred in programs, training methods, materials, knowledge, and legislation. Perhaps more important, the attitudes of the public toward early education and public child care have created new expectations about the right to obtain extra-family child care and education for young children.

Hundreds of studies have been conducted on the effect of Head Start (enrichment) programs upon the cognitive growth of children, and although researchers who review these studies correctly complain about inadequacies in their design and instrumentation, a number of consistent points appear in the results. New evidence will continue to come in—that is the nature of research—but some tentative conclusions are worth reviewing now.

Most programs show short term gains on IQ and school-related achievement tests—letter recognition, ability to label colors, recognition of shapes, ability to count and the like. These seem to appear in reasonably structured—that is planned and implemented—programs.

These short term gains usually do not persist more than a year after the children leave the program. It is not known if the

gains themselves are fundamental changes in the cognitive structures and capabilities or if they fade for lack of continuing support and stimulation.

Gains in social behavior—more adaptability to school expectations, more interest in school-related tasks, increased spontaneity in interaction with adults and other children—are reported by many studies. These also seem not to be permanent. The reliable assessment of social and emotional changes, however, is very difficult. The instruments of assessment and the methods of gathering data are not well developed. Also, although it is assumed that children who attend Head Start classes have special need for social and emotional intervention (paralleling the clear need for educational opportunity), the evidence for deficiency in these areas does not exist.

Indeed, several assumptions which were popular in early Head Start days are no longer tenable. The assumption of deficit, especially linguistic deficit, has been discarded by many professionals on the basis of new research data. Head Start has led to a dramatic change in our thinking of the processes by which language develops and the structure of dialect used by blacks, which is now seen as a language with its own set of rules and orderly usages. The effects of these discoveries has been profound upon early educational programs and especially upon programs for children who come from homes where some language other than standard English is spoken.

Another assumption about programs of intervention for young children is that the route to progress is more complex and takes longer than the designers of Head Start believed. Our knowledge in 1965 about the effects of poverty and discrimination was severely limited. Some reports about the pre-school experiences of young children in urban ghettos suggested that one of the significant problems they faced was a lack of familiarity with the basic materials and experiences that might facilitate initial school experience—little contact with books and other reading materials, little experience with crayons and other drawing and scribbling materials and other information that the teachers in first grade classrooms expected. Head Start, as the name suggests, was designed to fill in these experiential gaps.

One summer was sufficient to convince many people that the impact of poverty and social disadvantage was not superficial, and year round programs were soon developed. The first major evaluation, the so-called Westinghouse Study (1969) not only challenged the long term effectiveness of the program without follow up, it convinced many that summer programs alone were insufficient.

Additional evaluations, including that of Follow Through, offer convincing proof that no single dimension of a program or even concentrated structured programs can adequately deal with educational disadvantage. It is generally recognized that there must be a multiplicity of efforts to achieve real gains. These include health services, working with the families, economic support, community involvement along with direct efforts to provide educationally related instructional services.

One result of early educational intervention programs has been the increased involvement of families and community groups. The participation of parents, while a significant part of some programs of the mid-60s, has increased in scope and altered in the nature of their roles. Initially, the parent was seen primarily as a subsidiary target for intervention by the program staff. They were viewed as adult students, whose competence and experience was to be upgraded. With the experience of the past ten years, the family is seen much more often as a partner in the educational task and more often seen as having a degree of political control over the finances and management of the program. Groups of parents have developed programs of their own, with professionals providing resources and back up services. Parental involvement is now being mandated by local rules and by legislation. One major consequence of Head Start, then, is the greater recognition of parental roles in early education and their participation in planning and managing activities.

The rights of children have also become a focus of concern. Several organizations such as Children's Lobby have been created to promote legal services and rights for children. They also lobby for new legislation concerning children and children's programs. For the first time children, as a group in the society, are being represented in systematic and effective ways in the Congress and in state legislatures. Child abuse laws have been passed to protect children from their own parents. Many of the issues involved in this sort of advocacy speak to the quality of extra-family care and education of very young children and are thus relevant for teachers.

Public schools, in some parts of the country, are developing programs of early education which allow entrance of pre-kindergarten children into elementary classrooms. This trend seems to be encouraged not so much by force of research as by a public acceptance of early education as a good thing for children and for their parents. For economic reasons, some parents welcome the opportunity to send their young children to publicly supported school settings. The lowering of age of school entrance will also create many news jobs for teachers, some of whom may be reassigned from higher grades because of declining enrollment in the elementary schools. Positions may also be available for aides and teachers who now hold jobs in private schools or are training for work with young children.

There is a similarity between this trend—moving pre-school educational programs into the public schools—and the growth of kindergartens in the United States. Roughly one hundred years ago, there was intense social concern about the effects of urbanization and industrialization upon young children. Kindergartens were started with the financial aid of private foundations. These crusading efforts and the subsequent public acceptance of the idea of kindergartens led to the inclusion of kindergartens in the public school program in many parts of the country. The effects of a new lowering of school age entrance upon children is not clear and the prospect has both advocates and opponents. It is, however, a trend that has significance for teachers and other professionals in the field.

It is the emergence of day care, in its various forms, that represents the most dramatic and significant development in the field. Two events, among others, contributed to this shift in emphasis. One of these was the realization that the gains in cognitive and scholastic capabilities were less dramatic than had been expected and that more comprehensive and long term programs were essential. The second was the public awareness of the right of women who are in the labor force to have adequate facilities for child care. There is also a growing recognition of the demand for child care of women from all socio-economic levels who want to respond to their own desires for greater individual freedom and self-development. The public acceptance of the fact that greater equality for women can only be attained if more national resources are devoted to child care will probably allow or stimulate expansion of existing resources and create new institutional forms.

These trends reflect both the importance of early education and the continuing salience of developmental care for young children. The professional teacher maintains and renews her competence by watching the progress of these new features of the field.

SUMMARY

Operation Head Start, launched in 1965, recognized the importance of early education, especially for children from backgrounds of poverty. Prior to that time, little systematic work had been done on theory and research leading to development of effective preschool programs. Since then, many experimental programs of educational intervention have been designed, reflecting different theories and techniques. In order to more effectively select useful methods, the teacher needs to familiarize herself with various contemporary and historical points of view. This chapter examines the principal assumptions underlying programs designed for underprivileged children. Five approaches to educational intervention are described.

SOME POINTS
TO REMEMBER

1. Head Start was launched in 1965 as the first major national program of early education.
2. Intervention programs like Head Start stimulated much research in early education.
3. The knowledge gained from programs of early intervention is applicable to all children.
4. There are several quite different explanations about the effects of poverty on school achievement: (1) the child has not developed adequate skills, (2) the family and community have not provided him with appropriate experiences, (3) the school system has failed to reach the child, (4) the society is structured in ways that create disadvantage.
5. Several of these viewpoints were advanced by educators in the 17th and 18th centuries.
6. Language and dialect differences among poor and ethnic children create one of the most misunderstood discontinuities with the school.
7. The school, with its orientation toward middle class values, often ignores the culture of children from poor and ethnic backgrounds.
8. There are five popular approaches to educational intervention:
   (1) enriching the cultural and educational environment
   (2) engineering an instructional program
   (3) involving parents in the educational process
   (4) giving communities greater control over the school
   (5) beginning instruction at earlier ages
9. Evaluation shows that most intervention programs produce gains on IQ and achievement tests, but these often do not last without continued intervention.
10. New knowledge about dialects in black communities have changed the belief that black children from ghetto areas come to the school with a linguistic deficit.

11. To be effective, intervention programs need to be more comprehensive than many cognitively oriented (pre-academic) programs of the late '60's.
12. A significant result of Head Start was to increase family and community participation in early education.
13. Parental involvement in early education is now often mandated by federal, state, or local laws.
14. One current trend in child care is the establishment of organizations to protect and advance the rights of children.
15. Another trend is lowering the age of entrance into public schools to include pre-kindergarten children.
16. The emphasis on early education now includes comprehensive day care as well as cognitively oriented curricula.

REFERENCES

Bereiter, C. and Engelmann, S. *Teaching disadvantaged children in the preschool.* Englewood Cliffs, N.J.: Prentice-Hall, Inc., 1966.

Bronfenbrenner, U. *Is early intervention effective?* Office of Child Development, U.S. Department of Health, Education, and Welfare, Washington, D.C., 1974.

Fantini, M. D. and Weinstein, G. *The disadvantaged: challenge to education.* New York: Harper and Row, 1968.

Goodson, B. D. and Hess, R. D. *Parents as teachers of their children: an evaluative review of some contemporary concepts and programs.* Stanford University: Center for Research and Development in Teaching, 1974.

Hess, R. D., Beckum, L., Knowles, R. T. and Miller, R. Parent-training programs and community involvement in day care. In Grotberg, D. (ed.), *Day care: resources for decisions.* Office of Economic Opportunity, Office of Planning, Research and Evaluation. OEO Pamphlet 6106-1, June 1971.

Lyford, J. P. In my neighborhood an adult is a dead child. *The Center Magazine,* November 22, 1970, Vol. III, No. 6, 49–56.

Panel on Educational Research and Development. *Innovation and experiment in education.* Washington, D.C.: U.S. Government Printing Office, 1964.

Read, M. S. *Malnutrition and learning.* U.S. Department of Health, Education, and Welfare, Public Health Service. Washington, D.C. National Institute of Child Health and Human Development, 1969.

U.S. President 1963–1968 (President Lyndon B. Johnson). Annual message to the Congress on the State of the Union. *Congressional Record Proceedings and Debates of the 89th Congress,* First Session, January 4, 1965, Washington, D.C.: U.S. Government Printing Office, Volume 111, Part 1, 26–29.

U.S. President, 1963–1968 (President Lyndon B. Johnson). Toward full educational opportunity, Message from the President of the United

7 A New Era for Early Education

States. *Congressional Record Proceedings and Debates of the 89th Congress,* First Session, January 12, 1965, Washington, D.C.: U.S. Government Printing Office, Volume 111, Part 7, 589–592.

Westinghouse Learning Corporation. *The impact of Head Start: An evaluation of the effects of Head Start on children's cognitive and affective development.* Westinghouse Learning Corporation: Ohio University. 1969.

White, S. H., *et al. Federal programs for young children : review and recommendations.* Department of Health, Education, and Welfare, Washington, D.C. 1973.

Chapter 8   Programs are Tools, Not Religions

Chapter Outline

The Growth of Programs of Early Education

Recent Developments in Curriculum and Programs

The concentration of research and developmental efforts to create programs particularly effective with children from low-income communities had consequences for preschool children of varying backgrounds. Initially, these were experimental programs or modifications of established programs which had achieved a new popularity, as in the new impetus given curricula based on Montessori's theory and procedures. Although they were designed for disadvantaged children, the principles on which they were based and the imagination that went into their construction made them appropriate for children from a variety of ethnic groups and socio-economic origins.

The energy and interest that were generated by Head Start, as well as the experimental work that preceded this national effort, has taken many forms, most of which are variations on major programs. Some were created and used in local schools and received little publicity. The time pressure under which Head Start was organized made innovation necessary, and it is possible that a great deal of the imagination utilized in local programs was not publicly disseminated. Programs with a definite form, practice, and philosophy do not easily develop, and it was the combined efforts and funds of national educational projects that accelerated the emergence of special curricula and made them more widely accessible.

It seems likely that future historians of early education will regard Operation Head Start and Project Follow Through as the two major forces responsible for the growth of differentiated programs of early education in the sixties and seventies. Project Follow Through came about as an attempt to continue into the early grades the educational advantages of Head Start. It provided an opportunity to develop specific programs for children in the early grades from low-income communities.

At the invitation of the U.S. Office of Education, professionals who were working on experimental curricula and programs for young children were asked to develop these for kindergarten and the primary grades. The resulting programs were implemented under their supervision and sponsorship in schools in various parts of the country that were located in communities representing several different ethnic groups. The expansion and visibility of early education also stimulated the development of other approaches that later joined Follow Through as sponsored projects. The curricula and instructional methods of Follow Through, which were more specific and elaborate than most available preschool programs, were also adapted to age levels included in Head Start. This planned continuity between the two programs reduced the traditional gap between the preschool and the school curricula.

A part of the total Follow Through effort was an evaluation of the relative effectiveness of different approaches and curricular components. The results of this evaluation, as they are announced from time to time, will be of great interest to professionals in the field and will have a significant impact on the future of the programs involved—an impact that the teacher will have to consider carefully in light of his own and his school's objectives.[1] For example, results of one program may show impressive changes on one kind of behavior (number skills, letter recognition, IQ, etc.); others may be more effective in promoting affective and social development.

Publicity about evaluation programs in the mass media often simplifies and even distorts what a program has accomplished.

---

[1] For example, see References in Chapter 2, Stallings and Kaskowitz.

Announcements of evaluation results, therefore, should be examined with skepticism and great care (see Chapter 13).

These new programs were often presented, sometimes dramatically, with theoretical arguments and occasionally with research evidence as support for their merits. They offered solutions and supplied a need for specific information and effective procedures in the classroom. The field of early education, however, includes professionals with a wide range of educational philosophies and it was natural that teachers in pre-school centers and nursery schools would find some types of programs more appealing than others, depending on their own experience and beliefs. Techniques of teaching by using punishment or tangible rewards, such as M & Ms, seemed to work for some teachers but others found these approaches objectionable on philosophical grounds.

Teachers have strong emotional investment in their work and in their view of themselves as competent to do what is good for the child. They often took strong positions on the new programs and tended to align themselves with one or another. The desire to defend one's own convictions, however, makes it difficult to try out other approaches. A wider perspective, perhaps, in which the claims, points of view, and techniques of several programs are examined and considered may be useful. After all, it is the effect on the child that counts and skills are to be gathered from a variety of sources.

It is not possible to describe all the new and modified programs of early education that were inspired by the enthusiasm of the sixties, but some of the prominent examples will indicate the variety in point of view and practice that is available. The summaries cover basic issues in philosophy and implementation but do not attempt to describe parent-community involvement or in-service teacher training, all of which are used to different degrees in each program. Most of these programs have some objectives in common but differ in emphasis and manner of implementation. Some are widely known and may be identified by the sponsor's name.

The Tucson Early Education Model

Ronald E. Henderson
Arizona Center for Early Childhood Education
College of Education, University of Arizona
Tucson, Arizona 85721

Rationale and Objectives

Although this program was originally designed for Mexican-American children in the first through third grades, it is now

8 Programs Are Tools, Not Religions

being used in preschool through third grades with children of all ethnic backgrounds. The developers based the program on the belief that the lack of skills, particularly language skills, and low self-esteem have contributed to academic, vocational, and social failure among many low-income people. Four areas of activity are utilized to help prepare the children for successful participation in modern technical society: language competence, intellectual base (including skills such as planning, organization, and recall), motivational base (having a positive attitude toward school), and societal arts and skills (including reading and arithmetic).

Description and Implementation

Children in the program are not given a specified set of learning objectives but progress gradually according to their own pace of development. There is no ordered curriculum, and activities are designed in a way that allows many different skills and concepts to be taught at the same time. Most activities, for instance, are arranged around everyday experiences such as woodworking or cooking. A specific project, then, might be making ice cream, during which the children encounter new words and concepts; measure, multiply, and follow directions; and plan and work cooperatively. Afterwards, they write about the experience. Each project is designed to work toward all four principal goals of the program.

The physical environment of the classroom is organized into interest areas and is designed to promote interaction among the children themselves, between the children and the adults, and between the children and material objects. The teacher's primary role is that of organizer for the learning experience. There is strong emphasis on individual and small group instruction, modeling or imitation, and reinforcement. Spontaneity is encouraged, and the experiential background of the children is the source for many of the class projects.

The Behavior Analysis Model

Don Bushell, Jr.
Follow Through, Department of Human Development
University of Kansas
Lawrence, Kansas 66044

Rationale and Objectives

The Behavior Analysis Model has been used with low-income children from preschool through the third grade. Bushell feels that later academic failure can be avoided by instilling basic skills (reading, writing, spelling, etc.) and desirable classroom behavior (paying attention, self-confidence, cooperation, etc.) at an early age. The teaching strategy used is designed to identify for each child his present state of achievement, define his individual goals, and help him attain them, i.e., to bring him from where he is to where he should be. The method involves the use of systematic reinforcement or rewards to teach the child the needed skills. The rewards are individualized since it is assumed that what motivates one child to complete a task may not motivate another.

Description and Implementation

Rewards, in the form of tokens or plastic chips, are given frequently and immediately for accomplishments on the child's part. Then, at a specific time in the day, the child may exchange his accumulated tokens to participate in some desired activity, each of which has a cost. For instance, the child may earn twenty tokens by doing arithmetic problems correctly and spend fifteen of them to hear a story read. The student himself always determines when and for what to exchange his earnings. It is the teacher's responsibility to make sure that events are available that are important to the child. The tokens also remind the teacher to pay attention to each child and especially to those who are not earning much.

The Responsive Model

Masako Tanaka[2]
Far West Laboratory for Educational Research and Development
1855 Folsom Street, San Francisco, California 94103

Rationale and Objectives

The program was originally designed for children aged three through nine from low-income families, but the developers feel it could be used regardless of background. It is based on the idea that children learn at different rates and in different ways, but most importantly, they learn best when they are interested. Responding to children rather than requiring them to respond is a major part of the design. This follows the view that development of intellectual abilities (or learning how to learn) and a healthy self-concept are crucial to a child's success both in school and later in life. Problem-solving is seen as the essence of learning, and therefore the program emphasizes the development of skills and strategies, such as inductive and deductive reasoning.

---

[2] Formerly directed by Glen Nimnicht.

8   Programs Are Tools, Not Religions

Description and Implementation	The curriculum is organized into units called learning episodes that make use of specific toys and games. Very few printed materials like workbooks are used. The classroom is designed and equipped so that the child has many opportunities to explore and experiment, and great flexibility is allowed. The teacher selects what materials will be available, and then the child may choose to do whatever interests him and work at his own pace. An example of one of the activities is the learning booth, equipped with an electric typewriter that the child is allowed to explore, while the teacher names each of the letters and symbols the child types. The child then moves on to discriminating the letters himself, copying stories, and eventually to composing his own stories on the typewriter.

The Engelmann-Becker Model
(The Systematic Use of
Behavioral Principles)

Wesley Becker and Siegfried Engelmann
Department of Special Education
University of Oregon, Eugene, Oregon 97403

Rationale and Objectives	This highly structured, fast-paced program was designed for preschool through third grade, but children participate according to their level of achievement rather than age or grade level. The developers believe that mastery of basic academic skills is necessary for low-income children to compete successfully in school and achieve economic success in adult life. They see the preschool as a place where the disadvantaged child must learn twice as much twice as fast so as to be on a par with the middle-class child.
Description and Implementation	A complete curriculum (called Distar) in each of the goal areas (reading, language, arithmetic) has been developed. The lessons develop skills in small learning steps, with frequent testing so that the child can progress at his own rate. The lessons are presented in small groups, organized according to level of accomplishment, and the children sit in a tight semicircle around the teacher. All children in the same group should be progressing together. The program developers see the role of the teacher as that of a clinician, who responds in a premeditated and purposeful way. The importance of reinforcement is stressed and the children are often given rewards (perhaps in the form of a take-home worksheet) for correct responses. The curriculum calls for much repetition and rapid-fire drill, and art and music lessons are designed to reinforce academic lessons.

Primary Education Project

Lauren B. Resnick
Learning Research and Development Center
University of Pittsburgh
Pittsburgh, Pennsylvania 15213

Rationale and Objectives

This program (known as PEP) is aimed at developing an individualized education for children from preschool age through third grade. It has been specifically designed for urban areas. The developers believe that children learn best through active involvement, at their own rate, and with a large degree of self-direction. It is the role of a school to foster confidence in their ability to learn and to teach the basic skills they need to be effective learners. The project staff has developed a sequential curriculum that can be adapted to individual needs and abilities. Three classes of skills are included in the program's objectives: attending skills (listening, following directions); perceptual and motor skills (coordination, movement); and conceptual-linguistic skills (reasoning, classifying). After each child is carefully tested to determine her present level of achievement, the teacher will then define that child's individual goals.

Description and Implementation

Each child in the PEP project is tested often, and on the basis of test results the teacher prepares individual assignments. Because the instruction is constantly being revised, the child should always be meeting with success in the classroom, an important feature for building self-confidence. The daily classroom activities are divided into two different periods: the work period during which the child is involved in completing his individual assignments; and the exploratory period during which there are a number of different activities available from which to choose. The exploratory period is meant to provide the children with the opportunity to use their basic skills and develop new interests.

The Open Education Model

George E. Hein
Education Development Center
55 Chapel Street, Newton, Massachusetts 02158

Rationale and Objectives

The Education Development Center (EDC) has designed what is actually an approach to education rather than a program in the usual sense. It is based on the practices of British infant schools and advocates the development of a learning environment responsive to the needs of the children and the capabilities of the teacher. The EDC functions in an advisory role to assist teachers in setting up their classrooms and working out whatever problems arise.

The Open Education Model emphasizes developing the potential of the whole child. It is based on the belief that children teach themselves rather than being taught by adults. Learning grows out of the child's curiosity and interest in his environment, and the teacher is in the position of patterning or organizing the classroom to facilitate the child's natural tendencies.

Description and Implementation

There is no curriculum in the usual sense and there is no specific body of skills and concepts that children are expected to learn. The EDC approach, however, does emphasize communication skills (including reading, writing, and speaking) primarily in the context of children working with each other. They are encouraged to cooperate, discuss their work together, and learn from each other.

The classroom should be rich with materials for the child to work with, particularly common "junk" materials suitable for developing creative abilities. The teaching strategy is based on the concept of the open classroom where, in an atmosphere of mutual trust and respect, the child's learning is deeply rooted in his own experiences. It is emphasized that each classroom is individual and must be designed to be suitable to the needs and abilities of teacher and children.

The Bank Street Model

Elizabeth Gilkeson
Bank Street College of Education
610 West 112th Street, New York, New York 10025

Rationale and Objectives

The developers of this preschool through third grade program believe that, given a supportive and interesting learning environment, children will find learning to be a self-rewarding process. The design emphasizes the development of a positive self-image coupled with the ability for self-direction and works toward these goals by basing learning experiences on children's normal play activities. The approach assumes that each child has individual educational goals and that these goals evolve as the child progresses. The developers also believe that to emphasize compensatory measures or to develop only specific academic skills when working with low-income children is self-defeating; unless the whole child is considered and he learns to develop active, creative, thoughtful ways of dealing with his own life's problems, academic skills will prove useless.

Description and Implementation

The Bank Street Model offers no single approach to classroom learning. Methods are expected to evolve as a result of both the children's interests and the teacher's skills. Sometimes direct teaching methods along with preplanned lessons are appropriate, but often indirect instruction is used. No extrinsic rewards are used, because it is believed that children learn what and when it is important to them, not through having skills and knowledge imposed from outside authority.

The environment is planned to provide maximum opportunity for exploration and discovery, and the child has much freedom to choose his own activities. Group activities, such as cooking and building, are typical. These activities provide the learning context for concepts such as time and measurement as well as social skills in cooperation. Often one project will naturally lead into another, rather than there being sharp divisions between the day's activities.

Underlying Assumptions of Programs

A number of assumptions about teaching and learning underlie all contemporary programs of early education intended for low-income children. Some of these common views are described below.

Education Begins at the Level of the Child's Ability

Because what children learn depends largely upon what they already know, it is important to determine where a child is along the continuum of growth and development when setting up a program of early education. This is, of course, not a new idea. Maria Montessori, with her focus on individual learning, established procedures for evaluating the ability level of children in her classes so that instruction could begin with the child's edge of mastery. This basic principle of learning and motivation appears in many forms, especially in individualized pupil instructional programs, which plan sequences of learning steps that build on one another. Diagnostic examination to assess levels of mastery can provide the detailed information needed to determine children's capabilities. There are many ways to carry out this sort of assessment, some of which are highly informal and impressionistic, others formal and systematic. The principle, however, is that teaching most effectively proceeds from what a child already knows.

Teaching Should Adapt to the Needs of the Child

No matter how similar the experiences or endowment of a group of children, they differ greatly as individuals. Each will have his own store of skills, his own special interests and talents, his own worries about achievement. In order to be effective, therefore, teaching must be individualized more than it presently is in most classrooms.

A Child Learns Best When Motivated

Exposing children to numerous experiences, providing them with a wide variety of materials, or giving them the opportunity to participate in numerous activities, alone or in a group, does not always mean they will learn what you want them to, or be willing to learn at all. However attractive the environment from the teacher's viewpoint, many children need other stimulation; they require special direction in the form of a teacher's interest and enthusiasm, and they need help in finding out where and how to start, before they are capable of proceeding alone. Some children respond to rewards such as stars on a chart, a cookie or sweet, or special privilege. For others, social approval is sufficient. During the early stages, at least, choosing a technique that engages the child may be more important than utilizing one because it meets with universal or personal approval.

Children Must Learn the Role of Pupil to Succeed in School

Behavior appropriate to the role of pupil includes the ability to pay attention, to follow directions, to understand what the teacher expects, to work in groups, and to be able to take the initiative in learning situations rather than waiting passively for things to be done and or explained. The role of pupil also requires avoiding disruptive behavior, noise, fighting, teasing, shouting, or conversely, withdrawing or refusing to participate. To become a successful learner, the child must be able to master tasks as well as cognitive materials.

Disadvantaged Children Can Acquire School-related Skills and Concepts

Because of their record of low scores *on the average* compared with those of middle-class children, children from low-income backgrounds have sometimes been thought less capable of doing satisfactory school work. When children do not learn, however, the fault may be in the materials or the techniques of teaching, rather than in the children. Once dimensions of readiness have been ascertained, and subject matter has been chosen to correspond with their level, large numbers of disadvantaged children show themselves to be apt learners. It would seem that the learning capacity of these children has been grossly underestimated. The task may be to engage their interest and show them that learning is possible.

Issues That Differentiate Programs

Early educators dealt in various ways with issues involved in preschool education. Today's programs, whether innovative or based on old forms, take a stand on many of the same issues. These issues themselves provide categories by which programs can be classified or defined. The name, size, or location of a school tells very little about what its staff intends to do for its children. The stand a school takes on various basic issues, however, immediately gives a prospective teacher an idea of its philosophy and the direction her teaching will be expected to take. It helps answer the questions, "What kind of program is it?" and "What can be accomplished by working in this program instead of another?"

Structured vs. Unstructured Curriculum

One way to understand a program is to determine to what extent and in what ways it is structured.

The term *structure,* as applied to curriculum, is frequently used in discussions of early educational programs, but it means different things to different people. Most frequently, perhaps, it brings images of a rigidly disciplined, prearranged, organized pattern of activities in which the teacher directs the components of the daily routine. Unstructured may suggest free play and other activities that are initiated by the children and reflect their own preferences and interests. In general, traditional programs are thought of as having less structure (and being less cognitively oriented) than some of the newer, more innovative programs.

Some early educators had firm views on this subject. Pestalozzi (1746–1827) argued that teaching should proceed not from structured programs but from the unfolding of the child's natural interest and capability. Comenius (1592–1670), on the other hand, emphasized the importance of systematic early training and believed that all knowledge could and should be introduced early and systematically. Rousseau (1712–1778) was relaxed about the problem—he maintained that children would learn to read and write in due time according to their own inclination.

The term structure may have a negative connotation to some, because it suggests the image of mechanical, insensitive rigidity. This is only one meaning of the term and perhaps not the most significant one.

When applied to the arrangement of learning experiences, structure exists in two forms: 1) a constant *awareness in the teacher's mind* of an underlying design to a total curriculum, or 2) a prearranged *sequence of materials for presentation* to the child (Figure 8-1).

In the first form, the teacher keeps in mind overall goals that he uses to help organize and provide learning experiences for the child. The sequence of presentation of this underlying curriculum has not been arranged. (A casual observer might think it unstructured.) The teacher makes constant use of incidental experiences to provide teaching situations. When a child comments about her dress, for example, she may help him label colors, count buttons, and so on.

In the second form, the structure lies in the arrangement and presentation of information. This kind of structure may be highly similar from school to school and can easily be programed and used somewhat like a script. The most highly structured programs of this form utilize definite lesson plans in which one lesson is presented and presumably mastered before the next is introduced.

A truly unstructured program, in our view, is one in which *neither* is the implicit curriculum in the teacher's mind *nor* is the presentation organized and thought out. There is no statement of objectives in behavioral terms. Consequently, neither the physical nor the human environment has a design and the program lacks specified objectives. In programs of early education for children whose educational opportunities are likely to be limited, this is unacceptable no matter how skillfully a teacher might entertain her class and keep them interested and well behaved.

In the unstructured program, the teacher has little idea of the potential growth of the child so the curriculum as reflected in her behavior is not based on any systematic concepts of child development. Children may be happy, there may be administrative structure and rules, and there may be a good deal of interaction between teacher and children, but it is largely based on intuitive feel of the teacher and stimulated by accidental overtures and episodes of the day. It is, essentially, a custodial program.

Figure 8-1 *An example of a structured curriculum.*

This does not mean that the children are badly treated or unhappy but that there is no underlying concept of how to create an environment that will offer opportunities for challenge and growth in mental, social, affective, and physical phases of behavior.

There are, of course, programs in which children are not treated well, are neglected, and are exploited for the satisfaction of impulses and personal goals—economic, ideological, or emotional—of the staff. Such programs so obviously offend the sensibilities of an observer that they need no special description and condemnation here.

In some instances, the importance of structure in the presentation of materials has been overemphasized and the importance of structure in the teacher's mind has been neglected. A teacher who is able to use spontaneous experiences in the classroom to help teach concepts, and who knows how to serve as a model for

Figure 8-2 *A relatively unstructured activity.*

the children, may be very effective even though the learning situation itself has not been preprogramed.

Proponents of programs that are structured both in their underlying design and in the way of presentation to the child argue that the learning principles that such programs incorporate, such as properly timed rewards, make for more effective and efficient learning. Perhaps something can be said for giving an inexperienced teacher a script which relieves her of some of the responsibility for planning the children's learning experiences. It is more desirable, however, for teachers to have an underlying curriculum in their interaction with children. The most effective teacher can make use of a structured presentation of materials when this suits her purposes and can also utilize spontaneous opportunities to accomplish her goals.

Perhaps the real issue is whether the teacher is in charge of learning situations in the classroom, or whether decisions are made by some group who provides her and the classroom with predetermined educational experiences. A script strictly adhered to is better than nothing but not as desirable as a creative teacher with a curriculum in mind.

In gaining experience in evaluating the degree and kind of structure in a curriculum, it may be helpful to use a crude rating scale, similar to the one illustrated in Figure 8-3.

Depending upon the degree to which a program is structured, its staff emphasizes certain kinds of teaching and has specific goals and techniques. Evaluating a curriculum on each of the following dimensions adds perspective to the specific type of program.

Cognitive Skills	vs.	Affective Skills
Content	vs.	Process
Learn by Instruction	vs.	Learn by Discovery
Extrinsic Motivation	vs.	Intrinsic Motivation

(The order is not significant.) The two poles of each of these dimensions are not mutually exclusive. A program can teach both cognitive and affective skills, can emphasize content in one area and process in another. Usually, however, emphasis is placed more toward one side of the dimension than another. Where a program fits in regard to these dimensions can often be assessed by observation (and perhaps a few questions) if one knows what to look for.

Figure 8-3 *Rating scales for programs of early education.*

8 Programs Are Tools, Not Religions

"Teach them to think!" vs., "Help them feel and be!"

Programs that emphasize development of *cognitive skills* are likely to stress teaching of language, shape, color, concepts, and prereading skills. They may be prepared to teach reading itself. The staff will see that children work with numbers and number concepts. Children's speech habits will be closely attended and frequently assessed. In short, the teaching will concentrate on a curriculum that makes it possible for children to move more easily into the primary grades. At the other end of this dimension, a school will place primary emphasis on developing the child's *affective skills*. Teachers in this kind of program spend a major portion of their time helping children build positive self-esteem with some of the following activities:

1. displaying pictures of the children at child's eye level
2. constantly using children's names by labeling of coat lockers, art work, and through games, songs, etc.
3. placing of full length mirrors in dress up corners and encouragement of children to look and describe themselves and others
4. outlining child's body on large sheets of paper for child to paint and display
5. tape recording children's voices for identification and discussion in larger group

The primary concern of teachers in such programs is to develop the humanistic skills through activities that are designed to heighten a child's awareness of his feelings, of himself in relation to others, and of his own uniqueness and the legitimacy and value of his personal contributions to a larger group. Most programs emphasize both to some degree.

Content vs. Process

"Teach them!" vs., "Help them learn on their own!"

Some preschool teachers believe they should stress content in their programs by teaching specific information and academic skills. Others are less concerned with content, stressing instead the importance of *process*. Those who concentrate on content think in terms of what is learned and try to make sure that preschool children acquire skills and concepts and a store of specific knowledge. Those who focus attention on process think in terms of teaching how to learn. They attempt to start the young child on his way to becoming self-sufficient and autonomous in the school setting, and able to find and use information on his own initiative. In a program that emphasizes process, the

Table 8-1 *Examples of skills taught in content- and process-oriented programs*

When content is stressed	When process is stressed
Names of letters of the alphabet	Initiative in tackling problems
Identification of geometric shapes	Inquiry skills
Numbers and their ordering	Problem solving skills
Specific labels	Skills in carrying on a discussion and exploring meanings
Discrimination of speech sounds	Consideration of alternative solutions
Perceptual discrimination	Obtaining of information
Self-concepts (name, relationship in family . . .)	

teacher assumes it is more important to know how to solve problems than to store specific knowledge in one's memory, however efficient that memory might be.

These objectives are not contradictory and elements of both are found in many preschool programs. The teacher's having her own ideas about the importance of content and process is essential as she plans curriculum and makes decisions on how best to achieve the ends she has in mind.

Planned Instruction vs. Self Discovery

"Teach them facts and concepts!" vs., "Teach them how to learn!"

A third dimension along which programs group themselves concerns how learning and teaching can best take place. Do children learn best from specific instruction or by discovery? Is it better to give children information deliberately or to encourage them to find out what they are expected to know?

This is a question on which early educators had a great deal to say. Froebel (1782–1852), the founder of the kindergarten, argued that the child is the source of his own curriculum and that the teacher merely follows. In his view, learning takes place through following one's interests. He did see the need, however, for children to be presented with an orderly series of phenomena that challenged and stimulated mental activity and produced inner organization and integration, an idea developed in greatly elaborated form by Piaget (1952). In contrast to Comenius' position that knowledge should be introduced in systematic fashion was Rousseau's proposition that everything one learns should come from within, and that the child should be allowed to acquire knowledge for himself and acquire a power to learn on his own.

Two modern psychological theories—the learning theory associated with the American psychologist B. F. Skinner and the cognitive developmental theory based on Piaget's work—have widely influenced the more recent answers to this question but have by no means resolved the apparent difference in point of view. Skinnerians emphasize the acquisition of knowledge through instruction, while Piagetians stress the discovery-developmental method.

The Skinnerian holds that the goal of education is to produce specific behavioral changes. School programs based on this theory begin by determining the specific behaviors desired and proceed by building up the child's repertoire of responses one at a time. For example, in learning to write his name, a child would first need to know something about writing materials and their uses as well as the shape and sequence of certain letters. A child's responses are regulated by stimuli that the teacher introduces in a planned sequence. The process by which a child thinks is immaterial according to this view, since it deals only with what can be observed and controlled.

The Piagetian sees early learning as a matter of building cognitive structures in the child's mind. Rather than being governed by external stimuli, it is the child himself who controls stimuli. Through his own experience (discovery), structures emerge in his mind that guide further perception and the acquisition of concepts. The child can learn only if he has already built up the store of structures needed to master a new task. According to Piaget, children make their own contributions to the learning process. Therefore, teachers need to provide materials that serve the child's desire to see how new information compares with his present knowledge and concepts and that permit him to revise his ideas through examination and questioning. Only by changing internal structures does the child progress from one state to the next and so acquire new learning.

Because of the emphasis placed on the developmental nature of learning and its reliance on maturation, critics of Piaget's theory claim it does not permit teaching, that one waits for the child to reach a particular stage in order for learning to take place as the child explores and discovers the world about him. Those who favor the cognitive-developmental view tend to feel that the Skinnerian emphasis on "acquiring responses" is merely rote learning without understanding. To their way of thinking, it follows that without understanding (*i.e.,* relating new materials to what is already known), a child has not really learned.

Proponents of both theories agree that teaching must begin from where a child is when he comes into an educational program. To a Piagetian this means determining what a child is ready to learn by discovering his present level (stage) of understanding, and presenting materials appropriate to that stage. A teacher oriented to Skinner's ideas would attempt to find the child's present or basal level of skill or performance through diagnostic assessment, by using simple appropriate tests or performance measures, and begin the sequence of instruction at the edge of the child's knowledge and ability, without involving the notion of stages.

The effectiveness of both learning theories greatly depends on proper sequencing of tasks, but the Piagetian is inclined to be concerned with the total organization of thought, and the Skinnerian tends to deal with specific step-by-step increments. This latter approach recognizes that teaching a particular skill often depends on prior learning—for example, it is unlikely that a child could be taught the concept of equivalent sets without knowing how to do one-to-one matching—but the Skinnerian feels that once started, a child can be taken step-by-step through a well-designed learning sequence, regardless of "stage of readiness."

Extrinsic vs. Intrinsic Motivation

"Give them tangible rewards!" vs., "Help them enjoy learning!"

At some level, all educational programs are based on assumptions about what stimulates learning and what makes the acquisition of skill and knowledge a rewarding experience. There are several quite different conceptions about the motivational processes involved in learning and how they can be used to develop effective teaching procedures. No one disagrees that children learn best when they are engaged in the task and activities of the curriculum; the disagreement comes in deciding how best to arouse and maintain their interest.

One side of this second argument proposes programs (usually academically oriented) that emphasize the value of *extrinsic motivation*. Those who emphasize its use do not deny that children are normally curious and want to learn. They simply feel that children's interest should be aroused and their effort sustained deliberately rather than waiting for evidence of readiness or natural desire. In these schools the teaching includes some kind of tangible reward for the child other than satisfaction from completing the task. Although social reinforcement, such as words of praise and approval, or physical contact (pat, handshake) of some kind, is usually sufficient to keep a child working, in many instances, a more tangible symbol of approval is given. This is often candy, a cookie, raisins, a chip or token of some kind that can be exchanged for special privileges, or a toy or other object desired by the child. Occasionally some difficulty is encountered in deciding on what tangible reinforcers to use. Rewarding one child with a special mark that all can see may be so nonrewarding to all others as to defeat its total, broader purpose. Tokens have been shown to be effective not only in motivating children but also the teachers. The frequency of a teacher's attending individual children and praising performances increases sharply when she has tokens as well as words to give.

At the other end of the dimension of motivation are programs that emphasize the value of intrinsic motivation. These programs are based on the philosophy that learning and mastery of a new skill are basically satisfying experiences that are not only sufficient to hold interest, but may often be exciting to the child. In such programs, the teacher attempts to use the child's interest in activities and problems to begin the teaching experience. In this way, the mastery of the problem or completion of the task are goals that are set by the child and are themselves interesting and rewarding. One underlying principle of this approach is that mastering a task just slightly beyond the child's present level of ability or knowledge is sufficiently satisfying to make a child willing to continue learning. Tasks that are too easy fail to hold attention; those too complex are soon abandoned. The things that interest and motivate a child, in this view, are those that fit his present level of competence yet offer a challenge of mastery in which learning for its own sake can take place.

How can these dimensions be applied to ongoing programs? Figures 8-4 and 8-5 show two filled out rating cards. One represents the dimensions emphasized in a parent's co-op program, the other a compensatory program for three- and four-year-olds.

Compiling information of this kind from his own observation can give a teacher some idea of what to expect of a particular nursery school and a way of choosing a program in which he feels he can teach most effectively.

There are other dimensions, of course, for viewing a program of early education. Programs vary, for example, in the emphasis placed on diagnostic testing or parent involvement. But from the standpoint of teaching and learning effectiveness, the major differences are those discussed above. A teacher who is aware of the distinctions underlying various programs can more readily

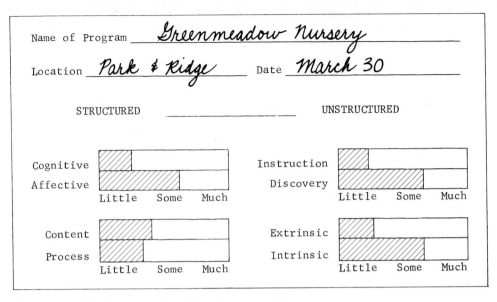

Figure 8-4 *Rating scale of emphasis in a parents' co-op program*

categorize the learning and teaching procedures of a school that he observes or hears described.

In every program, no matter how structured, there are occasions when the teacher is on his own or wants to work individually with a child for a specific goal. He must eventually come to his own conclusions as to what technique is most effective for that particular child. His judgment will be related to the characteristics and needs of the child at that time. By attending to individual differences he can be more effective in his teaching.

Controversy among proponents of the various programs sometimes polarizes feelings and loyalties towards one program or another. Attitudes of this kind may lead to a refusal to look closely enough to see the merits of a competing technique. For example, some teachers see the use of tangible rewards such as tokens or candy as materialistic and mechanical bribery. Perhaps before making judgment, these teachers might seek the opportunity to observe a program where tokens are used effectively. Or they might come to a conclusion about the usefulness of tokens by trying them and determining for themselves the various limitations and advantages. This same suggestion is perhaps worth following by anyone who so favors any single dimension or combination of dimensions over others.

The task of teaching young children is difficult under any circumstances and the problems of education are severe. No tool

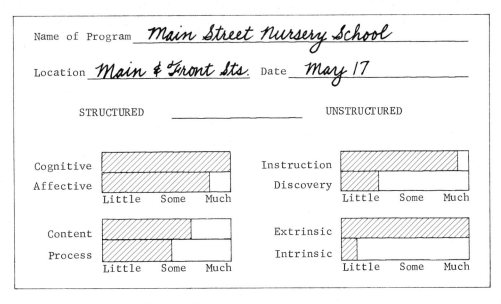

Figure 8-5 *Rating scale of emphasis in a compensatory program*

and no resource should be neglected that might help teachers be more effective in educating children.

The differing points of view in contemporary curricula and in the issues debated by educators during the past two hundred years offer remarkable parallels. Many of the same issues on which historical figures disagreed also divide our colleagues today. There is a shared concern about the need to provide conditions for optimal development of the child's resources, especially her mental faculties, but there is a dramatic divergence among them in theory and practice as to how this should be accomplished.

One finds it easy to be skeptical about whether recent findings and program developments have resolved these basic issues in any real sense. Perhaps the persistence of these problems and questions and the sharp disagreement among scholars and researchers about them means that they all represent different facets of reality and that, if we could gain sufficient perspective we could see that they are not really inconsistent but that we are too simplistic in our own interpretation and application of our knowledge. Perhaps some things are learned best by discovery, some best by direct instruction; it may be that intrinsic motivation may be ideal in one phase or situation and external rewards still are a necessity in another. It is possible that the question is not *whether* these different points of view are true but *when* and in what circumstances they are valid.

We must learn to think and work in a field that is becoming more complex and in which a mastery of our trade requires that we discard the simple solutions and absolute statements and make finer and more subtle discriminations in trying to comprehend the complexities of early learning and teaching. We can then select more freely from a range of techniques and strategies, viewing them as tools to use, not as articles of faith to defend.

SUMMARY

This chapter discusses the growth of early education and provides several examples of intervention programs, ending with a number of assumptions about teaching and learning which underlie all contemporary programs. Greater interest and research in early education have produced much data making the field more complex. It is important that the teacher remain informed and thereby better able to select from among a variety of techniques and strategies to use as tools rather than embrace a philosophy to defend.

SOME POINTS
TO REMEMBER

1. One major outcome of Head Start was the development of several experimental programs of early education.
2. Operation Head Start and Project Follow Through were two major forces in the growth and dissemination of experimental programs.
3. It is difficult to get adequate evaluation data on new educational efforts, and their evaluation results should be examined with great care.
4. There is a tendency for professionals to "pick a favorite" in adopting programs or program elements.
5. Experimental programs range from highly structured, teacher-directed, to informal child-oriented.
6. Most programs assume that (a) education must begin at the level of the children's abilities (b) teaching should be adapted to the needs of the individual child, (c) a child learns best when motivated, (d) children must learn the role of pupil in order to succeed in school, (e) all normal children can acquire school-related skills and concepts.
7. The degree of structure is a major dimension on which programs differ.
8. Structure is either (1) a constant awareness in the teacher's mind of an underlying design to a total curriculum, and/or

(2) a prearranged sequencing of materials for presentation to the child.

9. Programs may also differ in their emphasis on (a) cognitive vs. affective skills, (b) content vs. process, (c) instruction vs. discovery, (d) extrinsic vs. intrinsic motivation.

10. Some contemporary disagreements among professionals reflect differences in theories advanced by early educators during the past two hundred years.

11. Teachers may extend their competence by drawing from dissimilar programs, using a particular technique when it is most suitable.

REFERENCES

Chow, S. H. L. and Elmore, P. *Early childhood information unit resource manual and program descriptions.* Educational Products Information Exchange (EPIE) Institute, 1973.

Follow Through program approaches. Washington, D.C.: Follow Through Program, U.S. Office of Education, March 1969.

Follow Through program sponsors, Stanford Research Institute. Prepared for Bureau of Elementary and Secondary Education, U.S. Office of Education, U.S. Department of Health, Education, and Welfare, June 1972.

Maccoby, E. E. and Zellner, M. *Experiments in primary education.* New York: Harcourt Brace, Jovanovich, Inc., 1970.

Panel on Educational Research and Development. *Innovation and experiment in education.* Washington, D.C.: U.S. Government Printing Office, 1964.

Piaget, J. *The origins of intelligence in children.* New York: International Universities Press, Inc., 1952.

Pines, M. *Revolution in learning: the years from birth to six.* New York: Harper and Row, 1967.

M. S. Read, *Malnutrition and learning.* U.S. Department of Health, Education, and Welfare, Public Health Service, Washington, D.C.: National Institute of Child Health and Human Development, 1969.

U.S. President, 1963–1968 (President Lyndon B. Johnson). Annual message to the Congress on the State of the Union. *Congressional Record Proceedings and Debates of the 89th Congress,* First Session, January 4, 1965, Washington, D.C.: Government Printing Office, Volume 111, Part 1, 26–29.

U.S. President, 1963–1968 (President Lyndon B. Johnson). Toward full educational opportunity, Message from the President of the United States. *Congressional Record Proceedings and Debates of the 89th Congress,* First Session, January 12, 1965. Washington, D.C.: Government Printing Office, Volume 111, Part 7, 589–592.

Chapter 9 Growth of Language and Cognitive Abilities

Growth of Language Abilities

Recent debate over the usefulness of language training for young children, especially those from so-called disadvantaged backgrounds, has stimulated a great deal of research. These efforts have concentrated mainly on the processes by which language is acquired and the sequence and pace of language development.

Much progress has been made in documenting the growth of speech patterns in young children, especially in children from ethnic and low-income backgrounds. A number of educational myths have been exposed (such as the notion that black children who come to school speaking black English are linguistically deprived), but new questions have been raised and many familiar ones are still not answered. Some of the unanswered questions have to do with the processes through which children acquire speech, the influence of parents, mass media, and other adult sources of language upon the child's linguistic development, the long-term consequences of teaching preschoolers to read, the optimal time to institute bilingual training for children who come to school speaking a nonstandard form of English and in what way socio-economic and cultural differences in speech affect learning and cognitive development.

With so much still unknown, teachers may question the utility of concerning themselves with conflicting viewpoints and spending time reading about theories and research results that may be changed or reinterpreted in the near future.

Perhaps the best answer to this is that the teacher who has knowledge about current issues and viewpoints in a developing field is in a better position to make choices and is more able to recognize the significance of new findings. She also has a better perspective for evaluating the claims made by innovative programs that may be offered her. Obviously, when equipped with this knowledge, she can assess more adequately the language abilities of children and adapt her own teaching to their needs.

Language and Communication

The complex system of speech sounds that we call language is the basic channel for human intellectual and social interaction. Its obvious importance in academic accomplishment and in a broad sweep of human activities outside of school give it a particular value in programs of early education.

The usual description of the role of language, especially speech, in early educational programs is oriented to the view that it is a channel for the communication of ideas, information, and feelings. The way in which language is taught—that is, the treatment of the use of language in these programs—assumes that the speaker has the intent to transmit directly and straightforwardly the ideas that are in his mind. This perspective of language is too narrow; it ignores the additional utility of language as a more subtle strategy having an impact on the listener(s) which may be of a sort not conveyed by the words spoken. Filibustering is an obvious example of using speech as a strategy to achieve a purpose having little to do with communication. The words themselves are not important; the messages they convey are literally beside the point.

The uses of language to disguise meaning, to evade, mislead, impress, and arouse are well known. It may be less obvious that language used by teachers in a classroom may unintentionally create an impact quite different from the words which children actually hear. Such an inconsistency in speech can create confusion for both teacher and child.

A teacher who says, "Now, we all want to fold our hands and be quiet, don't we?" when she really does not mean to give the children a choice is forcing them to decode (that is, to interpret) the messages that come to them through nonverbal channels (intonation, gesture, timing, modeling, etc.) and abandon in part the meaning of the words for the meaning of the nonverbal signals. Another common example is that children are urged to say "I'm sorry," and "Thank you" and make other ritualistic comments even when they have dubious validity.

When children receive contradictory messages from different channels of communication (verbal messages vs. facial expressions, for example) they tend to discount the more positive information and assume the worst. This also happens with adults, but is more marked with children, who are less accustomed to sorting out and putting in perspective such apparent inconsistencies. They may not understand joking messages, for example, which give approval and disapproval simultaneously (Bugental, et al., 1970).

To an objective observer, perhaps, it might appear that the curricula and programs of language training for young children and the behavior of the teacher (and other adults in the child's life) are not entirely consonant with one another. In the midst of programs that urge the child to "Speak in complete sentences and say what you mean!" the adults around him are often talking to him using words that do not mean what they say. It is interesting to speculate on the logical problems that this poses for the young child and the contribution this discrepancy makes to his understanding of the nonverbal world.

Bill Cosby's record "Why Is There Air?" includes a band on which he describes his recollections of how he reinterpreted the teacher's words in order to psych out her meaning—a delightful example of cross-channel I-don't-mean-what-I-say messages. That children are likely to use similar tactics against teachers is often suggested in Schulz' inspired comic strip "Peanuts." Recall this exchange between Linus and a classmate at the beginning of the school year. Linus has submitted an essay about the joys of returning to school. Challenged by a classmate, he replies, "Through the years you eventually learn what sells."

Quite apart from the use of language to accomplish things not specifically indicated in the literal meaning of the words used, there is a flow of nonverbal communication that conveys messages without any use of words. Language training programs and curricula do not often include nonverbal communication, but it is nonetheless an important dimension of early learning. While this form of communication is not one that is taught directly, as spoken and written language are, the teacher's own behavior provides a model for the child to acquire techniques and skills in nonverbal exchange.

Language is present in every human society, yet no one is born knowing how to speak.[1] In order to acquire and use language, children must first learn a complicated system of sounds. Whether the sounds are those of Chinese, Swahili, Choctaw, or some other system, all children, barring physical or emotional disorder, speak at approximately the same age. They respond to and gradually come to use the speech of their parents and the "important others" with whom they are most closely associated, whether these people are wealthy or poor, educated or uneducated, young or old.

The first sounds a baby makes are the nasal sounds of discomfort closely followed by the cooing and gurgling associated with comfort and well-being. Around eight weeks of age she characteristically begins to practice vowel sounds and then consonants in a kind of babbling. From five or six months on, she may use her babbling purposefully to get attention and to signal her needs. She also begins to respond with sounds of her own to people who speak directly to her. By eight months her babbling rises and falls in very much the same intonation patterns as the speech around her. She then apparently becomes aware of syllables and other segments of sound distinct from intonation patterns and gradually arranges these into words.

An attempt to understand how children learn to speak must include a consideration of various biological factors. The exact nature of genetic influence on language ability is by no means clear. If there are genes for language, they have not been identified, although research studies on twins indicate that genetic endowment cannot be wholly discarded in favor of environmental influence.

Studies of twins (Lenneberg, 1969) show that the onset of speech occurs more nearly at the same time for identical twins than for fraternal twins. Also, if there is a delay in learning, it will be the same for both twins of an identical pair, while fraternal twins may sometimes experience the same delay, but frequently one twin will start later and learn more slowly than the other.

Because of his biological heritage the child responds to speech directed toward him, but how much he continues to respond seems to be highly dependent on environmental factors. During

---

[1] Linguists have identified approximately 3500 languages, many of which contain one or more dialects. About a third of these languages have a written form of some kind.

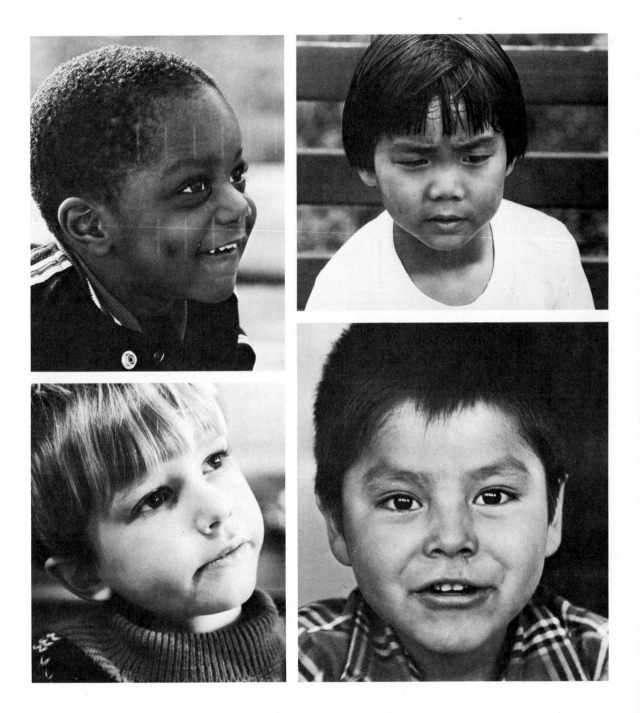

Table 9-1 *Children's progress in language ability*

Age	Ability
2 years	Should be able to follow simple commands without visual clues: *Johnny, get your hat and give it to Daddy* *Debby, bring me your ball* Uses a variety of everyday words heard in his home and neighborhood: *Mommy, milk, ball, hat* Shows he is developing sentence sense by the way he puts words together: *Go bye bye car* *Milk all gone*
3 years	Understands and uses words other than for naming; is able to fit simple verbs, pronouns, prepositions, and adjectives such as *go, me, in,* and *big* more and more into sentences:
4 years	Should be able to give a connected account of some recent experience: Should be able to carry out a sequence of two simple directions: *Bobby, find Susie and tell her dinner's ready*
5 years	Speech should be intelligible although some sounds may still be mispronounced: Can carry on a conversation if vocabulary is within his range

Adapted from *Learning to talk,* prepared by the U.S. National Institute of Neurological Diseases and Stroke, National Institutes of Health, U.S. Department of Health, Education and Welfare (Washington, D.C.: Government Printing Office, 1969), pp. 22–24.

the first three months of their lives, normal babies born to deaf parents obviously do not hear the same kind or amount of verbal discourse as children in families where the mother and father are not deaf. Nor are their normal vocalizations responded to as immediately. Yet it has been shown that their initial cooing and sound production are almost identical to those of babies born to mothers who can hear them and whose sounds the babies hear. As long as children of deaf parents hear language from others, their learning proceeds normally. Communication with their parents takes place through gestures and a repertoire of other nonverbal responses.

Most children who are born deaf may go through the cooing stage but since they do not hear speech, even their own, this behavior is soon extinguished and their introduction to language as a system does not take place until they reach school age, unless they have attended a special preschool. Blind children's learning to speak is closely related to physical maturation and follows that of children who have sight.

Observation of a wide variety of children shows that the acquisition of speech is a natural process that cannot be deterred.

Even when children have only minimum resources to aid them, they can and do learn to speak the language they hear.

The teacher's awareness of the social pressure exerted on those whose speech deviates from the forms of standard English often leads her to attempt to correct children's pronunciation and grammar. Even though a child may not have mastered pronunciation or postulated "rules" that permit his using the forms desired, she will often persist in presenting them, assuming that hearing and acquiring somehow take place simultaneously. But just as research shows that in the matter of grammatical form a child cannot go beyond the "rules" that he has worked out from his understanding of language, his ability to pronounce words is also limited to developmental factors. Some of these are summarized on this page.

The connotation of incompletely developed speech is more true in matters of pronunciation and vocabulary than in grammar, but teachers often assume an obligation to see that children learn to pronounce as well as to use words in approved ways. By so doing they feel they are helping the child avoid later discrimination based on speech differences. The notion of the need for grammatical correctness has been so strong as to form the basis for judgment of reading skill. If the printed page shows:

She goes to school every day and so does her brother.

and the child reads:

She go to school every day and so do her brother.

he is often held to be a poor reader, when in fact it is his regional or social dialect that is being judged, not his reading skill.

It is not yet known just why young children acquire certain language forms and not others, why those who spend many hours in a daycare center hearing only standard English, or who in their homes listen to more television talk than adult conversation, still speak as their parents do. Until the reasons are clear, however, teachers should not expect to be able to make changes in the form of a child's language if the change is not one he will regularly hear and use when he is not in school.

During his fourth year the child masters pronunciation of sounds represented by S and Z, of blends like TRain, BLow, faLLS, and of friction sounds requiring muscle coordinations as in Join, fuDGE, CHew, and maTCH.

People can usually comprehend all that a five-year-old says even though he may not pronounce every sound exactly as they do. He will use sounds represented by K, G, F, and V fairly consistently. These are difficult to make compared to sounds represented by M, N, P, and B. He may still have some difficulty with them in blends like GRass, CLean, and eLF. Sounds represented by R may not always be said correctly until the eighth year.

Learning the structure of a language

A child's ability to pronounce sounds and to order them into words does not mean he has learned a language. This kind of imitating is readily taught to various birds, and many kinds of animals can be trained to respond to words or word combinations. Only when a child himself generates and comprehends sentences he has never heard before can it be said he has learned a language.

The various stages a child goes through in learning the structure and use of his own language are similar for all children, but quite different from those experienced by an adult in acquiring a second language. For adults, language learning is likely to be an exercise in reasoning, imitation, and a feat of memory. For a child, it is learning to distinguish and vocalize the sounds of a language and then determining how various elements are put together to express meaning. It is a matter of discovering for himself how a language works. This is not to say that children never imitate sounds as they learn to assemble the elements of a language. Obviously they do. Their choice of speech sounds to express meaning seems to be accounted for by imitation. Likewise, the accumulation of vocabulary is largely a matter of imitation and repetition. But neither of these aspects of learning is the same as sensing the underlying principles of a language, or the ability to arrange combinations of sounds into meaningful patterns according to rules, even though the rules remain unstated.

As the child acquires tacit knowledge of the structure of language, he is likely to overgeneralize and say "He goed" and "This is mines," even though he never hears these verb and pronoun forms. Apparently he has grasped the regular endings which indicate past tense and possession and has formulated rules that he applies to his own utterances.

Despite the widely held opinion that children can be taught to correct their usage by hearing and then imitating desired forms, research has not shown this to be true. The following example represents how difficult it is to change behavior by attempted correction. It is a conversation with a four-year-old girl reported by Gleason (1967, p. 1.):

Child   My teacher holded the baby rabbits and we patted them.
Gleason   Did you say your teacher held the baby rabbits?
Child   Yes.
Gleason   What did you say she did?
Child   She holded the baby rabbits and we patted them.
Gleason   Did you say she held them tightly?
Child   No, she holded them loosely.

The child clearly heard and comprehended the accepted form "held," but even after repeated corrections she continued to speak within her own framework of language understanding. This is an example of evidence that challenges the theory that imitation is the only or primary way language is learned. Other students of language acquisition agree.

Early in their acquisition of knowledge of the structure of a language, children will apparently accept corrections of fact and make changes, and they will also substitute a "good" word for a "bad" word. But children gradually learn grammar, i.e., the rules of a language, on their own, and they are impervious to the type of correction and reinforcement so commonly carried on by adults. Their understanding and application of rules is a developmental behavior, one which all children apparently go through for themselves. The common "errors" in much of children's early speech, therefore, are seen to be overgeneralizations and are subject to adjustment as the child accumulates language experience.

Since language is a learned behavior, children who hear little or no speech, or who attend only to the speech of those who are limited in language development, will be likely to have a language deficiency compared with those children surrounded by conversation. On the other hand, fairly retarded children who have grown up in various institutions under the care of an older retardate (with limited skill in language) have been known to gain a good deal of language facility. When this has happened, it is thought that their learning might have been influenced by the television that was on all day long in the otherwise bare room where the children played (Lenneberg, 1969).

Children with a language deficiency are not necessarily incapable of language learning. To assess *capability*, the teacher should not count vocabulary items and usage errors, nor seek to determine the length and complexity of sentences children use. Results from this kind of evaluation probably measure the adequacy (or inadequacy) of the environment in which the learning took place, rather than a child's ability to learn.

A high correlation exists between chronological age and language development; an even higher one between language

Table 9-2 *Correlation of motor and language development*

Age	Motor Development	Language Development
6 mos.	Sits using hands for support.	Cooing sounds change to babbling with introduction of consonant sounds.
1 yr.	Stands and walks when held by one hand.	Duplicates syllables. Understands some words. First words used to signify particular objects or persons.
18 mos.	Creeps downstairs backwards. Walks.	Uses single words not joined in phrases. Understands well. Intonation patterns resemble those of adult conversation.
2 yrs.	Runs. Mounts steps one foot forward.	About 50 words: two-word combinations common. Interest in verbal communication heightened.
30 mos.	Jumps with both feet. Can stand on one.	New words every day. Uses three or more words in succession. Many grammatical constructions that are nonstandard. Understands well.
3 yrs.	Tiptoes, goes up stairs alternating feet.	Fewer "mistakes" in word forms. Most language intelligible. Language is systematic and predictable. 1000+ word vocabulary.
4+ yrs.	Jumps over rope, hops on one foot, walks line.	Language well established though may have a few unusual constructions and vocabulary choices.

Adapted from Lenneberg, Nichols, and Rosenberger, "Primitive Stages of Language Development in Mongolism" in *Disorders of Communication,* edited by D. Rioch, and E. A. Weinstein, Research Publications of Association for Research in Nervous and Mental Disorders, *42* (New York, Baltimore, Williams & Wilkins, 1964) pp. 128–130.

A Lack of Language?

Recent studies of peer groups in spontaneous interaction in Northern ghetto areas show that there is a rich verbal culture in constant use. Negro children in the vernacular culture cannot be considered "verbally deprived" if one observes them in a favorable environment—on the contrary, their daily life is a pattern of continual verbal stimulation, contest, and imitation. . . . There are many [other] speech events associated with the vernacular culture of the ghetto: jokes, songs, narratives, and of course the hip vocabulary itself. All of these reflect the value system of the vernacular, and because it is opposed in many ways to the standard culture of the school, it does not appear in school contexts.

From J. E. Birren and R. D. Hess (eds.), "Influences of Biological, Psychological, and Social Deprivation Upon Learning and Performance," in *Perspectives on Human Deprivation: Biological, Psychological, and Sociological,* 1968, pp. 122–23.

development and motor development. The information in Table 9-2 compares the language behaviors of a particular child with those of other children at the same stage of motor development.

The circumstance which seems most conducive to language learning is surrounding the child with what has been called "a sea of language." Exposure to a wide variety of conversation with a chance to enter at his own level from the beginning, listening to stories, hearing books read aloud, and having television, radio and records available, seemingly makes it possible for him to take from what he hears the elements he needs to build language for himself. The fact that no one yet knows exactly how this is done, or how it may be assisted, makes the achievement no less magnificent.

Language Learning and Socio-Economic and Cultural Differences

Many contemporary programs of early education place major emphasis on language training and the development of cognitive skills. This interest is reflected in highly engineered lessons with small groups of children, as well as in arranged environments in which every child is free to follow her own interests. To a great extent, this orientation toward language training comes from two sources: the widespread belief that children from poor and ghetto families come to school with inadequate language ability; and the theory that language development is a basic prerequisite to successful achievement in school and adult life. These beliefs are undergoing intensive investigation and it appears that both may be exaggerations, yet they have had an impressive influence on the field of early education. Whether or not the particular emphasis on linguistic skills in compensatory education programs is justified, language development is important.

As mentioned earlier, research shows no evidence that socio-economic and cultural differences affect children's capacity to learn a language. Nor do they determine the rate at which this learning takes place. The ability to learn a language at all proves a great deal of conceptual mastery on the part of the learner.

There can be no doubt about the ability of disadvantaged children to learn. In short-term memory skills and rote learning tasks, lower-class children perform at the same levels as middle-class children. But in specific abilities such as vocabulary size, and length of sentences, ghetto children score below middle-class children. What they apparently lack is the kind of language learning needed for success in a school system geared to the prior learning of middle-class children.

Explanations of cultural differences in language usage

NONSENSE SENTENCES
Yong tharsled the gringer.
Horbles jonkle zoperly.

In the search for an understanding of the school language problems of disadvantaged children, there are two explanations for the emphasis placed on language curricula in preschool programs. First, if it is thought that children have acquired "less language" than is needed to communicate effectively, then programs seek to provide the children with more language. Since he comes to school with a deficiency, he must somehow be given what he lacks as soon as he enters a program of early education.

But studies show that when tested with nonsense sentences, such as those illustrated, and asked to provide words that can be substituted for the forms underlined, lower-class and middle-class children of comparable ages did equally well in selecting nouns. In other tests, children from differing socio-economic levels showed no significant difference in their ability to generalize from nonsense words standard verb and noun endings to show tense, plurals, and possessives. Only when children were examined from the standpoint of the meaning of words were the middle-class children far ahead of lower-class children.

Some doubt exists as to whether low-income children know and use many words on which they are tested. Perhaps these children recognize and use as many words as middle-class children but not for school-related tasks. Also, little proof exists that simply adding more words used by middle-class children to a child's vocabulary will help his test performance.

Another basis for emphasis on language development in compensatory programs had to do with the notion of a "different language." Those who subscribe to this philosophy argue that all children acquire the structure of language at about the same age and rate, but that because some children learn a dialect of English that is not standard English they have difficulty communicating in school or anywhere that standard English is predominant. Much of the research in this area concerns dialects. A few of the more obvious differences between standard English and black dialect are listed in Table 9-3. Evidence has been growing that despite the differences in the two forms of language, ghetto children understand a great deal of language that they themselves do not use, and, more specifically, black children apparently understand the speech of middle-class teachers.

Situational setting as a cause of difference in language

Apparently the explanation for a language difference so severe that it causes marked school difficulties must be sought further. Courtney B. Cazden's study of language acquisition (1970, p. 83) suggests that one source may lie in the "effects of situations."

Both the less-language and different-language views of child language are inadequate on two counts. First, they speak only of patterns of structural forms and ignore patterns of use in actual speech events. Second, they speak as if the child learns only one way to speak, which is reflected in the same fashion and to the same extent at all times. On both theoretical and practical grounds, we can no longer accept such limitations.

Cazden makes clear that our understanding of the total range of children's language ability is far from complete and raises the

Table 9-3 *Some differences between standard English and black dialect*

Standard English	Black Dialect
"No one comes here anymore"	"Don't nobody come here no more"
"He works"	"He work"
"Why did you hit me?"	"Why you hit me?"
"Two fights"	"Two fight"
"He's working"	"He be working"
"If you're good"	"If you good"
"He's messing around"	"He messing around"

question as to what bearing the situation in which a child speaks has on his ability to use language. A summary of research on the influence of situation appears in Table 9-4.

Table 9-4 *Effects of a variety of situations (settings) on language use in groups of children*

Researcher	Children	Setting	Findings
Strandberg (1969)	4- and 5-year-olds with above-average IQ	Children presented with different kinds of pictures.	Talked more about a toy or a 20-second silent film presentation of the toy than about a color photo.
Strandberg & Griffith (1968)	4- and 5-year-olds from laboratory school	Children given simple cameras and shown how to take pictures.	Talked more spontaneously and used longer and more complex utterances discussing pictures they took than those taken under adult direction when learning to use camera.
Cowan et al. (1967)	Elementary school children	Children shown ten magazine covers that were in color.	Length of children's response varied with pictures.
Berlyne & Frommer (1966)	Children in kindergarten and grades 3, 5, and 6 in a laboratory school	Children told stories, shown pictures, and then told stories accompanied by pictures. When finished with each they were invited to ask questions.	Novel, incongruous, and surprising items elicited most questions.
Cazden (1971)	5-year-olds in two English Infant Schools	Setting A: Children given a book that contained blank pages, asked to draw a picture and then dictate story for teacher to write. Setting B: Each child had a word folder with store of basic words plus blanks for his personal choices, and a stand on which words could be set up and arranged as sentences. No pictures.	Setting A: All stories used simple sentences in form "This is a ____." One instance of sentence in another form: "This boy is dead." Setting B: Composed sentences of great variety and length, including questions.
Brent & Katz (1967)	White Head Start children	First asked to tell stories using selected picture—picture was removed and children were to tell story again.	Stories told without picture were superior in logic, explicitness, and length.
Cowe (1967)	Kindergarten children	Recordings were made of children's conversation in nine activities in the classroom.	In maturity and amount of speech, housekeeping activities and group discussions were most conducive to language use. Dance, blocks, and woodworking held least potential.

Adapted from a summary of research by Courtney B. Cazden, "The neglected situation in child language research and education," in *Language and poverty: perspectives on a theme,* ed. Frederick Williams (Chicago: Markham Publishing Company, 1970), pp. 81–101.

From what is known about language learning, children apparently acquire grammar on their own as they learn to speak; vocabulary and pronunciation are more a matter of imitation and repetition.

Teaching language at the preschool level, then, can best be accomplished by providing as much opportunity as possible for verbal interaction on a one-to-one basis. For example, teachers need to elaborate and qualify their answers to many of the questions a child asks. An instance of how this might be done is shown in the following report of a conversation:

Child   What's that?
Teacher   It's a pencil sharpener.

If the teacher's goal were greater use of language, she might have answered, "It's a pencil sharpener that Jack's daddy mounted for us. Now we have a way of sharpening pencils. Would you like to sharpen a pencil?"

If, as some researchers believe, the length of the dialogue children hear makes a difference in their language development, classroom routine on a casual, unstructured basis can be a rich resource for language growth. Table 9-5 contains examples of how this technique might be used.

Providing opportunities for children to learn language means reading aloud from a wide variety of sources: nursery tales, folk tales, verses, picture books, and children's dictation. In this way they hear a wide range of sentences and have a chance to think about their own experiences in comparison with those of the characters in the books. It means having formal and informal story-telling and discussion sessions. Children can make up

Table 9-5   *Providing language experience through expanded discourse*

Plain Discourse	Expanded Discourse
It's juice time.	It's juice time and today we're going to have pink juice and big, round crackers.
Bobby, will you help Maria put the blocks away, please?	Bobby, you put all the large blocks away on the bottom shelf. Maria, you can stack all the little blocks on the top shelf.
It's dark in here. Let's turn on the light.	It's much darker in here now than it was a little while ago. I wonder how we can make it lighter.

Figure 9-2 *Teachers need to provide specific and qualified answers to many of the questions a child asks.*

their own stories or repeat stories told to them. They enjoy talking about words, rhyming words, and expressing differences between word meanings such as *hit* and *spank, fly* and *soar, walk* and *tiptoe.* Just as children respond to beauty in nature and to elements such as color and line in art, and rhythm and melody in music, they also respond to the sounds and imagery of language.

Making records and tapes and books and pictures available to children encourages their interest in language, if there is also time for talking about what they hear and see for themselves. Helping children develop language ability means making sure they have many chances to interact on a verbal level with one another and with adults. Perhaps the best teacher of language is the use of language itself.

Growth of Cognitive Abilities

Cognitive ability refers to the mental processes that make it possible for human beings to acquire, store, arrange, and rearrange information. As the child interacts with the environment, old concepts are constantly modified, and new ones created. Language provides labels for these concepts and furnishes human beings with a means for communicating what they know. Therefore, as concepts develop, the meanings that the child gives to words also changes.

Because someone hands a child an object saying, "Look, here's a ball," the child doesn't suddenly know what is and what isn't a ball. To be sure, he has a word that names what he holds. But there is more to a ball than its name. An infant, having learned the word *ball,* and something about the shape of such an object, may point to the moon, to an orange, or to a box turtle and say, "ball," but a school child is expected to know the difference. Before a child can select another object and be correct in calling it a "ball," he must have some notion of what properties balls share (other than roundness) that makes them unique. He needs to have a concept of *ball.*

Through internal cognitive activity a child forms concepts not only of objects he perceives, such as balls, but also abstracts like *up, big, soft, first, good,* and *self.* In short, it is through cognition and the formation of concepts that children make sense of the world. Apparently some of what a child learns takes place by means of direct teaching. He is given labels and taught rules. But much of his knowledge is developmental, not imitative. He constructs on his own; that is, he makes his own sense of his experiences, and cannot be shown otherwise by adult intervention.

The Concept Ball

It rolls.
It is usually round.
People expect you to catch, throw, kick, and bounce a ball.
Balls come in many sizes, colors, and materials.
People don't eat balls—only food shaped like a ball.
A ball can be solid or hollow.
People play games with balls.
Balls can be light or heavy.

The evolution of children's use of language is an example of this kind of learning.

The ability to conceptualize begins as a child acts on objects in his environment and builds knowledge through sensory-motor activities and the accompanying modification of cognitive structures. What is learned at one stage is held to be the basis for learning at each successive stage. The age limits are not fixed, and the rate of movement, as well as the scope of development, varies according to individual children. The sequence of stages, however, tends to be consistent. In the development of intellectual functioning children usually go through the various stages in a relatively fixed order regardless of socio-economic or cultural differences. Socio-economic or cultural influences may speed up, slow down, or stop development. But they apparently do not greatly change its sequence.

Sensory motor is the name given the first learning stage in Piaget's theory of cognitive development.[2] In this period, which covers approximately the first two years of life, the infant interacts with the physical world through reflexes and perceptual-motor activities to slowly become aware of the physical world in ways that make more complete comprehension possible later. This is followed by the preoperational stage (2 to 7 years) during which the child is perceptually oriented. He makes sense of the world in terms of the way it looks to him, he usually centers on

---

[2] The extraordinary work of Jean Piaget provided the basis for much of the point of view and material of this part of the chapter. Only a small part of his theory of cognitive development is touched on here. Additional references appear in the bibliography of this chapter. Piaget's conceptions of the growth of intellectual capabilities have great appeal for many professionals but are not accepted by others, as the discussion in Chapter 8 indicated.

. . . Preschools must build a solid foundation for further development by going back to the sensory-motor period, and making certain that internal stages are not skipped or only partially achieved.

From C. K. Kamii and N. L. Radin, "A framework for a preschool curriculum based on some Piagetian concepts." *The Journal of Creative Behavior: 1,* 1967, p. 315.

only one variable or dimension (height only rather than height and width) at a time, and he has difficulty realizing that an object can possess more than one property. In the stage of concrete operations (7 to 11 years) the child can use more logical structures and classifications and view things from a perspective outside himself. In the stage of formal operations, he reaches the capacity for symbolic abstractions.

Human knowledge is structured from three principal sources:

Interaction with the physical world: physical knowledge
Interaction with others: social knowledge
Making sense out of experience: logical knowledge

Although the relationships among these sources are not entirely clear, apparently physical and logical knowledge underlie much of what is usually called cognitive development. The acquisition of these types of knowledge is the concern of the rest of this chapter.

The ability to form concepts is developmental; that is, it depends on physical and mental maturation *and* experience. The ability to work at the level of concrete experiences, therefore, isn't automatically assured simply because a child has reached a certain chronological age and is in school. In order to succeed in school tasks he must also have achieved a certain stage of cognitive capability before entering school.

To develop cognitive ability young children need multiple kinds of experiences and the chance to repeat these over and over. Such activities should not be hurried and it is important to make certain that the simpler levels are neither overlooked nor skipped. Constant observation and diagnosis by the teacher will help her set the needed pace and make effective choices.

Activities for Achieving Cognitive Goals

The activities that follow are examples of materials and procedures that can be used to achieve specific cognitive goals.[3]

Give the child a half stick of clay and ask him to tell you what it is. (If he cannot name it, identify it for him.) Then ask, "What is it for?"

Typical procedure

Over many, many sessions discuss any or all of the following in whatever order seems appropriate to the circumstances in which the questions are introduced. After each inquiry, give the child ample time to answer, and ask him to show or tell you how he knows.

COGNITIVE PROCESS
Gaining knowledge of the physical properties of matter

MATERIALS
Half sticks of modeling clay in different colors

1. Does modeling clay have more than one color? What are some of its colors? Can you mix the colors together? What happens if you do?
2. Can you change its shape? If you do, can you make it the same shape again? Can you divide clay into separate pieces? Will you be able to put the pieces back again?
3. Have him lick it and ask: What does it taste like?
4. Have him smell it and ask: Does it have a smell? What does it smell like? (He may not be able to tell how it tastes or smells, but he will know from his experience that it has taste and odor.)
5. What will happen if you drop it? Put it in water? Heat it? (Use sunlight, electric bulb, flame.)
6. Does clay move by itself? Can you stretch it? Will it bend? Break?
7. Is modeling clay smooth? Heavy? Cold? Sticky? (Have other materials available in like quantity for comparison since these qualities are relative.)
8. What happens if you hit clay with your fist? With another piece of clay? With a block?
9. Can you cut clay? Tear it?

The examples offered here simply seek to show the teacher one way she might initiate and maintain motivation for desired learnings. They are not scripts and should not be treated as such.[4] Research findings have shown that a child is bored by

---

[3] We have drawn significantly from the writings of Constance Kamii for interpretations of Piaget's theories and for adaptations of his concepts to curricula for preschool programs.

[4] Additional tasks based on Piagetian concepts may be found in the language and math sections of *An Activities Handbook for Teachers of Young Children,* 2nd ed. (by D. J. Croft and R. D. Hess, 1975), which accompanies this text.

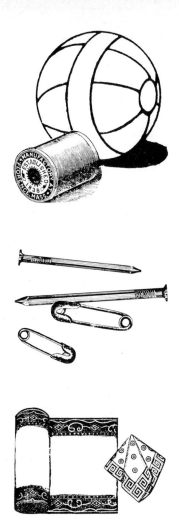

tasks that are too easy, and rejects tasks that are too difficult.

Teachers also need to remember that every question should be followed by the child's interaction with the object he holds. If he answers without physical involvement he should be encouraged to explain how he knows. In this way "errors" can be corrected —not by saying, "Oh, no. That's wrong—it's . . . ," but by having him manipulate whatever is involved so that he sees for himself that his answer is not borne out by reality. Dropping clay from a variety of heights allows the child to find out for himself whether clay breaks.

Another way to develop learning about physical properties of matter is to have small groups of children explore together. They might be provided with a collection of objects such as those pictured and encouraged to ask questions of one another.

1. What could we find out if we rolled a ball and a spool at the same time?
2. What could we find out if we put a little water on a paper towel and a paper napkin?

After each question the children raise, they should be given a chance to find the answer. The opportunity to make comparisons of these kinds brings knowledge they can depend on. Children can see the regularity of the physical world regardless of who performs the action. They can also see that objects themselves have certain characteristics no matter who pushes, pulls or drops them.

Learning situations similar to that of exploring the properties of clay can be brought about informally many times during a day, and the child's attention directed to a virtually limitless variety of objects. Teaching sessions do not need to be structured in any way except as the teacher deliberately gives the child a chance to find his own answers. The "lesson" can cease after only a question or two, or can continue as long as a child remains interested.

Children can and should be asked "What will happen if . . . ?" over and over but should not be asked "Why?" From their experiences they can learn to predict that blowing on a candle flame will extinguish it, but why this happens is beyond their ability to understand. When working with preschool level children, it is important to stay within the realm of their experience.

(Working with two or three children in a group)

1. Display one object from each set and give its name.[5] (If it is reasonable to expect that children might know, have them name the different objects.) Ask, "What can you tell me about this _____?" Wait for answers but probe as to color, size, shape, probable use, where found, etc.

2. Following brief discussion, display all the items in a random mix. Ask, "Do any of these look just the same?" Have child who answers correctly show the choice he made and tell how they are the same.

3. Without using the containers, sort items by kind and include one "mistake." Ask, "Are all the pieces where they belong?" Have a child make the needed change.

4. Ask one of the children to mix the pieces together and set out the containers. Suggest to the child that he put the pieces that are the same in these boxes.

5. When they have finished, have them look to see if the items are correctly grouped. "Are all the pieces where they belong?" ("Is every piece in this box exactly the same?")[6]

COGNITIVE PROCESS
Classification
(Grouping only)

MATERIALS
4 sets—each set containing
5 objects identical in size,
shape, and color.
Example: nails, bolts,
washers, nuts
or
various kinds of peas and
beans
or
various kinds of shells
(snail, conch, scallop,
clam)
4 open containers

DESCRIPTION
Classification is the ability
to group objects according
to similarities and
differences[5]

The progression suggested above, like that for physical knowledge, is to be thought of as an example, not a curriculum. Children need many individual and group experiences in separating objects according to different criteria before a concept of "class" develops.

Early practice in sorting lends itself to many routine nursery school procedures. Taking out and putting away equipment and materials by size, color, use, material; making sure Ronald has his jacket and not Buddy's; grouping by shape and degree of hardness; finding "five things bigger than this," etc., all provide needed experience. Simple games can be built around teaching similarities and differences based on choosing two of "this kind" and three of "another kind" from an array of highly different items. Putting objects in a bag and sorting by touch instead of by vision, gives children experience in sorting by still another

---

[5] This description is limited to the *preoperational stage.* Piaget holds classification to be an ability attained at the stage of *concrete operation.* Before a child can classify objects by both kind *and* number, he needs many opportunities to group them by their qualitative aspect(s) only.

[6] When working with several children, as often as possible have them correct one another—and the teacher! The notion of "correctness" however, holds only for grouping of identical objects. When more than one variable is present, the child's choice should be considered "correct" so long as it remains constant.

dimension. At all times children need to be encouraged to verbalize why they make the choices they do.

The idea of a *consistent criterion* is important and needs to be maintained when working with items that can be sorted in more than one way (by color, shape, size, etc.). Four-year-olds are likely to group a red square with a blue square "because they have the same shape," and then add a blue circle "because they are blue." Maintaining a consistent criterion requires that a child be able to remember why he made his first choice and then make all subsequent choices for the same reason.

Quite complex preoperational exercises in classifying need to be mastered before the child is asked to deal with both qualitative and quantitative properties. If shown a collection of 10 wooden beads, 2 of which are red and 8 green, and asked the question, "Are there more green beads or more wooden beads?" some will be able to consider both qualitative and quantitative aspects, but this ability is not often found in a preschooler. The foundations for classification need to be built early and carefully; the ability to classify both quantitatively and qualitatively is fundamental to many of the demands of schooling and other cognitive activities.

Three types of tasks encountered early in the development of seriation are:

1. Absolute Comparison
   Children identify large and small members of different pairs of objects—the biggest block, the smallest doll, etc.
2. Relative Comparison
   Children perceive the same object as now large, now small, relative to the size of another object.
3. Additive Seriation
   To a series of objects already ordered along a particular dimension, children add other objects and place them correctly.

Materials and procedures

COGNITIVE PROCESS
Seriation (at preoperational level)

DESCRIPTION
Seriation involves making two or more comparisons and ordering items along some dimension

Nursery schools have the variety of materials and the opportunities for sensory-motor activities that make it possible for children to identify differences and order objects in terms of these differences as a part of the daily program. Much of the equipment can be in two sizes (big and little dolls, blocks, plates, cups, paint brushes, etc.) and conversation can frequently be directed toward this relationship. "Kitty, you use the little swing and let Paul have the big one." "Do we need the little wagon or the big wagon for all these blocks?" Size comparisons should also include long or tall/short and narrow/wide.

Dimensions other than size (such as distance, loudness, hardness, amount of heat and amount of color) also lend themselves to comparison and seriation. Questions for diagnosing a child's level of development in seriation are indicated on p. 241.

Comparisons should first be made on the basis of gross differences and then gradually more subtle differences should be noted by matching pairs of elements for precise comparison. Dramatic play such as that which relates the size of objects to the needs of Mama, Papa and Baby Bear provides a meaningful base for many comparisons.

Another opportunity a teacher can create to give the child a chance to think about relative size is to have him add an item to an array of three of more ordered objects. For example, you might have him arrange three toy cars in order of size. Then give him a fourth that is either larger or smaller than the first three and ask, "Where should this go so it will be in the right place?"

A concept of relative size can be developed by having children learn they are taller than some of their friends, but also shorter than others. This can also be worked out with chairs, books, desks, cups, etc.

Seriation is a concept based on a system of relative dimensions, not just the comparison of two or three objects and their ordering. The ability to place items correctly along some dimension wherein they differ is closely tied to the demands of many school subjects. Its development should be constantly encouraged and sought at the preschool level.

Developing Elementary Number Concepts

Elementary number concepts such as "just enough," "the same number," "more," and "less," are an important part of logical thinking. Their beginnings are a natural part of nursery school activities. The child who holds up four fingers and says, "I'm four," when asked his age, or the child who can correctly count from 1 through 5, may or may not have number concepts. Unless he can also select 4 of something or know that by adding 1 more to 4 he will have 5, he lacks the elementary concepts of "the same number" and "more."

Before children can solve problems involving number—that is, quantity and measurement—they must be able to do more than count. They must be able to comprehend differences between big/little, full/empty, long/short, same/different, etc. Unless a child perceives these contrasts he will not realize there is a problem to solve.

The teacher might first ask, "Are these the same?" If the child answers "yes," she can ask "In what way?" If the child answers "no," she can ask "How are they different?"

If the question regarding size is not productive, she might ask, "Is there one that is bigger than the other? Which one?"

Classification and seriation abilities provide a framework for the kind of knowledge needed, but children must also have experiences leading to the achievement of specific number goals. In Piaget's theory of numbers, the first of these goals is establishing *numerical equivalence by one-to-one correspondence;* the second is establishing *conservation.*

Typical procedure

CONCEPT
Numerical equivalence by one-to-one correspondence

DESCRIPTION
Two sets are equivalent by one-to-one correspondence if each element of one set is exactly duplicated in the other, and vice versa

MATERIALS
Sets of identical small items that can be easily manipulated (bottle caps, checkers, game pieces, slugs, etc.), perhaps 5 or 6 different items per set

(Practice in linear ordering to make equivalent sets)

1. Make a row of items such as those shown and ask child to make a row just like it underneath.

2. When he has finished ask, "Do we each have the same number of pieces?" Then, "How do you know?" (Even if child can count he should be asked to show his understanding by matching one-to-one.) Repeat this many times with different arrangement of items and also having child arrange a line and check teacher's "wrong" matching.

MATERIALS
16 counters identical in all ways but color; half white and half green

DESCRIPTION
Conservation is the ability to know that the equivalence of two sets must *remain the same when their spatial arrangement is changed*

CONCEPT
Topological content
Transformation

CONCEPT LABEL
Above-below
Over-under
In-out
Behind-in front of
Disassembling object into smaller parts and reassembling to original shape

Children tend to quantify items by the amount of space an array occupies. Consequently, for a situation like the one illustrated, preschool children will probably say there are more hats in the top row than in the bottom row since they judge from the amount of space occupied rather than by number. Linear ordering and matching one-to-one helps build a logical rather than spatial basis for judging amount. Using dolls and hats and giving children opportunities to "find just enough hats for these dolls and not too many," or "just enough trikes for these children and not too many" (Piaget's *provoked correspondence*), strengthens the notion of one-to-one correspondence qualitatively as well as quantitatively. With mastery of numerical equivalence based on one-to-one correspondence, children are ready for simple addition and subtraction games.

Preschool children do not yet realize that when the shape or location of objects is changed, quantity is conserved since the original condition can be re-established. Although they are unable to consider destruction and re-establishment at the same time (*reversibility*), they can be started toward this kind of cognitive ability by being given practice in arranging, disarranging, and then rearranging. Thus, by proceeding successively in only one direction at a time children begin to understand that objects can be returned to the same spatial relationship and will also retain their original amount. The exercise that follows helps develop this idea.

Typical procedure

1. Ask child to make a row using all the counters of one color. Then have him make a row of white counters underneath the green without mentioning number. Ask "Are there the same number of green pieces and white pieces?" "How do you know?" "Make the rows so they have the same number."

2. Teacher then removes one counter. "Now are there the same number of green pieces and white pieces?" "How do you know?" She adds two, takes two, takes one from each row, etc., and asks, "Now are they the same number?" How do you know?" until the child has the notion of "same number."

3. Teacher: "Take all the pieces from one row and put them here." "Now are there the same number of white and green pieces?" "How do you know?" (If he does not answer the first question she might ask, "Are there more white pieces than green pieces or are there the same number?")

4. Teacher has child rearrange white pieces in a matching row and asks, "Are there more green pieces than white pieces or are there the same?"

Arranging, disarranging, and rearranging can be done first without matching—just by having child "put the pieces in another way" and then back again, over and over, in as many ways as the child can think of for himself or be prompted to do by the teacher. He should have a chance to explore these exercises with many kinds and numbers of objects. And he should be permitted to do them over and over but not made to continue beyond the level of his own interest.

Good practice can be achieved by changing plasticene "balls" into "sausages" and back, pouring liquid into different size containers and back, stacking blocks one place or another and then back. From such activities (some of which Piaget used in his classic experiments) children develop experience that enables them to predict results. Children must themselves be involved many times in order to internalize processes of this kind, and so come to perform by thinking instead of empirically. The most fundamental requirement is the child's active participation. At no time should the teacher perform the action and have the child merely observe.

Developing Concepts of Space and Time

At the preschool level developing space concepts includes the concept of *linear ordering*: Putting objects in sequence by some principle other than numbering.

The myriad motor experiences of children in nursery school build space concepts with topological content: putting objects *in* and taking them *out;* crawling *over, through, around,* and *under;* looking *high* and *low.* From these experiences children learn to recognize that even without their direct manipulation, a cup may be *in* or *on* the sink, a cookie *behind* or *in front of* a glass of juice. A child who has formed concepts of this kind can be expected to say, "The snowman has a hat *on top of* his head," when he sees a representation of this in a picture.

Puzzles, block structures, and flannel board stories that return to the first picture at the end of the story, provide a means for children to develop the concept of *transformation.* Further practice in building this idea of space comes when children cut pictures into several large pieces and put them back together.

The space concept of *linear ordering* might begin with the child copying the way a table is set for a tea party. Arranging identical supplies in identical order on different shelves, so that more than one person has the materials needed for a special project, also gives practice in linear ordering.

Young children's questions (such as those listed on p. 245) show their awareness of time. In general, *time concepts* involve:

Temporal order: first, next, last
before, after
sooner, later
if . . . then (cause and effect)

Intervals: minute, hour, day, week, year
sometime ago
in a little while

Studies made by Piaget and his associates indicate that a child's ability to structure uniform intervals comes much later than his ability to deal with temporal order. Therefore, at the preschool level it is desirable to help children develop time concepts based on sequence but not increments.

Many opportunities for children to learn relationships about time come through the teacher's emphasis on what is going on now, what has already been done, and what happens next. Telling a child, "We'll do that in an hour" carries little meaning. Explaining, "That's something for after juice time," relates a forthcoming event to his own experience.

Constant reminders about the regular events of the preschool schedule is one way of making children more aware of time. In addition, teachers convey ideas about time whenever they use expressions such as the following:

As soon as everyone's quiet . . .
When you go home at noon . . .
This morning we'll . . .
Tonight I'm going to . . .
Right now let's . . . then later on we . . .
Before you go out, be sure to . . .
When you come in . . .
First let's finish this and then . . .
Next time, why not . . .
It's Danny's turn first, Maurine is next, and Gerry can be last.

Preschoolers can also begin to develop concepts of time related to cause and effect. No special lessons need to be prepared since children best understand causal relationships as consequences of their own actions. When a child is using a crayon and it breaks, the teacher can simply ask, "What happens when you press too hard?" Likewise with chalk: "What happens when you drop a piece of chalk?"

Young Children's Typical Questions About Time

Is today a long time?
Is a year big? Is my birthday a year?
When will it be tomorrow?
When is it today?
How old will I be when I'm forty?
How much time is 10 o'clock?
What does 4:30 mean?

Children should have many experiences pouring liquids, stacking blocks, bouncing balls from different heights, shoving, pushing, pulling, fastening. In this way notions of cause and effect can begin to take form. From their own involvement children learn to predict the responses of their teachers, their classmates, and the world around them.

Some Issues and Principles of Cognitive Learning at the Preschool Level

The cognitive activity that takes place in the human brain makes it possible to store information received from experience. The structures already present (concepts, labels, patterns of stimuli) determine the way new information is processed. For example, although a big league baseball scout and an interested fan see the same baseball game, each will sort, select and store different details. Information that comes in that does not readily fit the concepts and logic already in use forces whoever is receiving it to examine and perhaps modify his internal structures. *Thus the reality of the external world is at least in part a reality of internal structures.* As these change, the external world is naturally seen in somewhat different ways. This is cognitive growth. The process of changing mental operations in response to externally derived information in turn changes the way the external world is seen and makes additional growth possible.

Although described separately in this text, the acquisition of physical knowledge and logical knowledge are inseparable. A child is not likely to form concepts regarding classification or spatial relationships without at the same time gaining understandings of physical properties. Although they occur simultaneously, acquisition of logical knowledge is more difficult to determine than acquisition of physical knowledge since the former is based on observation and interaction with the external world, the latter on consistency of internal processes. One can be verified, the other only inferred.

Conceptual development raises the basic issue of how much the growth of the mind and its abilities results from teaching and how much of it is an unfolding, maturational process. In other words, does the child best acquire cognitive ability when the teacher presents him with information step by step according to a preconceived curriculum, or when he himself deals with and logically orders changing cognitive structures? As more becomes known about how children learn, these different explanations may eventually converge; they may not be antithetical so much as simply different ways to think about a particular aspect of human growth and development.

For the young child, conceptual operations and cognitive abilities essential for future school success overlap and are less differentiated than they will be later on. Therefore teachers in programs of early education need to provide an environment conducive to a wide range of mental activity, rather than trying to concentrate on developing premath, prescience, or prereading skills. In the early formation of concepts, school-related tasks have common cognitive roots. It is important to recognize that the end points of the mental processes involved in forming concepts cannot be imposed without giving the child an opportunity to build the needed base. Unless the preschooler forms a wide variety of concepts, he is obviously limited in what he can gain from formal education.

The task of the preschool, then, should be to concentrate on the preliminary steps that make further learning more efficient even though the "teaching" may be gradual and undramatic. In these circumstances the importance of the teacher who knows something about how language and cognitive abilities develop cannot be overestimated. In many instances she, more than anyone else, is in a position to help children prepare for success, not failure, in the school years that lie ahead.

SUMMARY   This chapter deals with the processes by which children acquire language, and the influence of several features of early environments upon this development. Teachers can assist language development in several ways. The following section discusses the growth of cognitive abilities, with special attention to some of the work and formulations of Piaget. Included are illustrations of classroom activities and how they involve some of these cognitive operations.

1. Although language is only one channel of communication, it has been a major focus of research in designing new programs to facilitate cognitive development.
2. Even with preschoolers, language is often used to conceal or evade true meaning.
3. Both heredity and experience contribute to the time at which language is learned.
4. Acquiring speech is a natural process for young children; whether the language is simple or relatively complex, children learn to speak at about the same age in different cultures.
5. Children tend to learn the dialect of their parents even though they may hear standard English in day care centers and on the television.
6. Learning to speak generally follows the development of motor skills.
7. Children gradually learn grammar on their own and are often unaffected by the corrections of adults.
8. There is no evidence that socio-economic and cultural differences affect children's capability to learn a language.
9. The setting in which a child is asked to produce language affects the complexity and style of language he produces.
10. Teachers can best help language development by providing many opportunities for verbal interaction on a one-to-one basis.
11. A child develops cognitive operations both by direct teaching and his own act of making sense of his first hand experiences.
12. In the development of intellectual functioning children usually go through the various stages in a relatively fixed order regardless of socio-economic or cultural differences.
13. As a field, early education is concerned with sensory-motor and pre-operational stages of development.
14. Human knowledge is structured from three principal sources: (1) interaction with the physical world: physical knowledge, (2) interaction with others: social knowledge, (3) making sense out of experience: logical knowledge.
15. Physical and logical knowledge underlie much of cognitive development.
16. The ability to form concepts depends on maturation *and* experience.
17. To develop cognitive ability children need many opportunities to repeat multiple kinds of experiences.
18. Physical knowledge includes specific information about physical properties of matter such as hardness, color, shape.

19. Logical knowledge includes classification or grouping, seriation, equivalence and conservation.
20. The mental structures already present (concepts, labels, patterns of stimuli) determine the way new information is processed.
21. As the internal structures change, the external world is naturally seen in different ways.

REFERENCES

Almy, M. C. *Young children's thinking; studies of some aspects of Piaget's theory.* New York: Teachers College Press, Columbia University, 1966.

Birren, J. E. and Hess, R. D. (eds.). Influences of biological, psychological, and social deprivation upon learning and performance. *Perspectives on human deprivation: biological, psychological, and sociological.* Washington, D.C.: U.S. Department of Health, Education and Welfare, Public Health Service, National Institutes of Health, The National Institute of Child Health and Human Development, 1968, pp. 91–186.

Brearley, M. and Hitchfield, E. *A guide to reading Piaget.* New York: Schocken Books, 1966.

Bugental, D. E. et al. Child versus adult perceptions of evaluative messages in verbal, vocal, and visual channels. *Developmental psychology 2,* No. 3 (May 1970): 367–375.

Cazden, C. B. Language programs for young children: notes from England and Wales. In *Language training in early childhood education,* edited by C. S. Lavatelli, pp. 119–153. Urbana, Ill.: University of Illinois Press for ERIC Clearinghouse on Early Childhood Education, 1971.

Cazden, C. B. The neglected situation in child language research and education. In *Language and poverty, perspectives on a theme,* edited by F. Williams, pp. 81–101. Chicago, Ill.: Markham Publishing Co., 1970.

Cazden, C. B. Suggestions from studies of early language acquisition. *Childhood Education 46* (1969): 127–131.

Flavell, J. H. *The developmental psychology of Jean Piaget.* Princeton, N.J.: Van Nostrand Co., 1963.

Gleason, J. B. Do children imitate? Paper read at International Conference on Oral Education of the Deaf, June 1967, at Lexington School for the Deaf, New York.

Inhelder, B. and Piaget, J. *The early growth of logic in the child; classification and seriation.* New York: Harper & Row, 1964.

Kamii, C. K. and Radin, N. L. A framework for a preschool curriculum based on some Piagetian concepts. *The journal of creative behavior 1,* No. 3, (1967): 314–324.

Kamii, C. K. Evaluation of learning in preschool education: socio-emotional, perceptual-motor, cognitive development. In *Handbook on formative and summative evaluation of student learning,* edited by B. S. Bloom, J. T. Hastings, and G. F. Madaus. New York: McGraw-Hill, 1971.

Kamii, C. An application of Piaget's theory to the conceptualization of a preschool curriculum. In *The preschool in action,* edited by R. K. Parker. Boston, Mass.: Allyn and Bacon, 1972.

Lenneberg, E. H., Nichols, I. A., and Rosenberger, E. F. Primitive stages of language development in mongolism. In *Disorders of communication,* edited by D. Rioch and E. A. Weinstein. Research Publication of Association for Research in Nervous and Mental Disorders *42,* New York, Baltimore; Williams and Wilkins, 1964.

Lenneberg, E. H. On explaining language. *Science 164,* No. 3880, 9 May 1969, pp. 635–643.

Piaget, J. *The construction of reality in the child.* New York: Basic Books, 1954.

Piaget, J. *The origins of intelligence in children.* New York: International Universities Press, Inc., 1952.

Sinclair, H. and Kamii, C. K. Some implications of Piaget's theory for teaching young children. Paper prepared as part of the Ypsilanti Early Education Program. Ypsilanti, Michigan, March 1969.

Sonquist, H. D. and Kamii, C. K. Applying some Piagetian concepts in the classroom for the disadvantaged. *Young Children,* March 1967, pp. 231–246.

Sonquist, H., Kamii, C. K., and Derman, L. A Piaget-derived preschool curriculum. In *Educational implications of Piaget's theory,* edited by I. J. Athey and D. O. Rubadeau, pp. 101–114. Waltham, Mass.: Ginn-Blaisdell, 1970.

U.S., Department of Health, Education, and Welfare, National Institutes of Health, National Institute of Neurological Diseases and Stroke. *Learning to talk, speech, hearing and language problems in the preschool child.* Washington, D.C.: Government Printing Office, 1969.

Chapter 10 Social Concepts and Behavior

Chapter Outline

Growth of Self-Knowledge

The child gains knowledge about himself in the same way he initially learns about other aspects of the physical world. As an infant he plays with his toes and fingers, explores the contours of his body, pulling, poking, pushing, until he has satisfied his curiosity about where his body leaves off and the external world begins. Later, he can look in a mirror to help him know what he looks like. He needs labels, of course, but he can see for himself the color of his hair, whether he is big or little, what he looks like when he smiles or frowns, and so on.

But such perceptions, important as they are, contribute only partly to the development of self-knowledge. As a child grows, he acquires concepts of himself and his physical features, his worth, and an understanding of his place in the society.

In seeking to understand how to help children develop feelings about themselves, it is important for teachers to distinguish between *self-concept, identity,* and *self-esteem.*

Self-concept is a result of cognitive activity. It is the child's awareness of his own characteristics and of the differences and likenesses between himself and others. He learns to think of himself as "tall," "talkative," "red-headed," "strong," "right-handed," and the like. Even though he may not be able to verbalize the differences, he sees himself as separate from the adult members of his family, and distinct from other children. By three he knows whether he is a boy or a girl; his vocabulary includes the words *me, mine, I, you, yours,* and sometimes *we* and *ours.* This aspect of a child's self-knowledge indicates cognitive awareness of his characteristics, but includes no notion of evaluation, nor does it make clear his relationships to others.

Identity has a social connotation. While self-concept gives the child an image of himself as an individual, identity brings awareness of group membership. Understanding that possession of certain physical characteristics means "being a boy" precedes knowledge that there is a group called "boys" and that membership in this group carries with it certain expectations, privileges, and restraints. Without necessarily understanding the reasons, the child becomes aware of his membership in such a group. He first finds out he's a boy and then becomes aware of what it is that boys do.

A child's recognition that he has dark skin comes before an understanding that this may also mean he is a Negro, or that Negroes as a group often face discrimination and a set of expectations in white American society. Identity comes when some kind of sociocultural meaning is attached to elements of the self-concept. It is a process through which a child gains knowledge of such matters as his name, race, sex role, and social class.

Self-esteem is the level of regard an individual has for what he is and does. It reflects how a child feels about himself. Almost as soon as self-concepts form, they acquire positive or negative evaluations. For the child, self-concept and self-esteem are highly related since both have their source in feedback from people that are important to him. It is unlikely that children separate fact from evaluation when they hear, "My, aren't you a big boy!" or "Where did you ever get all those freckles?" Self-esteem may be *low* or *high,* self-concepts clear or incomplete, though this distinction is not always made. One is a level of regard, the other a cognitive grasp of characteristics.

Figure 10-1 *As a child grows, she develops a sense of self-knowledge.*

The building of self-concept is a cognitive operation carried out in much the same way as children form concepts of the physical world. The source of information for the physical world is much more direct, but the processes are not different. Based on a great deal of information from many different experiences, the child abstracts and generalizes—in one case about an object he perceives, in the other about himself, his behavior, and his feelings.

Self-concept and self-esteem originate from four major sources: (1) the impressions a child receives from others, (2) his own accumulated experiences, (3) his ability to live up to and internalize the goals set for him, and (4) the capacity to evaluate his performance on the basis of his own standards (Coopersmith, 1967). The impressions a child receives from those who are especially significant to him are very important. Their comments about him, their approval or disapproval of what he does, their concern for his welfare, their inclusion or exclusion of him from their activities all influence the way in which a child sees and values himself.

The child comes to know whether he is shy, aggressive, lazy, neat, willing, naughty, or good not from his own analysis, but from remarks made about him. The comments of people important to him are significant whether directly addressed to him or not. Indeed, children are sometimes talked about as though they were not present, as in the following conversation:

Mother   (while Cindy listens) I just don't know what I'm going to do about Cindy.
Neighbor Why, what's wrong?
Mother   Well, she takes forever to eat. And messy! You just can't imagine. By the time she's finished half of what I give her, it's either on the table or on the floor. You know, her father's just the same way. That's why I always use those washable table cloths. Have you ever tried them? They're . . .

In such instances, a child not only hears the words and ideas of her mother's conversation, but she also receives an underlying message that her mother doesn't care whether she hears her criticism or not.

A second source of the development of a child's self-concept and self-esteem is her accumulation of successful and unsuccessful experiences. As a child ventures into a world larger than her immediate family, she competes with others for rewards of many kinds. The child whose appearance and ways make a favorable impression sees herself as quite a different person from the one who meets with indifference or rejection. She may not realize what gives her this advantage, but her history of success in getting approval (even though this may only be sitting on a visitor's lap), forms a basis for high self-esteem. A cumulative effect of this kind is a powerful influence on the development of self-concept.

Success in school-related tasks also plays an important role in the development of both self-concept and self-esteem. Early in the primary grades, children come to see themselves as smart (or not) in the things the teacher requires. The familiar teaching technique of dividing the class into ability groups ("This group is the Redbirds; this one is the Bluebirds") indicating fast and slow learners is an early and dramatic feedback of the teacher's opinion of the child's ability. The teacher also gives individual evaluations of the child's behavior and performance in more subtle ways.

Failure in school plays its own damaging role. Thousands of children in this country do not do well in school and are reminded daily that they do not compete, cannot achieve. Success in school is great for children who do succeed, and we applaud the boost this gives their self-esteem. However, we often ignore the effect of daily failure on other children. What of their esteem?

A student teacher reports:

"I didn't realize I was showing so much favoritism until I read an observation of my work in the lab school. At first I was really upset to think that I would be unfair to some of the children. Then I felt angry at the observer for exposing me. After some discussion with my supervisor, I decided to consciously monitor my own behavior.

"I noticed that I held and touched little Edy several times while I worked at the puzzle table, and I even reached out to her when she made no gestures toward me. I asked her questions in an effort to get her to look at me and each time we had eye contact, I would smile at her. When Lisa sat down next to me, I practically ignored her. I answered when she asked me a question, but I didn't give her the sustained attention, the warmth and personal care that I gave to Edy. I guess I'm attracted to Edy because she's so cute, so well coordinated and speaks so clearly. Lisa is clumsy, kind of messy, and doesn't talk very much."

Very early in life children experience success or failure through the feed-back evaluation from adults in their world. By the time they begin formal schooling, their self-esteem is further enhanced or diminished by the competitive system of open rewards and grading prevalent in most school systems. Children who do well in at least some school areas can feel satisfied with their accomplishment (unless there is undue pressure from parents for even more outstanding achievement, such as competing with examples set by an older sister or brother), but children who are relatively low in their own classes may come to think of themselves as stupid or clumsy in the classroom.

One of the reasons that some professionals are reluctant to introduce an academic curriculum in the prekindergarten grades is that it may establish in the child's mind expectations (perhaps inaccurately) of competence or inadequacy before the child is ready to tackle solid academic tasks.

There is some disagreement among professionals in early education as to whether self-esteem contributes to successful performance or follows from it. One view is that children need to feel good about themselves and their abilities and this sense of confidence will enable them to achieve. The other view is that true self-confidence and esteem come from mastery of a task and the clear demonstration of skills. Otherwise the confidence is only a hope. The child who has learned to read or can count (or perform whatever task is set by the teacher) has a firmer sense of his competence because he has shown himself and others that he can perform valued tasks. The route to self-esteem is skill, in this approach, and we mislead the child if he is told he's doing fine when he isn't.

Teachers may find it difficult to take sides on this argument because both positions are appealing. Perhaps the solution may be to let the child know he is valued as a person but move immediately to help him acquire the skills he needs to maintain self-esteem.

The third source that strongly affects the formation of self-concept and self-esteem is the child's ability to live up to the goals set for him and internalized by him. If a child must be perfect in order to be content, self-esteem is likely to be very low. Even young children feel obliged to live up to certain expectations and standards, especially those established by a parent. Once this happens, they are often unable to accept what others say, and judge themselves only by this inner value system.

Five-year-old Marshall was such a child. He came from a family that insisted on excellent performance at all times and exemplary manners, including answering "Yes, sir" and "Yes, ma'am" at appropriate times. So strongly had the notion of doing something perfectly or not doing it at all been impressed upon Marshall that he saw himself as a failure in much he attempted on his own. He often went to the art table at school but could not bring himself to draw the dinosaur he really wanted because, he explained, "I can't make them good enough." Instead he contented himself with scribbling as he had when he was much younger.

Marshall and children like him will suffer from lack of confidence and self-esteem until they (or adults around them) set realistic standards and use them to evaluate their performance. This is the fourth source of feelings of esteem and self-concept. Standards that the child has set for himself help him maintain a stable self-esteem even in the face of criticism and other negative feedback. Very young children are unable to do this, but they can be helped to *decide for themselves* what success and good performance mean in the various things they do. Having done so they can recognize for themselves when they have accomplished something satisfactory.

Whatever their origins, a child's self-concept and self-esteem develop continuously. They cannot be taught in sessions of ten or fifteen minutes a day. The young child's awareness and evaluation of himself depend largely on the way others talk to him and about him, and how they behave toward him. Teachers aware of the processes involved recognize their part as significant people in the lives of young children.

Role-Taking Ability

Because she is likely to perceive the world from only her own viewpoint, the young child's initial role in the social world is that of observer. Her inability to comprehend social orientation is analogous to her struggle to deal with spatial orientation; imagining how another person feels and thinks is also difficult for her. Yet effectiveness in social relationships ultimately depends upon this ability to imagine how another person feels, to take into account his needs, to put herself into another's place, and to communicate with him accordingly.

The growth of this ability to take the role of another is thus a basic and important part of social development. It seems to be part of the ability to empathize and to sympathize with the feelings of others. Social communication is based to a large degree upon this ability. Indeed, we understand each other's feelings by recalling our own subjective reactions to things that happen to others. By projecting our own responses, we can say "I know how you feel" when we see others being rejected, put down, ignored, or winning a point or earning praise or compliments. What we should say, perhaps, is "I know how I feel when

I'm in that situation, so I think I know how you feel." These shared experiences allow us to have similar, shared feelings.

How do these capabilities develop and mature? Are they in part cognitive—that is, a matter of understanding as well as feeling? Some researchers have tried to examine these abilities in young children. The studies of Flavell (1966) are especially interesting in their description of what role-taking ability children acquire and approximately when it develops.

In one study he worked with 160 children from the second through the eleventh grades; in another his subjects were 40 preschool children aged three to six. The ability of preschool children to assume the role of another person was examined by means of the following situations:

1. Subject and experimenter sat facing each other across a table and the child was asked to place a picture so that the experimenter could see it right side up. This is primarily a matter of spatial orientation and has a basis in cognitive processes.
2. The sharpened end of an ordinary lead pencil rested in the hand of the experimenter. Its other end (with a cotton ball glued to it) rested in a child's hand. The child was first asked, "Does the pencil feel soft?" Then he was asked to tell if it felt soft to the experimenter. This requires the child not only to notice that the two ends of the pencil are different and that the experimenter is touching a part of the pencil quite different from that in the child's hand, but to be aware of how a sharp point feels and to project this feeling onto the experimenter. The question of how something feels is different in essential ways from asking what a picture looks like from another visual perspective.
3. As the child examined an array of objects he was asked to select one he might give to his mother for a birthday present. (Father, teacher, sibling and self also were included in the study.) His ability to choose a gift appropriate to the interest of the person named was held to be indicative of the level of his ability to role play. For example, the child who chose a truck for his mother showed poor role-taking performance.

This last situation also has essential elements of conceptual functioning. It draws not so much upon the child's shared experience and feeling with his mother as upon his knowledge about what his mother uses and wants. Some understanding of feelings is involved, however, in recognizing that a present should please the person getting it rather than himself.

1. What skills does the child acquire, in what order, and at what ages?
2. Does a high level of role-taking performance in one setting mean that use of the same components will result in an equally high level in another setting?
3. What effect does background and experience have on a child's ability to role play?
4. How is social behavior affected by the child's ability to role play?[1]

From this work and previous studies by others, Flavell observed that high performance in role-taking requires: first an understanding that there is a perspective other than one's own (that not everyone sees, thinks, or feels alike); second, realization that an analysis of the other perspective might be useful; third, possession of the ability to carry out the analysis needed; fourth, a way of keeping in mind what is learned from analysis; and fifth, knowledge of how to translate the results of analysis into effective social behavior—that is, into terms of getting along better with the person whose viewpoint is under consideration.

Of the factors needed for benefiting from role-taking, preschool children acquire only one—the ability to understand that there is more than one viewpoint.

The teacher can facilitate development of this ability by helping the child realize that others have different feelings, by asking the child to try to imagine how someone else feels and to remember how he feels when someone does to him what he has just done to someone else. This may help the child connect his own feelings with things he sees happen as well as things that he experiences himself.

The Self in the Social System

In infancy a child lacks the ability to distinguish between where his own body ends and where the world that surrounds him begins. The hand whose shape and texture he explores as he might a rattle or toy may be his own or his mother's; at first he does not differentiate or know. Repeated experiences and in-

[1] Adapted from J. H. Flavell, "Role taking and communication skills in children," *Young Children,* No. 3 (1966): 176.

creasing physical maturation lead him to see himself as an individual, one who shares characteristics with other individuals. He recognizes his membership in a group, and forms not only self-concepts, but concepts of his mother, his father, and the other members of his family. Through interaction with people he enters the social world.

Awareness of Group
Membership and Interaction

Once he recognizes himself and his immediate family as separate entities, the child becomes aware that there are still other people. Some of these others are like himself. They, too, have mothers and fathers. To his notions of "my mother" and "my father," therefore, he adds the new realization that there are *other* parents and arrives at the general concepts of "mother" and "father." These concepts, based on social knowledge, are developed by the same kinds of cognitive processes used to form concepts from physical knowledge and logical knowledge. Information from which to build social concepts such as "mother" and "father," however, is far more diffuse and difficult to get than information that enables the formation of concepts such as "chair" and "under," yet it is apparently processed in the same ways. The child continually receives, arranges, stores, and rearranges information as a result of his participation and involvement with humans, objects, and relationships.

Generalization about himself and those significant to him leads to an awareness of roles and social groups. The preschooler begins to understand not only that he belongs to a family, but will soon realize that the family itself is part of larger groups. It will be some time before he comprehends the religious, economic, or ethnic nature of these, but his awareness is nonetheless real.

The consistency of the relationships he has with others brings about realization that there are not only fathers and mothers, but neighbors, teachers, priests, storekeepers, nurses, bus drivers, dentists, aunts, uncles, grandparents, and so on. Until a later stage of his development he will not be able to separate the role from the person. Within the family he may be able to comprehend that his father also has a father and so is both parent and son. But he is usually not able to perceive that his father also fills the role of "mayor" or "clerk." To the child, his father is one or the other but not both simultaneously. Gradually his thinking develops until he is able to grasp the notion of people occupying multiple roles. This same inflexibility pertains to inanimate objects. The only "home" he knows is his own, or perhaps the house of a friend. Abstractions are not part of his mental processes. He deals primarily with the specific, the concrete—those matters he can know and verify from his own experience.

Gradually the child begins to see that families are composed of fathers, mothers, sons, and daughters; a school consists of teachers and children. His participation in groups shows him that the various elements within them depend upon one another and that groups themselves interact with each other to form larger entities—schools, communities, cities, nations. This kind of concept development is like other conceptual growth. It proceeds from personal awareness of repeated events and objects to an abstraction of their common characteristics and the application of a label. It is not something one learns and sets aside or forgets; it is an ongoing, continuous process beginning early in life and developing more completely during the school years.

Racial and Social-Class Awareness

Even as the child becomes conscious of himself as an individual, a member of a family, and so a part of society, she develops awareness of racial and social-class differences between herself and others. Children as young as three notice skin color, facial features, and hair texture. They look at, touch, and make comparisons regarding one another in much the same way that they explore the physical characteristics of any aspect of the world around them. Judgment is not involved, only a desire to determine what something is like by comparing it with what they already know. One of the ways in which young children explore these differences in racial characteristics is illustrated by the following observation:

During story time Janey, a blonde, blue-eyed three year old sits and stares at the four-year-old black girl, Denise, sitting beside her. Janey seems to have discovered Denise for the first time and obviously is unaware of the story being read by the teacher. Suddenly Janey remarks loudly enough to disrupt the teacher, "You should wash your hands. They're dirty." The teacher stops reading, but before she can say anything, Denise replies, "It don't come off." "Why not?" asks Janey curiously. By now the other children as well as the teacher watch and listen intently. "Cause I'm black." "She's born that way and her skin is naturally dark," adds the teacher. "Let's go see," says Janey, as she takes Denise by the hand and leads her to the bathroom wash basin. The teacher decides the whole group can go along to watch while the two girls wash their hands. After thoroughly washing their hands, Janey turns to Denise, looks at her again, then looks at her face, arms, hands, legs and feet and then remarks, "I believe you." Then, taking Denise's hand in her own, Janey looks down at both hands and says, "It doesn't come off on my hand." "See, I told you so," smiles Denise and both girls go with the others back to story time, holding hands and smiling at their discovery.

Realization of differences based on race makes little change in the children's behavior toward one another. Working with a group of three-year-old black and white children, Stevenson (1962, p. 118) found that "the interaction between children appeared to depend, as it does in most types of social interaction, upon the degree to which the relationship between individuals satisfied each other's needs." Various studies show that by age five labels such as "He's black," or "She's Chinese," or "They're Mexican," have discriminatory meanings and children of other groups begin to take on negative attitudes and behaviors toward those so labeled. Their prejudice is based for the most part on attitudes they have picked up from adults.

Children notice skin color differences from pictures before they think of themselves as white or nonwhite. In past studies, identification of others as members of a racial group generally took place earlier for white than nonwhite children. Whereas minority group youngsters rarely saw a white person before starting school, white children came in contact with the minority group members who worked in their neighborhoods. Changing attitudes toward racial identity in both white and ethnic communities and desegregation in schools are stimulating new research on racial awareness and its meaning for young children.

The preschooler's awareness of social class begins to emerge by noticing the various ways in which people live. Because of these differences he may categorize some people as "poor" and others as "rich" even though he isn't able to explain the meanings of these terms.

The chances are, though, that he has learned that it's better to be rich than poor and is thus beginning to evaluate others as well as himself. It is in such ways that social identity and esteem are formed. Also, a child may have a notion of status as it accrues to a family because of the father's occupation, but concepts of his own position in the social structure do not form until well along in the elementary school years. The realization that others have more (or fewer) toys than he is likely to be a greater factor in the development of the child's self-concept and self-esteem than the socio-economic status of his family.

Concepts of Social Relationships

An essential aspect of a child's social understanding and behavior involves learning and comprehending rules. From the time he first explores beyond the narrow confines of a particular play area, he is surrounded with verbal and physical constraints: "Don't touch!" "That's a 'No-No.'" "Use both hands." "Say, 'please.'" "Stay in your room." "Stop making all that noise." The list is long. Initially, regulations of this kind exist for the child's safety or are intended to "train him in good manners." Many are associated with the comfort and convenience of other family members. All are prohibitive in nature but carry little overtone of right or wrong. To most adults, behavior of a very young child is not judged from a moral standpoint. Gradually, he is expected to act in conformity with standards of the family group. He may be told it's wrong to hit his brother, he's a bad boy for pouring milk on the floor instead of drinking it, or it's naughty to play in the mud and get his good clothes dirty. Whether moral behavior is involved, or simply his safety and manners, the child often is scolded and punished in similar ways.

At a nursery school he gets new information about how he is expected to behave and what is considered right and wrong. Now he is judged from a much wider context. He must learn rules made by adults whose standards may be quite different from those he has known at home. Right and wrong have taken on a new dimension; however, they are still group standards imposed on the individual.

Some of these sets of standards are, of course, important— where to go to the bathroom, how to dress, rules of safety, etc. However, it may be that an even more important part of this early learning is the *fact that there are rules and standards* by which others will evaluate him. Along with this awareness is a realization that rewards and punishments may come as a consequence of his responses to these expectations.

In turn, both at home and at school, adults respond to the needs of the child. Thus, there exists a contractual relationship between the individual and the social unit of which he is a member.

Development of Concepts About Rules

Children acquire concepts about rules in a more or less predictable sequence but not in well-defined stages. Initially, children see themselves as subject to adult authority. Acts that are in accord with rules made by adults are right. The rule may not be a formal one in the usual sense; the child who "helps Mother" or "does what Daddy tells him to" is being "good" and doing "right" things. If he is punished, it follows that whatever he did must have been something "wrong."

Rules made by his parents guide his behavior until he accumulates the experience and maturity needed to formulate more sophisticated concepts of right and wrong. Adult authority in the form of rules continues to dominate the child's conception of morality until he is about eight years old. This is the first general phase of moral development. After this time the basis for conduct includes rules based on group agreement and cooperative action. Rules are less often seen as absolutes, but as something that can be changed according to the wishes of the members of the group involved.

Moral Development
Dimensions of morality

In general, morality is the outcome of the dimensions defined above. These are not independent of one another but parts of a whole. Knowledge, feelings, and conduct are all involved in the acquisition of morality. For example, suppose a child is told, "Do not steal." Before this ideal of appropriate conduct becomes part of his moral code, he obviously must know what stealing means. Is he stealing when he takes a toy from his shelf or only when he takes the same toy from a shelf at a store? Is he stealing when he shuts Mrs. Johnson's cat in his garage? What is stealing? What isn't?

Even though the child has a definition of stealing clearly in mind, if taking possessions that don't belong to him leaves him without a feeling of wrong-doing, morality is only partially developed. Unless the child feels guilty for his theft, or somehow virtuous when he refrains from transgression, he has not yet acquired a sense of morality. The rule must also serve as a guide to conduct. If the child knows he is stealing, feels guilty, but goes right ahead and steals, he has not developed morality. Knowledge, feeling, and conduct must all be present before morality is acquired.

At his stage of cognitive development, the preschool child cannot be expected to display morality in this complete sense. He may be made aware of the rules of the teacher and may know what pleases her and what kinds of things will cause her to punish him or withdraw approval. He may also behave accordingly or feel guilt if he does not. Although they are the beginning of a complex process, these are important phases in the development of genuine morality.

Dimensions of Morality

Moral Knowledge: Information about right and wrong behavior—specific rather than general

Moral Feelings: Inner reactions of guilt or innocence regarding one's behavior

Moral Conduct: Acting according to group standards of behavior

Limits of comprehension

Moral development in the sense of understanding, rather than merely acceding to principles associated with moral behavior, begins during the preschool years and continues long after the child embarks on formal education. Obviously understanding is limited at first. However, the child's primitive feeling of inner discomfort which accompanies having broken a rule may be similar or antecedent to his later orientation toward more sophisticated moral principles. Perhaps the initial learning is the awareness that there *are* rules that one must attend to in social interaction. This early response to underlying moral principles may be analogous to a child's use of grammatical rules. Long before he can define any aspect of syntax, he learns and applies rules that make verbal interaction possible.

Piaget's 1932 study of moral judgment shows that children judge "rightness" and "wrongness" according to how much harm has been done; older children take into consideration the intent of the actor. To confirm his theory, Piaget asked two different age groups of children to tell him which of the boys in the situations summarized below had been the naughtier.

The younger children (all under seven years of age) agreed that John was naughtier than Henry because he had broken many more cups. On the other hand, children ages nine and ten

Hypothetical Situations Used to Test Moral Judgment of Children

When John is called to dinner, on entering the dining room he inadvertently overturns a tray of fifteen cups and breaks them all.

While his mother is out, Henry goes to a cupboard and helps himself to forbidden jam. In reaching to the shelf where the jam is kept he knocks over and breaks a cup.

Adapted from J. Piaget, *The moral judgment of the child* (Glencoe, Ill.: The Free Press, 1948), p. 118.

were just as certain Henry's intent made him the naughtier child.

Extensive studies by Hartshorne and May as long ago as 1930 show that morality in behavior is not a general trait—that is, it does not apply to all situations. Although their work involved only school-age children (not preschool), it suggests principles with broad applications. Some 11,000 children were given a chance to cheat, lie, and steal in many different circumstances without fear of being caught or punished. To their surprise, the investigators found that even in closely related circumstances (a math test and spelling test, for example), a child would cheat on one and not the other. In other words, there was little relationship from one situation to another between behavior defined as "wrong."

The conclusion that children are not consistently moral in their conduct seems also to apply to the other areas of morality —emotion and knowledge or judgment. Studies of moral knowledge show some individual internal consistency but nothing of the sort of global, unifying concept of conscience and moral principles that is frequently assumed.

Other studies assessing the degree of guilt that accompanies different types of immorality indicate that there may be differences in feelings experienced in immoral conduct from one type of behavior to another and of one type of behavior from one event to the next. The conditions of the specific event, especially the likelihood of punishment or detection appear to be involved in the intensity of feelings of guilt (Brown, 1965, p. 413).

It is important for the teacher of young children to remember that the process of developing moral judgment is not a simple internalization of rules of the adult world or of conditioning through rewards and punishments. The conceptual component of morality continues through adolescence (Kohlberg, 1963) and probably throughout much of adult life as the individual struggles to sort out his own standards and values in the light of his own experience. A valuable part of that experience is having been with adults who made their rules and expectations clear and offered reasons for them. Moral judgment grows through the complex processes involved in other forms of conceptual development but with perhaps more difficulty. The knowledge and subsequent concepts gained from experience with the physical world begin with a firm base of physical tangible information. Social and moral knowledge are based on more ephemeral events and often come from experiences with conflicting evidence or values. The decisions many young men faced in the draft for the war in Vietnam, for example, were struggles between values of loyalty to their country and consequence for themselves and families as opposed to convictions that the war itself was not justified or moral. The development of a moral conceptual framework thus seems to be a matter of absorbing and reflecting upon experience, values of others, knowledge of consequences for oneself and others and beliefs developed in other ways. The preschool child is obviously merely beginning the process of constructing moral concepts and developing appropriate feelings and conduct.

The relationship between overt behavior and other dimensions of morality is not as close as one might think. Moral knowledge does not guarantee moral behavior, nor do feelings of guilt, although both are related to behavior. It appears that the child develops morality through different channels (Brown, 1965, p. 412). Moral judgment and knowledge are cognitive operations. Moral conduct is probably more often a result of reinforcement and imitation, and moral feelings appear to be in part a result of conditioning or association with painful experiences in the past. Feelings of guilt about misbehavior (however the act is defined) can be instilled by punishment, praise, approval, and disapproval, and especially, by withdrawal of love. Within limits these are useful.

A sense that there are right behaviors and wrong behaviors is separate from what the specific behaviors may be. It is a crucial phase of moral development to recognize that moral standards exist, but it is only preliminary and insufficient to learn moral rules as if they were a list of do's and don'ts. If a child is to become truly moral, he must acquire morality or moral judgment in part through his own cognitive prowess. The mature, moral person is one who is able and willing to regulate his behavior on the basis of his judgments about the rightness or wrongness of his behavior in terms of principles of justice and of conditions in the society in which he is living.

Patterns of Social Behavior

Social behavior occurs not only between two individuals, but also in a field of influences and social forces. A three person group is quite different than a two or a four person group, not because of the number of people and the amount of potential communication, but because of the structure of the set. For example, a three person group presents the greater possibility of an alignment of two against one, or an exclusion of one member. Group size is a critical factor in offering anonymity to an individual and diffusing the responsibility for actions. Groups, whether nations or gangs, may claim a turf or territory and create rules and tests of allegiance for individual members. A child-care center presents different dynamics if the child-adult ratio is 15 to 1 than if it is 5 to 1. These simple examples indicate the complexity of the nature of groups and of the different ways that individuals relate to groups and to others in groups.

Social Interaction

It is useful to understand some of the central elements that affect social interaction in group settings and exchanges. These concepts help explain behavior of individuals and may put it in a more neutral perspective. Behavior that might appear to be motivated by malevolence becomes a matter of following a principle of group rules and norms. This view of social behavior avoids some value judgments of whether the interactions are good in some moral sense and concentrates on attempts to understand some of the reasons why children behave as they do.

A central goal of a teacher is to understand the behavior of children in terms that put it in a conceptual context and give meaning to what they do. An identical social act will justify quite different interpretations from different perspectives. One adult may see a child's initiative in leading a group as decisiveness and leadership; another may see the child as bossy. Both may be correct. Concepts for viewing and interpreting social behavior thus add perspective and depth, giving the teacher more information on which to decide if a specific act calls for intervention, reinforcement, or serious concern.

It may be useful to think of social behavior in dimensions such as these:

1. Territoriality (establishment and maintenance of one's own boundaries)
2. Approach and influence behavior (attempts to obtain resources from others or alter the environment)
3. Alignment and cooperative behavior (joining with others for individual benefit or group goals)

Human behavior is so complex that it is difficult to analyze it without having classifications overlap. Some of these obviously do.

Territoriality is the cluster of attitudes and actions by which humans and other animals establish and maintain geographic and psychological boundaries (Ardrey, 1966). Just as though he had posted a private property sign, the young child takes possession of and will defend the physical space which he considers his. The area he chooses for his own may be a corner of a sandbox marked by a finger-swept line or a row of shovels and pails. It may be a bit of floor space outlined by blocks, a particular chair or place at a table, even just a favorite branch in a tree. He does not always occupy his chosen space alone; others play there with or without him, but they are there only with his consent.

In relationship to social growth, territoriality is not a matter of selfishness; rather it is a means by which children learn to defend their activities, interests, and property. In this sense it is natural and probably healthy behavior. Although it may lead to conflict if others intrude, or are in competition for the same

area, it is not in itself a problem. There may be a collision between the feelings of territory of an individual child and the needs of the group or the adults. This is to be expected and it is to be expected, also, that a child may feel wronged if his territory is invaded, even if for the benefit of the teacher or a larger group. As in all social systems, however, conflict inevitably occurs between individual aims and group goals, and social development is closely tied to the ability to resolve conflict of this kind.

In addition to geographical boundaries, children also seek to establish and maintain psychological space. This leads a child to claim "my teacher" and "my friend" as though these individuals were his and his alone. Sibling rivalries are of this kind; they, too, express possessiveness and a child's need to be wanted and loved.

Psychological as well as geographical boundaries bring children in conflict with one another. A typical verbal interaction along this dimension of territoriality is given on p. 270.

Approach and influence behavior

Maintaining boundaries of physical and psychological space involves another kind of interaction. As actors within their own territory, children turn to one another and to the adults for contact, for interaction, and for satisfaction of their needs. They approach one another with overtures, offers and demands, and requests for assistance, comfort, or rewards. Many of these contacts with peers and adults are attempts to influence the behavior of others to one's own ends or are responses to such attempts.

The ability to persuade or influence others in order to get a desired response is an essential part of the development of social competence. In turn, the ability to deal with the demands or overtures of others without surrendering one's own sense of direction or purpose is equally essential. A significant part of adult life involves approach and influence—from political campaigns and other attempts to gain power over large groups of people to the various strategies employed by both boys and girls in more personal and intimate interactions.

This particular aspect of development involves inner feelings of assertiveness, guilt, disappointment, and gratification. The development of techniques and strategies for dealing with these interactional issues and problems is a difficult part of early learning.

The teacher's role in the growth of this kind of social competence may take two forms. First, ways in which she gets children to do things and responds to their requests and demands

It is juice time and Sheila says, "Miss Cramer, I get to sit next to you today, don't I? It's my turn."

It is Rudy who answers, not Miss Cramer. "No, it's my turn."

Sheila disagrees. "No, it isn't. You sat by her yesterday."

Now Opal joins the conflict. "I never get to sit by her. It's my turn." There is more petulance in her assertion than conviction.

With this interference Rudy and Sheila join forces. "Yes, you do, Opal. You sit by her more than anyone else."

"No, I don't."

"Yes, you do!"

"No, I don't."

The teacher may elect to resolve the conflict in any number of ways, but her solution will invoke a rule the children can understand, such as "We have to take turns," or "Opal can sit next to me because she is new in school," or "I am going to choose a child who never asks to sit by me."

may provide a model for them (see examples on p. 271). Secondly, she can actively reinforce and support the behavior of children that shows effective styles of approach and influence. She will understand, for example, that there is a difference between attempts to manipulate others to one's own purposes—which she will not reward—and approaches that have goals such as interaction, mutual enjoyment, accomplishment of a task, which she will reinforce.

Alignment A third way to look at social behavior of young children is as a matter of *alignment*—the establishment of linkages and collaboration between and among individuals. Alignment may be the pairing of two children against a third or against a teacher; it may be the derision of boys by a group of girls; it may be the choosing of sides or identification with an ethnic group. It can be a relationship of temporary dependency when it involves a child's need to find someone who will push him on a swing or pull him in a wagon or perform any number of personal services that he cannot manage for himself, such as tying a shoelace, opening a cabinet door, or unscrewing a widemouth jar top. It is essentially a feeling of affiliation and may involve psychological dependence or mutual satisfaction and support in joint activities. More deliberate grouping and alignment begin in the later stages of the three-to-five period, although temporary alignments and loyalties develop in the classroom and on the playground for specific purposes. Alignment includes acts of friendship and companionship. It encompasses the form of sharing displayed when a child breaks off a piece of clay and gives it to the one who has none, or offers to squeeze over so that a friend can occupy the same mat or chair. (When children think and speak in terms of "our school" and "our teacher" and "our guinea pig," however, sharing may be thought of as a redefinition of territory.)

When a group of children play store or house together, build an elaborate block structure, or engage in dramatizing a story, alignment takes the forms of cooperation and collaboration. Yet children interacting in this way are also involved in approach-influence behavior whenever one of them attempts to persuade another to his way. And cooperation may be closely associated with territoriality since in cooperating, one child may be responding to another's claims regarding space.

Social behaviors are often so subtle, so interrelated, or so transitory as to challenge specific identification. Thinking of them as manifestations of territoriality, approach, and influence or alignment, however, gives the teacher a basis for understanding

---

Jennifer is passing crackers to the other children. She gets to Bobby who takes two large handsful, leaving three crackers in the basket. The expression on Jennifer's face indicates she is disturbed, but does not know what to do. Some of the other children call this to the attention of the teacher, "Look, Miss Cramer, Bobby took all the crackers." The teacher comments "Bobby, you'll need to put some of those crackers back and take just a few so the other children will have some too." The teacher's explanation is effective and Bobby keeps three crackers for himself while all the other children watch carefully.

The next day Bobby, who is passing crackers, can be heard saying, "You'll need to put some of those crackers back."

The teacher will not always see immediate results of modelling. Sometimes her own style is something a child may not adopt until much later, yet many examples and repeated exposure will have a long time effect.

"Teacher, I want you to carry me all day and not play with those other children," wails Susie.

"I know you want me all to yourself, Susie, and it will be hard for you to share me, but I need to spend time with the other children, too. I'm not going to carry you. I expect you to walk just like all the other children."

While Susie may not have an opportunity to imitate this type of behavior soon, the teacher has provided her with an example of how to say "No," while still accepting the other person's feelings.

---

children's attempts to relate to others and helps her find ways to meet their needs. She will also be more effective as she becomes aware of the techniques and strategies children use to achieve these goals through interaction with others.

Techniques and Strategies of Social Interaction

Children use a variety of techniques and strategies to pursue goals of territoriality, influencing, and alignment. These are rudimentary patterns of social behavior that can be taught and modified. On the whole they fall into two broad groupings: aggressive behaviors and persuasive behaviors.

Aggressive behaviors

Aggressive behaviors are among the most obvious as children interact with one another. They take a number of expressive forms which are often somewhat difficult to distinguish but which are quite different in their motives and consequences. *Assertiveness:* The child who insists on turning the pages of the book during story hour, or will use only a certain paint brush, or demands to pour the juice, is behaving assertively. Because he focuses on a particular goal his actions seem self-centered, rude, and often disruptive, although his intention may not be of this nature. Because he knows what he wants, he often achieves his immediate end but to the detriment of social acceptance.
Aggression: Aggression is a familiar response to threats to one's physical and psychological space. The child who "attacks another person, or by word or deed interferes with another, or threatens by word or gesture to do so, or tries by force or spoken demands to direct another's activities or to possess another's things in opposition to the apparent desire of that person" exhibits aggressive behavior (Debus, 1953, p. 95). His intention is to put down, discomfort, or even harm another, while defending himself. Feelings of aggression are as natural to young children as are those of friendliness—and as much a part of their social behavior. It follows, therefore, that the more contacts a child makes with others, the more likelihood there is that he will behave aggressively. In dealing with children's aggression, adults frequently react in terms of their own attitudes and feelings toward this form of behavior rather than by considering the motives and needs of the child.
Hostility: The child who deliberately and knowingly seeks to harm another child by pushing him into a box and closing the lid, by giving him pins or a knife to play with, or by doing anything to rid himself of the other child in such a way that the other child is injured, is displaying hostility. The orientation

toward destruction of another and the element of deliberateness and forethought make hostility different from either assertiveness or aggression.

True hostility is not often seen in young children; their mental concentration is too transitory to harbor the hatred and vindictiveness involved. However, preschool children frequently use assertiveness and aggression to achieve their ends. These forms of behavior need to be seen as symptoms, not causes. They spring from attempts to protect space, from frustration, rejection and feelings of inadequacy and ineffectiveness—human reactions not confined to childhood.

Persuasive behaviors

There is a temptation to think of persuasive behaviors as "positive" and "good" and of aggressive behaviors as "negative" and "bad." Persuasive behavior, however, can often be as difficult to handle and as undesirable in terms of the development of social competence as many acts of aggression and assertiveness.

It is true that the most common and most effective forms of persuasion are behaviors such as smiling, hugging, laughing, cheerfulness, cooperation, politeness, and acts of friendliness. But whining, persistence, dawdling, and arguing are persuasive strategies, too, and as frequently used as the more agreeable methods, if a child finds them to be effective. An observer has only to stand beside a gum ball machine to decide which of the two techniques illustrated in Figure 10-2 children use most frequently to get gum.

The values adults put on different kinds of behavior have little to do with children's techniques and strategies. If a child is concerned with getting a piece of gum or having the first turn on a swing, or finding just the truck he needs for a garage he built, how he reaches his objective is often of little consequence to him. The means will concern him only when his goal shifts to wanting approval and acceptance *more* than immediate gratification.

Socially active children use many forms of both aggressive and persuasive behaviors in their efforts to establish individuality, develop self-esteem, and yet relate acceptably to adults and other children. The teacher who recognizes the various techniques and strategies children use can help each child learn ways that will meet his needs and help him become socially competent in long-term and immediate situations.

One of the central concerns of parents and of teachers in early educational programs is whether young children will learn to "get along with others" and develop social skills and compe-

Figure 10-2

tence. This is sometimes accompanied by a belief that a child who is not popular and socially active is not developing properly. The initial question of social interaction, then, is how much a child interacts or wants to interact with other children. As professionals we possibly place too much value upon group activities and social exchange. It is as normal for children to play alone and avoid social contact at times as it is for them to seek companionship. Beatrice de Regniers (1954) recognized this when she wrote:

But sometimes you just want everyone to leave you alone.
No children. No grownups.
You just don't want anyone to bother you.

A child who plays alone frequently is not necessarily anti-social, rejected, lonely or without resources. The teacher who recognizes this aspect of social behavior realizes that her intervention may not be needed and will wait for other signs that something is wrong before interfering.

Age and sex differences One can easily observe children's behavior without being aware of age and sex differences. Given a nursery school scene such as the one shown above, it would be interesting to note if an inexperienced observer would be able to differentiate the youngest from the oldest children. However, it is during the preschool years that the patterning of age and sex-related behavior begins to appear in more obvious forms.

A child's age affects the amount of cooperative play he engages in and how much he plays alone, watches others, or contributes to group activity. Older preschoolers not only seek the approval of others more actively, but also do more to avoid disapproval.

During the preschool years, competition increases with age. Two-year-olds show far more interest in the materials they are playing with than in what others are doing. Rivalry exists between three-year-olds, but not really at the level it reaches among those who are four or five. Studies show less frustration among older children and fewer conflicts, but the conflicts that occur last longer.

Twos and threes tend to have preferences among their playmates, but their choices usually last only a short while—perhaps no longer than a day or two, sometimes only a single morning. Older preschoolers often form strong attachments, some of these continuing into elementary school, even though each child also interacts with many other children.

The younger child's lack of motor development and muscular strength obviously limits the activities in which he engages either alone or with others. Yet his smaller size may mean his inclusion in older children's activities even though he does not initiate the contact. When a "baby" is needed for a realistic game of "house," or the firemen need a child to rescue, the two- or three-year-old may be persuaded to become a member of a group. Also, the younger child is sought out as a companion by the older child who finds it difficult to relate to children his own age.

To call a three-year-old boy a girl, or a girl a boy, is to elicit vigorous denial. By this age they know and care. However, it is not so clear how they acquired this knowledge or what their feelings are concerning their sex role and the behavior it requires of them.

Every society differentiates in some way between the sexes. Since the assigned roles often differ so greatly from society to society, many people believe that sex-role development is a purely cultural matter. Adults in Western society transmit expectations for boys.and girls in the areas such as those shown on p. 277. Not only are certain characteristics considered feminine (tenderness, emotionality, intuitiveness) and others masculine (dominance, vigor, courage), adults expect children to show these behaviors to demonstrate their sexual identity. They compare and judge children's behavior against such stereotypes, approving appropriate sex-role behaviors and either punishing or withholding approval for opposite sex-role behavior.

Areas Involving Sex-Role Expectations

Clothing styles and colors
Hair styles
Kinds of toys
Kinds of games
Roughhousing vs. decorum
Types of emotional expression

Those who hold that sex-role development is innate—that is, biological in a fundamental sense—point out that in addition to obvious anatomical differences, other apparently genetic factors probably exercise control over sex-role behavior. More males are conceived than females, but they have a higher infant mortality rate and a lower life expectancy. The bone composition of boys changes at a rate different from that of girls, and boys mature physically a year or two years later. These suggest, to some, a strong biological influence upon behavior, as well.

No firm evidence exists to show the ways that biological differences may affect the sex-roles of boys or girls or influence self-concept, although the difference in age at which sexual maturity occurs directly affects behavior patterns during the adolescent years. As far as the early years are concerned, the greater facility of girls in language and reading skills as well as their greater interest in people influence intellectual performance, social behavior, and views regarding sex-roles.

It is well-known that children tend to identify with the parent of like sex, and that as early as three they choose friends of their own sex more often than those of the opposite sex. It is not known, however, what behavior girls would consistently engage in because they are female, and what interests boys would have in the preschool setting because they are male if they were not exposed to cultural expectations. Even for twos and threes, adult expectations are already so strongly operative that the answer is obscured.

Regulating Behavior and Developing Social Competence

The process by which a child gains social competence and acquires acceptable patterns of social behavior depends not only on his energies and efforts but upon the environment provided for him by the adult world. If this physical and social environment is confining and restrictive, it may frustrate and irritate the children and induce "discipline problems," or if it is rewarding and open, it may tend to encourage less difficult forms of behavior. Since teachers control the environment of the nursery school to a great extent, it follows that they share responsibility with the child for the behavior that develops as a consequence of his interaction with them and the world they have provided.

Ways to Regulate Behavior

Every teacher has his own particular techniques for regulating classroom as well as individual behavior. Through careful planning and monitoring of activities, he attempts to anticipate problems, while knowing that the unexpected is as much a part of school life as is daily routine. (This aspect of the teacher's task is more fully described in Chapter 12.)

Children tend to do better as a group if the rules they are expected to follow are the same for everyone, and if everyone knows the rules. Therefore rules need to be specific, concrete, simple, and inclusive and part of everyday conversation—rather than an impressive list filled with exceptions and posted on a bulletin board.

Remarks such as those listed above reinforce the rule-learning of not only the children to whom they are directed, but all within hearing. They also provide needed alternatives for the "Don't Do's." As discussed earlier in this chapter, rules inform children what is "right," and preschoolers know well the approval that accompanies doing "right" things.

Just as a well planned room contributes to more orderly "traffic" and helps determine the kinds of activities that go on at

---

Conversation That Reinforces Rule-Learning

"Good for you, Lennie. You remembered to keep your trike on the pavement, didn't you?"

"Sally, I think you're forgetting you're not supposed to climb on the fence. How about climbing to the top of the jungle gym instead?"

"Marcy, I like the way you used both hands going up the ladder this time."

"I noticed everyone finished juice and crackers without getting up from his seat today."

"It's okay to run, boys, but not inside. There's plenty of space for you outside."

"Vincent, I'm really proud of the way you let Jenny work with your group in the block area today."

---

the same time, teachers can exercise control by the variety and amount of materials they put out. Plenty of paper, scissors, and paste can mean fewer arguments. Removal of a trike or other piece of equipment that inspires competition does away with a cause of fighting. Drums need not be put out every day and all records don't have to be loud and fast pieces; the number of parties and holiday occasions can be limited. By such means, perhaps unintentionally, teachers regulate the arrangement of stimuli and opportunities, and so control behavior in their classrooms.

When children behave in ways that do not contribute to the objectives the teacher has in mind, she can ask consciously, "What happened to bring this on? What can be done so there won't be a next time?" Whether desirable or undesirable, behavior doesn't take place at random or without cause. Therefore, the teacher who is alert to the situation that brought on a disruption of a peaceful scene is in a better position to regulate the behavior that goes on in his nursery school classroom.

Setting Behavioral Objectives

A child's behavior is in part the responsibility of the teacher. Surely no teacher needs to be told that unless he has a clear idea of the social behaviors he wants children to display, he isn't likely to know whether his efforts to help them develop these behaviors have been successful. The more uncertain he is in this matter the less he can be sure what needs to be done. Even though a teacher has certain goals in mind, such as those listed in Table 10-1, he must have some way of measuring the results in order to know whether he is modifying children's behavior in the desired direction.

Objectives need to be stated in terms of observable behavior; that is, they must specify exactly what behavior is expected.

Table 10-1 *Examples of goals and behavior indicating their achievement*

Goal	Behavior Indicating Achievement of Goal
Learning that something can be achieved in more than one way	Child chooses an alternative action if he is unable to solve a problem through his original means
Learning to defend interests and possessions	Child defends himself or his possessions verbally or by force if words are ineffective

Since a nursery school is concerned with the growth and development of individuals, objectives will be specified differently for each child. Rather than calling for understanding, or acceptance, or initiative, teachers need to define precisely what they want a child to do to show that he has learned what is intended. In this way the teacher can observe the degree to which a child attains the desired behavior. The objectives should concern only behaviors that are within the standards of conduct accepted by the society in which the child is being trained.

Although adults expect children to be responsive to their rules, some are reluctant to set behavioral objectives. The idea of being able to control human behavior in a positive sense somehow introduces a question of ethics. Even though these same people admit they regularly influence and are influenced by others, being in control of human behavior makes them uneasy. But knowledge and use of the techniques that most effectively guarantee learning is neither moral nor immoral. It is a matter of necessity if children are to receive the help they need to survive and succeed in a complex world of social and cultural upheaval.

Modifying Behavior

Unlike some aspects of children's growth and development, a good deal is known about ways to modify behavior. Two of the more powerful techniques are: (a) imitation and modeling, and (b) systematic reinforcement (or withdrawal of reinforcement). The first is especially significant in eliciting desired behaviors, the second in encouraging desired behavior and discouraging undesired behavior.

Imitation and modeling

Most of us would agree with the familiar saying "Actions speak louder than words." Yet it is easy to disregard its validity when involved in training young children. The research and writings of Bandura and his colleagues at Stanford University (1961, 1961a) have been particularly effective in showing how models influence the behavior of young children. Using adults in staged situations, films, and television programs, Bandura has established that children will imitate and take on the behavior that they have seen in others they respect, admire, or whose behavior has been particularly impressive. In these studies children have imitated aggressive verbal and motor behavior, particularly if they think that the actor they observed was rewarded for his behavior. These studies have given tremendous weight to the old dictum that young children are

> *Young children re-enact everyday experiences over and over as they play "house," "doctor," "store," "welfare visit," and "vacation trip." Much of their conversation and action imitates what they have seen and done themselves or observed others doing.*
>
> *Children frequently repeat the social conversation they hear, imitating both tone of voice and mannerisms as well as exact wordings.*
>
> *As they watch their three's and four's discipline a doll or stuffed toy, some parents become aware for the first time of the way they sound to their children in the same kind of situation.*

much more likely to acquire behavior that they see than to take on the behavior they are told to adopt. Teachers of young children can scarcely overestimate how much their own actions, especially aggressive and destructive behavior, are likely to be imitated.

Systematic reinforcement[2]   Since behavior is learned, it can be strengthened, extinguished, or maintained by its consequences. If a child is systematically reinforced (rewarded) for hanging up his sweater when he comes to school, the behavior will likely become habitual. If it is not reinforced, eventually the child will make no attempt to hang up his sweater. Punishing him for failing to do so will have only a temporary effect on his compliance. Since rewards (attention, approval, food, privileges) during the training of young children come from adults, adults must also train their own responses so that they remember to reinforce at appropriate times and in effective ways.

To succeed, reinforcement must be seen as rewarding by the child, and it must be timed correctly. Young children initially respond well to external material rewards such as sweets, toys, stars, and tokens, and to external social rewards like praise, affection, or special privileges. In time, through development of interest and skill, certain behaviors supply effective internal rewards, and the child's pleasure and pride are self-reinforcing.

Internal rewards are especially effective in strengthening behavior when they are occasionally reinforced with external approval of some kind. The young child who waits cheerfully for his turn on the swing should at first be rewarded each time he

---

[2] Material in this section draws from the work of Glorianne Wittes and Norma Radin, Ypsilanti Public Schools Early Education Program, Ypsilanti, Michigan, 1968.

does this, and then intermittently until the behavior becomes strong enough to be a habit. It should also be rewarded as the child does the waiting and not as a casual afterthought when he is ready to go home. In this way the child sees the reward as a consequence of his behavior.

Many teachers are faced with the combination of a "mess" and children who have no idea they are expected to clean up or how to begin. A teacher will be more successful in teaching them a new behavior if she begins by thinking of the separate tasks involved in restoring order. Then by first rewarding a child for whatever effort he makes, even if it is only to screw a lid back on a paste jar, she will be gradually preparing him to pick up the paper, put away paste, scissors, crayons, etc., and wash off the table top. Rewarding him for each level of effort eventually leads a child to keep trying until he masters the total behavior desired. The child also achieves inner satisfactions from having mastered this kind of skill and contributed to the efficient running of his school.

Behaviors are weakened and eliminated in the following ways:

1. *Providing undesirable consequences* such as ignoring the behavior (few persons persist in behaviors that do not pay off), or punishing the behavior. Punishment usually just represses behavior, creates anxiety, models aggression (in the case of physical punishment) and sets up a poor relationship between adult and child. Punishment used for quick training, such as for matters of safety, can be effective if it is administered immediately after the behavior occurs and is accompanied by an explanation.

2. *Reasoning* so that a connection can be made between the behavior and its consequences. Explanations provide the child with language that he needs for thinking about why his behavior was unacceptable. This thinking in turn helps him learn to anticipate the consequences of his act and eventually leads to the development of self-control so that he can avoid undesirable consequences.

3. *Providing alternative behaviors* means giving children knowledge of behaviors that meet with approval as well as those that don't. The child should be able to express his anger and exuberance in acceptable ways. Thus, the teacher should see that he has places to climb other than fences, objects to hammer and hit besides his classmates. She can also provide some quiet activities and areas as retreats from the more demanding kinds of interaction. Alternative behaviors

also enable him to help make decisions that meet with approval—a step toward the self-reinforcement and self-control he needs for school achievement later on.

Effective modification of behavior based on systematic reinforcement requires clear objectives, determination, and consistency on the part of the teacher. In this way children learn to expect certain consequences as a result of their behavior. By being rewarded and not rewarded for what they *do*, they also learn that it is their behavior and not their person or their feelings that bring about the desired or undesired consequences.

In helping children develop social competence, teachers do more than reward and model specific styles and skills. They also help the child learn to confront and resolve conflicts, isolation, and rejection as well as to master the social graces. True social competence involves understanding oneself and knowing how to relate to people, not merely being accepted by a group. It involves deeply private communication of interpersonal experience and, perhaps most importantly, the ability to share one's own self with others.

SUMMARY

This chapter begins with definitions of self-concept, identity, and self-esteem and a discussion of the four major sources contributing to their development. An important part of the child's social development is the ability to imagine how another person feels. There follows a discussion of role playing and its implications for the teacher. The child's social development is described in relation to social class awareness and learning rules which guide his behavior including the growth of moral judgment as a long and complex process. Patterns of social behavior may be thought of as an attempt to establish territory, to approach and influence others, and to align and cooperate with others. The final section discusses some of the principles involved in regulating behavior in the classroom.

SOME POINTS
TO REMEMBER

1. A child's knowledge about his social world and himself is learned through interaction with his social environment.
2. Self concept, identity, and self-esteem are different concepts. Self-concept is awareness of one's own characteristics; identity is awareness of group membership; self-esteem is the degree of regard an individual has for what he is and does.

3. The origins of self-concept and self-esteem are: (1) the impressions a child receives from others, (2) her own experiences, (3) her ability to live up to goals set for her, and (4) capacity to evaluate her behavior on the basis of her own standards.

4. Building self-concept is a cognitive operation not unlike the building of concepts about the physical world.

5. One unsolved issue in early education is whether teachers should build self-confidence or children in order to help them learn, or teach them skills in order to build self-confidence.

6. Self-esteem cannot be "taught" in the usual sense; it develops slowly over a period of time as a result of interaction with important other people.

7. Social communication is based to a great degree upon the ability to take the role of another.

8. The ability to take the role of another person is based upon a cluster of skills such as the comprehension that there is a perspective other than one's own.

9. The teacher can facilitate this aspect of development by asking the child to imagine, by playing games, asking him to remember how he felt when he had been treated in a particular way.

10. Around age 5, most children begin to develop an awareness of racial and socio-economic differences.

11. Children observe racial differences before they are aware of their social meaning.

12. Children acquire concepts about rules in relatively predictable sequence.

13. Young children cannot easily distinguish between the rules of adults and things that are "right" and "wrong"—breaking an adult rule is "wrong."

14. Morality involves knowledge about "right and wrong" behavior, reactions of guilt or innocence, and behaving in accordance with standards of conduct.

15. Three major dimensions of social behavior are: (1) territoriality, (2) approach and influence behavior, (3) alignment and cooperation.

16. Territoriality is the behavior which establishes and maintains geographic and psychological boundaries.

17. Approach and influence skills (or the ability to persuade others in order to get a desired response) is an essential part of the development of social competence.

18. Children may learn this kind of competence from the teacher's response to their request and by watching her techniques.

19. Alignment is collaboration between and among individuals.
20. Assertiveness, aggression and hostility differ from one another primarily in their intent and in the feelings involved.
21. During the preschool years, competition increases with age.
22. Two powerful techniques for changing children's behavior are (1) imitation and modeling, and (2) systematic reinforcement (or withdrawal of reinforcement).
23. Behavior is weakened in the following ways: (1) providing undesirable consequences, (2) reasoning, (3) providing alternative behaviors.

REFERENCES

Ardrey, R. *The territorial imperative; a personal inquiry into the animal origins of property and nations.* New York: Atheneum Publishers, 1966.

Bandura, A. and Huston, A. C. Identification as a process of incidental learning. *Journal of Abnormal and Social Psychology* 63, No. 2 (1961): 311–318.

Bandura, A., Ross, D., and Ross, S. A. Transmission of aggression through imitation of aggressive models. *Journal of Abnormal and Social Psychology* 63, No. 3 (1961a): 575–582.

Brown, R. W. *Social psychology.* New York: The Free Press, 1965.

Coopersmith, S. *The antecedents of self-esteem.* San Francisco, Calif.: W. H. Freeman and Co., 1967.

Debus, R. L. Aggressive behavior in young children. *The Forum of Education* 11 (1953): 95–105.

de Regniers, B. S. *A little house of your own.* New York: Harcourt, Brace and World, 1954.

Durkin, D. Children's concepts of justice: a comparison with the Piaget data. *Child Development* 30 (1959): 59–67.

Flavell, J. H. Role taking and communication skills in children. *Young Children* 21, No. 3 (1966): 164–177.

Hartshorne, H. and May, M. A. *Studies in the organization of character.* New York: The Macmillan Co., 1930.

Hurlock, E. B. *Child development.* 4th ed. New York: McGraw-Hill, 1964.

Kohlberg, L. The development of children's orientations toward a moral order: I. Sequence in the development of moral thought. *Vita Humanae,* 1963, Base 1.

Piaget, J. *The moral judgment of the child.* 1st American edition translated by Marjorie Gabain. Glencoe, Ill.: The Free Press, 1948.

Stevenson, H. W. Studies of racial awareness in young children. *Journal of Nursery Education* 17 (1962): 118–122.

Wittes, G. and Radin, N. *Helping your child to learn: Parent education handbook No. 1, The reinforcement approach.* Ypsilanti, Mich.: Ypsilanti Public Schools, September, 1968.

Chapter 11 Versatility of the Arts in a Preschool Program

The Place of the Arts in the Curriculum

In this chapter the term *the arts* refers to those activities that a teacher uses to help children develop and recognize inner responses to external stimuli and to express these responses in some perceptible or tangible form. In this sense, the teacher's efforts to arouse curiosity, kindle interest, stimulate imagination, stir emotion, and otherwise enhance perceptual awareness lie within the arts. Her comment about the color and design of a dress or jacket, her choice of a picture to familiarize children with the work of a famous artist, and her request, "Show me how this kind of music makes you feel," are as much a part of the arts as providing a listening corner with a record player and records, or making available paints, brushes, and paper. Each furthers the goal of the arts program—that is, it helps children become aware of their feelings and develop artistically. To the degree that producing and responding to music, rhythm, drama, and visual art are a part of the human experience, the arts have a legitimate place in programs of early education.

The widespread preoccupation in the 1960s with cognitive development of young children and with academically oriented programs resulted in a demand for curricula that would prepare children for success in school and would develop their mental abilities. In the midst of the flurry of academically related activity, those aspects of the preschool program that allowed the child freedom to engage in dramatic play, finger painting, music, and other things referred to as "the arts," lost favor with some professionals and became the target of disdain.

Other educators, however, found some of the new academic programs narrow in scope, mechanical, insensitive to the child's feelings, and overly concerned with school-related skills, which in their view were best taught later in the early elementary grades.

The debate that arose over the place of the arts in relation to systematic academic instruction forced many professionals to reexamine their programs. This controversy is still lively and is not likely to be settled soon, if at all. Educational priorities, especially at the preschool level, are usually expressions of the

Table 11-1 *Example of picture song card and description of Froebel's materials*

Play Songs	Gifts	Occupations
These were originally prepared for use by the mother but were later employed by teachers in the kindergarten when Froebel observed children spontaneously joining hands in a circle as they played and sang together. He placed chairs in a circle and engaged the children in singing games and stories using his picture song cards.	These were a series of play materials that fitted into boxes as units. They were used for creative play but primarily to encourage certain kinds of learning (development of concepts and cognitive skills). The concept of a ball was basic to the understanding of the relationship and form of a unified whole—this unity was basic to all of Froebel's work and philosophy.	Children engaged in each or all of the following activities freely, but the materials were presented in a somewhat sequential manner. Clay modeling Dot patterns Pricking cards Bead stringing Sewing cards Paper weaving Paper folding Drawing Coloring Tracing Pasting Making gardens Nature study

Picture song card reprinted with the permission of Holt, Rinehart & Winston, Inc., from *The History of Education: Socrates to Montessori*, p. 537. Copyright 1950 by Rinehart and Company, Inc.

philosophy and preference of the school staff and participating community members. It seems unlikely, therefore, that a consensus will be reached soon.

Although this is not an area in which final answers are available, it is useful for the teacher to become familiar with several disparate points of view. Such familiarity with the issues will put her in a better position to evaluate her own philosophy and to use the arts to accomplish her own purposes without need for apology.

Do the arts have a place in an up-to-date, informed, and focused program and, if they do, what emphasis should be given them? This is not a new concern. Frederick Froebel (1782–1852), founder of the "kindergarten," created materials that he called *play songs, gifts,* and *occupations.* These presented an orderly series of phenomena designed to challenge the children's abilities, stimulate mental activity and produce inner organization and integration (Table 11-1).

Many of Froebel's "occupations" can be found in today's nursery schools, but they do not always serve his educational purposes. The question of how art should be used and what aspects of the arts should be emphasized is of concern to modern day teachers.

The issue is illustrated in this informal after-school conversation in which several teachers were discussing their role as instructors in the arts program:

"Frankly, I'm confused," Miss F. announced. "Rich's mother visited today and saw him at the easel. He was painting those figures he's been doing so much of lately. You know, the kind with big heads and enormous eyes but no bodies and just long lines for arms and legs. I was clear across the room but I heard her say, 'Rich, you know better than that! That's not what people look like.' You should have seen his expression. Poor little guy—he was really crushed."

"What did you do?" Bill S. asked.

"I went over and tried to explain that it's quite natural for children to draw people this way at a certain stage, but she wasn't at all impressed. She wanted to know what he was learning from this experience."

"What did you say?"

"Oh, something vague like 'He needs to have lots of opportunities to explore with the materials in order to express himself.' This obviously didn't satisfy her. She complained that we should at least point out to him that people have bodies."

"That's a fairly common complaint," Miss L. remarked. "I've been here five years and I remember how helpless I felt the first time one of the parents confronted me with 'Just what do you teach the children in this school?!'"

"I think Rich's mom is unhappy with us because she can't see the value of an exploratory kind of art activity. I know she is anxious to have him learn to read and write and doesn't want him to 'waste his time' here," commented Bill S.

"I don't want him to waste his time here either," interjected Mrs. A., "but I happen to believe that painting and other art activities are not a waste of time."

"I agree," said Miss L., "but we haven't convinced Rich's mother, and I really think we're doing her a disservice if we ignore her concerns and treat her as if she didn't know anything."

"Look," Miss F. said. "I have to admit that I often wonder just what the kids are getting out of their experiences, especially when they're splattering paint around in the art area and jingling bells like crazy in the music room."

"What's all this got to do with teaching art?" Bill S. insisted.

"We have to be more clear about our own goals and the ways in which we achieve them," said Mrs. A. "I think the reason we feel threatened by people like Rich's mother is because we aren't sure about what we are doing."

This kind of shop talk is fairly common among teachers of young children and represents some of the problems that concern them. The comments of Rich's mother also represent attitudes of some parents who see school achievement and the "3 R's" as essential to success. Unless they are used to develop cognitive abilities, art and art activities have little or no place in a curriculum that is intended to help their child prepare for more formal schooling. The early years ought to be spent on the apparently more important skills such as learning letters and numbers. In this view, children are expected to achieve at a faster than normal rate through a highly selective, structured, and teacher-directed curriculum. The arts are a luxury.

The teachers in this vignette seem more representative of the view that the curriculum should incorporate activities that develop the whole child, with the arts being as important as the cognitively oriented tasks. Art, along with social activities, should be spontaneous and expressive and children should be involved in each of them in their own individual ways.

These two viewpoints are apparently contradictory and perhaps cannot be reconciled completely even though, as is discussed later in this chapter, art activities can be used to serve *both* cognitive and artistic goals. In planning a program the staff must decide whether activities oriented toward artistic experience and expression are to be given a place in the curriculum and if so, what it will be. If they include art activities they have an additional decision to make about how structured and purposeful they will be in teaching artistic abilities and responses.

The academic aspects of preschool curricula have been given priority in the recent past; perhaps the arts will soon come into their own. If so, it will be because teachers and other professionals take them seriously, place explicit value upon them, and use them as well as other activities to develop aesthetic and humanistic dimensions of human capability.

The Purposes of an Arts Program

Some teachers may think of the arts as independent, specific activities. Painting is done at a particular time in the paint corner; the product is to be taken home and prized. During the Christmas season, handprints in plaster of paris may be taken home as gifts. The dittoed turkey page is an art activity used to teach about Thanksgiving. At music time, children may be given rhythm band instruments to beat in time with a record. Art, to these teachers, is material bound, constrained to predefined acts, areas, and even times. The end of the specific activity is the end of the art lesson or experience. To other teachers, an art experience is where one finds it. It may be in the design of frost on the window, the pattern of a foot or hand in the sandbox, the rhythm of a swing. Many experiences may contribute to increase the child's awareness of his feelings and to stimulate his inner responses to the external world. No part of the curriculum is excluded from the arts.

The distinction between the arts as a cluster of pre-selected activities and the arts as *any* activity that accomplishes a particular goal of artistic response or expression is an important one.

It means that the teacher selects and plans tasks not because they are done in other nursery schools, nor because they are ends in themselves, but because they are oriented to the effects she wants to achieve. This emphasis on effects and goals rather than on activities themselves frees a teacher to be more flexible in utilizing the many resources, both planned and spontaneous, at her command.

As an example, imagine a visit to two different nursery schools, both of which use play dough as one of their art activities. Ask the teachers why they have play dough. One will say it is an easy activity to supervise; the children like it and play quietly with it for long periods of time.

The other teacher will agree, but in addition will say that the child learns about texture, consistency, color, and shape from play dough. She helps to create these experiences by having the children help her mix the play dough in different consistencies, textures, and colors. She also makes it a point to ask questions as the children are manipulating the dough, and she helps them to talk about their discoveries.

The scenes in both schools may look alike to an observer, but the expected outcomes of such experiences will be different. The distinction between the casual orientation toward the arts (where the teacher provides an activity because it keeps the children content or is an interesting thing for them to do or because other schools do it) and one in which the teacher uses an activity—any activity—because she has some desired goals in mind, is that in the latter case the teacher will have a clearer idea of what she hopes to achieve and just how she plans to achieve it. This does not detract from the pleasure the children will have, or inhibit their spontaneity in play. Nor does it suggest that one teacher is necessarily warmer or more child-oriented than the other or that one teacher intervenes or manipulates the child in such a way that he is deprived of spontaneous exploration.

It does mean, however, that one teacher has a more complex, wider range of goals and purposes in mind. She senses, in even the daily routine, more possibilities for developing the child's capabilities. It means that she preplans and selects activities that will entice children to make discoveries related to the outcomes she has in mind. It also means that she is sensitive to the child's reactions, and that she responds or questions at appropriate times. The outcome of an activity is more predictable and less likely to be left to chance or come as a lucky surprise to the teacher who knows what she wants and how she intends to achieve it.

The intent of this chapter is to consider some of the ways a teacher may utilize the arts to achieve her goals; it is not intended as an enumeration of the activities themselves. There are many sources for "recipes" and specific tasks, including the handbook of curriculum activities prepared as a supplement to this text. Those described here are selected to illustrate how a teacher may choose tasks to accomplish specific objectives.

A versatile and imaginative teacher will probably use art activities in several different ways. First, she may use them in pursuit of art-oriented goals, i.e., to develop responses to artistic objects and events and to provide experience and training for artistic expression and judgment. Second, teachers may utilize art activities to achieve goals unrelated to art, such as the teaching of cognitive, school-related concepts and skills. Third, the teacher may see art activities as vehicles for humanistic experiences and use them to allow children an opportunity to experience the immediate gratification and release they offer, or to soothe, or to stimulate. Fourth, in some instances and perhaps in desperation, a teacher may use art activities to keep children busy, to occupy time, and in other ways to help regulate the activities and tone of the group.

This chapter, then, is oriented toward the issues and purposes that are involved in the use of the arts in a preschool program. The teacher must eventually decide for herself what her own philosophy will be. Once she has established her goals, she can utilize a variety of techniques and activities to achieve them and can also use the same activities for other purposes.

The staff who wants to give the arts an important place in its program will find that there is a diversity of thought as to how the arts can best be implemented. Here again, the teacher faces two different, almost inconsistent, points of view. In one school, the parents and administrators may feel that the child's artistic ability develops best on its own in a free environment. This assumes to some extent that the ability is inborn and will, at an early age, develop naturally. The teacher's responsibility is to facilitate the child's efforts; he should be allowed to express himself freely without the imposition of adult standards or direct teaching. This approach sees art as a behavior that can best be developed through providing the child many opportunities for direct interaction with his environment.

Another orientation toward the use of art materials suggests that perceptual skills are more fully trained with instruction than without, and that this training can be effective even with quite young children. The teacher provides specific experiences and directly teaches certain aspects of the arts such as relationships and patterns, and how to begin to use form, line, color, and texture. It is argued that some types of instruction are more helpful than others in promoting children's artistic development.

Every teacher needs to consider what she expects to accomplish within a given framework of instructional philosophy. The following description of interaction between a four-year-old and his teacher is an example of what can happen when a teacher either has no specific objectives in mind, or fails to think of ways to achieve those she *has* formulated.

INTERACTION	TEACHER'S THOUGHTS
(Robert stands at an easel, a paint brush in each hand, vigorously stroking heavy, vertical lines on his paper.)	
Robert *Look, teacher, look what I'm doing!*	
Teacher *Mmmmm—you're using both hands, aren't you?*	*I wonder if it's all right to let him paint that way. Maybe he should have only one brush.*
Teacher *Robert, why don't you use just one brush?*	*If I can't stop him he'll make an awful mess. How can I get him to stop?*
Robert *I don't want to.*	
(Robert keeps on dipping and slapping.)	
Teacher *But you're making such a mess.*	*That's not what I should say, but how can I get him to stop?*

Robert *I like making a mess, it's fun.*

Maybe I should just let him paint the way he wants to. He really isn't doing any harm. How can I make this a learning situation? Maybe I should talk about circles, or thick and thin lines.

(Robert switches to painting large, drippy circles accompanying each stroke with a loud ZOOM-ZOOM.)

Teacher *I see you're making circles.*

What do I do now?

(As though he hadn't heard, Robert continues to apply paint in rhythm to his ZOOM-ZOOM.)

Teacher *Are you finished now, Robert?*

Thank goodness the paint's almost all gone.

(Without answering, Robert drops his brushes and runs off to play.)

What a relief to have him stop. I don't think I handled this situation in the best way.

Fortunately, this teacher had a supervisor with whom she could talk about the incident. From their discussion and her own reflection she realized:

1. Her feeling of inadequacy was based on the fact that she had no objectives in mind for Robert—only her own desire to have him stop.
2. She had no understanding of Robert's behavior. Why was he painting that way? Why couldn't she control him?

When the supervisor asked her to restate the objectives that had vaguely come to mind, and then to list what she might have done to achieve them, the teacher prepared the following summary:

POSSIBLE OBJECTIVES	POSSIBLE WAYS TO ACHIEVE OBJECTIVES
Robert should be allowed to paint without being made to feel guilty.	Encouragement *Sometimes it's fun to make a mess, isn't it?* *It's okay to do that but you'll need to keep the paint on the paper.*
Robert should have opportunities for being "messy."	Presentation of attractive alternative. *I'll bet you'd like using finger paints even better, Robert. Let's go see.*

Robert should develop concepts about shapes.	Calling attention to and reinforcing specifics *That's great, Robert—you just made some circles. Now, make another circle for me.* *Good work! Now I'd like you to make a square—two lines the same length side by side but with space between them—and two lines to join the ends.*
	Using questions
Robert should be helped to acquire art techniques.	*(Pointing) First you drew a _____?* *And then you drew a _____?* *Now, tell me, which one is made with straight lines?* *What do we call the shape you drew using a curved line with the ends joined together?*
	Modeling *Robert, show me if you can hold your brush like this.* *Let's see what a line looks like when you hold a brush this way. What do you think a line will look like if you turn your brush this way? Let's try it and see.*
	Questioning *Can you think of another way you can make a line? Are both lines the same? Which one is thicker?* *Draw another thick line.* *Draw another thin line.* *What did you do to make one line thicker than the other?*

As the teacher and her supervisor went over the list, they discussed each of the objectives from the standpoint of Robert's needs. With knowledge of what would most contribute to his development, the teacher's choices became clear. By the time she completed her analysis she realized that having in mind what she wanted for Robert would have helped her use the art activity more effectively.

Ideally, a teacher at any moment in the day should be able to see a stop-action, instant replay of her work and be able to identify what she is doing and for what purpose in any area. Her purpose might be general or specific—that is, she could have in mind smoother, less noisy transitions from one activity to the next as an intent, or "getting Marita" to use more than one color as a specific objective. Knowing what she is trying to do alleviates feelings of helplessness, makes decisions easier, and provides a way to assess her effectiveness in the use of the arts.

Until a teacher has time to observe the children in her class, she cannot plan for individual needs. She can consider the overall goals of the program in which she is working, however, and gradually prepare objectives for individuals within the framework of those goals. Overall approaches for developing competence in the arts may include the four categories listed on p. 297.

Developing Awareness of Inner Responses to External Stimuli

For all their curiosity and activity, many children have never really looked up at the sky or down at the earth long enough to become aware of what they are seeing or to realize their response to these experiences. They have never run their hands over a stainless steel surface nor touched the bristles of a brush. They haven't thought about the sensations they experience when they put their feet in cool mud or warm sand. Some have smelled their mother's perfume and their father's shaving lotion but may not know the odors of paper, paste, leather, wood, fruit, or flowers. They hear noise but have never listened to silence.

Even when they have done such things, experience alone is not enough. Teachers can help them recognize and talk about how these experiences make them feel and become aware of their responses. Children need to know, too, that their responses are important, and that inner feelings can be expressed in many, many ways.

By nature children are curious and eager for knowledge. To help them develop an awareness of their inner responses the teacher should start simply and be willing to take time. No script is necessary, but some general strategies are useful. The teacher may make use of familiar experiences and events and then get the child to focus on some aspect of the experience he may not have noticed before. She may ask him if he can see a face or an animal shape in a cloud, or tell him to put his head back and look at the sky while he is swinging. This first strategy is to get the child to experience sensual stimuli aesthetically and in a new way. A follow-up of this is to ask the child how events or experiences make him feel or whether he likes something he has observed and why. This "How-does-that-make-you-feel?" approach has many variations and can be used in many different situations.

Another strategy is to reinforce a child's expression of response to art experiences and to make it clear that such responses are appropriate, welcomed, and rewarded.

The following is an example of how a teacher might help a young child develop awareness of inner feelings.[1]

Goal
To develop awareness of internal response to external stimuli

Objective
To get Opal to express in some overt way that she realizes there is a difference in the way two everyday objects feel to the touch

Miss P. watched three-year-old Opal tentatively run a pudgy finger along the edge of a hardwood block. The child picked up another and did the same thing. Then she spread her hand and rubbed it across the top surface of the block as one brushes crumbs from a table. Leaving Opal for a moment, Miss P. went to get a piece of rough bark, slightly curved and not as thick as the block, but about the same size. She put it in the deep pocket of her smock.

When she returned she sat on the floor beside Opal and said, "I like the way you're playing, Opal. What does it feel like when you rub your hand across the top of a block?"

Opal smiled but did not answer.

Miss P. picked up a matching block and held it out. "Rub your hand across the top of this block, Opal."

Opal willingly followed her teacher's instruction.

"Do both of them make you feel the same way when you rub them?"

Opal smiled but did not answer.

Miss P. began swishing her hand like a metronome across the floor. Happily Opal joined in this new game. Swish-swish.

"Does it feel the same when you rub your hand across the floor as it does when you rub your hand across the top of a block?"

Opal answered by rubbing first the block and then the floor but she said nothing. Instead she began stacking pairs of blocks. Every so often she took time to rub one with her hand.

Miss P. watched. Waited. Slowly she took the bark from her pocket and placed it on the floor between them. Opal reached over, picked up the bark, and rubbed her hand across the top. She frowned and rubbed it again. She gave her teacher the bark and picked up a block.

"Do they feel the same, Opal?"

Opal shook her head, her eyes puzzled. "No," she said.

"You're right, Opal. They feel different. The block is SMOOTH. The

---
[1] For further ideas see Croft and Hess, *An Activities Handbook for Teachers of Young Children* (2nd ed.) Boston, Mass.: Houghton Mifflin, 1975.

bark is ROUGH. I'm glad you noticed they were different. Here, feel them again. This block is smooth. The bark is rough."

Opal looked, but put her hands behind her back and said nothing. Miss P. smiled. Then she got up. As she rose she gave Opal an affectionate pat. "Good girl," she said, and walked away. A start had been made; it was all that was needed for now. There would be time enough to engage Opal's interest in the different properties and kinds of wood and bark, in having her find out where bark came from and in getting her to make other comparisons later on. But for now she felt she had made the right start by gaining Opal's confidence and waiting until she was willing to express her response to the way two different objects felt.

Objectives for Developing the Child's Awareness of Inner Responses to External Stimuli

1. *Examining the qualities of objects, both natural and manmade*
2. *Using more than one modality to investigate properties of objects*
3. *Developing sensitivity to more subtle differences in each of the five senses*
4. *Learning to notice shapes, colors, textures of natural objects such as flowers, leaves, etc.*
5. *Seeing and thinking of objects from different perspectives (above, below, inside, outside, etc.)*
6. *Sharing the child's responses to artistic stimuli and interesting features of the environment*

Development of tactile discrimination between "smooth" and "rough" may seem far removed from the arts in the traditional sense. But from such simple beginnings, from a stirring of interest and a conscious realization of differences, come other responses with new experiences. Once children are aware that they have responses, then through music, painting, and other art forms they can be helped to find ways to express their inner feelings and the thoughts that accompany them. Using the arts is not just a matter of putting a crayon in a child's hand and saying "Draw a picture," or asking children to clap time to music. The arts are a resource for helping children to develop sensitivity and competence in aesthetic activities.

In the next scene, a teacher uses a wider range of experience and technique to help a boy learn to express his reaction to certain kinds of music.

Jack, a sturdy five-year-old, sat listening to loud music with a pronounced beat. After the third playing of his record, Mrs. N. joined him.

Goal

*To develop awareness of internal
response to external stimuli*

Objective

*To get Jack to express freely his response
to feelings engendered by music, either
by body movement or in words, or both*

"You like that record, don't you, Jack?"

"Yeah," Jack answered, ready to drop the needle for a fourth time.

"How does the music make you feel?"

"I like it."

"Does it make you want to do anything?"

"I don't know."

"Does it make you want to get up and march or dance or anything?"

"I don't think so. I just like it."

During the conversation Mrs. N. had sorted through several other records and found one she knew had low tones and a slow rhythm. She handed it to Jack. "Here, play this one. I'd like to listen to it with you."

"Okay." But halfway through the music, Jack stopped the machine. "I like the other one better," he explained. "I'm going to play mine again."

"All right," Mrs. N. agreed. "But tell me, do the two records make you feel the same?"

"I guess so. No. I don't know."

"Look, Jack, let's play the one you like and you show me how it makes you feel. Move around any way you want to."

Mrs. N. could tell from Jack's expression that he wasn't just sure he wanted to follow the suggestion. She smiled and asked David to join them. "David, we're going to play Jack's record and I'm hoping he'll show me how it makes him feel. Will you do that, too?"

David liked the idea. With the first note or two he began to shuffle his feet, wriggle his hips and soon was slapping his thighs calling out, "Man, man!" Clearly David recognized his feelings and found them easy to express.

Jack watched David for a moment and then began to move about. His motions were awkward but the beat caught him up, too, and by the end of the record his response was almost as vigorous as David's. He grinned happily.

"That was fine, boys. Just fine. I could certainly see how happy this kind of music makes you feel. Now I want to play the other record and you show me how that makes you feel." Sensing Jack's hesitancy, she added, "Here, Jack, you put it on for us."

This time several measures went by before either boy responded. David was again first. His shoulders drooped, his head fell forward and slowly he let himself down to the floor where he lay sprawled like a rag doll. Jack watched and imitated. But when both were lying down, it was Jack who got to his knees and began to rock back and forth in time to the slow music. The sounds stopped before he did.

Mrs. N. made no comment. She sat quietly waiting. Jack straightened up and came over to her. "I liked the record better this time," he said.

Mrs. N. put her arm around him. "How did it make you feel, Jack?"

The boy hesitated, uncertain, uncertain not of his response but of the teacher's. "It was like being in a rocking chair," he said.

Jack's interest in music enabled his teacher to make him aware of his inner response and to encourage him to express how he felt through body movement. In this instance, the arts also included David's response and the teacher's affective behavior. By having in mind what she wanted to do, the teacher was able to take advantage of a combination of resources in order to achieve her objective.

Inner responses to art need not be treated as though they were separate from thought. In fact, a teacher can often help children to feel and think about an object at the same time. The following is an example:

Goal
To develop awareness of internal response to external stimuli

Objective:
To have child use thought and feeling at the same time

Miss B. was standing next to Jerry when she saw him stoop to pick up a leaf. "What a beautiful leaf, Jerry," she commented.

Jerry held his leaf at arm's length, twisting and turning it as though it were a gigantic butterfly whose red and yellow wings flashed in the sun.

"How does it make you feel when you see a leaf like that?" she asked.

"I like to look at it. I think it's pretty."

"I do too, Jerry. What do you suppose makes it so pretty?"

Jerry looked at the leaf, turning it over and back again, but didn't say anything.

"It's the kind we call a maple leaf, Jerry. What do you notice that makes it different from leaves on that tree over there?"

"It's red and yellow."

"What's different about that?"

Jerry grinned. This was a game he'd played with the teacher before. She knew, but she wanted him to tell her. "You can see that the leaves on the tree are green," he said.

"That's right, Jerry. They have a different color." She stopped and picked up a dry leaf and held it next to Jerry's. "Which of the leaves has brighter colors? Yours or mine?"

"Mine."

"Which leaf is bigger?"

"Mine."

"How do you think the outside edge of your leaf feels?"

Jerry's finger slowly explored the outline of the leaf. "It's bumpy," he said.

"I agree. It's bumpy," his teacher said. "Is the leaf round?"

"No."

"Is it square?"

"No. It has points."

"Hmmmm. Points. How many?"

"One-two-three-four-five."

"That's right, Jerry. We've noticed a good many things about your leaf, haven't we? It has bright colors. Its edges are _____; and there are five _____. Was it a big leaf compared to this one of mine?"

"Yep," Jerry said and ran off for a turn on the swing.

From the thoughts adults express in their interaction with children, the child learns ways to think about and communicate his experiences. He can be shown meanings and be helped to develop concepts. This won't happen all at once, of course. It will be a result of many opportunities for the child to consider his inner responses and to think about the information his senses bring. The information he receives through sensory experience acquires additional meaning from interpretation by adults. For this reason it is important for the teacher to use every opportunity to help a child realize he can both respond and think about his responses at the same time. Providing children with many experiences is important, but unless they are also helped to identify and interpret these experiences, their learning may be limited.

Developing Children's Competence in the Arts

For many children, preschool is their first introduction to a wide variety of materials and equipment. As with anything new and strange, this experience can be puzzling as well as pleasurable. Because they don't know how paint acts, how music is created, or what will happen if they leap, some children are slow to explore and learn to use what is available to them. Some also hesitate to move around and try things until adults assure them that what they are doing meets with approval. Gradually, however, on their own initiative or by watching others, and with suggestions from the teacher, most children begin to experiment with paints, respond to rhythms, try out the hammer and saw, and use other available materials.

Having plenty of materials is desirable, but simply providing an impressive assortment is not enough. Some publicly funded programs have had money to buy adequate or even fancy equipment, but sometimes much of it was not used or was misused— books torn and thrown around, records damaged, blocks splintered, etc.

Competence in the arts comes through guidance by the teacher, who makes suggestions and gives instructions at appropriate times. Equally important is the fact that she provides the child with plenty of time to learn about the properties and uses of materials.

Teaching a child about consistency of materials, for example, is much more meaningful than giving him thick and thin paint with appropriate labels. If developing competence in making something thick or thin is the desired effect, the child must first have many opportunities to experience and explore qualities of thickness and thinness, such as mixing dirt with water to make mud, stirring a thick batter for muffins or a thin batter for crepes, mixing water and flour and oil for thick play dough, or beating cream to make butter.

Teaching competence in the arts does not mean allowing completely free, undirected "messing around," nor does it mean following formal, organized units of instruction. The teacher must combine appropriately selected materials, guidance, and plenty of time and opportunity for the child to satisfy his curiosity.

A teacher using shapes of faces on a flannel board can give children an opportunity to learn to use lines to indicate feelings; a line curved downward for the mouth and eyes to express sadness, or curved upward for a smile. Artists often use lines to communicate feelings. The soft curved dark lines and three-dimensional effect of Rubens' "Head of a Negro" are used effectively to draw attention to the sad facial features of the subject. Miro creates humorous effects through designs that use straight bright colored lines and dots to represent eyes, nose and mouth. (See pp. 316–320 on aesthetic sensitivity.)

A seemingly simple skill such as learning how to use a hand punch to make holes in paper can be highly satisfying to a child. Learning how to use scissors to cut in the direction he wants to cut adds to his feeling of competence. A child who knows not only the names of the colors and what color he wants to use, but also how to mix a new color with what he has, possesses a great degree of competence. The teacher might suggest that he mix and stir the primary colors at the easel; or she might choose to give him food colors and test tubes of water and eye droppers with which to experiment under her guidance. His ability to mix colors and create new ones gives him added skills, satisfaction in his own accomplishments, more alternatives for choices, and control over what he wants to express through the arts.

Development of skills aimed at achieving a desired effect can be begun in preschool through manipulation and conscious selection of materials. These skills need not be achieved at the expense of the child's freedom to explore. A perceptive teacher is cognizant of the child's need to learn through physical interaction with his environment.

Some recent research in art education for young children indicates that children's perceptual abilities are enhanced when they are motivated to look for components of an artistic creation such as color, line, texture, and form. Grossman (1970, pp. 421–427) reports on a 1967 study by Douglas and Schwartz in which professionally made ceramic pieces were used to illustrate some basic ideas to a group of four-year-olds. Four of the basic ideas were:

1. Art is a means of non-verbal communication.
2. The art product is the result of the artist's idea.
3. The artist uses what he sees, thinks, and feels to create art.
4. There is a great variety of materials available to the contemporary artist.

The children were able to understand these ideas and used them to interpret their own as well as other works of art.

On the basis of studies by Wachowiak and Ramsay (1965, pp. 25–27) and research by Torrance (1963, pp. 110–117), Grossman (pp. 425–426) suggests that "an effective way of developing young children's artistic expressive abilities is to provide them with real and immediate objects or experiences, and teach them to explore these objects or experiences through all their senses."

Teachers adapt their styles to the type of activity in which they are working. In one school that served predominantly minority children, the teacher complained that even though the playhouse area was well stocked with a large variety of dress-ups, dolls and puppets, etc. for dramatic play, a small group of children played "cops" all day, arresting other children and putting them in jail. She wondered how she might help them achieve more competence and skill even in this area by giving them a less simplistic view of this role.

She invited a policeman to visit. He arrived in a patrol car, let the children take turns getting in and listening to the two-way radio; he let the children wear his badge and hat and gave them a book of tickets similar to the real tickets he had to write. He also told them about the reports he had to fill in and the routine calls he made during the day. After his visit, the children's dramatic play took on new dimensions. They began to incorporate the ideas provided by the policeman's visit. The teacher had helped them gain greater "skill" and competence in dramatic play through additional information about how to portray a single role.

A teacher with five years of experience describes her first attempt to help children learn to use woodworking tools:

"When I first started teaching nursery school, I remember being assigned to supervise the carpentry table. I had no idea what to expect. I got the children to help me push the wood box and tools out and before I knew what had happened, someone ran to the sandbox with a saw and a couple of other children had started hammering on the cement and trikes.

"I was really frightened. I ran after everyone, grabbed the tools from them and put everything away. I went home that night and decided I couldn't avoid potentially dangerous situations like that. I thought a lot about just what the carpentry activity is for, how I can best help the children participate in this activity and how I can help them gain competence in the use of the carpentry materials.

"I learned from experience that I had to start simply. The rules for safety had to be clear for the children and me. For example, I brought out the wood box and suggested that children select a piece of wood first, then I let them select a tool—(sometimes I left the saws in the shed until I was sure the children knew how to use a hammer first). I used to let them bang around on the wood and try to get the nail in as best they could (or I would just end up doing it for them).

"I noticed many of the children, especially those who had never had any experience with carpentry before, would take a whack at the wood, fool around with a saw and leave the table; others would get frustrated and complain or wait for help. I gradually began to give more specific supervision. That is, I would hold my hands over the hands of a child and gently guide his movements while he was hammering or sawing. I would help him get the feel of the activity. I tell the children to keep their eyes on the nail when they are hammering and show them how they can remove a nail.

"I remember one little boy who was particularly frustrated one day because he wanted to 'build a barn' by nailing a piece of wood onto the narrow edge of another piece. The wood kept slipping and he couldn't get the nail started while holding the two pieces of wood together with his other hand. I showed him how he could start the nail in one piece of wood and hammer it in until it went through and then nail it onto the other piece, which he could attach to a vise. He was so excited when he discovered he could indeed achieve his goal with his newly acquired skills that he went around for days offering to teach the other children how to 'make a barn.' I find that children are more likely to stay with a project and experiment more readily if they feel competent with the tools and materials they have at hand."

Objectives for Developing Competence in the Arts

1. *Learning to communicate internal responses graphically (paintings, drawings, etc.) and physically (dance, movement, music)*
2. *Beginning to be aware of differences of color, line, form, texture and how they are used to create different effects*
3. *Learning to use a variety of tools and equipment and recognize their properties and purposes*
4. *Acquiring specific skills in music such as responding to rhythm, keeping time, recognizing harmony, tone, etc.*
5. *Learning how to mix materials to produce new creations (mixing paints to achieve a new color, cooking, etc.)*
6. *Developing skills in use of materials to facilitate expression of feelings and ideas*

As children experiment with materials, the teacher can guide their natural interest and responses in a sequence of activities designed to extend their range of experience and stimulate growth in particular areas.

In the area of music, for example, she might help them learn to listen, to sing, to play simple instruments (tambourine, drum, wood blocks, bells, etc.) and to respond to different kinds of music through body movement. Following is an example of some specific goals in music:

GOAL	ACTIVITY
Melody	Identify several songs or themes by name
	Indicate by difference in body response that one melody is different from another (high, low, gay, sad, etc.)
	Compose own melodies and sing or play them
Harmony	Signal chord changes they recognize while listening
	Tell whether a piece consists of only a melody or melody plus chord accompaniment
Tone	Identify various instruments by name as they are played
	Tell whether one or more than one instrument is playing
	Recognize loudness and softness in music by clapping or stamping feet in similar volume
Rhythm	Clap, beat time, rock body to different tempos
	Mark out musical accent with hand or foot movement
	Create own rhythm patterns with instruments or clapping
	Draw attention to rhythmic sounds heard in the environment and identify source (clock tick, raindrops, traffic hum, typewriter . . .)
Form	Signal awareness of a repetition of melody or rhythm pattern

Musical goals are only partially accomplished by having groups of children listen, sing, and move about for fifteen or twenty minutes each day. They are also achieved by surrounding the children with a great deal of music and encouraging active response through humming, singing, dancing, and moving to sounds. Having a variety of instruments available to play, touch, and ask questions about also helps greatly.

Most of the activities of a school can become an expression of the art curriculum and can be used to serve artistic goals. For example, a group of students assigned to visit six different schools were asked to list in order of preference which schools they would like to attend if they were four years old. One student's description of the school that was the unanimous choice of all the students suggests some of the ways an imaginative staff can exploit the versatility of the school's resources.

The main room of this school was no larger than the others we had visited, but somehow it seemed more spacious and cheerful. Low shelves were neatly arranged and activities were all equally inviting so that small groups of four to six children were congregated in different parts of the room.

In one area I noticed the children helping themselves to paper and collage materials from the low shelves that were clearly labeled with pictures of the items, such as scissors, paste, crayons, etc. The children didn't have to read in order to know where things went. The easels were designed so the children could remove their own paintings and hang them over a large drying rack without help from an adult. Some of the older children were showing the younger ones how to pour more paint from the supply shelves. Examples of the children's art work were displayed at the child's eye level.

In another part of the room two children were working at a small sink, measuring flour and water into a large plastic container. Posted above the sink at their eye level was a "picture recipe" for play dough illustrating the number of cups of flour and water, and the number of spoons of salt and powdered paint to use in mixing the dough. The children worked cooperatively without any adult supervision.

Adjacent to this area was a long low table where several children were shelling peanuts, grinding them, and making peanut butter to spread on crackers. A teacher was helping two of the children count the number of crackers needed for snack time.

I shut my eyes and listened to the sounds in the room, just as I had done at the other schools. The level of noise felt comfortable to me: muted voices coming from various parts of the room interspersed with occasional laughter, disagreement, or a plea for assistance. I was struck by the fact that adult voices in this school did not dominate the sounds, nor were there any extremes in the children's voices—shouting, screaming, crying. This school was neither too loud nor too quiet.

During a large group activity one of the adult volunteers projected some slide pictures on the wall while the teacher played some recordings, including Ravel's "Bolero" as well as The Beatles' "Hard Day's Night." Each child whose painting or art project was shown created a dance for the group. It was a most impressive experience with the lights turned off, the large projection of a colorful painting and a child's silhouetted dance movements superimposed on his creation. The teacher made comments like "Jamie's painting has lots of movement to it, just the way he's dancing." "How does your painting make you feel, Rodney?" "Quiet," was the reply. "Can you do a quiet dance to show how your painting makes you feel?" "I can," volunteered Janey. "O.K.

Rodney, would you and Janey both like to do a quiet dance?" Both children create a slow, gentle dance using graceful movements while the rest of the group watch intently. "I like the way you stretch your arms, Rodney. Just like they're attached to a big rubber band. Janey looks like she's slowly tossing a huge balloon up in the air and stretching on her tippy toes to catch it." When the session was over, the children rushed off to the art areas to make something for the next time.

The staff in this school spend many hours planning activities that encourage imagination and independence and that allow the children freedom to explore and to express their feelings in constructive ways. The arts in such a curriculum become a natural part of the child's total environment.

It is important for the teacher to know that many aspects of children's artistic responses are based on developmental patterns. Children's expression through the arts follows specific steps that are correlated with growth and development as well as experience. The work of Rhoda Kellogg in the field of children's art has focused attention on these developmental patterns. Her analysis shows that children everywhere scribble before they draw, and draw outline shapes before they reach a representational stage. Even at this level the child draws not from the way things are, but from the way he sees objects and events, or would like to, and concentrates only on what is important to him. In this light children's art can be understood for what it is—spontaneous creation.

Piaget's studies provide information as to why children produce art in the forms they do. He found, for example, that during the sensory motor stage, children explore objects systematically, especially by sight and touch. From this visual and tactile perception they acquire initial knowledge of geometric forms and space relationships. Although a child does not draw before the age of two, and may not create shapes meaningful to adults before four or five, it is from perceptual learning during his early years that the child eventually produces representational images.

The ability to represent what he has perceived through his senses comes during later stages of development. A brief summary of Piaget's findings regarding children's ability to draw during the first two substages is given in Table 11-2. It is during the preoperational substage that children

. . . make drawings of men by attaching four lines to an irregular circle, and sometimes they put other circles inside a large one to represent eyes and other facial features. But, when the child attempts a

Table 11-2 *Summary of Piaget's findings regarding children's ability to draw during the first two substages of the concrete operations period*

Preoperational Substage (2 to 4 years)	Intuitive Thought Substage (4 to 7 years)
Up to 3 can only scribble.	From 4 to 5 begins to make straight lines, squares, triangles, houses, tables, in his drawings. Figures have little thoughtful organization.
Between 3 and 4 can indicate open and closed form figures in unorganized attempts at symbolic representation. Makes irregular circles and shapes that enclose other shapes but not straight lines.	From 6 to 7 begins to coordinate mental image of the world. Understands topological relationships of human figure.
	Spatial relationships of single objects well developed. House will be on a baseline next to other houses, people and trees, yet separate. Proportions are likely to differ from reality and child does not use perspective.

Adapted from Kenneth M. Lansing, "The Research of Jean Piaget and Its Implications for Art Education in the Elementary School," *Studies in Art Education* (Publication of the National Art Education Association) 7, No. 2 (1966): pp. 35–38.

complicated human being at this stage, it is clear that his concepts of topological relationships are not *fully* developed, because he may place the mouth over the nose or draw the ears detached from the body. Although his visual concept of proximity, separation, and enclosure is fairly well formed, his mental image of order and continuity is still poor. Thus, he cannot retain in his mind the correct sequence of mouth and nose along a vertical axis, nor can he imagine a man wearing a hat to be a continuous unit. Consequently, he draws the hat above the figure but not on it (Lansing, 1966, pp. 35–38).

Adults frequently urge children to copy rather than to express their own responses and ideas. However well-intentioned, an adult saying, "No, dear, you don't have it right. You didn't make the tail long enough. Here, I'll show you," is almost certain to be ineffective in producing a change in a child's work. He may dutifully copy and try to do as he is told, but Piaget's findings show that a child's work in art is not improved by criticism of his visual symbols. During his early development the most effective way to change his work is to help him build additional concepts. In working on aesthetic development, the teacher's goals must be limited because young children can acquire only concepts that deal with actual objects and events. They are less capable of forming concepts of abstracts such as beauty, joy, courage, or pride. However, Piaget's work and that of others suggests that children can be provided with activities that will increase perceptual knowledge and so add to artistic development.

The Development of Pictorial Form

If left to develop on their own, with no formal teaching, children show growth in the portrayal of form from simple to increasingly complex patterns.

1. *Children's first drawings may be thought of as* recorded gestures. *As a child makes visible signs of his hand, arm, and even body movements, parents and teachers will first observe random rotations, sometimes called* scribbles. *Soon zig-zags will fill spaces, then circles close and shapes appear.*

2. *The child discovers the lines and shapes he makes and his control over them. He produces endless quantities of* undifferentiated shape, *mostly circular forms, the simplest possible shape. These shapes are undifferentiated in that they stand for any form at all.*

3. *Children add shape to shape, producing* constructed shape, *a combination of constant elements. Simple directional relationships are built. Forms become more elaborate. Still, the shapes are not so much representation as presentation.*

Adapted from R. Arnheim, *Art and visual perception* (Berkeley: University of California Press, 1967) p. 174.

    The ideal sequence corresponds only roughly to what happens with a specific child. Different children cling to different phases for different lengths of time. Phases overlap. An older child's highly developed drawing may be followed by a scribble. Differentiation in size, color, and dimension develop in a manner similar to the development of form in children's art.

Dramatic Play

In many countries perhaps the most common form of self-expression engaged in by young children is that of dramatic play. Between the ages of three and five children are still in the process of becoming social creatures. They are learning to interact with other human beings. They are finding their own individuality. Dramatic play and other forms of pretending permit children to recreate for themselves what they see all around them. By *trying on* a role, they learn through vicarious experience about themselves and their reactions.

The child of three participates in simple imaginative play. He or she may put a dolly to bed, cover it, kiss it goodnight saying "Night, night," or "Baby, go to bed." By four the imaginative aspects are more detailed and complex but they remain within the same framework. Dolls are now fed, elaborately talked to, and nurtured. Conversations such as the following are not uncommon: "Now you have to eat all your food and then take a bath and go to bed before Daddy comes home. Tomorrow we will take you on a nice trip and if you're good you'll see Grandma and she'll give you some cookies." Fours may work out aggressions and hostilities through spanking, scolding, and even throwing around the dolls they so carefully tend at other times.

At five, make-believe of this kind often involves other children and long processes of "pretend." Typically, several children gather in the housekeeping corner making plans for complex imaginative play involving daddies, mothers, uncles, siblings, and friends. All are an extension of the child's real world. Cul-

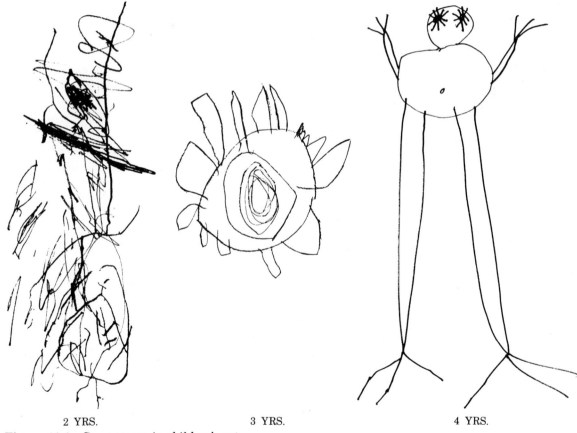

2 YRS.   3 YRS.   4 YRS.

Figure 11-1 *Some stages in children's art*

tural differences are evident in children's imaginative play at this level. Those who see policemen as nonthreatening agents of society create helping roles for them in the scheme of their play. Other children pretend to hide from the "fuzz" and act out being put in jail by "cops" who have caught them. Imaginative play affords children an opportunity to relate to one another and to develop ideas as to how others think and feel. Children learn from one another through the enactments of typical situations.

Children often deal with problems of emotional development by creating imaginary playmates. Three-year-olds who need companionship they are not finding elsewhere, who need someone to look up to, to dominate, or to do things for or with, often create imaginary playmates. By four, many of these needs are closely bound to everyday occurrences in the life of the child. The creature he imagines goes through all the familiar routines with him and has equal rights and needs.

Four- and five-year-olds frequently use imaginary people and animals to play out fears and desires that are unacceptable in real life. Beating a doll is permissible, beating one's baby sister is not, no matter what the provocation. Antisocial talk meets little opposition when you are a Badman, whereas a boy or girl is scolded for the same behavior. By five, most imaginative play is closely tied to the world of reality, with children endlessly re-enacting the events of their daily lives or pretending to be familiar figures, such as family members, firemen, grocers, and nurses.

Although little formal study has been made of preschoolers' dramatic play except in the field of therapy, one cannot observe children of three to five very long without realizing that such activity is central to both group and individual behavior. In all its forms, dramatic play is a means by which children come to understand their environment and the people in it. Acting out feelings and impressions externalizes emotions, as does participation in art and music activities. Dramatic play helps children to distinguish between reality and fantasy, and to come to terms with both. It serves as yet another means of socializing the child and teaching her to find her place in the world.

Dramatic play takes quite different forms in different cultures and in dissimilar political systems. In some countries, China, for example, children are taught the values of the nation through skits, plays, songs and dances. These are, in a sense, forms of dramatic play but they are designed to socialize the young child toward national goals. In the U.S. individual expressions of fantasy through play are more typical. However, even in individual play one sees the process of socialization.

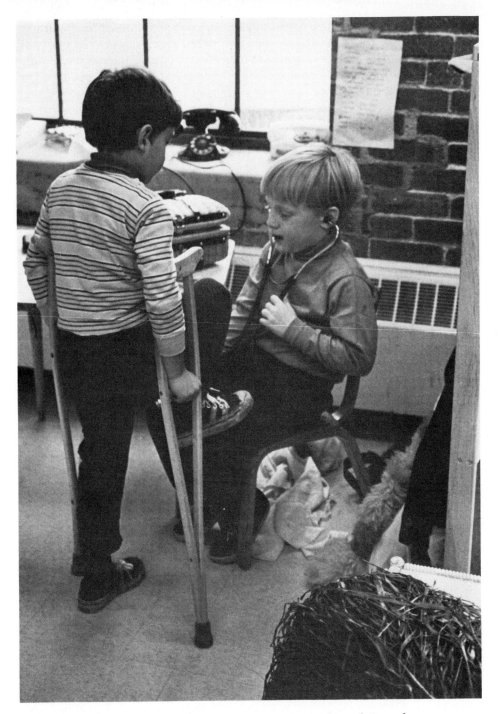

Figure 11-2 *Dramatic play helps children to express themselves and relate to their environment.*

The Arts as Development of Artistic Capabilities

Young children act out characters they see on the mass media (Kung Fu as well as Sesame Street). This type of play, which has a powerful appeal to children, is one of the most effective techniques of socialization at the disposal of adults working with the young.

Developing Awareness of
Cultural Heritage

Every human society has used the arts to express the hopes and aspirations of its people and to record historic events. The walls of cave dwellers carry a pictorial history of the prowess of their hunters. Trajan's column in Rome tells the story of his military conquests. The temples of Greece reflect a people's love for beauty combined with their worship of many gods. Great works of music reflect people's joy and sorrow, their fear and longing during particular periods of time. They reveal how humans perceive their world. To the knowing ear, a Gregorian chant has as much to say as an English madrigal, an Italian aria, or a modern country ballad. Children are capable of recognizing the differences in these various forms even though they cannot define them.

Jazz music covers more than just one style. It is more than just popular music, though jazz is popular music. It is a distinctive art form that owes much of its popularity to the way it can communicate the human emotions we all understand, and to the way it appeals to a basic love of rhythm which seems instinctive in most humans.

From Charles Boeckman, *Cool, hot, and blue* (Washington, D.C.: Robert B. Luce, Inc., 1968), p. 4.

Even very young children can be given some idea of the forms of art that are the particular products of their culture. American children have an especially rich heritage to draw from since their culture includes music, dance, and art from the various ethnic groups who settled the country. In addition to this unique heritage, America has native art and music forms that children should know about. They need to hear and learn to distinguish jazz, soul music, Indian chants, cowboy songs, and modern rock music as well as melodies of the classical composers. The work of American artists should become a part of the child's experience, for it has a great deal to tell her about herself and the world she lives in. Artists such as Grant Wood,

Winslow Homer, Frederic Remington, Mary Cassatt and Andrew Wyeth speak to children as well as to adults.

This is not to suggest that a picture or piece of sculpture should be displayed and the class asked to join in a group discussion about it. Nor that a classroom needs to be turned into an art gallery of Americana. But a teacher bringing in one example at a time on a rotating basis and making a point of engaging children in casual conversation about certain details that are characteristic of the artist, telling a little bit about where the artist lives and when and how he happened to draw the picture, can begin to build a foundation of cultural knowledge. And the teacher should always ask, "What do you see? What do you think this artist has tried to tell you?"

In introducing music and music listening, the teacher need not limit himself to records that are presumably prepared for young children. Using pieces that form a part of children's culture—a well-known aria, folk song, or march—are as likely to elicit responses and at the same time build artistic knowledge. A teacher's choices in such matters are not difficult if he has in mind what he is trying to do.

There is no need to wait until children are old enough to take art appreciation before introducing them to art forms that have won recognition in the adult world. No special time of day or week needs to be set aside for this exposure. Children can be as constantly surrounded by art and music as they are by blocks and swings and sand boxes.

Identification of works of art and music and the names of famous artists and composers is a useful goal in itself. When one picture or piece of music can be recognized as separate from all others, art takes on a new meaning. To give a child the opportunity to be aware of the artistic products of her society and to become acquainted with great art and artists, is to give her access to a wider area of human experience. The teacher will have time to use only a little of the vast amount of material available to him; his most difficult task will be to choose exactly what he wants to do and to confine himself to the resources that will be effective for his purpose. A child's recognition that she is part of a particular society, and her resultant interest in learning more about the people in that society, and thus of herself, can begin with a teacher's choices. A teacher's choices are determined in part by the values of his own society and his desire to pass along these values to the children in his class. These values—moral, religious, patriotic, social—are embodied in the arts as well as other parts of the curriculum.

Objectives for Developing Awareness of Cultural Heritage

1. *Learning to look at details in a variety of art forms*
2. *Learning about artists, musicians, sculptors, etc., as occupational roles*
3. *Beginning to understand how artists contribute to a culture*
4. *Becoming familiar with some of the social, cultural rituals, celebrations and historical records through works of art (weaving stories into rugs, folk songs and folk tales and their origin, painting, carvings, etc.)*
5. *Learning that adults and children have been producing art for a long time*

Developing Aesthetic Sensitivity and Discrimination

Helping a child experience and become aware of inner responses and getting him to develop preferences are first steps toward the ability to recognize the variety of patterns, forms, color, etc., in his experience. By careful planning and skillful questioning, together with a genuine interest in the child's answers, a teacher can guide a child's initial discriminations. These discriminations form the basis for later responses to a variety of aesthetic experiences.

For example, a teacher's skillful questions about contrasting pictures can teach a child to notice that some pictures are brighter than others; some have people in them, others do not; in one the lines may be mostly straight, in another predominantly curved; some pictures may have many details, others almost none. The teacher will know he has observed the differences and is beginning to make judgments by his answers to questions such as the following:

1. How many colors do you see? Do the colors in this picture make you feel the same as the colors in that picture? Which colors do you like best? How do they make you feel?
2. What do you think the artist is trying to tell you? What does he want you to know about the people (animals, flowers, buildings, etc.) in his picture?
3. Are the people in the different pictures drawn the same way? What are some of the differences? Do they have the same kinds of hands? Of eyes? What are the differences? How are they the same?

At first the child's discriminations may not be very fine, but gradually, after repeated exposure and chances for comparison, he will know that a Van Gogh is not the same as a Rembrandt, nor a Modigliani the same as a Miró. He will also be able to tell which one he prefers though it may take many experiences and conversations with his teacher before this happens. A traveling *gallery* of art reproductions prepared by one school district[2] consists of portraits of children and of adults, along with suggestions for helping children develop artistic awareness and judgment. Some of the objectives suggested are listed below:

OBJECTIVES	COMMENTARY
To encourage acceptance of the unfamiliar and unusual	When we look at children we see that they do not always look the same
To develop awareness and sensitivity to feelings reflected in the face	If you are sad your face will look a certain way. (Have children demonstrate and examine expression in paintings) What makes you feel that way?
	If you are feeling especially happy your face might look quite different. (Have children demonstrate and consider expressions in paintings)

Adults as Subjects

American Gothic	*Grant Wood, American*
Puppet Show Woman	*O. Masara, Japanese*
Head of a Negro	*Rubens, Belgian*
The Postman Roulin	*Van Gogh, Dutch*
Señora Sabrosa García	*Goya, Spanish*
People and Dog in the Sun	*Miró, Spanish*

Children as Subjects

Girl with a Broom	*Rembrandt, Dutch*
Portrait of a Boy	*C. Soutine, Russian*
Girl with a Watering Can	*Renoir, French*
Don Emanuel Osorio de Zúñiga	*Goya, Spanish*
Girl with Braids	*Modigliani, Italian*
Head of a Young Boy	*Rouault, French*

[2] Information used by permission of the Palo Alto Unified School District, Palo Alto, California.

Figure 11-3 *Development of aesthetic judgment begins with exposure to a variety of art forms.*

Before they saw the portraits the teachers helped children realize that people perceive the same objects differently, in different settings. For example, it was suggested that teachers have children look at one another in a darkened room and then with bright light; that they look at objects close up and then from a distance; that the size of a person or object be considered relative to various larger and smaller objects nearby. Young children can develop preferences concerning works of art. The two groups of portraits described on this page were displayed in a nursery school where children could see them at any time. At various moments individual children were brought to see them. After talking informally with each child about the first group and then the second, and attracting his attention to various likenesses and differences, the teacher asked:

1. Do you like the pictures?
2. What do you like about them?
3. What don't you like?
4. Which picture do you like best?

All of the children were able to form an opinion; the older children, however, were more unanimous in their preferences than the younger. The choices made were as follows:

Selection	Younger Children (17) (3's and 4's)	Older Children (28) (4's and 5's)
Adult portrait most liked	Miró (7)	Van Gogh (16)
Child portrait most liked	Renoir (7)	Renoir (14)

A child can develop aesthetic responses to things other than recognized works of art. The qualities to which he responds in a Van Gogh or a Renoir exist all around him. An arrangement of flowers, designs on book covers, patterns of sunlight and shadow, the curve of a staircase, can all be viewed and talked about from the standpoint of their effect on the viewer. Asking, "How do they make you feel?" and "Which do you like better," and then accepting the child's answers frees him from fear of being wrong or ridiculed. Children can be helped to see details of color, line, texture, and form in their surroundings as well as in pictures. They can be asked about their artistic preferences and can gradually build judgments on what they like and dislike and why.

Objectives for Developing Sensitivity and Discrimination

1. *Understanding that people respond in personal (unique) ways to the arts*
2. *Becoming familiar with a variety of art forms and growing in acceptance of different modes of expression*
3. *Becoming aware of, identifying, and responding to some of the specific characteristics that comprise a work of art or expression (color, line, texture, brush strokes, etc., of paintings; timbre, pitch, melody, tempo, etc., of music; gestures, manner, tone of voice, subject matter, etc., of stories; movement, mood, gestures, etc., of dance)*
4. *Beginning to articulate and justify judgments with some specificity*

From his response to music a child will show he has learned to recognize not only that there is a difference between the Beatles and Bach, but also between "Skip to My Lou" and "The Blue-Tail Fly." Even quite young children move about very differently to different tempos and rhythms. Once a child demonstrates his realization that not all music is the same, he can be expected to answer questions such as:

1. What do you like about it?
2. Which piece goes faster?
3. Which one is louder?
4. How does it make you feel?

Helping a child recognize differences in his responses to various stimuli, and asking him to consider whether he likes or dislikes something and why, encourages his making simple judgments about himself and his world. It will be some time before he is able to form an objective evaluation about whether the art he sees or the music he hears is good or bad. But this is not expected of him at the preschool level since he has not had enough experience to permit judgment of this kind.

Relationship of the Arts to Cognitive, Affective, and Social Development

A well-planned arts program brings children in contact with a wide variety of materials and sensory experiences. What the child gets from these experiences is not haphazard; it is up to the teacher to decide how to utilize them in keeping with her educational goals. In some instances she will have in mind the child's artistic development, emphasizing different features and aspects of the arts themselves. In other instances, she may arrange the experience so that it relates to cognitive or affective and social development of the child. At such times the particular form of art she chooses as a resource will be incidental to her objective. She may, of course, wish to keep in mind both purposes at once. On the whole, however, she will tend to emphasize one more than the other during a single instance of instruction.

Teachers as Labelers

The arts offer teachers a wide range of vocabulary to share with children. There are all the terms peculiar to the activities involved—the names of the activities themselves, colors, shapes, instruments, materials, tools, methods, and techniques. In addition, she has many ways to describe what is being done. For example, children need not just put objects together. Materials can be made to fit, match, adhere, hold, cleave, cling, or stick to one another. These joinings can be accomplished by using string, nails, pins, dowels, thongs, rubber bands, cement, glue, solder, adhesive, scotch tape, and staples as well as paste.

For example, suppose the teacher has decided that a particular child needs help in building concepts about shapes. He likes to draw and often works at the easel. The teacher can help him label and observe the various properties of the shapes that he is drawing, or she may ask him to consider squares, triangles, and circles that are apparent in other pictures. She may or may not at the same time seek to interest him in color, brush technique, or the characteristics of an artist's work.

Contribution of the Arts to Cognitive Growth

There are various ways in which the teacher can use the arts to encourage cognitive development. She can use the arts to increase vocabulary, to give the child many new opportunities for gaining physical and logical knowledge. She can help him realize he may both affectively respond to something and think about it at the same time.

Increasing vocabulary and developing concepts

When interacting with children, the teacher provides many labels to help them increase their vocabulary and to make it possible for them to reflect upon and communicate their experiences. The following remarks are typical of the kind teachers make in order to point out similarities and differences and to increase vocabulary:

1. I see you're using a *wide brush* today, Laura.
2. What *bright tempera colors* you chose to paint your picture with, Charles.
3. Do you want me to help you move that *heavy easel*, John?
4. That's certainly *lively* music, isn't it?

A child doesn't have to know he's using a wide *brush* filled with *bright tempera color* in order to paint a picture on a piece of paper that's mounted on an *easel*. Nor does he need to be told that music is *lively* before he will start hopping or dancing to its rhythm. However, by labeling, the teacher makes it possible for children to acquire the vocabulary which helps them sort, organize, classify, and keep track of the vast amounts of information they accumulate as they participate in art activities. The vocabulary she provides also aids in the gradual development of a store of concepts by which children order new experiences.

Gaining physical and logical knowledge

The child's approach to painting and clay modeling, to using musical instruments and record players, to the props for dramatic play—in short, to any of the materials provided in the arts program—is initially one of investigation, not expression. The description above summarizes the way in which children typically acquire physical knowledge from their experiences with an art form.

Gaining Physical Knowledge from Clay

If you hand a young child a piece of clay, it will be a long while before he makes a pot or figure with it that you will recognize if this is his first experience with clay.

He will explore its properties. That clay will be rolled, squeezed, slapped, smelled, and perhaps tasted. He will pull it, drop it, throw it, take tiny pieces from it and then put it all back together again.

Once satisfied as to how clay feels and what he can do with it, he may use it to make "balls" or "cakes" or perhaps simply roll out an endless supply of rope-like pieces for which he has no use. He is unlikely to seek labels for what he does or to talk about his activities.

Later, he may use clay to represent objects, though what he depicts may or may not be recognizable to anyone else. Only after many experiences of this kind is he ready to create something of his own choosing.

Children derive a great deal of physical knowledge from the materials that are part of an arts program in a nursery school;

the arts lend themselves to the acquisition of logical knowledge. Many drawings involve shape and space relationships; music and finger games bring understanding of counting, adding, subtracting and seriation; dramatic play encourages categorizing and transfer; and, as mentioned earlier, all of the arts help children acquire labels and develop concepts about in-on-under-around-over, fast-slow, loud-soft, happy-sad, up-down, etc.

Miriam Stecher (1970, p. 148) reports the following example as one of the ways she and her associates have used free movement as a means for children's acquisition of logical knowledge:

The kindergarten was exploring the concept of *lightness* and *looseness* through movement experience with tension and relaxation.

Teacher *Hug yourself very hard. Harder. That's very tight. Let go! That's not tight at all now, is it?*
Katy *It's loose.*
Teacher *Do it with your hands. Can you make a fist like this? Make it so tight that I can't open it. (She tried to pry open Peter's fist.)*
Pete *It's like a knot in my shoelace.*
Tony *B-o-i-i-n-g. (He fell down and remained there limp.)*
Teacher *What's that?*
Tony *The knot busted.*

Both teacher and children were delighted with the image and together proceeded to develop it, first with isolated parts of the body, then the whole body, and finally tying up with a partner. At a signal (a glissando on the piano) all shouted "Boiing!" then, falling suddenly, they lay quietly and limply loose. Later, when the teacher wished them to relax again after vigorous galloping, she asked them to lie down and "be loose like a busted shoelace."

Questions for Encouraging Physical Activity

1. *Can you walk quickly?*
2. *Can you walk less (more) quickly than that?*
3. *Can you walk quietly?*
4. *Can you walk less (more) quietly than that?*
5. *How would you walk to show you're happy? (angry, frightened, sad, tired, in a hurry, afraid of getting wet in the rain, being blown by the wind?)*
6. *Are there ways to move without moving your feet? Show me.*

Relationship of the Arts
to Affective and Social
Development

The nursery school has traditionally emphasized the affective and social development of children, with the arts considered as one means for achieving this purpose. The use of music, art, drama, and other artistic activities is often initiated by individual children with development left to their own imaginations. Thus, the use of the arts is frequently unsystematic even though there may be an established daily routine. As more is known about the value of a more structured approach to furthering affective and social development, hopefully the arts will assume the place of importance that is rightfully theirs in programs of early education.

*Physical and emotional
release*

The arts provide many opportunities for children to release energy, and teachers make use of them for this purpose. It is natural for a child to want to wriggle and jump and run and climb and move about. Children can be encouraged to march, skip, clap, and dance to music; to beat and stomp to the sound of drums, to recreate the gait of animals in dramatic play, to manipulate clay and other modeling materials freely, and to draw and finger paint with broad movements.

In addition they can release physical drives by experimenting with the use of balance beams, obstacle courses, hula hoops, ladders, climbing ropes, and other playground equipment. When appropriate to the child's interest, the teacher might ask questions such as those listed on page 323. From these and many other experiences involving movement, children can become more and more aware of themselves as human beings with bodies that can be controlled and used the way they wish. Through physical experiences they develop skills that lead to self-confidence and ways of expressing themselves through movement.

The arts also provide channels for emotional release. Young children are not always aware of their emotions, do not always know why they cry, strike out at others, are restless or feel good-enough-to-burst at times. Few have the ability to recognize feelings of these kinds or the verbal skills to express them in words. But they do have emotions. Yet almost from infancy pressure is often placed on children to conceal their emotions, especially those expressed loudly or accompanied by tears. Adults are intolerant of what they consider too much noise, and unable to control their own reactions to the sight and sound of crying.

Thus children repeatedly hear instructions such as "Be quiet," "Don't cry," "He won't hurt you" or "You don't have to worry." As can be noted, sometimes he is even told not to have an emotion. Yet how should he respond to experiences such as confrontation with a large animal, being left alone in the dark, or having to stay with strangers?

The child's affective development needs to include opportunity for him to recognize and express feelings. Psychologist Arthur T. Jersild of Columbia University states:

If an older person wishes to understand a child's emotions and to help him cope with the conditions that arouse emotion, it is necessary to encourage the child to face feelings rather than to falsify them or run away from them. But to do this requires courage on the adult's part, the courage to permit the child to allow his feelings to show and the courage to face feelings that are aroused within himself when the emotions of someone else appear in raw form (Jersild, 1968, p. 312).

It is clear that the arts give children a means to express emotion outwardly. An angry child who paints a picture and covers it with masses of dark color, or stomps his feet as he marches to music, is often finding a way to vent his frustration. But he is not engaging in art experiences or artistic expression and development. Realizing that emotions can be released and expressed through the arts, the teacher needs to be careful not to misinterpret behavior. Masses of dark paint do not always signify hate and anger; some children simply like these colors; others use them liberally to represent rain or night. A child who stamps his feet and clenches his fists as he marches may be imagining himself a giant, not reacting to hurt or disappointment. It is up to the teacher to be sure she knows the difference before she decides whether to help a child control his emotions or provide encouragement to further his artistic development.

Social experiences

In discussing music as a universal language, Florence Foster said:

Music has an integrating power on the individual and the group. The withdrawn child tends to relax his guard and is more ready to participate with the others, while the hostile child seems to be less aggressive, so that each is helped to become a contributing member of the group.

Here is one task in which all can cooperate to produce something mutually pleasing (Foster, 1965, p. 375).

Singing and listening to music, participating in finger games, acting out "The Wheels of the Bus Go Round and Round" or some other action song, and playing in a rhythm band are often the first, and for some time the only, group activities in which young children join. Until three or four they engage in most experiences, including those of the arts, as individuals, or with an older person.

Gradually, however, the arts provide many opportunities for interaction. Talking about stories or poems and pictures, dramatic play (even though some children act out their role alone and say nothing), a construction project, and planning and making decorations for a "party," lend themselves to a good deal of conversation and social experience.

Not all children in a preschool are ready for group experiences, and the teacher will help decide which part of the arts program best meets the child's social needs. Using the child's experiences as a medium for her own interaction with him may be all that is required. In time he can be encouraged to make more and more contacts through interest in the arts and through the universal appeal of music.

By her understanding of their potential, the teacher can use the arts as a means to further children's total development. However, to use them most effectively she must have goals in mind and know the needs of individual children. Her responsibility in the arts program is both to impart knowledge and to further children's response to the world about them. Rather than seeking to make children into artists, musicians, or craftsmen, she should strive to help them develop as social beings with capacity to observe, to respond, to communicate and to learn to experience the world aesthetically.

SUMMARY   The arts and their appropriate place in the program involve a question of whether such humanistic activities should have priority over more school-related cognitive elements of the curriculum. Also considered is whether for a preschool child art activities should be seen as spontaneous expressions of inner feelings or include skills which should be taught systematically. Goals of an art program can include both, and art can be used to

11 Versatility of the Arts in a Preschool Program

promote cognitive development. Suggestions are offered for using such activities as music, creative movement, and describing well-known paintings to develop inner responses to external stimuli, awareness of cultural heritage and more specific competence in art. Art activities can be related directly to cognitive, affective, and social development.

SOME POINTS
TO REMEMBER

1. The purpose of teaching the arts is to help children recognize and express inner responses to external stimuli.
2. Frederick Froebel, founder of the kindergarten, used the arts as a basis for his curriculum almost two hundred years ago.
3. There are two major issues which divide many professionals with respect to the use of the arts: (1) whether the arts are as important as cognitively oriented tasks, (2) and what the specific goals of an art program should be.
4. Five common goals of an art program are (1) to develop responses to artistic objects, (2) to provide experience and training for artistic expression, (3) to use art as an aid in teaching school-related concepts and skills, (4) as vehicles for humanistic experiences, and for fun, and (5) to keep the children occupied.
5. There's evidence that training promotes artistic capabilities, even in young children.
6. An art program offers the opportunity to develop an awareness of cultural heritages.
7. Young children can begin to develop artistic judgment and standards even at the preschool level.
8. Competence in the arts for very young children can be developed in such specific ways as learning about differences in color, texture, acquiring specific skills in music and movement, etc.
9. Children's artistic ability follows a developmental pattern.
10. Through dramatic play young children learn about their social environment.
11. Because dramatic play is so appealing to children adults can use it as a powerful socializing technique.
12. Using the arts to aid in concept development is essentially a matter of pointing out or emphasizing cognitive features—color, shape, rhythm, etc.

REFERENCES   Arnheim, R. *Art and visual perception*. Berkeley, Ca.: University of
                California Press, 1967.

                Boeckman, C. *Cool, hot, and blue*. Washington, D.C.: Robert B. Luce,
                Inc., 1968.

                Carson, R. L. *The sense of wonder*. New York: Harper and Row, 1965.

                Cole, L. *A history of education: Socrates to Montessori*. New York:
                Rinehart and Co., Inc., 1955.

                Croft, D. J. and Hess, R. D. *An activities handbook for teachers of young
                children* (2nd ed.) Boston, Mass.: Houghton Mifflin Co., 1975.

                Douglas, N. K. and Schwartz, J. B. Increasing awareness of art ideas of
                young children through guided experiences with ceramics. *Studies
                in Art Education* 8, No. 2 (1967): 2–9.

                Foster, F. P. The song within: music and the disadvantaged preschool
                child. *Young Children* 20, September 1965.

                Grossman, M. Art education for the young child. *Review of Educa-
                tional Research* 40, No. 3 (June 1970): 421–427.

                Hartley, R., Frank, L. K., and Goldenson, R. M. *Understanding chil-
                dren's play*. New York: Columbia University Press, 1952.

                Hess-Behrens, B. *The development of the concept of space as observed in
                children's drawings: a cross-national/cross-cultural study*. Wash-
                ington, D.C.: U.S. Department of Health, Education, and Welfare,
                Office of Education, National Center for Educational Research and
                Development. May 25, 1973. (Final Report, Project No. RO
                2-0611, Grant No. OEG-0-72-4524.)

                Jersild, A. T. *Child psychology*. 6th ed. Englewood Cliffs, N.J.:
                Prentice-Hall, Inc., 1968.

                Kellogg, R. *Analyzing children's art*. Palo Alto, Ca.: National Press
                Books, 1969.

                Lansing, K. M. The research of Jean Piaget and its implications for art
                education in the elementary school. *Studies in Art Education* 7,
                No. 2 (1966): 33–42.

                Lewis, H. P., ed., *Child art: the beginnings of self-affirmation*. Berkeley,
                Ca.: Diablo Press, 1966.

                Stecher, M. B. Concept learning through movement improvisation: the
                teacher's role as catalyst. *Young Children* 25, 148, January 1970.

                Torrance, E. P. *Education and the creative potential*. Minneapolis,
                Minn.: University of Minnesota Press, 1963.

                Wachowiak, F. and Ramsay, T. *Emphasis: art*. Scranton, Pa.: Interna-
                tional Textbook, 1965.

Chapter 12 Crisis in the Preschool

Crisis Doesn't Mean Failure
Inevitability of Crisis

Janet Fong had been an assistant teacher for almost six months. Today she was assigned to supervise outdoor activities, one of her favorite duties. She moved leisurely about the playground, stopping to admire Sally's sand cake, then over to the swings to push Kevin. Even though he might not rise high enough to see "rivers and trees and cattle and all," at least with a little help he'd be able to glimpse that busy part of the world which lay just over the fence of the Lincoln Street Nursery School.

Between Kevin's regular ups-and-downs she caught sight of the new boy maneuvering a wagon under the jungle gym to use as a mounting block. Giving Kevin a final push, she started over to move the wagon

Figure 12-1 *Stress is part of the daily routine.*

and explain the rule of "nothing under the jungle gym," noting as she went how quickly the child had climbed to the top. But she was too late; even as she approached him the boy failed to gain a handhold, and tumbled to the ground.

An outstretched arm slapped against the wagon with such force that Janet never understood how the fall resulted only in a bad bruise. As she hastened to help him, the stunned child struggled to his feet and began to scream. Anxious to reassure him without alarming others, Janet gently but firmly lifted him into her arms and carried him to the office. The crisis was not over, but at least the situation was under control.

Crisis and stress are part of the routine of a preschool as surely as they are part of the life of a family with young children. No matter how experienced and competent a teacher may be, or how carefully she plans and works, she will frequently have to deal with crisis and may herself occasionally be its cause.

Several features of the preschool make it virtually inevitable that such tension will be a normal, though unplanned, element in the schedule. First, for both educational and developmental reasons, the child obviously needs an environment in which he can freely explore and manipulate a variety of materials. Given such opportunity, he often shows remarkable ingenuity for arranging things in ways that physically endanger himself and/or others. In addition, situations arising from coincidence, equipment breaking, falls, and other accidents, mean that children will be hurt despite all precautions. A second potential source for crisis at the preschool level is illness. Illness presents a physical hazard not only for the child directly affected, but also for others who are exposed to infectious or communicable diseases.

The responsibility of the teacher to be custodian of young children, both on school grounds and during trips or outings, is a third source of potential crisis. It is particularly critical because it is bound to legal liability. Other potential sources of crisis include psychological and social pressures arising from value differences between teacher and parents and emotional problems that parents or children bring to the school from family interaction. Of course, there is always the possibility of personal difficulties and staff tensions. Individually or collectively, these potential sources of trouble are not entirely avoidable. The only certain way to avoid crisis in a preschool is to close the school.

The teacher who is experienced and prepared sees these situations as a natural part of her job. Since they pose specific threats to her, she obviously has an interest in learning how to deal with them, in knowing what the possible consequences will be, and in learning how they can be avoided. She has a legal responsibility and will feel severe psychological distress if a child is hurt or not properly taken care of and she is at fault, especially if she faces court action. She also has an investment in her reputation as a teacher, which affects both her own self-esteem and her career.

The teacher's primary interest, of course, is the care and education of the children for whom she is responsible. In order to meet her responsibilities, she will orient herself toward crisis by familiarizing herself with the major types of critical incidents that can arise and learning how to avoid or minimize crisis and deal with its effects.

Difficulties in Identifying Crisis Situations

Crisis is not an "all or nothing" matter. Stressful situations and events range in severity from the obvious one of severe physical injury, through subtle signs of a child's or parent's inner turmoil, fear, or depression; in addition there are the normal stresses of social interaction and socialization. While we may think of crisis generally as something that interrupts the routine of the school and demands some attention, a comprehensive definition of crisis is probably not possible.

Some elements can, of course, be identified. There is an element of threat to someone or something; there is usually some urgency for immediate action to keep conditions from getting worse; and there are likely to be other, more serious consequences if no action is taken. The teacher is the judge of the seriousness of the circumstances; her competence and effectiveness as a professional are reflected in her ability to deal with the unexpected and difficult.

The task of evaluating the seriousness of a situation is complicated by the fact that the symptoms of distress—crying, hysteria, accusations, threats, pleas for help, and complaints of various kinds—do not always mean there is a crisis and, conversely, a crisis may exist without these cues. While these indicate that something is wrong, they do not clearly signal a crisis or reveal the nature or extent of the problem. A crying child may be one who is frightened by a fall; a child who acts subdued after a tumble may be more seriously hurt. Noise and emotion may easily distract the teacher from her task of assessing a situation accurately. A mother who gets upset when a child throws sand in the sandbox can create the impression that (a) the child is the only one creating the problem and (b) the problem and danger are severe. Actually, it is also the mother who creates the stress by making an unnecessary emotional fuss, threatening or accusing a child, and overestimating the physical dangers involved. The experienced teacher recognizes that the mother is herself part of the problem and avoids turning against the child as a way to deal with the minor uproar.

The analysis of crisis takes into account the different interests of those involved and the fact that they see the problem and its seriousness from their own perspective. To a degree, this implies that particular events present crises to the child, others to the parents, still others to the teachers, staff, and administrators of a preschool. All involved recognize and share concern about the difficulties that others have, but initial reactions most often reflect their individual viewpoint. The lists on pp. 337, 338, and 340 present some common crises as seen from differing points of view.

Although the teacher cannot entirely avoid defining a particular crisis in terms of who will be affected by it, her role is to assess a situation both from the viewpoint of the child and other participants. Her action, however, is based necessarily on her responsibility to the child, even though this may mean that she gives a parent, aide, or volunteer less attention and support than they feel they deserve. In addition, she has the task of keeping her own response from contributing to the crisis.

Analyzing Crises   A preschool is a complex organization and many different kinds of crises can occur. General questions or guidelines may be useful in sizing up a crisis or potential problem. Suppose, for example, a group of mothers hears that a school plans to bus in children from a minority neighborhood and they let the teacher know that they oppose this change in policy. What threat, if

12 Crisis in the Preschool

any, does this represent to the teacher? To the school? Will the consequences of the new policy be severe or minimal in economic or other terms? Are there obvious solutions to decrease community resistance? What are the consequences for all the children involved? How soon must a decision be made? It may be useful to apply these analytical questions, which are summarized in the list below, to several hypothetical situations. As you study each situation, consider whether it is a genuine crisis and how it should be assessed in light of the checklist of questions.

Situation one

Leon strides boldly to the sandbox where Jeff is busy digging a "tunnel." Grabbing Jeff's shovel from him he raises the tool threateningly, stomps on the tunnel and loudly orders "Move over, stupid, so I can build a battlefield."

A teacher quickly walks over to the boys and puts her hand on the shovel saying, "Give it back, Leon. Jeff had it first. You'll have to wait your turn."

Rather than doing as he has been told, Leon snatches the shovel from the teacher, very nearly striking another child in the eye as he does so. "Get away from me," he shouts. "You're not gonna boss me." To emphasize his remark he spits at her, then runs away, shovel in hand.

Checklist for Dimensions of Crisis

1. *Who or what is threatened? The child? The teacher? The parent? The school?*
2. *How severe are the consequences likely to be for each one involved?*
3. *How obvious is the solution (or solutions)?*
4. *How urgent is it that a decision be reached?*

Situation two

It is almost the end of nap time in a small, private nursery school. The owner has not returned from a series of errands and the assistant teacher is busy helping children put on shoes and sweaters so they can go out to play. The older children are already at the far end of the yard on a nature walk with Brad, who comes in two afternoons a week. The teacher looks up to see a well-dressed man walk in and hears him say, "How do you do. I'm Jennifer Hamilton's father. I realize it's a bit early, but I've come to take her home."

Hearing his voice, Jenny runs to him crying, "Oh, Daddy, come look. I did a painting today." At her urging, Mr. Hamilton accompanies Jenny to see her work and all the areas of special interest to Jenny. The teacher hastens to get Jennifer's coat and mittens and to speed the girl and her father on their way.

Within moments of their departure Jennifer's mother arrives. She is horrified when told that Jenny's father has already taken the child. She becomes upset, cries, and then threatens to sue the teacher and the school for releasing the child to her former husband, who has been denied custody and visitation rights. She knew he might "kidnap" Jennifer, because he'd threatened to do so unless she would agree to what he considered a more reasonable settlement. All of this had been explained to the owner. By the way, where was the owner?

Situation three One morning when Pam, aged three and a half, is brought to school, her mother stays to visit. In honor of the occasion, Pam's mother has dressed herself and her daughter in matching new outfits. Eager to show her mother what she has learned to do, and before any of the teachers can help her into a smock, Pam rushes to the finger paint table and immerses both hands in the colorful "goo."

At her mother's shout she withdraws her hands and hastily wipes them down the front of her dress. "You naughty, naughty girl," her mother scolds as she drags the cowed child toward the washroom. "You know you're not to get your clothes dirty."

The mother's anger continues all through the clean-up process. When she has finished berating her daughter she starts in on the teacher who has been trying to help by supplying extra towels. "You spoil the children here. It's easy for you; you don't have to wash and iron their clothes. Believe me, I'm not paying good money for my child to learn how to make a mess!"

These situations are obviously of varying degrees of severity, with quite different consequences, and involve the teacher and other participants in different ways. Are they all genuine crises? How urgent are they? After evaluating them by the basic questions for assessing crises, how would you react to each situation if you were the teacher involved?

Some critical situations seem to combine all the elements of crisis—physical injury, psychological and social stress, and possibility of legal action. Consider one such incident and how it was handled. This involved a young college student hired as an aide.

Ted lived in the neighborhood of the nursery school where he worked and knew many of the children and their families personally. He enjoyed the children's affection for him and willingly joined in playground supervision, pleased that so many of the children seemed to like being with him.

He initiated games, roughhoused with the children, organized "races," and was the center of one project after another. The head teacher suggested he do more guiding and less directing, but Ted felt he wouldn't be doing his job if he "just stood around and watched." Besides, when he tried to follow her advice, the kids spent a lot more time arguing and fighting, and he couldn't stand that. Kids should have fun together.

One day, while pushing Lester and Ellie on the swings, he noticed how much hitting and shoving went on as the other children waited their turns. He felt he had a good solution to the problem when he thought of putting one of the climbing boards across the swings so that as many kids as could hang on to the board or each other could have a turn.

The children responded enthusiastically, eight of them finding places for the first turn. "Higher! Higher!" they shrieked, their excitement matching the request. Amidst the screaming and shouting Ted suddenly heard another sound, a thud. Susie had somehow been hit by the end of the board. A moment ago she had been walking around the swing; now she lay motionless.

"Stop! Stop pumping!" Ted shouted. "Susie's hurt!" His fright communicated more quickly than the command. As the board slowed the children slid off to cluster around the limp form. Rufus spoke Ted's question. "Is she dead?" he asked.

In answer, Ted stooped and took Susie in his arms. Too confused to think what was best, too frightened to remember what to do, oblivious to the others, he knew only his own fault, his own guilt. Her parents would never forgive him; he would never forgive himself.

The two children closest to him began to cry. Several of the boys shoved forward demanding to see. Attracted by the noise and confusion, the director came quickly to see what was wrong. As she took in the situation she spoke quietly.

"Ted, put Susie down carefully. Everyone else, inside, and Miss Lewis will read you a story."

Dutifully the children moved toward the classroom, only to turn back

---

Teachers' View of Crisis

1. *Inability to reach parents when child ill or hurt*
2. *A bleeding or badly injured child*
3. *Sand or soap in a child's eye; choking, nosebleeds*
4. *Children running out of the room and refusing to return*
5. *Child who loses control of himself*
6. *Wrong person taking child home*
7. *Volunteers who don't show up when expected*
8. *Child's work discarded by mistake*
9. *Children arguing adamantly over toys or equipment*
10. *Mother upset about a classroom situation as reported by her child*
11. *Supplies and materials not available when needed*
12. *Collapse of play equipment*
13. *Small child bullied by larger child*

---

as they heard Ted remonstrating with the director. "Susie needs help bad . . . her parents won't ever . . . to the hospital. I'll drive her myself. I'll take care of her. I'll . . ."

Noticing that Susie had begun to stir, the director again gave instructions. "Ted, stay with her. I'll be back in a moment." Then calling Miss Lewis to take the children in for a story, she went to summon both doctor and parent.

A director's calmness and positive course of action had restored order, but a crisis may not be over once order is restored. There are other things to be done. The children should have a chance to talk about and to learn from the accident. The concern of the parents and their attitude toward the school must be considered. Any fears that Susie might have about being hurt again after she returned to school would need to be overcome.

The person who brings on the crisis is also its victim. Ted would need help. His poor judgment had contributed to the crisis, as had his inability to deal with his own feelings in reacting to the emergency. Once the extent of Susie's injury was known and her care assured, the director and Ted would talk about what had happened. They would also talk about his feelings and what he had learned about his own reactions in emergencies and how to improve his work with the children.

One of the features of crisis is that it often represents a mingling of several types of potential damage to the people and institution involved. The incident brought about by Ted included physical injury, danger of lawsuit over carelessness or incompetence, and psychological trauma to Ted as well as others. It also created stress within the staff, as well as between the parents and the school.

Parents' View of Crisis

1. *Severe illness or injury*
2. *Children fighting, hitting, biting one another*
3. *Child striking a teacher or parent*
4. *Re-adjustment due to teacher change during the school year*
5. *Temper tantrums*
6. *Child released to unauthorized person*
7. *Not enough supervisory staff due to absence of teacher*
8. *Other parents not doing their part in co-op program*

Each of these four different kinds of stress—psychological, social, medical and legal—has its own consequences. They often overlap, but it is useful to consider them as different components of a stressful situation when trying to decide how to cope with a possible emergency.

The Major Areas of Crisis
Psychological and Social Crises

The difficulties that arise in psychological and social types of stress are often closely related. In a general sense, *psychological* stress refers to feelings of strain or tension, fear, extreme anxiety, and other internally traumatic conditions. The *social* aspects of stress include straining of social ties, morale of staff, and community pressures such as protests from parents or groups of parents. The problem extends beyond the internal feelings of individuals involved to possible changes in relationships, reputation, income, and the like. Because they are often intimately related however, psychological and social stress will be discussed together.

Psychological and social situations are not easily categorized into positive and negative instances. When a child gashes his chin or complains, "I don't feel well" and his temperature reads 102°, the teacher has fairly clear evidence of a problem that should be alleviated, although she may not know how serious it is and what measures to take. Broken equipment left unrepaired, or failure to report an injury clearly invite charges of negligence. Where there is doubt, professional advice is available to give the staff or teacher expert consultation about the seriousness of the crisis and the probable consequences of different courses of action.

Unlike medical and legal problems, various kinds of psychological stress are not only inevitable but may be a necessary part of human development. Interaction with others almost necessarily involves frustration of a wish or need. And learning ways to deal with disappointment, frustration, and failure may well be a part of normal growth. Internal stress in a psychological sense may not be a crisis if it is within limits, although it obviously can also reach traumatic proportions.

In similar fashion, social interaction within the staff and between the staff and parents cannot always be smooth and satisfying. There may be instances in which parents need to be told something less than pleasant about a child or face disappointment if they have expected too much from the teacher and the school. In short, unlike the stress inherent in medical and legal situations, the stress resulting from social and psychological problems may not require positive action. Emotional responses that are natural for one child, for example, may create a psychological crisis for another. Psychological situations call for an on-the-spot judgment in order to decide whether there *is* a crisis or whether the stress may have positive consequences. The decision on medical matters is less complex because, in most instances, it is a matter of deciding how *severe* the problem is.

Children's View of Crisis

1. *Separation from parents*
2. *Loss of bladder or bowel control*
3. *Arbitrary attack by other children*
4. *Being called "names"*
5. *Parents forgetting to pick them up at going-home time*
6. *Deviation from usual routine*

In all types of crisis situations, the teacher is called on to make prompt decisions that usually require an evaluation of the circumstance and what action if any should be taken. Much as he occasionally would like to let things settle themselves, the teacher cannot avoid a decision of some kind.

It isn't enough to get busy and start tying shoe laces, or help a child put a book on the shelf as though nothing had happened. In a psychological crisis, *not* doing something about a situation is just as much a decision as taking positive action. Although a teacher may have little time to weigh the appropriateness of what he does, or to assess the consequences of adopting one procedure over another, the choice is his. The decision he makes may later be overruled, but its effect cannot be changed.

In dealing with social and psychological crises it is difficult to assess whether a decision was right or wrong. For example, a teacher who had been concerned about Lyn, an unusually dependent four-year-old who had recently enrolled in the school, decided it was time to help Lyn gain some experience and confidence on her own with the other children. Despite Lyn's clinging, he put her with a group of children at the play dough table. Lyn was obviously even more upset and sat quietly not playing and scarcely moving. Even though the teacher returned to her after a few moments, Lyn seemed more shy and dependent than before. Had he done the right thing, he wondered, or made the situation worse?

In psychological crises, the teacher's own feelings may be part of the problem. Obviously, if he gets upset about what the situation may mean to him and his job he is not in a position to make the necessary decisions. Personal feelings of resentment against a child or parent may make him more sensitive and less objective in response to a crisis involving that particular family. His own response to attack by a child or parent, or to criticism by other staff members may contribute to a crisis and affect his ability to deal effectively with tension.

For the teacher, psychological crisis is frequently based on a conflict in values. No matter how well-trained he may be, or how objectively he approaches his work, the actions or words of children that clash with his sense of values will distress him. A teacher who has grown up believing that swearing, name calling, defiance of authority, and various sex and toilet behaviors are taboo, won't find them easy to accept or ignore in the classroom.

One of the most distinctive features of psychological crisis is the ripple effect—the way one situation brings about another or spreads until a chain reaction is set in motion. The examples given earlier in the chapter illustrate how this may occur. The chain reaction may not be immediate. Suppose Mr. C., a teacher, intervenes when Frank and Andrew start hitting each other on the head with wooden blocks. He may feel a satisfactory solution has been reached if he gets the boys separated—Frank in with a group of children in the housekeeping corner and Andrew outside kicking a ball. However, that night a phone call from the head teacher makes him realize the parents are anything but calm. They want to know why their son was told he had to play house with the girls; they aren't about to let anyone make a sissy of Frank.

Naturally their attitude has upset the head teacher but she listens without comment to the explanation. Even though she says she feels the situation was properly handled and that the parents are being unreasonable, Mr. C. finds himself worrying about how he will react to Frank the next time he loses control of himself, and whether the head teacher really still has confidence in him. Next day, in his desire to keep everyone under control, he is on edge and so are the children. The crisis has gone full circle—from child to parent to school to teacher and back into the classroom.

A teacher must learn to deal with children's physical problems—ranging from minor bruises to traumatic injury. The demands that these make on the teacher, and the possible dangers to the child, vary enormously. Every wound, sniffle, exposure to measles or mumps does not constitute a crisis. There are, of course, potentially severe consequences, and part of the teacher's role is to judge the severity of the situation and know when to soothe and when to call for professional aid. The familiar medical situations are described below.

Eye, ear, nose, and throat infections

To some parents, nursery schools are breeding grounds for colds, coughs, sore throats, and all the familiar childhood diseases. Parents are probably right in thinking that a young child does get more colds and illnesses when he first goes to nursery school. The reason for this is his exposure to so many children in a confined area, rather than the school program itself. Also, whether or not mothers realize it, the child isn't getting the *same* cold over and over. Each time he has been infected by a new virus, he gets a new illness. As he builds up antibodies to these, he also builds up immunity and eventually cuts down on the number of illnesses he contracts.

Most colds are not communicable after the first three days. After that, the child's nose may be running, his throat sore, his spirits low, and he may be more susceptible to other illness, but he is not likely to infect another person. (See Table 12-1)

Colds are a problem in the classroom only if a child's sniffling and sneezing interfere with his activities or make the teacher uneasy about parents' reactions to allowing children with cold symptoms to be in school. Response to the concerns of parents often guides school procedure. In addition to the rule "Keep a child home the first three days of a cold," some schools have a uniformed nurse on duty each morning. Even though nurses are not required by state or local health regulations, having a nurse on hand means that the parent is more likely to keep a child home during the first few days of a cold rather than risk his not being admitted. The nurse can also give professional answers to parents' questions about health and encourage good habits on the part of the children.

Tonsillitis (inflammation of the tonsil) may be caused by bacteria or viruses. A viral tonsillitis must run its course but the

---

[1] Information in this section is based largely on lectures by Dr. Birt Harvey, assistant clinical professor of pediatrics, Stanford University School of Medicine, Stanford, California.

period of communicability is usually short. A child may return to school when his temperature has been normal for 24 hours. Bacterial tonsillitis is most commonly caused by the beta hemolytic streptococcus, which responds to antibiotics. (See Strep Throat and Scarlet Fever, Table 12-2.) A child with bacteria tonsillitis may return to school a day after treatment is started if he feels well and his temperature is normal.

The most common types of eye infection in young children are *conjunctivitis* (pink eye) and *sties*. Pink eye is highly contagious and is almost always accompanied by discharge and crusty matter around the eyes. In general, as long as there is a discharge the mother should be requested to keep the child at home while the infection is being treated by a doctor. With antibiotics it can usually be cleared up very rapidly. Sties are not communicable.

Allergies may also cause children's eyes to tear and redden and itch, but they are not transmittable. Even though they are noncontagious, allergies do have a potential for crisis: some children develop acute allergic reactions to insect (especially bee) stings, certain foods (including chocolate), animal dander, and inhalants (sprays, etc.). These problems should be noted on the child's records together with whatever emergency treatment is prescribed. Naturally every effort should be made to avoid exposure to potentially dangerous situations, but if it occurs, the parent should be notified and the instructions on the child's record followed. Obviously, the school staff should not administer medicine, either prescription or nonprescription, *without written* authorization from parents or legal guardians.

Earaches occur frequently in young children. They are almost always secondary to a common cold. A child may not be able to locate the point of his distress but can be observed tipping his head to the side that hurts, rubbing the area, and exhibiting

Table 12-1 *The common cold*

Cause	Average Occurrence	Incubation	Symptoms	Contagion	Duration
Various viruses	In young children, 4 to 6 per year—usually in winter	From several hours to 2 or 3 days	Sneezing, runny nose, eyes tearing, fever, letdown feeling	Spread through droplets from nose and throat to those nearby Uncovered cough or sneeze extends radius of infection to 12 feet	Few days to several weeks

Table 12-2 *Communicable diseases common among preschool children*

	Chicken Pox	German Measles	Measles	Mumps	Strep Throat and Scarlet Fever	Tuberculosis	Whooping Cough
Cause	Virus	Virus	Virus	Virus	bacterium beta hemolytic streptococcus	Tubercle bacillus	Pertussis bacterium
How spread	Droplets in air from sneezing, coughing, or from rash	Droplets from nose and throat of infected person	Droplets from talking, breathing, sneezing, coughing	Droplets from infected person's throat	Droplets, and direct contact with contaminated food and milk	Cough	Droplets and direct contact with discharge
Incubation Period	Usully 14–16 days; maximum 21 days	Usually 17–18 days; can be 13–21	Usually 11 days; can be 7–14	Usually 18 days; can be 11–26	Usually 2–4 days; can be 1–7	Usually 6–8 weeks; can be 2–10 weeks	Usually 5–7; can be 5–14 days
Symptoms	Fever, rash, itching; bite-like eruptions starting on face and trunk	Usually mild: swollen lymph nodes, low-grade fever, rash, cold or merely a stiff neck	Red eyes, runny nose, cough and high fever for 3–4 days, then rash.	Swollen, tender glands in front of and below ear, fever, general discomfort	Fever, headache, vomiting, sore throat (rash, flaking skin in scarlet fever)	Persistent cough, low-grade fever, weight loss, or no symptoms	Mild hacking cough or cold followed by spells of heavy coughing; maybe vomiting
Possible Complications	Skin infection	If pregnant, injury to fetus	Many, including pneumonia and encephalitis	Injury to testes and ovaries and (rarely) encephalitis or deafness	Inflamed glands, sinuses, pneumonia, kidney disease, Rheumatic fever	Damage to brain, liver, kidney, intestines	Pneumonia, bronchitis
Communicability	1 day before rash until last lesion crusted	Usually 3–7 days	Especially during first few days of "cold" symptoms; 7–8 days total	2 days before swelling starts until swelling gone; 5–7 days	7 days unless penicillin given; then 1 day thereafter	At any time by active case, especially during coughing	5–6 weeks

general fussiness. Ear infections are not contagious, but the child is generally more comfortable at home. The common belief that the infection will be prevented by having children wear hats or turn up their collars to cover the ears is incorrect. The cause of ear infection is obstruction of the Eustachian tube that blocks the normal drainage from the middle ear.

Reportable Diseases: When a child in nursery school contracts one of the communicable diseases described in Table 12-2, the school should report that child's illness to county health authorities and notify parents of exposed children immediately. Parent awareness of exposure is particularly important in the following cases:

German Measles: Mothers should be notified because those who contact German measles during the early months of a pregnancy may give birth to babies who have defects of the brain, eyes, ears, heart, or other body systems.

Measles: This is a dangerous disease in childhood and the death rate can be high. Complications can be drastically reduced if gamma globulin is given early after known exposure.

Strep infections including scarlet fever: When suitable drugs are administered at the onset of illness, kidney involvement and rheumatic fever are usually avoided.

Tuberculosis deserves special attention in the nursery school because it is easily spread to children and the disease often manifests itself in particularly severe form in children. Adults with the disease who may not feel or act ill are the chief threat to children. Yearly chest x-rays or tuberculin tests should be required of all adults who interact with children at school including volunteers serving on any regular basis.

The incidence of many of these diseases in a school can be reduced by requiring immunization before admission (Table 12-3).

Immunizations

Many states require immunizations before a child is accepted into a daycare or nursery school program. In addition to the diphtheria, pertussis (whooping cough), and tetanus immunizations (commonly referred to as DPT) many schools now require polio and measles vaccine. (See Table 12-3)

Broken bones and head injuries

Those who work with young children must be cognizant of the constant threat of serious injury to youngsters. Because motor control, balance, and physical strength are undergoing rapid change, falls are common. Children have little understanding of safety for themselves or others, and are therefore careless about leaving equipment in hazardous places or throwing toys and tools without thought of the consequences. The wonder is that there are so few accidents in school resulting in serious injury to children. Proper precautions and knowledge of procedural steps can alleviate many of the anxieties of both child and teacher in the event of an accident.

Table 12-3 *Immunization guide*

Immunization	Ages	Initial Series	Booster(s)
Diphtheria	Persons 6 weeks to 7 years of age get DPT Vaccine	3 immunizations one month apart. 4th immunization one year after 3rd	5th immunization upon entering school
Tetanus	Persons 6 weeks to 7 years of age get DPT Vaccine	3 immunizations one month apart. 4th immunization one year after 3rd	5th immunization upon entering school
Pertussis (Whooping Cough) There is a 3-in-1 type vaccine called DPT and a 2-in-1 called Td.	Persons 7 years of age and older get Td Vaccine	2 immunizations one month apart. 3rd immunization one year after 2nd	Td booster every 10 years
Polio (Live Sabin Trivalent Oral Vaccine)	Persons 6 weeks to 19 years of age	2 doses two months apart. 3rd dose 8 months after 2nd	Booster upon entering school.
Measles (Rubeola) (Live Vaccine)	Persons 12 months or older	One immunization	No booster needed

Broken bones are not always readily detectable, unless there is a compound fracture, i.e., a breaking of the skin. When a child falls it is best not to be too eager to pick him up. If he is out of danger, let him lie still until he attempts to rise on his own. Serious injury to an ankle, a knee, or a leg means the child won't be able to stand up. Breaking a collar bone, rib, arm, or wrist usually means too much pain for the child to want to move this part of his body.

Directing a child to point to where it hurts, gives some idea of what may have happened. If after a few minutes everything seems to be all right, it is probably safe to let the child get up and continue whatever he was doing when the interruption occurred. He should be watched carefully until the teacher is sure his activity seems normal. Whatever type of accident report is required by the school should be filled in (Figure 12-2) and a copy given to the parent when the child is dismissed for the day. Time should be taken to tell the parent what happened, too.

When the consequences are more serious—a bone broken or a child obviously in pain or distress—the child should be made as comfortable as possible and the instructions on the child's emergency card followed immediately. No matter how well-trained the teacher is in first aid or how many similar experiences she has had, she should not try to diagnose or minister

```
┌─────────────────────────────────────────────────────────────────────┐
│                                                                       │
│                    GREENMEADOW NURSERY SCHOOL                         │
│                                                                       │
│                         ACCIDENT REPORT                              │
│                                                                       │
│  Date_____ Approx. Time of Accident_____  │
│  Name of Child_____ │
│  Address_____ Phone_____  │
│  Accident Reported By_____ │
│  Nature of Injury:_____ │
│       Location_____ │
│       Type: Bump____; Bruise____; Scratch____; Blister____; Abrasion____; Cut____; │
│            Laceration____; Suspected Strain or Sprain____; Suspected Fracture____; │
│            Burn____; Bite____; Other_____ │
│       Extent of bleeding_____ │
│       Estimate of extent and severity_____ │
│                                                                       │
│  DESCRIPTION OF CHILD'S OVERT REACTION TO INJURY:                     │
│  DESCRIPTION OF FIRST-AID MEASURES                                    │
│                      First-Aid Given By:_____  │
│  DESCRIPTION OF ACCIDENT:                                             │
│  DISPOSITION OF CASE:                                                 │
│       Parent or doctor not notified____. Reason_____  │
│       Parent notified____. Parent's Instructions_____  │
│                                                                       │
│       Family Physician Notified____. Name_____  │
│       Other Physician Notified____. Name_____  │
│        Reason_____  │
│        Physician's Instructions_____  │
│                                                                       │
│       Child remained at school____; was taken home____; was taken to_____ │
│       for medical attention by_____ (Name of Person Transporting Child). │
│       Other disposition_____  │
│                      Head Teacher_____  │
│                      Director_____  │
│  USE REVERSE SIDE FOR ADDITIONAL INFORMATION PERTINENT TO CASE AND   │
│  DISPOSITION.                                                         │
│                                                                       │
└─────────────────────────────────────────────────────────────────────┘
```

Figure 12-2 *Example of an accident form report*

to the child beyond doing whatever might be needed to preserve life (as in the case of serious bleeding or asphyxiation).

Inexperienced teachers often misinterpret the seriousness of head injuries. Because the scalp has more blood vessels than any other part of the body of similar size, even a minor blow to the head may easily form a large bump. *Where* the child is hit, and the amount of swelling have relatively little bearing on the degree of injury. What needs to be known is whether internal bleeding is taking place. After any head blow, three significant signs should be watched for:

1. Initial unconsciousness
2. Progressive lethargy
3. Recurrent vomiting

Even if a child is unconscious for only ten or fifteen seconds after a fall or blow on his head, this fact needs to be reported. Normally the family should be notified immediately and their instructions followed. If the child must be kept for a time, however, and he becomes very lethargic or starts to vomit recurrently call the doctor and follow his suggestions. The teacher needs to keep an exact record of what she does and when. This should be given to the parent or the person taking over the treatment of the child.

Vomiting immediately following a head (or any other) injury is frequently an emotional reaction and may have little significance, but it should be recorded. Vomiting that occurs after half an hour later is considered significant.

What seemed to a teacher to be an inconsequential head injury brought serious consequences to a three-and-a-half year old girl, her family, and the owners of a nursery school. The details of this event are described fully in the section on crisis and the law.

DO'S and DON'TS in Cases of Severe Injury

1. *DO keep the child quiet and someone with him until his or her parent or a doctor takes over*
2. *DON'T try to diagnose or repair damage*
3. *DO follow the procedure given on his emergency card*
4. *DON'T neglect the other children in the class*
5. *DO make a complete report to the parent and for the school records*

Minor injuries   Many common emergencies in nursery schools present little threat to an experienced teacher even though she knows the consequences could be serious for the child and herself depending on how she handles each situation. Wherever there are children, there will be a certain number of cuts, scrapes, bruises, eyes with sand in them, nose bleeds, abdominal pains, etc. Every school provides first aid supplies and has them readily available. However, the head teacher, or the teacher most likely to see the parent after school, should have knowledge of even the most minor bumps or bruises so she can enter them in the school record and inform the parent. It is advisable to inform the parents of every accident lest they discover even a small injury later and be disturbed both by the accident and by the teacher's failure to notify them. Of course, in the case of serious injury, the parent or indicated guardian should be called immediately.

The following are descriptions of common minor injuries and remedies with which the teacher should be familiar:

CUTS
(knife, glass, paper)

If there is any possibility that stitches are needed (to avoid scar when healed), parent should be notified. Otherwise clean with soap and water and protect with bandage.

SCRAPES

If gravel, sand, or any foreign substance is deeply imbedded, call parent. (The injury may need a doctor's attention in order to avoid infection or scarring.) Otherwise, clean *thoroughly* with soap and water. It is important to remove all foreign matter. Cover lightly.

BURNS

If a burn blisters, call parent. While waiting, keep area under cold water or wrapped in clean cloth. Do not apply any ointments. If burn is minor and small in area, soothe with cool water. Area is already bacteria-free from the burn itself.

SAND-IN-EYE

Not harmful but quite irritating to child. Wash eye(s) with plenty of cool water.

NOSE BLEED

Can usually be stopped by keeping child quiet and squeezing nostrils together for a few minutes. If bleeding persists or recurs, call parent.

ABDOMINAL PAIN

Pains in the abdominal area are often related to infectious diseases, in which case there will be other symptoms present. If the pain is connected with appendicitis, child won't want to move and he'll probably have fever and vomiting. Abdomen will remain rigid and painful when touched, particularly low on the right side. Parent should be called in either of above circumstances. Common "tummy ache," which often accompanies anxiety, comes and goes but while present is very real to child. Can be alleviated with judicious amount of reassurance. Report to parent.

CHOKING

Can be very serious if foreign matter gets into lungs or air passage is completely blocked. Enforce simple rules in the nursery school:

1. Sit to eat
2. Avoid giving foods such as raw carrots, peanuts, bacon, popcorn (exceedingly difficult to remove once in the windpipe)

If child is choking, try to hook finger into mouth and around whatever is caught in throat. Pull forward. When this is ineffective or impossible, sit down, place child face down across lap and give sharp "whack" across his shoulder blades. If still gagging, get medical help immediately. Notify parent.

Miscellaneous medical problems

Teachers hear about the following group of medical problems far more than they encounter them. Yet because these conditions sometimes represent serious problems for young children, teachers understandably want to know how they can identify them, and in what way they should attempt to help.

SKIN DISEASES

Children suffer from a wide variety of skin diseases. Those caused by fungi are probably the most widespread, including athlete's foot (tiny, itchy blisters between the toes) and ringworm (circular, scaly lesions on the body and in the scalp). They are difficult to cure and a physician's advice is needed in determining whether an infected child should be in school. Impetigo, a bacteria-caused infection, is characterized by yellowish crusted sores anywhere on the body, but especially at nostril openings. It is highly contagious and if not cured may occasionally lead to erysipelas or kidney diseases. Until all infected areas are healing, children should probably remain at home, although a day or two after proper treatment the disease is not communicable. Boils, an infection at the root of a hair, may be caused by the same bacteria responsible for impetigo. They start as a red swelling, fill with pus, and are quite painful. Their treatment should be left up to the child's family and agreement reached with them as to whether the child should be in school.

LICE

Infestation with lice is not uncommon whenever there is a shortage of soap and laundering. Unwashed hair, unwashed bodies, and unwashed clothes furnish perfect breeding places for head and body lice. They usually are found in a child's hair or the seams of his clothing, where they cause severe itching and irritation. Although lice rarely carry disease, they need to be removed. This can best be done by disinfection—a task not usually handled by the school.

BITES

The bite of any sharp-toothed animal can be quite painful, may become infected, and generally brings discomfort to the person bitten. When the skin is broken, whether by guinea pigs, rats, or any other animal, including a human being, tetanus or other infections may result and make the victim ill. Wash the area thoroughly with soap and water. A physician should determine if a tetanus injection is appropriate.

CONVULSIONS Convulsions are spasmodic muscular contractions that come without warning and cannot be stopped. When having a convulsion the child falls unconscious, his muscles stiffen and then relax and start a series of somewhat rhythmical contractions. When the attack is over, the child sleeps from a few moments up to an hour or more. The attacks themselves may be brief or prolonged. During an attack the child needs to be protected so that his breathing is not impaired (by vomit or the tongue being swallowed) and so that he does not bruise himself by his movements. Until help comes he should be placed face down on a soft surface with his head to one side and a rolled-up cloth between his teeth. Seizures of this kind accompany certain sudden high fevers and are also associated with epilepsy.

Safety for You

1. *Sit down to eat or drink*
2. *Keep sticks, balls, and all foreign objects out of your mouth*
3. *Keep wheeled equipment on the paved areas or in the sheds*
4. *Walk around swings*
5. *Use both hands when climbing*
6. *Use tools properly and keep them where they belong*

CHILD BEATING Occasionally a teacher suspects that a child is the victim of brutal treatment. She may notice welts and bruises, find him crying for no apparent reason, or hear his innocent remark, "They hit me all the time." If tactful questioning and further observation confirm her suspicion, she should immediately see that the proper authorities are notified. Usually this means a call to the Department of Dependent Children of the local welfare office. Many of these groups are now in a position to take over with no further involvement on the part of the teacher. Some states have laws that protect the teacher from lawsuit.

Seeking help from an outside agency is considerably facilitated if the school and agency personnel have already met and are familiar with one another's work and jurisdiction. Prior introduction of this kind, whether formal or informal, makes it possible to give maximum help to children if and when it is needed.[2] Additional references on this important topic are listed in the bibliography.

---

[2] A good source for materials on this subject is Children's Division, The American Humane Association, P.O. Box 1266, Denver, Colorado.

Prevention is perhaps a teacher's best strategy as far as medical crisis is concerned. She probably can do little beforehand about the illnesses children bring to school, but is in a position to do a great deal about injuries at school. Careful maintenance of equipment, strict enforcement of safety rules (such as those listed above), and consideration for the rights and comforts of others are effective ways to eliminate many of the accidents that all too often precipitate crisis.

When the teacher must deal with illness or injury, she needs first of all to remember that she is neither parent nor doctor. Other than providing simple first aid and large quantities of reassurance, her primary responsibility to the child is to notify the parent and follow the instructions on the emergency card. She should also make the child as comfortable as possible until someone who is responsible arrives and can take over.

Neither during the time of crisis, nor in the normal routine of the day, should the teacher administer medication (including aspirin) without written permission and instructions from a parent. Some children, such as those with certain allergies, are on a schedule that requires dosage during the time the child is in school. When this is the case, the teacher should act only upon explicit, written procedures worked out with the parent and kept on file at the school. Teachers should not make medical decisions regarding the kind of care a child is to receive when he is ill or injured. Both the child and the school are best served by following instructions exactly as they are given in the child's records.

Fortunately, real medical crisis is rare in a nursery school considering the number of hours and the number of children involved in routine procedures. When a child is hurt or ill, the time it takes to decide what to do, and how the decision is to be implemented, are not likely to be the critical factors. The crisis is far more likely to rest in the psychological effect on the staff, the child, and the parent. This aspect of crisis is discussed later on in this chapter.

Crisis and the Law[3]

Suppose that in the nursery school where you work a child is injured:

1. By a child who has previously been cooperative, pleasant, and quiet

_____

[3] Information in this section is based on lectures by Richard G. Mansfield, Attorney at Law, Palo Alto, California.

2. By a child whom you know is destructive and physically aggressive
3. Because of a defective piece of equipment (a slide that has a sharp edge, a jungle gym that collapses, etc.)
4. Through his own carelessness and in violation of school rules that have been explained to him
5. Because of your carelessness or that of another teacher

Who is liable?

When the owners of a nursery school occupy a facility and enroll students, they establish a relationship recognized by law. The owners automatically assume certain responsibilities, whether or not these are written into the school records. The same is true for a person who agrees to teach in a nursery school. By law, in many instances, a teacher may also share in the responsibility for what takes place during school hours even if she is not directly involved. In essence, the administration and staff become liable for the health and safety of the students and, if legally challenged, must provide suitable explanation for the way they met this responsibility.

General principles of the law

Nursery school liability is essentially different from that of other schools, because when a young child is injured, there is deemed to be no contributory negligence on his part. If older children are injured, lost, kidnapped or in some way harmed while at school, the courts hold that they may conceivably have contributed to their condition. In cases involving nursery schools, however, the law is clear that young children are not expected to be able to take care of themselves. Because caretaking, not education, is interpreted to be the primary purpose of a nursery school, a special burden is placed on the school and its teachers. Although a given situation may not in any sense be an emergency, the threat of a lawsuit constitutes a crisis for many teachers. The anxiety resulting from the prospect of court proceedings is very real not only for the teacher but for the child, the parents, and the school as well.

The case of Fowler vs. Seaton, involving action against a nursery school, brings out the broad range of responsibility that lies with the school. The plaintiff, Jenny Gene Fowler, at the age of three years and ten months was a student in a private school that provided day care for children of working mothers. Mrs. Seaton, the defendant, was the owner of the school.

When picking Jenny Gene up one evening, the mother was told there had been an accident—Jenny Gene had wet her pants. This was unusual but not alarming as far as the mother was concerned. What was alarming was the fact that at supper an hour later the parents noticed that Jenny Gene's eyes were crossed and that there was a large lump on her forehead. The mother immediately called Mrs. Seaton, asking what had happened. The owner then explained that another child "who had nothing in his hands" had struck Jenny Gene in the forehead.

Jenny Gene eventually had three operations to correct the crossing of her eyes, and the parents sued the school, alleging negligence resulting in personal injuries to their child. At the time of the proceedings the child's eyes were still crossing. After a judgment by a lower court, in favor of the owner of the school, a higher court reversed the verdict in an opinion that included these points:

Thus, it appears that the school was a preschool nursery operated for profit. We know, as a matter of common knowledge, that such schools are primarily intended to give the children an opportunity to engage in supervised group play and other supervised activities. Such schools hold themselves out as furnishing supervision for the children. *Furnishing supervision is the basic service for which these schools charge. It is their main function.*[4] The duty owed by the operator of such a school to the students in attendance is substantially different in degree from that owed by schools whose primary function is education, where the children are much older, and where supervision is incidental. *The supervision required must be commensurate with the age of the children and with their activities.* Thus the several cases cited by respondent relating to the duties owed to grammar and high school students are not in point. (61 C. 2d 681; 39 Cal. Rpts. 881, 394 P. 2d 697, p. 688).

Certainly it is true that this was an unusual occurrence. *While it may be common knowledge, as contended by defendant, that in the normal course of play children suffer bumps, bruises, and scratches, it certainly is not a matter of common knowledge that children normally come home from a nursery school with concussion of the brain and crossed eyes. If that were "normal" or "usual," nursery schools would not stay in business very long. Such a school, as already pointed out, by its very nature, holds itself out as a place where children can be safely left and carefully supervised.*

Of course, in most *res ipsa* cases, it is incumbent on the plaintiff to show that the actions of the plaintiff did not contribute to the injuries. Here it was shown that plaintiff is of an age that, as a matter of law, she could not be guilty of contributory negligence, and also that, as a result of shock caused by the accident she cannot remember or communicate the cause of the accident. Under such circumstances, of course, she is entitled to the presumption that she exercised due care for her own safety. (61 C. 2d 681; 39 Cal. Rpts. 881, 394 P. 2d 697, p. 690).

---

[4] Italics ours.

In *Fowler* v. *Seaton* the California Supreme Court found that the facts justified application of the doctrine of *res ipsa loquitur* to require the Happy Day Nursery School to produce evidence that it was not careless. This doctrine includes three central conditions:

1. That the plaintiff for some good reason really does not know or cannot say how he was injured and cannot produce witnesses of his own to tell what happened
2. That the plaintiff's injuries are of the sort which are usually caused by carelessness or negligence
3. That if anyone was careless, it was probably the defendant

The teacher or nursery school director or owner should understand that if a situation analogous to *Fowler* v. *Seaton* should occur, and the three elements of the doctrine of *res ipsa loquitur* apply, the school will have to prove its innocence. If, on the other hand, the doctrine does not apply, the burden will remain upon the child and his or her parents to demonstrate that the school staff was careless.

In general, the following principles of law apply to nursery schools:

1. Children in the nursery school age group are too young to be required to take care of themselves, therefore no doctrine for contributory negligence exists because nursery school children cannot be negligent.
2. Care is the predominant principle. The law views the nursery school as a place that cares for children primarily and only secondarily educates them.
3. The employer is liable for the acts of his employee. If a teacher or other employee is involved in harming a child, either negligently or intentionally, the owner is usually also liable if the employee was in the scope of his employment. It does not, however, release the employee from liability.
4. The standard of care that must be exercised in providing for the safety of a child increases as the child's capacity to take care of himself decreases.
5. Waivers signed by parents or guardians do not release the teacher or nursery school operator from liability. The child is considered a ward of society through the courts and even the parents cannot waive a child's rights. However, from a psychological standpoint, it is always a good idea to require signed permission slips or detailed releases for field trips and

emergency treatment. A release prepared by the school with details of every field trip should be signed each time; a general release for all trips is not adequate.

The teacher's responsibility

Since the courts have established that nursery school owners and teachers are responsible (and therefore liable under the law) for the health and safety of their students during school hours, the staff of a school must be able to show they have consistently done all that is reasonably required to maintain the health and safety of the children in their school.

Teachers should not wait until something happens before meeting their responsibility. A great many practical steps can be taken to protect those in charge, should they become involved in legal action, steps that often discourage the initiation of such action. Even though the final decision of the courts may be favorable to the school, the inconvenience, expense, and emotional strain of a suit can be very great.

In order to lessen the dimensions of a potential legal crisis, a school should constantly observe the following measures:

1. Adequate and consistent recording and reporting
2. Comprehensive safety measures
3. Realistic insurance coverage

Many errors can be avoided in a nursery school if its records for every child are complete and up to date. A teacher needs to have information available regarding whom to call in case of an emergency, who is responsible for each child when he is not in school, and who is authorized to pick up the child. The school should also have on file any limitations on the child's diet or physical activity and a record of any family beliefs that take precedence over usual school procedures.

Written reports made at the time of illness or injury at school and filed as a matter of record can be an important resource if a teacher's actions are questioned later on. Regularly reporting to parents any unusual occurrence or any emergency action taken, and involving them as much as possible in the affairs of the school, build support rather than suspicion, and show good faith on the part of the school and the teachers.

A school's safety program indicates as much as anything the extent to which it meets its responsibility for the children in its care. In addition to establishing simple rules which are easy to remember (see p. 351), enforcement should be carried out in such a way as to make the staff and children mindful of safety.

Who is Liable?

Whatever equipment is provided should be sturdy and bought or built with consideration for safety features as well as economy. Because of the danger of children being hit in the mouth or face, swing seats should be made of canvas or soft material, never of wood or metal. Teeter-totters are a poor choice of equipment for similar reasons. Raised sandboxes are more likely to cause tripping than sunken ones (see Chapter 3 on impact of physical environment). All permanent supplies and equipment should undergo regular inspection and constant upkeep and should not be allowed to break or wear out.

A realistic insurance program must cover teachers as well as the owners of a school in a variety of ways and for many contingencies. It lessens the fear of the consequences of unavoidable accidents such as loss by fire, or injury in a car accident while on a field trip. When a teacher is hired, she should determine what insurance coverage a school has and in what way, if any, it protects her.

The consequences of critical situations, of course, can be tragic for all involved, including the teacher. She need not be apprehensive; with good training, reasonable precautions, and sensible reactions, she will be able to deal effectively with crisis.

How to Deal with Crisis

Crisis is an unscheduled part of a preschool program and the alert and prepared teacher will have several strategies for dealing with it. The consequences are, to a degree, within the capability of the staff to control.

Even though some stress and an occasional emergency will be inevitable, this does not mean that they are to be awaited with a passive philosophy of "Accidents will happen." Crisis is not only accidental, it may come from carelessness, neglect, and lack of foresight or experience. An apparently smooth, safe, well-run school is never accidental.

The basic rules of safe equipment and procedures were discussed in the sections on legal and medical crisis. In addition to these elementary principles covering physical injury or illness and liability, the teacher can avoid crisis and stress by *creating an environment in which accumulated frustration is minimized.* The teacher can provide many safe places for play, many acceptable outlets for aggression. Trees to climb, dirt to dig in, clay to thump, nails to pound, drums to beat, balls to kick, dolls to spank, mattresses to jump on, paint and paste to smear, and water for washing, splashing and bubbling provide opportunity to work off a great many aggressions without extra help.

The teacher who praises and spends time with children when they are engaged in approved behaviors is likely to minimize stress in her classroom. This may be especially important for those children who come to school with fears and basic frustrations. These children often need more help than those who have been allowed to explore and share a variety of experiences with other children their age.

In a program of early education there are many experiences that are naturally frustrating to children. Someone else wants what they want; the teacher expects them to pick up after themselves, to wait until later, to take turns; they aren't strong enough or skilled enough to pursue many of their interests; they ask questions that no one answers; they want to read but the book they're looking for isn't on the shelf where it belongs; when they need a red crayon the only ones left are black, blue, or green. Just when it's their turn on the slide, it's time to go home. Even an environment that is designed to meet the needs of children seems to induce frustration. Anything that can be done to help reduce frustration can help deal with crisis.

Psychological and other stress in the classroom, while often not severe, is a persistent source of potential crisis. It is more readily avoided or resolved if the teacher understands children's natural eagerness in pursuit of what they want and recognizes that aggression and passivity, anger and withdrawal may be brought on by frustration. She needs to accept children as they are and lend her support, at the same time working to give them an understanding of more acceptable behavior.

One teacher may find it helpful to concentrate on relating a goal or rule to the child's true feelings and needs. Using a comment such as "I'm sure you won't mind letting Julie have a turn" is less mindful of the child's feelings than "I know you don't want to give up the swing, but it is time to let Julie have a turn now."

The latter statement recognizes and accepts a natural response on the child's part, yet is firm about letting the child know what is expected of him. The teacher may still have to remove the child from the swing, but her technique will be based on an understanding of needs and expectations and confident follow through. Sometimes the best solution to a fight or an act of defiance is to find a compromise and go on from there; at other times it may seem best to ignore it or to direct the children's attention to a new activity.

Each of the examples in Table 12-4 illustrates procedures teachers find useful in dealing with potential problems. Some are teaching techniques; others are simply ways of terminating a situation and going on to something else. They represent how some teachers handle various aspects of crisis resulting from children's behavior.

Some principles in dealing with crises

When a genuine crisis cannot be avoided, the teacher's response to it may be more effective if she acts on the basis of two general principles. The first of these is that a crisis has a number of consequences that follow the event itself—the ripple effect described earlier. In dealing with a stressful event the *attention* should be paid to *other persons* who may not be the central focus but who are affected in various ways. The incident involving Ted, for example, illustrated how the director or head teacher needed to attend to his reaction and those of the other children as well as the injury to the girl. A child who hits another may also need help in dealing with his own reactions as he sees the response of other children and adults to what he has done. Parents whose children have been involved in a crisis may need reassurance and information.

Another general principle in dealing with social and psychological stress is to *follow up* in a day or two—and perhaps again later—by contacting persons outside the immediate staff with information about how a crisis turned out. Word of how an injured child is doing, comments about whether safeguards have been taken to avoid future accidents, or sharing the resolution of a problem can give people a much needed opportunity to express their concerns, which they may not otherwise have had occasion to voice.

Table 12-4 *Examples of techniques for dealing with potential problems*

Situation	Alternatives	Examples
Three children who are playing store refuse to let a fourth join them	Suggesting a solution	"Maybe Billy can deliver groceries for you?"
	Diverting	"It's almost juice time. Billy, you go call everyone and the rest of you can come help get out the juice and crackers."
Two boys claim the same post in the tree house and start pushing one another	Explaining property rights	"Kenny, Steve was there first. It'll be your turn next."
	Enforcing rule	"No pushing when you're up high."
Jane is sweeping and Margie grabs the broom from her. Jane complains to teacher	Encouraging experimentation in coping with problems	"What are some of the things you can do to get it back? What do you think will happen? Let's try it."
	Offering a substitute	"Maybe you would like to use this mop until Jane can trade with you."
A group of children are acting out the song, "Row, row, row your boat." Much to Lisa's annoyance, Danny insists on holding her hands to do the rowing	Interpreting	"Danny, I think Lisa wants to do her rowing alone."
	Separating	"Danny, you move over on this side, please."
Wendy has carefully collected all the plastic tiles and sorted them into two piles. Paul approaches, eyeing the piles longingly. He is not a patient child	Encouraging sharing	"You've done a fine job, Wendy. Which pile may Paul play with?"
	Restraining, should Paul start to grab	"Wendy is playing with these, Paul, and I can't let you take them." (Teacher would probably also suggest a solution or divert Paul to another activity.)
Child falls while running down grassy slope—breath knocked out and frightened—but otherwise okay	Child's feelings recognized	"That was pretty scary, wasn't it? Let's try it again. I'll hold your hand so you won't fall."
	Warning	"You're okay. Try not to run so fast next time—you don't want to get hurt."
About an hour before closing time, both Gloria and Helen want to wash a large rubber doll. In their determination, the water is spilled and the doll's arm is pulled off. As the teacher attempts to restore order, Helen kicks and shouts obscenities	Making acceptable behavior clear	"I know you're angry, Helen, but I can't let you kick and use words like that." (Teacher is prepared to remove Helen from the situation.)
	Ignoring unacceptable behavior	"Let's mop up the water and decide how you both can wash the doll."

The teacher's skill in coping with crisis may in itself be useful in dealing with the effects of stress. Studies of disaster, for example, show that adults who remain calm instill similar behavior in children; when they become openly frightened, children also react in frightened ways. In the classroom, children obviously imitate their teachers. In times of stress they are especially in need of models as to how to respond.

Dealing with crisis is partly a matter of experience, and the teacher will find it useful to find time to reflect on what has happened once the situation has passed. She needs to review the circumstances that led to the event and her own response to it. She may then consider alternatives, and decide whether she handled their feelings and those of the others involved as effectively as possible. Every crisis should become a learning situation and provide a background for sound action in the future.

SUMMARY Crisis is an inevitable part of working with young children and deserves careful consideration. In general it comes in four different types: (1) physical injury, (2) psychological trauma, (3) social stress, and (4) lawsuits. The role of the teacher in recognizing crisis, assessing its severity and dealing with it are discussed in this chapter. The unique legal liabilities of those who care for young children are described and illustrated by an actual lawsuit brought against the director of a private child care facility. Some medical problems and their symptoms common to young children are identified. The teacher can take steps to decrease the possibility of crisis and there are things she can do once it has occurred to minimize its impact on those involved.

SOME POINTS
TO REMEMBER

1. Crisis is an inevitable part of any curriculum dealing with young children.
2. An environment with sufficient exploration opportunities for young children will necessarily contain possibilities for crisis.
3. It is up to the teacher to judge whether there is a crisis and if so, how severe it is.
4. The major elements of crisis are: physical injury, psychological trauma, social stress, and possibility of legal action.
5. In a psychological crisis, doing nothing is as much a decision as taking positive action.
6. In psychological crises, the teacher's own feelings may be a part of the problem.

7. Familiarity with medical problems common to young children will help the teacher deal with medical crises more effectively.
8. When a young child is injured, there is deemed to be no contributory negligence on his part.
9. These principles of law apply to programs caring for young children:
    (a) Young children are not expected to be able to take care of themselves.
    (b) Centers and nursery schools care for children primarily and only secondarily educate them.
    (c) The employer is liable for the acts of his employee; this doesn't release the employee, however.
    (d) The standard of care that must be used in providing safety increases as the child's capacity to take care of himself decreases.
    (e) Waivers signed by parents do not release the teacher or school from liability.
10. Measures for reducing potential crisis include: (a) adequate reporting and recording; (b) comprehensive safety measures; (c) adequate insurance coverage.
11. Teachers can avoid crisis and stress by creating an environment in which accumulated frustration is minimized.
12. Crises often have ripple effects that involve persons not the most obvious victims; the teacher may need to attend to their needs also.
13. After a crisis, the teacher needs to follow up in a day or two with inquiries and information about how the crisis has been resolved.

REFERENCES

Child Welfare League of America, Inc. *Child welfare league of America, standards for child protective service.* New York: Child Welfare League of America, Inc., 1960.

De Francis, V. *Child abuse—preview of a nationwide survey.* Denver, Colo.: The American Humane Association, Children's Division, May, 1963.

De Francis, V. *Interpreting child protective services to your community.* Denver, Col.: The American Humane Association, Children's Division, n.d.

Fowler v. *Seaton.* (61 C. 2d 681; 39 Cal. Rpts. 881, 394 P. 2d 697) San Francisco, Ca.: Bancroft-Whitney, August, 1964.

Karelitz, S. *When your child is ill: a guide to infectious diseases in childhood.* rev. ed. New York: Random House, 1969.

Chapter 13 The Challenge of Evaluation

The Inevitability of Evaluation
    Attitudes and Apprehensions
    Summary Evaluation versus Formative Evaluation
Evaluation as Critical Judgments
    Informal and Formal Evaluation
    Techniques of Formal Assessment
    Instruments for Testing
The Purpose of Evaluation
    Evaluating Program Effectiveness
    Evaluation of the Side Effects of Programs
Research as Evaluation
    The Interdependence of Evaluation and Research
    The Goals of Research
    The Ethics of Research
    Using Research Results

The Inevitability of Evaluation

Attitudes and Apprehensions

Whether by formal procedure or informal conversation, teachers and their programs are evaluated by staff, parents, colleagues, teams of evaluation experts, and others. This evaluation is essentially a judgment of the quality of the staff and its effectiveness and training. It may also be a comparison of the usefulness of alternative programs and curricula or an examination of student achievement. It is often uncomfortable and sometimes threatening to be evaluated. However, the process may be useful to the teacher who understands the basic issues and procedures involved.

Newspaper and magazine editors know the attraction of popular quizzes that claim to reveal personality, talent, social effectiveness, insight, or compatibility as a partner. People respond eagerly to them; their consequences are minimal, and lives and behavior change little no matter what the results may indicate.

The response to this form of self-evaluation is probably an indication of a mild kind of competition such as wanting to know how one compares with some presumed norm of desirable behavior.

Evaluation of one's self, however, is a sharp contrast to evaluation by others, especially those whose judgment is respected or who are in a position of influence and power. Suppose, for example, that you are teaching in a nursery school program and your director has just said, "Tomorrow Mrs. G. from the superintendent's office is coming in. She's making the annual assessment. I'll post a copy of the evaluation form on the bulletin board." (See Figure 13-1.) How would you feel? What would you think?

Many teachers, even experienced ones, become apprehensive when they know that their professional skills and personal qualifications are being assessed. This is a natural response, one conditioned by years of school grading, selection procedures, entrance tests, verbal recommendations, and the like. In such a situation it is easy to raise questions about the legitimacy and adequacy of the evaluation.

For example, is it fair for an outsider to make judgments when a visit lasts only an hour or two, and each part of the program is observed only a few minutes? What kind of person is Mrs. G. and what are her feelings about a particular type of program? Is she really up-to-date on the new trends in the field or will she reject innovation? Has she ever taught kids like these? Who will read her report, and what effect will her comments have on someone else's job?

Many people find the prospect of evaluation disturbing, regardless of how well they may be doing. When they feel they are being judged by a particular standard, no amount of reassurance puts them at ease. Nonetheless, evaluation of some form is a part of every profession. The teacher's task is to become aware of the kinds of evaluation that will be made of her and her school, to prepare herself to deal with them and to use the information she gains as a means of improving her teaching.

Since evaluation is inevitable, how should the teacher respond? Different kinds of evaluations will ask for different responses and activities. In some—for example, when the teacher wonders if she is doing a good job and is evaluating herself—her strategy will have little resemblance to her behavior when an outside group or person comes to conduct a more formal evaluation. She will respond differently to a new parent inquiring about the qualifications of the staff than she will to the questions of a representative from the licensing section of the

Program No._____

Date_____

Time Observed_____   Name of teacher_____

Observer_____

PERFORMANCE

   Efficient

Excellent	Good	Fair	Poor

   Imaginative

Excellent	Good	Fair	Poor

   Maintains
   good control

Excellent	Good	Fair	Poor

   Dependable

Excellent	Good	Fair	Poor

ATTITUDE

   Responds
   well to
   suggestions

Excellent	Good	Fair	Poor

   Happy, warm
   personality

Excellent	Good	Fair	Poor

   Sympathetic,
   sensitive

Excellent	Good	Fair	Poor

   Relates well
   to children

Excellent	Good	Fair	Poor

   Relates well
   to staff

Excellent	Good	Fair	Poor

PERSONAL QUALITIES

   Sense of
   humor

Excellent	Good	Fair	Poor

   Self confident

Excellent	Good	Fair	Poor

   Appropriately
   dressed

Excellent	Good	Fair	Poor

   Well modulated
   voice

Excellent	Good	Fair	Poor

Figure 13-1 *Example of a teacher evaluation sheet*

state department who has come unannounced to inspect the files, examine the physical facilities and observe the activities of the staff. She will be more helpful or cautious in some situations than in others, depending on what is at stake.

When a curriculum or program is evaluated, e.g., the effectiveness of a new pre-reading program, assistance in obtaining data may be requested. Tests may be administered to children in the program, sometimes at the beginning of the year and again months later to see if there has been a measurable effect of the new curriculum. Teachers may be asked to participate by filling out questionnaires, making ratings of children or parents, or cooperating in other ways such as providing information about themselves and the program. In research studies, teachers may also be invited to engage in specific, predefined interaction with children in order to generate research data. At these times, they may not know exactly what it is that the researcher has in mind and what he or she is looking for.

But evaluation is a two-way street. While it may occasionally be uncomfortable, it can also be very useful if the teacher knows how to utilize the information it offers. A first step in using evaluation, instead of letting it use you, is to understand some of the purposes, the procedures, and the possible abuse of evaluation and other research. This will make it possible for you to collaborate effectively and recognize the ways that you and the families in your school can benefit from evaluation and research.

Summary Evaluation versus Formative Evaluation

In its traditional meaning, evaluation is rather like a final exam. It was and is used to examine the effectiveness of a curriculum, such as the new math, or a national program like Head Start. In these study designs, it was essential that the program or curriculum be continued *unaltered* from the beginning to the end of the study. A program that was not working well from the standpoint of the teacher, nonetheless, might continue unchanged so that the study design would not be lost. The evaluator then could ascertain if the new program realized its intended outcome.

One obvious problem with this design is that changes could not be made during the course of the program. New information is not allowed to influence the curriculum until the study is ended. This means that the turn-around time in modifying the program is relatively long and revisions are slow and delayed.

The dissatisfaction created by this model of evaluation led to a new concept, called *formulative evaluation*. In these studies, the information gained about the operation and effectiveness of a program is immediately fed back to the program planners and teachers so that changes can be made. This is an appealing strategy; however, it is more difficult to determine just what elements of a program make it successful if the program has been modified in midstream.

Evaluation as Critical Judgments

Informal and Formal Evaluation

Evaluation ranges from informal and even casual comments about the behavior, performance, and characteristics of another, to formal testing and assessment programs carried out by teams of experts. The major distinction between formal and informal assessment is in the methods by which comparisons are made and how systematically data or impressions are gathered and processed. One parent informally asking another, "How do you like the new teacher?" is essentially the same kind of inquiry as a formal rating made by an official observer from the State Department of Education on the item:

Overall effectiveness of teacher _____

                                Excellent   *Good*   *Fair*

Other differences between formal and informal assessments lie in the way the evaluation is used, how it is processed and reported, whether it is made public, how much confidence is placed in it, and the consequences it will have for those who have been assessed.

Informal evaluation

Although this discussion deals for the most part with formal evaluation, the informal evaluation system also deserves attention. Teachers and school staff members make informal evaluations of themselves and one another. These, too, can create anxiety. For example, shortly after starting to work on a new job, Alice H. overheard a group of teachers casually discussing the problem of a child to whom she'd been giving extra attention.

"You know," one of the teachers said, "I can't decide whether Harry has a speech impediment, doesn't hear well, or what's happening. He seems happy here at school, but something's wrong."

"What do you mean?" another asked.

"Well, I noticed Alice spending extra time with him, but he still doesn't talk very much. When he does speak, you can hardly understand what he's trying to say."

"Maybe Alice should have the kid tested by the speech consultant. That's probably the only way we'll be able to find out what's wrong."

In this kind of situation, the teacher may feel that the staff is actually talking about her, as well as about a particular child. In effect she hears: "The new teacher really isn't doing a very good job." Or she senses that her work is likely to be criticized when a consultant comes to make a diagnosis. Even though the comments are impersonal and casual, some teachers may be upset by implications they imagine.

Many informal evaluations are carried out by supervisors. Directors assess teachers and staff, head teachers assess assistants, aides, and volunteers. Part of the job of each person in any hierarchy is a continuous appraisal of the performance and personal qualities of those for whose work they are responsible.

Figure 13-2 *Mothers' answers to questions regarding teacher evaluation*

How do you evaluate a teacher?	What makes a good teacher?
I watch to see if she hears the children and gives her undivided attention when she listens to a child or speaks to him.	She attends to the needs of the children.
	She is firm without being mean.
I depend on the judgment of my friends if I am not able to observe for myself.	She doesn't hold a grudge or play favorites.
I notice whether or not she treats children as individuals or always as members of a group.	She gives of herself to every child equally.
I expect her to talk to me as an equal and not to make me feel she knows much more than I do.	She is able to handle unexpected situations smoothly and doesn't let herself get excited in emergencies.
I wait to see if she stoops down to put her arm around a child and look him in the eyes when she talks to him.	She makes learning situations out of every "problem."
	She watches and listens and concentrates on the children.
I don't want her to tell me everything is "just fine" when I know it isn't.	She gives me specific information about my child and helps me learn how to teach him what she wants him to know.
I keep track of how often she touches and holds them and lets them be near.	She reinforces what I think is important for my child to know.
I look to see what she does with quiet children.	She is warm and friendly and smiles sincerely.
I count how often she tells the kids what to do.	
I think she should punish children and not let them get away with things.	

Figure 13-3 *Fathers' assessments of what makes a good teacher*

What makes a good teacher?

A male teacher who would handle the children differently from the way women handle them in rough and tumble play.

A teacher who is not afraid to get dirty.

Someone who will positively reinforce good social behavior and negatively reinforce antisocial behavior.

Someone who is patient and has a lot of confidence in himself.

Someone physically affectionate.

A man who is not afraid to be gentle and affectionate.

A teacher who is not afraid to be firm and discipline the child.

A teacher with a sense of humor.

Someone who can create a special bond with each child.

Someone with varied interests and an eager, joyful outlook on life.

Someone who isn't all hung up with a sexist role.

The consequences of this kind of evaluation, of course, are related to the person who is making the evaluation and the resources for change that he commands.

Parents evaluate the program, the teacher, and the school. The comments they make among themselves and to others about what the school offers, the way a teacher looks, and what the program is or isn't doing for their children, have consequences for the reputation and image of the school. These consequences are reflected in increased (or decreased) enrollment, changes in staff and program, offers of help and cooperation and requests for parent conferences and meetings. Figures 13-2 and 13-3 contain information indicating the things some parents notice and what they expect of teachers.

Although their appraisal may not be as clearly defined as the examples given in Figures 13-1, 13-2, and 13-3 children also informally evaluate their teachers and one another (Figure 13-4). Whether expressed in words or actions (such as acceptance or rejection), evaluation of this kind usually brings about at least subtle changes in the behavior of the person assessed.

Another type of informal evaluation that preschool teachers frequently face is an appraisal by outsiders who come to visit or to do research. The effect on a teacher may be more readily understood by considering what each of the following persons might find of interest if he or she were to come into a nursery school some morning and observe the program as it is shown in Figure 13-4.

1. Owner of the school
2. Mother who has not yet enrolled her child
3. Mother whose child is smallest in the class
4. Visitor from a low-income area
5. State Welfare Department representative
6. Doctoral candidate doing research for his thesis on the effects of school discipline on children's curiosity

Informal evaluation goes on all the time and cannot be ignored by the teacher who wants to become competent in her field. The fact that it frequently poses a threat signifies, of course, that the teacher has a sense of standards and quality and that she wants to think of herself as doing a good job.

Figure 13-4 *Children's assessments of what makes a good teacher*

A good teacher:
Holds you and reads to you
Sings songs to you
Doesn't slap you
Pushes you high on a swing
Goes to meetings
When you have a hurt finger she puts a band-aid on it right away
Smiles at you
Doesn't make you sit still or be quiet
Wears pretty beads
Lets you play with her hair
Helps you
Fixes bikes
Doesn't get mad
Works hard
Builds with us
Makes you laugh

Formal evaluation of a school program or of the teachers and children in a school is based on data obtained by various kinds of tests and techniques. The teacher should become familiar with these—their purposes, uses, and limitations—so that he can recognize what resources are available to him and how he can best use them.

Techniques of Formal Assessment

Formal evaluation is usually based on data obtained from standard measurement techniques. Some of these methods are general and are so frequently used that examples and descriptions may be helpful to teachers in the classroom when they come into contact with evaluation and research studies.

Data for evaluation are usually gathered in these ways:

1. By asking persons who have experience with the programs of children to make judgments about them by ratings or by rankings (Figures 13-5, 13-6, 13-7).
2. By asking persons involved in the program to describe themselves or aspects of the program or children in an interview.
3. By asking persons involved to report information about themselves or the program on a questionnaire with predetermined questions.
4. By direct observation of a research staff member.
5. By testing a child's or teacher's performance, as in a prereading test or an intelligence test (Figure 13-9).

The information gathered may be of an artificial (also called experimental) situation devised to serve a particular purpose or may be from a regular part of the program, sometimes called a "naturalistic" situation. Experimental situations may be children or adults responding to pictures shown to them or a teacher interacting in a special, requested way with a child. Evaluations are most useful to the teacher when they report on things that occur as part of the regular program. Artificial situations are most frequently useful for specific research purposes.

Ratings and rankings

One popular method for obtaining data is to ask staff members to make ratings of the performance and behavior of individuals. Ratings are usually done on a scale which presents descriptions of the behavior to be rated (Figure 13-5, Figure 13-6, Figure 13-7). The judgments called for by this method are summaries of observations, impressions, and interpretations that have accumulated over a period of time.

OBSERVATIONS OF SCHOOL STAFF

School:_____

Staff Member:_____

Observer:_____

Date:_____

    Circle the number on each line that describes most accurately the behavior and performance of the staff members in carrying out their assigned tasks and duties.

1. In working with the group, the staff member is:

     strict   1 2 3 4 5 6   permissive,
                               ———————————   easy going

2. With respect to racial and ethnic history and customs of children and parents, the staff member:

     promotes ethnic   ignores or puts down
     pride and   1 2 3 4 5 6   ethnic background
     awareness   ———————————   and behavior

3. When the staff member is together with the children, in a relatively free and unstructured situation, she is:

     warm and outgoing   distant, detached,
     to the children and   1 2 3 4 5 6 stiff
     other staff members ———————————

4. In the daily curricular routine schedule, the staff member:

     selects and directs   1 2 3 4 5 6 lets the children
     most activities   ——————————— pick their activities

Figure 13-5 *Examples of scales for rating staff performance*

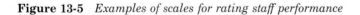

    Thus, a teacher may be asked to rate a child on the extent to which he works independently or depends on her or others for assistance. She can make a general judgment on such a global

BEHAVIOR RATING FORM

Instructions: Please rate the way this child behaves by circling one of the numbers on each line.

	Very much	Quite a bit	Slightly	Not at all
1. Talks easily to adults about what he thinks and feels.	1	2	3	4
2. Attempts to work out things for himself rather than ask for help	1	2	3	4
3. Has little respect for others' rights: takes toys, tries to get to head of line, etc.	1	2	3	4
4. Reacts to frustration by becoming aggressive or angry	1	2	3	4
5. Shows creativity in his use of materials and toys	1	2	3	4

Etc.

Figure 13-6 *Examples of scales for rating children's behavior*

Figure 13-7

Children's pre-math skill by rank
(From highest to lowest)

1. Halle
2. Mary Lou
3. Isadore
4. Ellen
5. Alice
6. Karl
7. Paula
8. Willie
9. Carlotta
10. Michele

cluster of behaviors only if she has seen the child in many different situations, and if she can average out in her own mind the different expressions of independence and dependence that she has observed.

Another procedure for evaluation is ranking. An example of ranking children by pre-math skill is given in Figure 13-7. Rank does not need to involve an entire group, nor must it be confined to people. A director might ask her staff to pick out what they consider are the two best ways to help children learn to ask questions, or the most and least successful means of teaching a song. Factors to consider in making choices may or may not be defined, although ranking of particular skills is often carried out by using scores on formal tests.

Recording data about behavior from direct and immediate observation is another formal method for evaluation of early educational programs and their specific activities. One might look, for example, for all acts that indicate cooperation between children, noting who initiates them, what the response is, and whether they lead to cooperative activities. Or, the observer might watch the teacher to see what his response is to acts of aggression in the group. Does he respond (reward) with attention? Is his attention a punishment of some kind, an attempt to distract, or some other behavior?

An alternative approach is to record all the "significant" types of behavior that occur in a particular time span, or in successive time spans. One pattern would be to observe a given child during a 30-second period once every five minutes in order to get cross sections of his behavior during an hour, day, week or even longer period. As an evaluation technique, observation is a more flexible approach than the use of rating scales. It is useful to teacher, researcher, and parent as well.

Questionnaires are written lists of questions, usually with multiple choice or short answer possibilities for response. They have the advantage of being easily scored and easily administered and of presenting standard items from one person to another. They are especially useful in obtaining information that is specific and not sensitive. Data about the number of children in a program, facilities of the school, demographic aspects of the community, and the like, are easily measured by this form of evaluation technique. Attitudes and feelings that are personal and confidential are not.

Interviews are less frequently used in research and evaluation than are other techniques primarily because of the time and expense involved in both taking the interview and in analysis of the data. Interviews are less structured, typically, than are other forms of data gathering and are most useful when the information to be gathered is relatively diffuse or impressionistic and may cover a wide range of possible answers. Some interviews, as in public opinion polling, use specific direct questions, with a limited set of possible responses from which the respondent must select. These are really verbal questionnaires. The less structured interview is useful when the topic to be discussed is broad. It permits the interviewer to follow up an answer to explore attitudes or information more thoroughly.

Assessment also may include measures that are less immediate and direct, sometimes called unobtrusive measures. These are measures of one type of behavior from which fairly clear inferences may be made about some other area of behavior. They can be as useful as ratings, rankings, and observations. The morale of a project staff, for example, may be indicated by turnover rate among the teachers. The eagerness of teachers to sign contracts, as shown by the time it takes to get all staff positions filled for the coming year, is another example.

Parent interest and involvement may be shown by the number of offers for volunteer work, the number of times parents keep their children from school to involve them in other activities, and the like.

Another example of an indirect measure of evaluation are the records showing absences or lateness. Although perhaps not critical in a preschool program, student attendance has a bearing on the effectiveness of a total program and on staff performance and may therefore indicate a need for change of some kind if it does not meet certain standards.

Unobtrusive measures are handicapped by the fact that the behavior observed or recorded is connected with other behavior only by inference. High teacher turnover rate *may* indicate low morale but may also indicate other conditions, such as a well-trained staff that is motivated to go on for additional training or is hired away for promotions that the school itself could not provide. This type of measure is useful but should be interpreted cautiously with alternative interpretations kept in mind.

Instruments for Testing

Educational and performance tests, as we know them today, were introduced in Europe early in the 1900s. They received great attention in the United States where they were further developed and widely used for the evaluation and selection of recruits during World War I and subsequently for the evaluation of student achievement and ability in the schools. At the present time, testing and the sale of a wide variety of tests are major industries, whose growth was accelerated by the development of the IBM punch card and scoring sheet.

Tests and test scores are typically based on the principle of comparing individuals to group norms. That is, a child is considered not on an absolute standard of mastery, but in relation to what has been found to be typical for an age or sex group. This is not true of all tests, but it is the premise on which a large part of the testing movement has been developed.

Some evaluations of performance, however, are based on the concept of mastery of a given subject matter. For example, there are tests that indicate whether a child has learned to count and/or how far he has learned to count, whether he can identify colors, how many objects he can name, etc. Standards of this kind apply to a child without regard to where he stands in relation to other children. Subsequent interpretation of such data, however, is almost inevitably made in terms of the performance typically expected of children his age.

Literally thousands of tests are on the educational market, hundreds of which apply to evaluation of preschoolers and programs of early education. Probably the best known and most controversial in the United States are those developed to measure intelligence. Even though there have been numerous attempts to put IQ into reasonable perspective, many parents and teachers still regard this measure as having finality and permanence.

Tests designed to show academic achievement at all school levels, and various personnel tests, have also captivated the public. Unfortunately they have sometimes been misused and misinterpreted. It is particularly tragic when they are used early in a child's educational experience to put him in a "track" or otherwise label him as "slow" or educationally retarded in some way. These reputations may influence the child's learning and achievement all his life. This is especially true when the teacher represents a test score as indicating an inherent disability when it may actually indicate the quality of the education provided and the experience offered by the society.

Bias in testing   Traditionally, achievement and IQ tests have been constructed by professionals who come from academic, white middle-class society. Their beliefs of what children should know are in part a product of their middle-class environment, status, and experiences. Results of efforts at the state and local levels to force a more equitable means of assessing children's ability are shown in Figure 13-8, p. 377.

A child's IQ may change considerably as he or she grows older and there is no justification for discrimination, for example, between children with an IQ of 96 and those with an IQ of 102. Placing children into ranks or streams within a grade on the assumption that a given IQ test score represents an absolute and total potential may adversely affect a child's self-esteem and consequently his motivation to learn. A child so labeled may be given a significantly false impression of his talents, which will be difficult to overcome. It should be remembered that tests, to some extent at least, inevitably reflect the values, life style, and experiences of the group that has created them, and of those who administer and evaluate them.

SF Schools Halt Negro IQ Testing

SAN FRANCISCO (UPI)—Board of Education members voted unanimously today to stop administering intelligence tests to students by groups.

Also voted was a moratorium on individual intelligence tests for Negro children unless their parents requested them.

Those actions came after repeated demands by Negro organizations which asked moratoriums on both intelligence tests and achievement tests, contending they were culturally biased against black students.

The board decided, however, to continue achievement tests.

It also decided to employ consultants "who have expertise in test development and knowledge of ethnic minority backgrounds" to find means of testing the intelligence quotients of black and other minority students.

Among the organizations that objected to standard intelligence tests were the Association of Black Psychologists, the Urban League, the National Association for the Advancement of Colored People and the Neighborhood Legal Assistance Foundation.

School administrators were ordered not to put the results of either group or individual IQ tests in a child's permanent record folder and a committee was appointed to find ways of getting existing test scores out of such folders. (Palo Alto *Times,* July 17, 1970, p. 2.)

Figure 13-8 *Efforts to force more equitable assessment sometimes have dramatic results*

Tests in programs of early education

Teachers in preschool programs should become familiar with the tests commonly used for evaluating young children and with the kinds of goals and behavioral objectives considered to be relevant criteria for evaluation. The use of tests assumes the existence of standards of measurement—that is, behavioral objectives. Goals inherent in the test may not coincide with those the teacher has established and those the program tends to foster. A nursery school program that encourages children to play, to build with blocks, and to get along well together, should obviously be evaluated in terms of how well the children engage in play activities, build with blocks, and accept one another.

There is little justification in measuring such a program with a test that scores the ability to recognize letters of the alphabet and to count. Tests are usually designed to measure cognitive performance because affective performance does not easily lend itself to testing. This doesn't mean that affective behaviors or goals are any less important. There is simply a temptation to find situations that call for the instruments on hand, much as the small child armed with a hammer goes around looking for something to hammer. Characteristics and qualities for which measures have not been devised can easily be ignored despite their importance. Thus ignored, they tend to lose value in the mind of the professional and fail to be built into future program objectives and evaluation procedures.

UNITED STATES DISTRICT COURT
NORTHERN DISTRICT OF CALIFORNIA

DIANA, *et al.*, Plaintiffs,
vs.
STATE BOARD OF
EDUCATION, *et al.*, Defendants
C-70 37 RFP
STIPULATION AND ORDER

Dated Feb. 5, 1970

(Excerpt from Agreement) . . . The State Department of Education . . . shall require districts to get statistics sufficient to enable a determination to be made of the numbers and percentages of the various racial and ethnic groups in each Educable Mentally Retarded class in the district . . .

(Excerpt from Exhibit A) . . . If the primary language used in the home of the minor is a language other than English, the minor shall be tested by a school psychologist or other qualified person. . . . in both English and the primary language used in his home and shall be permitted to respond in either language during the testing session. . . . The school psychologist or other qualified person giving a test . . . shall be competent in speaking and reading the language used by the minor in his speaking and cognitive activity.

(Excerpt from Exhibit B) . . . It is the intent, of the State Board of Education that all children who come from homes in which the primary spoken language is other than English shall be interviewed, and examined, both in English and in the primary language used in his home. The examiner should take cognizance of the child's differential language facility. Any assessment of the child's intellectual functioning should be made on the basis of the spoken language most familiar to the child. In determining the intellectual functioning of a child whose primary language is other than English, it is recommended that the examiner utilize more than one instrument and include tests with performance scales.

Figure 13-9 contains examples of typical kinds of items used at this time in the evaluation of early educational programs. These are adapted from many different types of tests and are shown for illustration only.

The Purpose of Evaluation

Although an assessment usually carries with it the possibility that some change in program or behavior may be indicated, the specific purpose of each evaluation depends upon the persons responsible for the assessment plans and procedures. Many of the reasons for evaluations fall in these two categories:

> To determine the effectiveness of the program or some of its elements
> To obtain research data

In the recent past, there has been a growing resistance to research in low-income and minority communities. Arguments against research include accusations that the information gained has not been used to assist the community or change the educational opportunities of children from poverty areas. Other objections to the use of test data have been raised in debates about differences in performance between ethnic groups and children from white communities. Funds for research are often considered secondary to improvements of educational programs.

Evaluating Program Effectiveness

One of the most prominent types of evaluation of early educational programs is oriented toward an assessment of the success of different approaches and major programs. These evaluations are inspired by pressures from political sources and desires to determine program efficiency. They fall into the following somewhat overlapping categories.

Desire to know what has been done and how well

One response to increased educational costs and higher taxes is that voters are more likely to ask, "What are we getting for our money?" And many are following up this question with another: "Are we getting what we want?" School bonds and higher taxes have been justified by school officials on the presumption that educational benefits would result from increases in expenditures. There have been many public attacks on the school in the mass media and in books, and the questions that have been raised have given school communities a sense of caution and skepticism. They are now beginning to ask for an accounting, at least in the sense that they want more evidence that additional funds or new programs have some chance of accomplishing their aims. Questions regarding the problems of preparing youth for a complex society, and the increased political activity and new behavior codes among young people (as reflected in their attitudes toward protests, sex, drugs, etc.,) have motivated many taxpayers to call for evaluation of the schools to determine whether they are doing an effective job in this society.

Figure 13-9 *Examples of testing methods used in evaluation of preschoolers and preschool programs*

Skill and level	Setting	Procedure	Response expected
Naming Objects from Memory 3- and 4-year-olds	Child and teacher are seated across from one another at small table In a concealed location teacher has six different items commonly used by child and whose names he knows 　　Example: doll, book, ball, spoon, car, crayon	For a total of six different trials, teacher places any two of the objects in front of the child, side by side Teacher: "This is a game where I'm going to take one of these away while your eyes are closed" "Look at the objects and think what they are" "Now, close your eyes and don't look while I take one away" "Open your eyes. What did I take away?"	Child should *name* the object that the teacher removed If he simply points to where the missing object was located, teacher should rephrase question so that he understands he is to *tell* her *what* she took away 　　Example: "What was here a moment ago that isn't here now?" *Score:* 　　1 point for each name correctly given
Simultaneous Voluntary Movement 5-year-olds	Child seated at table has box approximately half the size of a shoe box in front of him; at either side of box there are ten small items such as bottle caps, checkers, scrabble-type squares (total of 20)	Teacher: "Pick up a checker in each hand and put them in the box at the same time until all the checkers are in the box"	Two by two, child should put all pieces in the box using both hands simultaneously He is successful if he can do this in one out of two trials
Digit Span Preschool	Teacher and child in conversation together Teacher has list of number sets which vary according to quantity of numbers; three examples of each set—sets to go as high as 7 numerals 	4	2, 5	8, 1, 6	4, 7, 2, 1
9	6, 3	7, 8, 2	9, 6, 8, 3
1	4, 8	5, 9, 4	5, 8, 1, 4		Teacher: "Whatever numbers I say, you say them, too" She then says, "4" or whatever number is first on her list. She gives all numbers in the set with just 1 number, then all in the 2-set, the 3-set, etc., until child fails all items of any set	Child is to repeat the numbers after the teacher in the same serial order *Score:* 　　1 point for each correct repetition

Figure 13-9 (*Continued*)

Skill and level	Setting	Procedure	Response expected
Visual Perception Preschool	Teacher and child sit facing one another across small table Teacher has nine different cards with four pictures each The pictures are geometric figures, letters, words, numbers, shapes, and/or colors; one of the pictures on each card is the same as the first one in its row	Teacher places the cards in front of the child one by one Pointing to the first picture in the row (to the left for the child) she asks, "Which picture in the row is most nearly like the one I am pointing to?" If child has had training in matching she can say, "Which picture matches the one I am pointing to?"	Child is to point to his choice *Score:* 2 points for each item matched without hesitation; 1 point if child was unsure or simply guessing
Visual Discrimination 3 to 6 years	Teacher and child sit facing one another across small table Teacher has 33 different cards each containing four pictures of the same object; picture at top of each set serves as model The objects are identical but differ in position	Teacher places the cards in front of the child one by one For each card she points to the model picture saying, "Which of the other pictures is most like this one?"	Child is to point to or in some way select picture of his choice *Score:* 1 point for each correct identification
Letter Recognition 5-year-olds	Teacher and child sit facing one another across a small table Teacher has 3 cards, each containing 6 lines of letters with 4 letters per line Letters are both upper and lower case Child has cardboard strip big enough to cover one row of 4 letters and a pencil for marking answers	Teacher puts cards in front of child one at a time She shows child how to use the cardboard strip he has to cover line *below* the one he will be working on Then she says, "Put a mark on the letter I name. If you are not sure, mark the one you think it might be." As child finishes one line he goes to next below in each column	Child is expected to mark (or cross out) his choices *Score:* 1 point is given for correct choice

(Visual Perception row illustration:)

■ ▲ ▇ ●	3 386	Z FNZ

(Visual Discrimination row illustration:)

(Letter Recognition row illustration:)

H EXR	Wid L
Sp Kn	om Br
N h AV	C ek a

Figure 13-9 (*Continued*)

Skill and level	Setting	Procedure	Response expected
Stimuli Recognition (Vocabulary) 3½ up	Teacher and child face one another standing or seated From different items in 20 specific areas such as parts of body, classroom objects, foods, sounds, amounts, occupations, household items, teacher asks a total of 100 questions (number of questions during any testing time varies with maturity of child; each area has 5 items) Half of items are directly visible, the other half of a general nature	Teacher calls child by name or talks to him so she knows she has his attention, then asks a series of questions waiting for child to answer one before going on to next Examples: "What is a person who fixes teeth called?" (Touching knee) "What part of my body am I touching?" (Holding up picture of girl roller-skating) "What is this girl doing?"	Following each question, child is expected to name the object or activity indicated *Score:* 1 point for each correct answer
Self-Concept Preschool and primary	Child and teacher are seated together side by side Teacher has photograph of child. She also has a written list of questions designed to test child's concept of himself, and how he thinks his mother, teacher, and peers perceive him The questions consider pairs of bi-polar adjectives—one of which describes a socially approved quality Self-referent questions are used first	Photograph is shown to child and teacher asks him to tell her whose picture is shown ("Who is this a picture of?") Before going further, teacher makes sure child recognizes that what he sees is a picture of himself Pointing to the photo she asks questions such as the following, using child's name —he is here identified as Tom "Is Tom sad or happy?" "Does Tom's mother think he is neat or messy?" "Does Tom's teacher think he's quiet or noisy?" "Do Tom's friends like to play with him or dislike to play with him?"	Child is to respond verbally choosing one of the paired adjectives as criteria *Score:* 1 point for each answer in which he uses the positive adjective to represent how he sees himself, and how he thinks others see him Note: Keeping track of the number of times child is unable to respond helps make total evaluation more realistic

Figure 13-9 *(Continued)*

Skill and level	Setting	Procedure	Response expected
Concept of Social Relationship Preschool	Teacher and child seated beside one another Teacher has 8 cards each with 6 identical circles except first which contains a picture representing a stimulus person—mother, father, teacher, friend; each stimulus person is used twice	Teacher shows child one card at a time As she does she says, "Pretend this circle is your mother (pointing to circle on left and naming stimulus person). "Show me which circle would be you" When child chooses she says, "I'll write your name in the circle you chose"	Child points to or in some way indicates his choice *Score:* 1 to 5 points from nearest to farthest away from stimulus picture High score shows least identification

Skill and level	Setting	Procedure	Response expected

Ordering-Sequencing
 	
5-year-olds
	Teacher and child seated across from one another at small table
	
	Teacher has sets of pictures of recognizable objects, varying in size, shape and number
	
	Child will be asked to order them by
	  shape
	  size
	  number
	or a combination of these factors
		Depending on skill to be tested, teacher gives child an appropriate set of items or shows him pictures
		
		Example: "Here are four pictures of trucks; put the pictures in a line so that the one with the most red trucks comes first, and the one with the fewest red trucks comes last"
			Child should order, or attempt to order items as directed.
			
			In example given, scoring would be as follows:
			
			3 points for correct ordering
			2 points if end sets correct but middle reversed
			1 point for attempt but no success
			0 points for no attempt

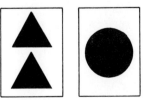

Figure 13-9 (*Continued*)

Skill and level	Setting	Procedure	Response expected
Recognizing Ordinal Numbers Preschool	Teacher and child at table or on floor together Teacher has 5 open containers (trucks, boxes, cups, dishes, etc.) lined up in a row She also has a checker or marble or object that can easily be placed in any of the containers	Teacher hands the checker (or whatever item) to child saying, "Put this in the fifth dish" (or whatever container used) Teacher removes checker from whichever container child put it in and hands it to him again asking that he place it in the following ordering: 5th, 4th, 1st, last, 2nd	Child is expected to place the marble in the location asked for *Score:* 1 point for each correct placement

Skill and level	Setting	Procedure	Response expected
Matching Quantities 5-year-olds	Teacher and child sit facing one another across small table Teacher has 4 cards, each with 5 sets in the arrangement shown. Center picture used as model	Placing a card in front of the child teacher says, "I will point to a picture; put your finger on another picture that has the same number of objects"	Child is to put his finger on the matching picture. *Score:* 1 point for each correct answer

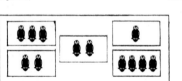

Skill and level	Setting	Procedure	Response expected

Parallel Sentence Production
 	
Preschool
	Teacher and child seated together in any comfortable arrangement
	
	Teacher has 22 cards—two of which are samples. Each card has two drawings on it. One drawing illustrates a clue sentence, one the sentence desired
	
	Some require only simple word substitution, others require more elaborate word substitution
		Teacher shows one of the sample cards to the child and gives the clue sentence; she then points to other picture and gives parallel sentence; repeats but asks child to give parallel sentence; if child's answer is incorrect, she uses second sample card; she does not begin until child has responded correctly
		
		She then shows each of the 20 cards, gives clue sentence, and waits for parallel sentence response before going on
			Child should give sentence called for with whatever word substitutions are needed
			
			Score:
			   1 point for each parallel sentence
			
			Teacher is to record any deviation from sentence expected. Example:
			   The girl is standing still
			   The boy is running

Figure 13-9 *(Continued)*

Skill and level	Setting	Procedure	Response expected
Verbal Facility Using Parts of Speech 5-year-olds	Teacher and child seated comfortably together Teacher has list of 40 questions—one for each of 40 pictures which are designed to elicit word responses containing various parts of speech 	While child looks at a picture teacher asks question associated with it and calling for answer that contains desired parts of speech Example: What is the girl doing? (crying) What is different about these two circles? (one is bigger) 	Child is to give verbal answer in appropriate word form *Score:* 1 point each correct answer
Knowledge of Word Meaning Preschool	Teacher and child seated facing one another across small table Teacher has 10 cards each of which contains four pictures —all elements essentially alike in each set of pictures but arranged in different relationships Examples: over, on, under, with, beside, around, in, through. . . .	Teacher asks child to look at each card, one by one; as he does she reads a sentence describing one of the pictures Example: The cat is in the barrel Then she says, "Put your finger on the picture that shows what I said about the cat" 	Child is expected to put his finger on picture asked for (or to point to it) *Score:* 1 point for each correct answer (If child does not respond, sentence and instruction may be repeated)

Figure 13-10

SACRAMENTO (AP)—The state's superintendent of public instruction says he is setting up a special evaluation unit to determine if new school programs are doing what they're supposed to do.

"If they're not, we'll cut them off," said Wilson Riles in an interview. "Funds are scarce."

Riles commented Tuesday on a report by Legislative Analyst A. Alan Post that said California public schools are wasting large amounts of money through misguided efforts to improve education.

Post mentioned such programs as smaller classes, hiring more consultants and higher teacher pay.

Post said there has been no indication that all these special programs—some of them federally financed—have improved the pupils' performance in school.

"The problem," he said, "is a lack of yardsticks to measure the effectiveness of the programs."

Riles commented, "Accountability is what we have to have to get the job done."

Riles had no quarrel with the study, conducted while the State Department of Education was under his predecessor, Max Rafferty.

Evaluation and approval unit he is setting up for special programs will have authority to "determine whether the new projects are coordinated with anything else," Riles said. "If not, we'll disapprove them."

"We should put all our funds together in some kind of comprehensive thrust so that we're dealing with something you can handle, not in bits and pieces," Riles said.

Post has been a frequent critic of the State Department of Education's organization and handling of projects such as the special federal programs. (Associated Press, June 23, 1971)

Demand for cost-benefit analysis

Staff members of governmental and other fundgranting agencies are particularly interested in the economic side of education and are inclined to see the need for evaluation from an additional viewpoint. They are concerned with students' achievement, the efficiency of the schools, and the cost of increasing their effectiveness. They want to compare results of alternative ways for accomplishing the same end to see which method gives the greatest return for the money spent. In effect, they ask, "It has cost x number of dollars to obtain these results, how much more will it cost to increase achievement even more? What would a different way cost?" The unit of measure may be IQ points, the number of children reading at grade level, or the proportion completing high school. In any event, their reason for assessing a program is closely tied to an analysis of cost-effectiveness.

Guarantee of contract performance

Evaluation is obviously a part of the philosophy of *performance contracting*. Within the last few years, education has come to be looked upon by some groups as a commodity—as something that can be bought and delivered on a guaranteed basis. For example, various private organizations are now advertising that for a given number of dollars and within such an amount of time they will teach a child to read. Parents who respond to this kind of promise are paying money for which they expect certain guarantees in return. An obvious reason for evaluation, therefore, is to determine whether a child has learned what the agency has contracted to teach him.

Follow-up of large-scale programs

Large-scale, publicly financed, innovative projects have brought pressure for evaluation to determine whether they have achieved their intended goals. Quite logically, researchers and administrators responsible for these undertakings want to know how well they are going. Funding is generally year-to-year, and at renewal time legislators and their constituents are naturally curious to know what has been accomplished. In appropriating money to launch efforts such as Head Start, Follow Through, and Sesame Street, Congress said in effect, "We're convinced the need is great. Here's the money to get started on a solution to our problems. Be sure to let us know what happens." Accordingly, programs of this magnitude have evaluation provisions incorporated into the original proposals—evaluation that is to be carried on by outside agencies and not the people receiving the funds. In this way innovators recognized the need for objective assessment.

The results of an evaluation of a program mean different things to different audiences. These results do not interpret themselves but are given meaning by those who write the report, by mass media, and by informal discussions. An evaluation of a program must be interpreted in light of the program's original intentions. In this case, the instruments used for evaluation and the criteria of performance applied are limited to those agreed upon in advance. This is perhaps the most "fair" type of evaluation, but rarely is a program director or teacher given sole authority to say in what terms his or her results will be measured. Programs designed to raise self-esteem will probably be assessed by pre-academic measures, such as pre-math skills and pre-reading skills. The interpretation of results does not always make this clear, especially if there is publicity through mass media.

An essential principle in interpreting evaluation results, then, is to consider the criteria used and the standards against which the quality of the program is described. In other instances, the reader might want to take into account the length of time the program had been underway and the opportunity that had been provided for staff training and curriculum development. It is wise to be skeptical and withhold judgment about a program's effectiveness until opportunity has been given for the results to stabilize and to discover if gains can be obtained by more than one program staff or teacher.

Evaluation of the Side Effects of Programs

Evaluation of national educational efforts typically takes into account the success of a program in terms of its own goals. However, large-scale programs such as Head Start may have unexpected side benefits. An example is the wealth of research data that has come and is still coming from Head Start and Follow Through. In 1965, when Head Start began, relatively little was known about poor children in the United States. Since that time, knowledge has been tremendously increased in areas such as language development, family interaction, and physical, cognitive, and emotional growth of children from ghetto areas.

Another example is the impact of highly visible programs upon the attitudes and expectations of the general public in a neighborhood, state, or nation. The publicity accompanying Head Start in its early years and the orientation of much of this publicity toward ghetto neighborhoods aroused increased concern among adults about the educational opportunities available to their children and a greater desire to participate in this sort of effort. The long range effects of this sort of community interest are difficult to measure but are nonetheless significant. The teacher whose goal is "to involve mothers in the school program" can evaluate whether or not this is being accomplished in her particular situation. Without the teacher's knowledge, however, a mother may continue to participate in school-related concerns throughout her child's educational development because of having become involved at the preschool level. The teacher may learn of the mother's involvement if the family continues to live in the same neighborhood and has younger children who are subsequently enrolled at the preschool level. But she may never be able to assess the total results of her plan "to involve the mother" once she loses contact with the family.

Another unanticipated result of Head Start, which did not appear during the formal evaluations of the program, was the considerable increase in the number of professional men and women from other fields who became both interested and active in the field of preschool education. Within a short period sociologists, psychologists, linguists, anthropologists, and people highly trained in related fields brought considerable talent and experience to bear on the problems associated with early education.

There is often so much overlap between research studies and evaluation efforts that it is difficult to see the difference between them. Similar procedures are often used in both, the tests or instruments may be identical, and the type of persons who do both often have similar training and qualifications. They may indeed be the same person. However, they do serve somewhat different purposes. Research, in the ideal sense, is a search for new information; evaluation always comes after some effort to reach a goal. It is intended to show whether the purposes of the educational effort were achieved.

There has been an enormous increase in both research and evaluation in early education since the creation of Head Start and other large-scale programs. A great many experimental projects were begun and many new procedures have been developed and introduced into preschools in the past few years. One of the principal aims of evaluators has been to discover which types of programs are most efficient in reaching specific kinds of objectives.

New information is also needed about the children themselves, the processes through which they learn, and the things that influence learning. Researchers attempt to discover this basic knowledge. The discovery that mothers affect the cognitive behavior and academic achievement of their children long before they send them to school led to a number of parent-involvement programs and to the development of toys and other devices that mothers might use in the home to encourage the growth of school-related skills. Evaluation of these programs attempted to reveal how well they worked. This new information may itself tell both researcher and evaluator significant things that lead to additional research and to modified programs or both.

Even basic research can serve evaluation purposes. If a graduate student from a nearby college is sent to collect research data by observing the instances of warm exchange and punishment between the teacher and her students, this information is also an indirect assessment of the teacher's effectiveness.

A researcher who examines the pattern of sociometric choices (which children play together, which are isolates) and finds that there are several children who seem to be left out of the group has revealed a finding that could be interpreted as an indirect criticism of the teacher's techniques for promoting group interaction or her sensitivity to the needs of the children in her class. The research intent may have been to look for the effects of social interaction upon verbal behavior of children.

When she is involved in the process, the teacher may learn a great deal about the children with whom she works. Evaluation and research thus may also serve diagnostic purposes for the teacher.

The Goals of Research

Research is a term that means many different things. To some, it is a symbol of the scientist in her laboratory, discovering radium, or an astronomer examining the temperature of stars a thousand light years away. To others, it is a market survey to determine how an advertisement should be phrased in order to increase sales. For some it may be an experiment on perception or memory with rigorous controls of all the research conditions. Or, it may be a summary of a group of interviews that are loose, unstructured, and casual. Research is all of these and more. Until you know what has been done in a given study and are informed about the qualifications of the persons doing the work, you cannot make a judgment about the quality of any work that someone chooses to call research.

In straightforward terms, research is a systematic attempt to discover new information about a topic on which information often is already available but on which there is a need for more. Research thus builds on present knowledge. The rocks brought back from the moon are significant obviously because of knowledge we already have regarding the age and structure of rocks on earth. The moon rocks provide more knowledge, which fits into a larger field of information. Usually, each study adds a little data and gives a better base for the next study. Knowing that more boys than girls are reported to have reading and speaking disabilities leads to the question: why? Studies that attempt to show why (is it the attitudes of female teachers toward small males or is it something physiological or genetic) would lead to another question: can it be prevented? This desire and need to learn more about human behavior is the challenge of educational and social research. It ultimately has meaning for the teacher when he or she can recognize a situation and realize that she has the knowledge and skills to take some effective action. This is the bridge between the researcher and the teacher.

If we agree that research on human behavior and on young

children and their teachers may ultimately contribute to the growth and development of young children, it does not follow that all research is equally useful. Nor does it mean that all research with these goals is automatically to be accepted and encouraged by the staff of a child-care center or nursery school. Some important studies have goals that have little direct relevance for young children. Others may serve primarily the aims of the researcher. Some studies are poorly designed and will result in no useful findings of any kind. Other projects are done with such little consideration for the subjects on whom the research is conducted that they may do more harm than good.

While few teachers are in a position to evaluate and modify a research goal or design, there are, nonetheless, some general guidelines that will help make the study more effective and protect the interests of the teacher and the children in her class.

The Ethics of Research

Researchers sometimes create the impression that the children and the staff on which they do research are guinea pigs whose importance comes only from the fact that they are available as subjects. The feeling of being used is sometimes part of the research experience and may be the cause of resentment and misunderstanding. People do not need to be treated as guinea pigs or to feel that they are. When this happens, it most likely comes from the inexperience, ineptness, or carelessness of the researcher. You can help avoid such research experiences for yourself, your students, and the parents in the community.

For many years, researchers were not trained to take seriously the feelings of people on whom they did research or consider the consequences of research for subjects involved. Most researchers, of course, showed courtesy and consideration for the subjects and for the cooperating schools. A few abuses of research in medical science and in the social sciences, however, jolted the researchers and the public and led to the establishment of guidelines protecting the rights of human subjects in research. These guidelines are now applied to all research funded through the United States Department of Health, Education, and Welfare and are usually administered by the sponsoring college or research institute. Some states, like California, have legislation regulating the kind of research that can be conducted in the public schools without express, often written, consent of parents. These regulations are beginning to create a climate of greater communication between the researcher and the schools. They provide a basis for discussion about research expectations and consequences.

The staff of a school invited to participate in research or evaluation has the legal and ethical right to set conditions under which research can be conducted. Each staff may want to draw up guidelines suitable for their own needs and school. These general principles may be useful in evaluating the acceptability of a study.

1. The researcher will specify in advance the exact nature of the study, the time to be involved, the number and approximate schedule of testing sessions, and the qualifications of the research staff.
2. The director and staff of the school will have an opportunity to examine the testing instruments and to invite a group of parents to examine them if there is question about the study.
3. The children and/or their parents are to be fully informed about the purpose of the research and the procedures involved.
4. The parents must give consent for their children to participate or will have delegated this responsibility to the director and her staff.
5. The procedures of the study will not inflict physical, emotional, or mental harm on the subjects.
6. The information sought will not touch on personally offensive topics or invade the privacy of individuals or their families.
7. Information obtained about individuals or families will be kept confidential, and will be protected from inspection by unauthorized persons.
8. The results of the study, if published, will not cause harm to the reputations or self-esteem of the children, families, or staff.
9. Results that identify an individual or a school will not be reported without express consent of the subjects or school *after* they or their parents have had opportunity to read or view the report and findings.
10. The participating school and parents will be provided with a report of the study and a description of the relevance of the findings for education and child development.

These guidelines are a sensible expression of the principle that research subjects should not suffer negative consequences as a result of participation in a study. When in doubt, ask yourself how people will feel when they have been through the research experience and when they see the results.

There is a potential problem with studies that give parents information about the stage of development or achievement of their children. Test scores or developmental growth charts, whether for physical, social, or mental characteristics, may serve to make parents anxious about the status and competence of their children. Especially when the children are young, parents are developing an impression of their intelligence, physical talents, and social skills. Information about the performance of their child in relation to others in the class reflects favorably or adversely on them as parents. Children, after all, are the published testimony of their parents—the evidence of both their genetic stock and their emotional maturity. It is difficult to overestimate the sensitivity of parents to information about the achievements of their young children.

Be prepared for strong parental reaction to research, whether it is part of your program or the study of an outsider, that compares children in any significant way. Be especially cautious about letting parents know how the children of other parents perform. These comparisons have social significance for adults quite apart from the meaning they have for children.

Using Research Results

Both research and evaluation results can be used by the teacher to gain both a more complete perspective on the program in which he is participating and information about the children in his class. Research results can add to his professional understanding of the field of early education and child care, and help keep him in touch with recent developments in the field.

Some studies will be more useful than others, of course, and the results of studies done in his school can be more helpful if they are prepared with the needs of the staff in mind. In negotiating with researchers who want to use staff, children, or parents in their studies, one of the requests should be for a written report of the results with the implications for teachers clearly described. In some instances, the researcher will agree to meet with the staff and perhaps with groups of parents to discuss the results and show how they may be useful or of general interest. Most researchers will not be inclined to suggest this themselves, but will agree if it is made a part of the conditions of the study. If the project is conducted by a student, it may be wise to be in touch with the faculty advisor or sponsor in deciding what the conditions of the study will be.

When the study, whether research or evaluation, involves testing or observing children, the information provided may be of specific, direct relevance to the teachers and parents. Where this type of testing is involved, two things are essential; first, be certain that you know in advance just what information will be obtained, and second, find out if the information about individual children will be available to you for the school files. Of particular significance, obviously, is information that reveals some disability or problem requiring special attention. The evaluation or research thus becomes part of a total diagnosis of the developmental progress of the child and can be used to provide individual help for him.

In summary, these guidelines may be helpful in establishing conditions for research.

1. Find out what types of data are to be obtained and from whom.
2. Inquire whether the information about individuals can be made part of the school records.
3. Reach agreement on whether the information can be shared with parents.
4. Agree on the kind of feedback to be given the school and research subjects.
5. Get a commitment from the researcher as to the type of feedback to be given and who is responsible for giving it.
6. Keep a file of studies done, including who was responsible for the study, the personnel who carried it out in the school, the type of feedback, and the usefulness of the study to the staff and families.

Seen in their proper roles, evaluation and research are, at worst, necessary nuisances and, at best, resources for the teacher to use in perfecting his skills and understanding. They may carry a bit of a threat, but if the teacher understands why they exist and if the mystique is evaporated by an understanding of what is involved, he is more likely to accept evaluation as a challenge.

SUMMARY   Evaluation is frequently a part of programs of early education and child care. It is less threatening if the procedures and purposes are understood. This chapter describes various aspects of evaluation including its purposes, rationale, and instruments for collecting data. Research may be one form of evaluation although it may have other goals. Research studies should be regulated by a code of ethics which protects the rights of the people on whom the research is done. The teacher who knows how to use research reports has an additional resource for improving her own skills and keeping informed about new developments in the field. The chapter includes a section describing types of items used in tests for young children.

1. If the teacher understands the procedures of evaluation she may find the process less threatening.
2. Summative evaluation is used to study effectiveness of a program after it has been completed.
3. Formative evaluation is ongoing, providing feedback to the program and allowing changes to be made while the program is in progress.
4. Informal evaluation includes casual comments of praise or criticism and other types of incidental assessments.
5. Formal evaluation is based on data obtained through tests, observations, ratings, interviews, questionnaires, and other standard measurement techniques.
6. Tests, by their design and conceptualization, represent the cultural biases of the test makers. This has been recognized by court decisions as to the uses that may be made of test results in public education.
7. Popular tests in early education include language, memory, perceptual abilities, letter recognitions and many more. The teacher should know something of the range of tests in order to select the one that examines the particular skill she is trying to assess or diagnose.
8. The two purposes of evaluation are: to determine program effectiveness and to obtain research data.
9. In programs using public funds, there is a strong demand for evaluation to determine if the cost of a program is justified by the results.
10. Research and evaluation have similar methods and overlap in types of data gathered.
11. The goals of research are traditionally set by the researcher; teachers need to know what these goals are before approving studies with their children.
12. There are ethical principles governing research with human subjects. Teachers need to be familiar with the central features of these principles in order to see that the school staff, the children and their parents are adequately protected from invasion of privacy, harm, undue publicity and other potential consequences.
13. The teacher who takes time to become familiar with the general procedures of research can use research results to keep informed of new developments in the field.

14. Teachers should take particular care to inform parents about testing programs and research studies in which their children may participate.

REFERENCES

Association for Supervision and Curriculum Development Yearbook. *Evaluation as feedback and guide.* Wilhelms, F. T. (ed.). Washington, D.C.: National Education Association, 1967.

Bloom, B. S., Hastings, J. T. and Madaus, G. F. *Handbook on formative and summative evaluation of student learning.* New York: McGraw-Hill, 1971.

Mager, R. F. *Preparing instructional objectives.* Belmont, Ca.: Fearon Publishers, 1962.

Paulson, C. *Strategies for evaluation design.* Monmouth, Ore.: Teaching Research Division, Oregon State System of Higher Education, 1970.

Popham, W. J. and Baker, E. L. *Establishing instructional goals.* Englewood Cliffs, N.J.: Prentice-Hall, 1970.

Chapter 14 Self Evaluation: The Art of Developing Your Own Resources

When You're on Your Own

Being on your own on your first job can be a frightening experience. Just as the teacher in Chapter 1 had to make quick decisions on her own, you will be in many situations that compel you to act on your own initiative. After you have made a decision you may wonder, "How would my teacher have handled this?" Or, "Now what was it that the book said about this sort of problem?" You may wish you had a chance to talk with your classmates or a faculty member about what you've done. If only your new job had the same comfortable routine of the training schedule you know so well! But things are different, and you are now on your own and must develop other sources of evaluation, information, and training.

Every other teacher has been through this kind of experience. They learn, however, that they are not without resources and are not alone. Just as they have found ways to develop greater professional competence, you too will learn to rely on yourself more and to use your experiences to grow. In effect, you will learn to be your own teacher.

You will decide on the job what is important for you to master. Although others may make suggestions or offer opinions, seldom will other teachers or a director make systematic efforts to help you become a professional. You will begin the important task of developing resources for self-teaching. Learning doesn't stop with graduation or the offer of a job. In many important ways this is when your learning will really begin.

After graduation, the center of control is in your hands. Your future accomplishments and competence rely heavily on your own efforts. To a large extent, the opportunities you have will be the result of a willingness and an ability to teach yourself.

If you teach yourself, you must also evaluate yourself. How do you learn to stand aside and ask yourself how you are doing? First, you can learn to pick up cues, even subtle ones, from others that will give you valuable information about your performance. And while your ex-teacher's feedback and friendly criticism will no longer be there, you can learn to give yourself unwritten and unspoken grades and comments. You are now working not for grades but for long-term rewards that carry more weight than did your semester marks.

An experienced teacher develops over the years a history of experiences. From these he or she learns what sort of teacher he or she is—what her or his strengths and weaknesses are. You too have developed a similar sense of how well you have done in your training program. Many of these impressions come from the direct, explicit feedback of the teachers with whom you have worked, grades you have received, comments on a class paper or project, evaluations of your work with children. But you are also probably aware of more subtle cues—how the children respond, the enthusiasm of your fellow students, the behavior of parents toward you. In short, you are beginning to be aware of your competence through information gained from a variety of sources, both formal (grades, direct criticism of your work, etc.,) and informal. You have developed an internal system for judging your work. You take seriously what others tell you, but you also have your own evaluation of your competence. It may be somewhat tentative and cautious, but it is there.

As a professional you need to develop a more effective way to read the external cues and to set your own standards of performance. Much of the learning you will do comes directly from experience. If you begin to work out a set of goals and standards by which you will evaluate yourself, you will be aware of what you have learned from your experiences and see how they fit into your own professional growth.

Why bother to go through the hassle of self-evaluation? For one thing, the field is growing and changing. It is not easy to keep up with new ideas and programs. Federal projects, state programs, local child-care activities, and an enormous growth of professional literature and research are stimulating development in the field. Social changes, especially those associated with the family and the role of women in this country, are influencing the field of child development and early education. These affect both the curricula and the definitions of jobs. Early education and child care are probably the most rapidly changing areas in education and there is no guarantee that they will become static after you take your first job. If they seem to do so, it is because you are isolated from what's going on.

The competition will be tough. Programs for training teachers of young children are being constantly updated and improved. New research and new teacher techniques are constantly being fed into these programs and into inservice training, too. In some areas, parents are gaining more information about early education and will bring a more informed attitude when they visit your classroom. These changes are dramatic. They are exciting, too, and can be part of the basis for your developing competence as a professional. They will be one of your resources in your program of self-teaching.

You will also keep yourself growing and learning for the sake of the children. You came into early education because you believed that you could influence the children in some positive way. To reach this goal, you need to keep yourself in shape. Like any professional, to be your best, you need to be well informed, to keep thinking, keep learning.

How Do You Know You're Doing a Good Job?

In China, there is a self-awareness process for teachers called Struggle, Self-Criticism, and Transformation. Students and teachers criticize one another in order to improve the achievement and performance level of the group. This is not an individual effort; the beliefs of the Chinese about achievement are such that individuals must be open to comments and suggestions for improvement from their students and friends. This is not an easy task. Attitudes of competition in this country are such that we are much less likely to use this route to improve the quality of teaching. It is more an individual matter. The penalty for not growing is much more subtle, and likely to be delayed.

Nonetheless, you are constantly being evaluated. Whether you choose to acknowledge this or deny it is up to you.

A number of programs of early education rely on team teaching, and parent and community involvement. Cooperation and mutual support for effectiveness in these programs are desirable but certainly not universal. In these situations, a teacher should be able to rely on others for reinforcement of teaching methods and for achieving goals. Nonetheless, the environment may be such that she can easily avoid self-criticism or ignore and discount the comments of others. She then must take responsibility herself for getting the sort of feedback that will help her to be aware of her own areas of strengths and weaknesses.

Sources of Feedback

Where should the teacher turn? What are the sources of information that will tell you how you are doing? Where are the cues you will need to piece together the feedback that will show you how you look to others? The cues exist all around. There are many sources of information on how well you are doing.

The Children

First, and most available, are the children. In indirect (and sometimes almost too direct) ways they are the mirrors of your behavior. Their smiles, eagerness, reticence, and problems carry messages not only of rejection or affection but of your effectiveness as a teacher. For example:

Norma came into the teachers' room a little louder and more active than usual. Those who knew her sensed that she was concerned.

"I hate to serve juice. Every time I sit at a table, the children all go to other tables and have their juice with someone else."

"Why do you think they might do that?" asked the Director. "I really don't know. Maybe the other teachers bribe them." There was a moment of silence. Then, in a quieter voice, she said a little sadly, "I really don't know. I like kids but maybe I can't relate to them. I guess I have bad vibes."

The Director looked thoughtful. She pondered the list of things that might be said. Norma was loud, too busy, too little aware of where the children were and how they felt. But it would do no good to say these things. Instead she said, "Let's think of some ways that we might work with you. The first thing is that you are aware that you want to be more effective. That means you can begin to find some answers. Maybe we can help you get some specific ideas about how you interact with the children. Maybe one of us can observe you and make some useful comments. For example, perhaps you might wait a little longer for the children to respond when you say something to them. Sometimes I think you rush the conversation a bit and the children don't get a chance to say things they want to say. If you want, I think things can work out."

Norma's trip is a painful one. Recognizing a problem is a difficult but essential first step of the self-evaluation process. The observations and the supervisor's comments would be tough to take. They might even make her more self-conscious and stilted for a while until she got over her embarrassment. She would need some time to come to terms with her situation and the understanding support of her supervisor during this time would be essential. But the comments and the specific suggestions she received might help Norma see how she could conceivably change her techniques of relating to the children. The first cues as to what was wrong, however, were the acts of the children themselves. It was on this information that the process of developing competence began.

Not all clues will be as obvious as in Norma's case, but the sensitive and knowledgeable teacher will learn to look to the children for signs that may carry significant bits of information.

Do the children initiate contact with you? Do they do things like touch you, climb on your lap, touch your hair?

Do they show any signs of affection—hug you, smile at you, and in other ways let you know that they are glad you're around? Are they eager to share experiences and bits of information with you?

Do the children look to you as a resource? This is more than an affectionate gesture. It is an expression of trust in your strength and helpfulness. Do they rely on you and ask for help or information?

Are you effective in redirecting the activities of children and still maintaining a positive relationship when you need to be firm?

The information you get from children's responses has to be interpreted. Your goal is not merely to be popular and have children follow you around. It is important to be liked, but your responsibility as a teacher extends far beyond this feature of your relationship with them.

Popularity is not the only criteria for being a good teacher, but it is unlikely that a teacher the children do not like can be effective for very long.

"Mrs. D., I have a confession to make," confided the student teacher. "Yesterday I watched you handle Eric very firmly when he was throwing blocks and he yelled that he hated you, but a half hour later when he got frustrated with his wood collage, he adamently refused any help from me or the other teacher and insisted on carrying all his wood and glue bottle out to you in the yard to ask your help. I was awfully curious to find out just what it is that you have going for you, so I followed him out and pretended to be busy at the sand box while I observed you. I watched you get down to his level and really concentrate on him like he was the most important person in the world. You looked at him and listened to him and then you suggested he do as much as he could and you would help him when he needed it. You really shared his concern and interest in a caring way. I feel like a phony when I see you in action."

"Well, I'm flattered to hear your report, but maybe I can add one more thing to your observation," replied Mrs. D. "Eric and I have had some really heavy confrontations over his aggressiveness. I have always tried to be honest with him in letting him know that I don't like his negative behavior but I make it a point to be as supportive as possible in letting him know I intend to stay with him until we both work the problem out. He knows he can count on me and I do use lots of praise when he does good things. I have found that the children and I usually end up with a closer relationship after we have survived some battles together."

A teacher who is concerned with winning popularity contests by resorting to superficial tactics to manipulate others will be exposed as a phony in short order. The teacher who places real concerns for the mental and emotional growth of her children first will recognize that accepting and absorbing hostility is also an important part of a genuine relationship.

These bits and fragments of informal feedback from the children are a valuable source of information about some aspects of your job. As with other impressions you receive, they are most useful when assessed against a matrix of goals and objectives you have for yourself and for the children.

Colleagues

A second source of information about your performance is the opinions of other professionals. Your supervisor, the other teachers, the aides, and the volunteers with whom you work can give you quite varied and more informed opinions and reactions.

One way to get ideas from your peers is to ask, directly or indirectly, for comments or help, as Norma did. There are several ways to do this. You may ask for observation of your work. You might ask for suggestions before you tackle a difficult task. You may find it useful to ask more than one of your colleagues about some aspect of your job in order to get a different perspective. There are ways, however, to read cues from other teachers that are more subtle.

For example, what happens to the suggestions you make for changes in schedule or other features of the program or the center? Are they discussed? accepted? ignored? Do other teachers welcome your opinion? How does the director or your supervisor respond? If your ideas are not taken seriously, however, it may be that the other teachers cannot accept initiative from junior staff members. You may want to reserve judgment for a while to see if there is a consistent pattern in the way others react to your ideas. One or two responses are not sufficient for you to make a judgment. Again, the critical process is how you interpret the information you get from others.

Do other teachers seek you out? Do they confide in you? Do they share information about the children and the parents that will help you do a better job? When was the last time one of your colleagues asked for your opinions or ideas?

You can also learn from other teachers by watching them do things you may have difficulty with. How do they engage the children at story time? How do they greet parents? Obviously, this does not mean that you should attempt to imitate them, but sometimes there are clues that you can pick up that tell you things about what you do. Perhaps their techniques may be those you want to adopt. Or, there may be behavior you want to avoid. In any case, their techniques help you become aware of what you yourself do.

Betty watched Tim asking Nora, the other teacher, to tie his shoe. Betty felt herself beginning to reach down to tie the muddy, stepped-on shoelace. But Nora didn't move. Instead, she said, "Tim, you're a big boy now. You show me how to tie your own shoe."

Tim did. Betty thought to herself, "Maybe I should encourage more self-reliance and independence in the children by encouraging them to try to do more things for themselves."

The next time one of the children asked for help with working a zipper, Betty said, "Try to do as much as you can by yourself. I'll help you if you still need me."

Betty had learned something about herself by contrasting her own behavior with that of someone else. This may mean that she will imitate, or adopt what she sees to suit her style. Or it may mean that she will congratulate herself on her own ability to do the same thing in her own effective way.

You may be aware of subtle messages that other teachers send. An oblique remark, an overheard (perhaps intentional) comment to another teacher or the director. A question or a wisp of praise about something you have done can be eloquent. The comment about a child with whom you have been working, "He requires a lot of consistency," may be a comment about the boy, or it may carry a message about your own ability to handle a child of his particular temperament. These clues are spontaneous and sometimes should be ignored. But they are information for you to gather and consider. We'll discuss later how such information might be used in self-assessment.

Parents

Parents are another good source of information about both your interactions with the children and your effectiveness in the program. How often have parents looked right past one teacher in preference for another teacher they have learned to trust and like. They will sometimes ignore new, young teachers until they prove themselves. Observe any classroom or children's center where there are several staff members. You will notice that parents may tend to confide in and chat more informally with one teacher than another. There may be outward signs of more smiling, praising, thanking, and sharing with some teachers than others.

Parents provide a good barometer of your effectiveness. Watch their subtle messages, such as knowing and calling you by name, or bypassing you to talk with someone else or the more blatant ones of bringing gifts or inviting you to dinner. Of course, sometimes they simply tell you that they like you. Or that they don't. Sometimes the most candid parent evaluations take place just outside the school doors at going home time when parents have a chance to get together and share their complaints and compliments.

Often it is a considerable task to learn how parents feel. Many parents may not have much time to come to the school to help or to respond to requests for formal written evaluations of the teacher, but their opinions are important. Teachers in all-day centers where working parents take their children are often frustrated by the lack of communication. One teacher says,

"They're too tired by the end of the day, and so are we, to do much talking. Our evening and weekend meetings are poorly attended, and we just have to resort to all kinds of ways to be in touch."

One teacher reports that it is worth the extra effort to get feedback from the parents. "I find from experience that I get the best results when I use positive examples at first. Sometimes I'll call a mother or father at home and report something amusing and clever. That often leads to questions from them about the program and how their child is doing. They may also make some comment that tells me if they like what I'm doing and how our school is run. If they say nothing about how they feel . . . well, that tells me something, too. Sometimes the most important things are those that are *not* said."

"Other times I'll send home a short note and I always read it to the child first so he will know what it says. I try to leave them open-ended so the parents can respond if they wish. I really appreciate getting notes from the parents and I let them know that nothing is too insignificant to share with me."

Dear Mrs. Carter,
Jimmy did a beautiful job of teaching some of the other children how to separate eggs today during our cooking project. He tells me you know how to bake the best cake in all the world. Maybe you can share the recipe sometime. It's obvious that Jimmy enjoys helping you with the cooking at home. I miss not having a chance to chat with some of our parents and sharing some of these experiences, so I hope you don't mind a note from me once in a while. Please feel free to call me or drop me a note any time.

Sincerely,

"This mother called from work the next day to give me her recipe and when I asked if she had any concerns she admitted she never would have called me about it, but since I asked . . . she had some minor complaints about the routine when she picked Jimmy up each day. He seldom had his shoes or jacket on and his paintings and other work were often scattered so no one could find them. She felt no one really cared enough to get Jimmy organized when it was time to go home. She was grateful to have this opportunity to express her feelings and asked me to continue to write notes so she would have an excuse to call."

When given the opportunity, parents provide a good source of information about teachers and programs. Sometimes a great deal of significant evaluation takes place in the public park, the grocery checkout line, and other such places where parents are likely to meet informally. The wise teacher will help to channel some of that information her way and use it to correct misinterpretations and to evaluate herself and her program.

Yourself

The best source of information about yourself is yourself. You can keep track of your own behavior and make your own opportunities for self-study and reflection. You are in the best position to see if your progress matches your hopes and aspirations. You are the best judge of yourself if you get and use wisely the information around you.

One way to do this is to make a list of your priorities and then keep a log of how you spend your time when you are on the job. The ways you allocate your time reveal what your true, underlying priorities are. For example, you might start with a simple list of things you ought to do in order to be a good teacher, such as: (1) spend time interacting with every child; (2) observe some of the problem children more closely; (3) have many positive experiences with quiet children; (4) plan more individual creative activities. The log you keep needn't be a minute-by-minute detailed account, but should give you an accurate picture of how you actually have allotted your time.

Suppose you discover that a large part of your day is spent in the kitchen preparing activities and cleaning up; another large part spent in talking with parents or other teachers, and only a few minutes spent in group activities with the children. The discrepancy between your list of priorities and the things you actually do can provide you with a means for reassessing yourself. Maybe your assigned duties do not permit you to work closely with the children, or is it possible that you have been retreating to these duties in order to disguise some of your fears or hidden motives? Most teachers have experienced times they frantically busied themselves tying shoe strings or wiping noses when they felt inadequate to handle a more serious situation. It happens to the best of teachers. This discomfort may be the impetus you need to sit down and redesign your work schedule or discuss with your supervisor how you can allow time for your stated priorities. In any event, the way you actually spend your time is one of the best indicators of your sense of values and competence. A sure sign of the need to reassess your goals is when there is a great discrepancy between what you do and what you say you really want to do.

If you are lucky enough to have access to a videotape machine you can arrange to see yourself as others see you. One teacher, knowing she would be self-conscious and unnatural if the camera followed her, chose to be videotaped during a particular segment of her creative dance time with the children when she thought she was particularly effective. She replayed the tape several times and made notes that helped her improve her methods. In most cases, it may be least painful to start in areas where you feel you are most capable. Then as you begin to get helpful feedback from your self-assessment, you will be more likely to look at other areas of your teaching where you are less comfortable.

Use an audio tape recorder to hear yourself interact with others. One teacher used a miniature recorder with built-in microphone to tape sharing time without any distraction to the children. "I knew I would never let anyone else hear it so I didn't have to be fake in order to impress someone else. I left that tape around for two weeks before I had the nerve to listen to myself. Yuck! I really sounded like an old nag. I would have hated to have me for a teacher. That first tape helped me identify lots of poor teaching strategies and I have since taped myself at least once a week and don't mind sharing and discussing the tapes with others."

Having a friend or volunteer write an observation can be helpful, especially if the observer confines his report to objective data; what you and the children actually did and said. Subjective opinions ("She was nervous and should have been removed from the group") are of questionable value, especially if the observer is unfamiliar with your teaching situation. Suggestions can be helpful but the teacher should rely on her inner standards to assess the comments offered by friends, whether they are critical or flattering.

Use your co-workers and other professional colleagues as sounding boards. It's often helpful to toss out an idea you've been considering before you've become so committed to it or so ego-involved that you don't want to hear any criticisms. You can play around with ideas in the comfort and safety of your own imagination but how do they appear when these same ideas are reflected against someone else's perspective? You don't have to accept their point of view, but you can learn from it.

Keeping a diary can provide an excellent basis for introspection. Like the teacher who knew she would not share her tape recording with anyone, your diary can be your private affair. Keeping a record of your discomforts and how you felt can be a therapeutic experience. Most of us try to suppress the painful things that happen to us. We want to ignore the negative signs, hoping they are not true and will go away. Usually they don't. You can utilize and exploit these experiences.

Keep a record of situations that have made you uncomfortable or seem to reveal some lack of competence. Over a period of time you may see a pattern. Maybe an honest expression of your feelings toward aggressiveness is your problem; or perhaps children who whine really turn you off. A diary can help reveal some of your vulnerable spots and help you develop ways to deal with them.

Excerpt from a teacher's diary:
Thursday, May 8—That brat, Jonathan, got me so upset today I broke down and cried! I hate him. I wish he'd drop dead, or at least move away! He seems to sense that I have a hard time handling noisy aggressive boys. Too upset to write any more.
(Later, same day) I really had a good cry—took a long walk and sobbed. I felt so alone and helpless but I feel much better now. I don't recall ever crying so hard. It's a good release for my pent-up frustrations. I realized that I'm always telling the children, "It's all right to cry. It's OK to let people know how you feel," and here I am holding back all my feelings just because I'm afraid of being a failure as a perfect teacher! Well, I'll restrain myself appropriately, but tomorrow Jonathan is going to learn something about my honest feelings!

This teacher still had many moments of uncertainty and her teaching methods were revised many times, but she later wrote of this particular experience.

. . . for the first time I immersed myself totally in feelings of helplessness, anger, and frustration. I came out of that experience knowing that I could deal with those feelings and I may have many more experiences in my teaching that will lead to similar feelings, but I'm stronger for having dealt with them. I guess I've lost a lot of the fear of having to confront situations that bring about those feelings of helplessness. I think I'm much more honest and sympathetic and therefore more real and effective now than a year ago.

Not all of a teacher's insights have to come from negative and painful experiences. Equally important are those times when everything runs smoothly. Too often, a teacher will lose a good opportunity to learn from a positive, rewarding situation by simply viewing it as good luck.

When the day has gone well or some activity you planned and supervised turned out to be even more successful than you had hoped, do a mental replay and try to isolate and capture the exact combination of ingredients that will enable you to do it again. Perhaps it was the combination (or separation) of certain children, or the way you introduced the activity. Maybe you made your limits clear and reinforced them at appropriate times. It could be all these things or a combination of many others, but the time you take to debrief yourself will help you be clearer about identifying your teaching methods.

Talk aloud to someone else or to yourself about the high points and the low points of the day and ask how you might have handled the situation better or what you did to make it go well. Compare in retrospect your behavior and techniques with those of others. Learn to look at yourself and to be honest in confronting your own reality. Self-assessment through systematic methods such as those described can be highly rewarding.

Information gained through these self-monitoring techniques can be helpful only if you use this information for improvement and professional growth. It's no fun to see yourself in a negative light, nor is it useful to distort your self-image so that you delude yourself into thinking you're a great teacher.

Self-evaluation is most beneficial if the teacher can share her information with others who are striving to improve their teaching methods as well. Just as Weight Watchers set observable goals and applaud each other in a supportive manner for individual efforts and gains, teachers need also to share their concerns and be supportive. Too often, the work environment fosters competitiveness and individual achievement. Helping your colleagues to improve is not often rewarded.

Teaching in a competitive environment can be a lonely affair and many teachers report that one of the most important factors in job satisfaction is the friendliness and cooperation of the other teachers with whom they work. Students who first enter the field report that salary is one of the most important considerations in job hunting, but after a few years of experience, they place "compatibility of other teachers" above salary.

The task of self-evaluation requires determination, consistency, and a real desire to improve, but the teacher who develops systematic techniques to aid her in professional growth will realize one of the greatest satisfactions in teaching—the development of her inner resources. A teacher who is skilled in monitoring herself will have the confidence to make decisions based on accurate self-knowledge and thus be able to rely on her own inner strength and self-confidence to develop and use effective teaching methods.

Clues, be they subtle or blatant, do not themselves tell you all you will need to know to develop greater competence. The signals you get need to be sorted, assessed, and fit into a systematic framework, which will help you evaluate your performance. To evaluate means to place a value upon, to judge yourself against some standard of behavior that you value and wish to attain.

If children crowd around you, begging for your attention, you may feel pleased. But what do you do with this information? Perhaps the first question is to ask: Is this really what I want? This means that you must have a fairly clear idea of your goals for the children and for yourself.

Getting information about yourself is only the beginning. The next step may be the most difficult. It is the first phase of a continual, growing process. If the information pleases you, you still have the task of sorting out your own satisfaction from the more important questions about how this affects the children, influences your own growth and career, and supports the goals of the program and center. If it is painful news, you have a more difficult task of sorting out the pain from the other reality and deciding whether you need to try to change your behavior. Dwelling on popularity or on attack or criticism isn't really very productive. You need the information you have gathered to make decisions and take some action.

For example, if a parent complains to you that her child never brings home things that he has done in school, your initial reaction may be to feel guilty and to see to it that the child produces something to bring home. But on reflection you realize that this is not one of your goals. You want the children to do things for themselves, but for their parents only if they take the initiative to do so. Your response is to assess the information as relevant because it tells you that there is a dissatisfied parent. It does not suggest, however, that you should take steps to change your own behavior. The information about the parent's feelings toward you is useful only after it has been assessed against your own standards.

Or, if a parent compliments you by saying, "My girl really loves you. She talks about you all the time and always wants to be with you. She can hardly wait for the weekend to be over so she can come back to school. Her highest point of the day is when she sits on your lap at juice time." You may feel pleased at first and recognize later that the child may be more attached to you than she should be. You want to develop positive relationships with the children, but this one sounds as if you may have encouraged a dependency that is not to the best interests of the child. You recall that, indeed, this girl has such appeal that you find yourself doing things with her more than with other children. Perhaps other children are being neglected. Your initial response of pleasure and satisfaction turns out to be unreliable. By assessing information against your own professional objectives, you may or may not alter your own behavior to develop further competence.

To be useful, the information you get from monitoring your own behavior has to be put into a critical framework. That framework is a well-defined set of goals and objectives. What is it you really want *for* the children and what do you want *from* them? Have you thought out clearly what you want to achieve with the group and with individual children? And, especially, what do you want for yourself?

As you acquire experience, you accumulate a history of feedbacks, which gives you a sense of competence and self-esteem. You can't always depend upon opinions of others. You will learn to trust yourself more and more. You will be able to attend to messages from others but not be overwhelmed by them if they are not complimentary, or if they are too effusive. You balance what you hear against your own knowledge of yourself. Sometimes you will handle a situation very poorly. So does everyone else at one time or another. But that won't mean disaster since you know what your usual style can be and you can pick up the pieces and go on.

And there are times when the best and only thing to do is to hang on to your own sense of worth and competence and wait out the stormy situation you find yourself in. At such times, try to find a trusted friend or teacher to talk with. Allowing grievances to accumulate and fester is not usually very productive.

Setting Goals for Yourself

In a sense, the teacher of young children leads a double life. She has plans and goals for the children in her care, but she also has goals for her own personal and professional growth and career. These two sets of objectives are intermingled and rarely do they conflict. They are different, however, and both contribute to the professional behavior and success she seeks.

A student teacher complained that during her work day in the lab school a group of children always ran through the art area and disturbed the other children who were working quietly. "I tell them to stop running but they don't pay any attention." Some of her co-workers suggested she state her objectives in positive terms and tell why she wanted to achieve them. "I want the children to stop running through

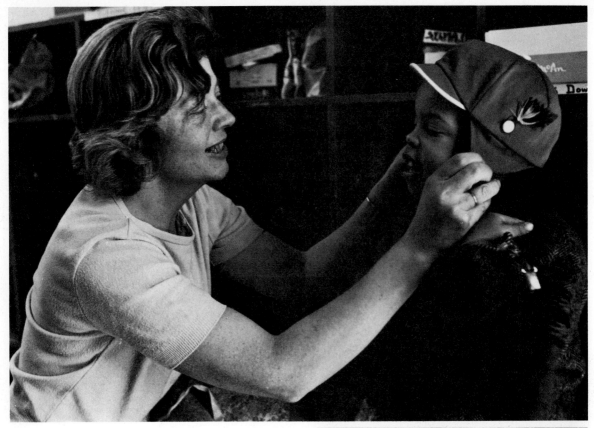

Setting Goals and Assessing Progress

the art area. That's my first and most important objective. I also want them to get involved in quiet, creative play. My reasons are simple—I don't want them to be noisy and disruptive and I also hate policing them by scolding. I think there's something wrong with my role as a teacher if I have to yell and scold all the time."

Further discussion resulted in her recognizing that running is quite natural for young children, and many of the children in this program did not have many opportunities to do much running in their neighborhoods. The teacher had no difficulty finding an appropriate place for them to run, outdoors, where she encouraged specific tasks requiring the use of large muscles ("run as fast as you can," "take giant steps backwards," "crawl on your tummies as fast you can—as slow as you can," "show me how you do somersaults," etc.).

She then set up some natural obstacles indoors by rearranging the art area so that the broken space would not be so conducive to running. In clarifying her objectives, she was able to rechannel the children's energies into acceptable activities and eliminated the need for "policing." She was more comfortable about setting limits she felt were reasonable so she could firmly and positively say, "I know it's fun to run, but I can't let you do it in here. There's a special place outside where you can show me how well you can run."

Setting goals and clarifying objectives helped this teacher acquire additional competence in her teaching techniques.

Whether you are concerned with your own objectives or want to identify those you set for the children in your class, you will find that it helps to be explicit and definite. Knowing what you want to accomplish and developing competence to get it done go hand in hand. Indeed, the ability to set goals and to be aware of what you are trying to do is a long step toward acquiring the skills you need to carry them out.

One instructor in a teacher-training program asked all the beginning students to list three wishes. Most of the wishes indicated a desire to "change the world," "to make the future brighter," "to make a positive impact on society through better teaching."

At the end of the first and second year of training these same students were given opportunities to make three more wishes. Many were revised to reflect shorter term goals such as "to graduate," "to find a good job with excellent pay," "to get married and have healthy children."

Revising goals does not have to mean that you lose sight of your dreams. Setting goals should be a continual process in which you revise, assess, and set new goals. Some of the immediate goals you set are realistic and have a good chance of success. But don't be afraid to set goals that are more difficult to attain, those that will challenge you and push you to achieve. Recognizing the difference in types of goals and being realistic is important, too. You probably won't change the world in a year or five years, but . . . .

No matter what kind of work you are doing now, relate some of your goals to present opportunities. If you are working in a program where you don't agree with the philosophy, use the opportunity to develop skill and gain competence in case you want to know more about it or use some form of it in the future. See how you can adapt the situation to fit your style. Try it on for size and reflect on how flexible you can be. Identify the areas of comfort and discomfort.

One teacher who wanted to have an open classroom where the children could be flexible in their activities ran into direct conflict with his school's philosophy that emphasized the children's development of cognitive skills. He reports, "These 5- and 6-year-olds were identified as 'slow learners' and I was expected to force-feed them on school-related skills. I was really discouraged at first and figured that my personal goal would have to be discarded, but then I gave it lots of thought and decided it would be worth a small risk to try to combine both goals. Besides, I knew that I would not be satisfied with my job for long if I felt that I had to defer all my ideas in preference for some externally imposed criteria.

"First I talked with the other teachers and agreed that the concern of the parents to have their kids succeed in school was quite understandable. I really didn't object to emphasizing cognitive skills. My conflict (and that of the parents) was in assuming that these skills couldn't be taught in less traditional ways. I knew for certain that my teaching would be successful only if it was natural for me."

The example of this teacher shows how he related goals to his present opportunities. If you are working with someone whose teaching philosophy differs radically from yours, take this as an opportunity to learn something about another approach, even though you do not expect to use it yourself. You will gain from understanding a different perspective.

Set some short-term goals that have definite time limits. You can assess progress more readily and keep closer check on your performance.

Cling tenaciously to your long-term goals. Events and experiences of the moment can buffet you so that you lose sight of the things you want to achieve in five or ten years. Occasionally review your long-term objectives and see how much closer you are to them at the time than when you first committed yourself to them.

Use short-term objectives to reach long-term goals. If you want eventually to be a head teacher or a director, set goals for yourself that will train you to accept more responsibility at some future time.

Setting goals and revising them through experience and feedback is a long-term, continual process. As you grow in experience and get information about your performance from your children and peers, use this as formative feedback to revise your aims and help identify what situations you want to place yourself in so that you can gain new experience and growth. This is a life-long task but a rewarding one.

Developing Objectives for Your Children

Identifying what it is you want for yourself is intimately related to the task of setting goals for the children with whom you interact. It is through monitoring progress toward these objectives that you can be aware of your success as a teacher. Clear statements of your aims make it possible for you to see in specific ways just how far a given child has progressed toward some goal you have set for him or have set with his help and cooperation. This procedure also helps you recognize your failures and problems and points out areas in which you may turn to others or to self-assessment techniques in order to clarify the problem and begin to plan ways to deal with it.

The primary task of education requires that some clear and specific goals be established for the group and for the children as individuals.

Some Comments About Self-Change

So far in this chapter we have discussed four steps in the quest for self-evaluation and change. The first was to recognize the need for self-evaluation and a continual renewal of competence, which are a necessary part of the professional life in early education. The second was to recognize how to seek and to read clues from others and from yourself about your performance. The third was to set goals and objectives for yourself and your class. The fourth was the evaluation of your own performance and behavior in light of what you want to do for yourself and for the children in your class.

These are essential steps in the self-correction and self-renewal process but they are not sufficient. The additional stage is one of working to change your behavior and to come closer to the level of competence and confidence you desire.

The Desire to Do Better

A significant part of the change process is included in the phases already described. A teacher who does not want to alter her style or develop new techniques will not bother to read the clues that tell her that change is needed. She will not be sufficiently concerned to set objectives and match her behavior against them. So if you have done these things, the most difficult part may be behind you. The fifth component, then, is the desire to do better in whatever you are doing.

Sometimes this is provoked by your own perceptions, sometimes by a discomfort that comes from criticism from others. A complementary part of this first stage, then, is a genuine, sometimes severe, discomfort with yourself and the way you are doing things now. By discomfort, we do not mean despair or feelings of worthlessness. Change and growth are best built on the foundation of a sense of worth and a feeling of competence, at least in some areas. You are not starting from scratch. You have competence and skills and confidence or you would not be in a job in a children's center or preschool. Too much confidence or too little both make change more difficult; a mixture of both is often an indicator that you are on your way.

Focus on Specific Ways to Get Help

Discomfort in itself is not enough. Nor are expressions of feelings sufficient. To see things in your behavior as a teacher that you genuinely want to change and to confront yourself with your own problems is not in itself necessarily helpful. We each have our own egos to protect and we stubbornly guard our sense of worth. To admit failure can be unproductive; to be forced to admit it can be damaging unless there are additional steps that lead to a way out of the self-doubt.

One of the most useful of these steps is to focus upon the exact nature of the skill or problem that you are confronting. A general sense of having handled a situation poorly won't help. Exactly what was it that went wrong? What did you do that turned off a parent? What did you say to a child that led to dependency? Or, what should you have said to avoid the temper tantrum? In short, the sixth step is to *focus* upon specifics. Resist generalized feelings of self-blame. Identify as precisely as you can what you are not doing or what you should or should not have done.

This is a process in which you may want help. A more experienced teacher, a supervisor, a friend can sometimes see the source of the problem before you can. Ideally, such an outside person can also give you some affective support and encouragement. It is difficult to change in an atmosphere of criticism and blame. You can learn to recognize situations in which change will be relatively possible and where it really cannot occur. If you are battling a supervisor or a group and feel that there is little encouragement to change and little sympathy for your point of view, it isn't likely that such a group can be of much help. You may occasionally find yourself in a situation that is not conducive to growth. Sometimes the only realistic alternative is to leave and find a more compatible place. This takes both judgment and good luck (jobs are not always easy to find) so be prepared for occasional times when the affective climate isn't supporting. Find a supportive person or group that will offer both constructive criticism and encouragement.

Some skills are more easily changed than others; some behaviors are more easily shed than others. Perhaps the seventh component of the change process is to assess the type of change you are trying to make. How fundamental is it? Does it involve your total personality? Or, is it a skill or habit that can be easily modified? Styles of relating to children or adults are examples of behavior that is persistent; learning how to teach geometric shapes is much easier to acquire. Learning how to play a few chords on a guitar and memorize some songs is a relatively easy task; learning to be more flexible in your techniques of controlling children is a long-term task. This component, then, is to assess the difficulty and nature of the changes you want to make.

Watch Others

One of the best ways to acquire new behavior is to watch someone who can do what you want to learn. Modeling someone else is a classic learning technique, and intensive research supports the confidence we have had in learning by watching. It is especially useful when you are ready for change—when you have convinced yourself that you really want to do something in a different way. Modeling gives you an opportunity to practice and to check your behavior against the model. Find a model; watch and practice, watch and practice. This is an example of the eighth component—find or create a learning situation.

There are other useful hints in establishing a setting in which to learn new behavior or change old patterns. One is to alter the physical environment and to establish new social patterns and relationships. The environment supports and reinforces your past behavior. Change the surroundings and you enhance the possibility of changing yourself.

Decide the Task

Another tactic is to divide the task into more manageable parts. If it is a skill, set short-range milestones and keep track of your progress. If it is a social behavior, try to keep careful track of how often you behave or don't behave a certain way. If you find that you interact conversationally with children by asking questions and that you make few statements of your own, begin to keep track of the number of questions you use in keeping a conversation going. Then keep track of the assertive statements you make. This helps you monitor yourself as you go along. In effect, you are dividing the task by making each comment a specific part of the total habit you want to change.

Changing is not an easy experience. Despite the cluster of books that offer suggestions about changing your life and the publicity about encounter groups and other social situations that are presumed to help, changing one's own behavior is one of the most difficult tasks any of us face. If it were easy, there would not be so many professionals devoting full time to assisting people deal with behavior that they would like to change. Our behavior, whether or not we like it, has served some purpose for us in the past. It has helped us avoid pain or to gain some reward. And, above all, it is what we know. It is comfortable and familiar. Behavior once established has its own inertia. It tends to resist change. But it can be modified, sometimes with ease, sometimes not. You may feel that you are taking a risk, exploring new areas about which you may be apprehensive. Willingness to take risks is part of the challenge of self-evaluation. It can be a rewarding venture.

The Social Responsibilities of Teaching

Teachers of young children are expected to help produce perfect adults. The hopes and dreams of our generation for a better future are expressed through the expectations we have for our children. Parents, supervisors, the church, the community all look to the teacher to provide the young child with the intellectual and social skills both to succeed in life and to solve social problems.

In a society that values diversity and individualism, the important socializing agents in each child's life—his home, family, church, friends—often send him confusing and contradictory messages. "Learn to get along peacefully with others!" "Defend yourself!" "Demand your rights!" "Make lasting relationships!" "Don't play too much with only one child!" "Have fun and enjoy yourself today!" "Compete!" "Cooperate!"

How then does a teacher bring some consistency to such a fragmented social world? Faced with changing priorities, inconsistent values, and many confusing alternatives open to the young, the teacher needs more than ever to be familiar with those significant people in the child's world who help shape his life—those people and institutions that are meaningful to him.

To be effective, the goals that the teacher sets for herself and her children must also reflect the child's larger community. The most useful goals are those that the community and the teacher share.

The teacher of today cannot indulge in the luxury of operating in an environment designed to recognize only her goals. She must be aware of a larger society; she must continually seek new information and sort out what is important; she must establish and reestablish priorities based on lasting values. And through it all, she must be prepared to face the painful prospect of change.

Through her expertise in the field, her concern for quality in teaching, her dedication to children and to her profession, the teacher will indeed be a determining force in shaping the future of our society.

Dear Mrs. C,

Now that I have been teaching for two years I promised myself and you that I would try to write down some of the things I learned since graduation. Remember when I first applied for the program and you asked me why I wanted to be a teacher? I said the same corny thing that everyone else said. "Because I love little children. They're so cute!" I think of that often, because in these past two years there have been many days when I didn't love little children and I definitely didn't think they were so cute! This may seem contradictory, but I think I'm a better teacher for being able to say that.

When I first started I thought I knew an awful lot about child-rearing and what was good for children, and in a way everything I learned in college was valuable, but now that I assess it all a bit more objectively, I can see that what I learned takes on a new perspective as I gain more experience. I see things differently now than I did two years ago. I guess that is what you would call growth. It hasn't been painless!

Now that I look back, I can tell beginning students that it takes lots of hard work, determination, and willingness to change to be a teacher. When I first started working I recall listening to myself and hearing only my biased opinions about how great my own training was and how others were wrong. I tolerated the parents and was critical of those who didn't agree with me. I'm still critical (justifiably so at times) but my listening is more and more concentrated on self-improvement. I seem to be reacting differently to what I hear.

Let me give an example: two years ago one of the things I hated most about going to work was 4-year-old Chris and his gang of friends who never failed to disrupt my whole day with their bad behavior—hurting other children, not minding me, etc. It was like a vacation when Chris was absent. I felt guilty about hating that kid and I spent a lot of time blaming his parents, his friends, and him for his poor behavior. I soon realized that there's a Chris in every classroom and in every year of a teacher's life. Oh, what a period of discouragement when I had to grope with that realization!

I still have a long way to go, and I can recognize the Chris's in my life (only this year it's Valerie). But I learned to use that list of ways a teacher can monitor herself, and to my surprise it really helped! Last week I taped Valerie and me during story time when I could count on her to be disruptive. Later on she and I listened to it and I was amazed at how I sounded. I didn't realize I was scolding and threatening so much and she seemed surprised to hear herself. We talked about feelings and she was much more perceptive than I gave her credit for.

Today I had one of the parents write an observation of my story time and we will read it out loud to the story group. It really helps the children and me to see ourselves in a more detached way. This may not make a big difference immediately, but I feel as if I am in control of my teaching techniques and what I do.

Just one item to add to the list of "How Do Teachers Monitor Themselves and What To Do With The Information." Tell them not to be afraid to take a chance and look foolish by trying something new and having others watch. I have discovered that all the teachers here feel helpless more often than we are willing to admit and we try to cover up by acting like we know what we're doing. Since we all started monitoring ourselves and using some of these observations for self-improvement, we feel less self-conscious and much more willing to talk about our need for help.

More next time . . .

Love,

Ali

P.S. I read some pages from my diary of two years ago. What a change! I'd forgotten my reactions to incidents that I see differently now—and, I'm sure, will see differently next year.

SUMMARY

This final chapter speaks to the teacher who wants to know how well she is doing and how she can improve her skills in a systematic way. She can get information about her performance from several sources and can begin a program of self-monitoring which can provide her with the information she needs to evaluate her own performance. This information is more useful if she has specific goals for herself and a desire to develop competence in areas where she is not doing as well as she would like. There are resources she can use to achieve the goals she has set for herself.

SOME POINTS
TO REMEMBER

1. A teacher on her own gradually learns, one way or another, what her strengths and weaknesses are.
2. With experience she can work out a set of standards by which she can evaluate herself.
3. Self-evaluation is necessary for professional growth and because of competition in the field.
4. The main sources of feedback for the teacher are responses of the children, colleagues, and parents.
5. The most important source of information is yourself.
6. There are several specific ways to be systematic in assessing

yourself: (1) keep a log of how you spend your time on the job, (2) use a videotape, or audio tape recorder, (3) have a friend or volunteer observe you, (4) use co-workers for feedback, (5) keep a diary of your personal feelings about your failures and successes.

7. The information that you obtain about yourself must be judged against what you want to accomplish.

8. The effective teacher has two sets of goals, one for the children, and another for her own professional career and growth.

9. Changes and growth are not easy, but there are specific techniques to help the teacher achieve her goals.

Credits

Cover photo by Michael McGuire
Drawings by Jeanette Kehl

CHAPTER 2 The Bettmann Archive, Inc. **p. 16**
Culver Pictures, Inc. **p. 16**
Culver Pictures, Inc. **p. 16**
Brown Brothers **p. 17**
Brown Brothers **p. 17**
Culver Pictures, Inc. **p. 17**

CHAPTER 3 Lucia Woods / Portogallo & Galate **p. 56**
Frank Siteman / Stock, Boston **p. 57**
Lynn McLaren **p. 69** (*photo essay*)
Robert Overstreet **p. 70** (*left*)
Jack Prelutsky / Stock, Boston **p. 70** (*right*)
A. J. Sullivan **p. 71** (*upper*)
Julie O'Neil **p. 71** (*lower*)
Mel Malinowski **p. 72**
Julie O'Neil **p. 73** (*upper*)
Cary Wolinsky / Stock, Boston **p. 73** (*lower*)
George S. Zimbel / Photo Researchers, Inc. **p. 74** (*upper left*)
George S. Zimbel / Photo Researchers, Inc. **p. 74** (*upper right*)
Marion Bernstein **p. 74** (*lower right*)
Julie O'Neil **p. 75**

CHAPTER 4 Mary M. Thacher / Photo Researchers, Inc. **p. 83**
Christopher Morrow / Stock, Boston **p. 84**
Marion Bernstein **p. 89**

CHAPTER 5 Doreen Croft **p. 110**
Mel Malinowski **p. 111**
Mel Malinowski **p. 119**
Marion Bernstein **p. 121**
A. J. Sullivan **p. 124** (*left*)
Laszlo Hege / Photo Researchers, Inc. **p. 124** (*right*)

Index

Bugental, D. E., 218
Burns, 349
Bushell, D., Jr., 195

California, 386, 391
Carson, R., 325
Casler, L., 18
Cazden, C. B., 229, 230
Central nervous system, effect of malnutrition on, 18
Certification requirements, for teachers, 50–51
Child abuse: teacher's reporting of, 93, 351; legislation against, 187
Child care, as school purpose, 54
Children: and media-transmitted information, 5; and technology, 5–6; socialization for change, 7–8; and physical or learning disabilities, 11; basic needs of, 19–20; and socio-cultural factors, 139–40; protection of rights of, 187; onset of speech, 220, 222–23; learning language, 224–25; growth of self-knowledge, 250–58; group membership and interaction, 259–60; racial and social-class awareness, 260–61; concepts of social relationships, 262–63; moral development, 263–66; patterns of social behavior, 266–77; regulating behavior and developing social competence, 277–83; evaluation of teachers, 369–70; and feedback for teachers self-evaluation, 400–402. *See also* Self-knowledge
Children's center, organizational structure, 60
Children's Lobby, 187
Child Study Association of America, 53
Child Welfare League of America, 53
China: self-awareness process for teachers, 399
Chinese: population, 57; and involvement of apprehensive mothers, 116; prejudice and discrimination against, 148–49; ranking of mental abilities in study, 162
Choking, 349–50
Church groups, enrollment policy, 55
City school system, administrative organization of, 149
Classification ability, acquisition of, 238–39
Clay, gaining physical knowledge from, 322–23
Cloward, R. A., 155
Cognitive achievement: and curricula, 25; growth of abilities, 233–35, 245; and the arts, 321–23

Cognitive-developmental view of education, 209–10
Cognitive goals: activities for achieving, 235–45; and physical knowledge, 236–37, 245; and logical knowledge, 238–39, 245; and seriation, 239–40; and elementary number concepts, 240–43; and concepts of space and time, 243–45; and the arts, 289, 292, 321–23; cognitive growth, 245
Cognitive skills, 207; and educability, 120–21; versus affective skills, 207
Colds, 342, 343
Coleman, J. S., 162
Colleges, 161; and training of nursery school teachers, 50
Comenius, J. A., 16, 171, 202
Commercial nursery schools, purpose of, 54
Common cold, 342, 343
Communicable diseases, and preschoolers, 344–45
Communication, and language, 217–19
Community colleges, and training of nursery school teachers, 50
Community control of schools: attempts to increase, 77–81, 182–83; responsiveness of schools to, 164; effects of shift to, 183
Community Coordinated Child Care, 164
Compensatory educational programs: growth of, 6; described, 11; federal guidelines for hiring teacher's aides, 42–43; purposes of, 54; enrollment policy, 55; early hopes for, 164–65; rating scale of emphasis, 213; and language development, 228–29
Conferences, teacher-parent, 107
Conflict, staff, and role expectations, 35
Conjunctivitis, 343
Content versus process, 207–8
Convulsions, 351
Coopersmith, S., 253
Cosby, B., 219
Cost-benefit analysis, demand for, 386
Crisis in the preschool: inevitability of, 329–32; potential sources of, 331–32; identification of, 332–33; analyzing of 333–39; psychological and social, 339–41; children's view of, 340; legal liability 352–57; *Fowler* vs. *Seaton.* 353–55; reduction of potential legal crises, 356–57; coping with, 357–61. *See also* Medical crises
Croft, D. J., 52

Kindergartens (*cont'd.*)
11; professional requirements for teachers, 51; growth of in United States, 188
King, C. S., 155
King, M. L., 155
Klaus, R. A., 23
Kohlberg, L., 265
Koos, E. L., 156
Krech, D., 18
Kugelmass, I. M., 18
Kung Fu, 314

Laboratory (demonstration) school, described, 11
Language: as basic channel of communication, 217–19; learning structure of, 224–27
Language abilities: growth of, 216–17; children's progress in, 222
Language development: correlation with motor development, 226; emphasis in early education programs, 227–29; and situational setting, 229
Language learning: by adults, 9; by deaf children, 222; by retarded children, 225–26; and socio-economic and cultural differences, 227–30; teacher's role in, 231–33
Languages: number identified, 220
Language usage: contrasts between home and school, 174; discrepancies between training programs and teacher behavior, 2, 18–19
Lansing, K. M., 309
Learning disabilities, children with, 11
Legal responsibility, 47, 352–57
Lenneberg, E. H., 220, 226
Lesser, G. S., 162
Letter recognition, testing of, 381
Levenstein, P., 131
Lewis, O., 153
Lice, 350
Licensing requirements: for nursery school teachers, 50–51; for schools, 58
Light, and emotional climate of school, 65
Linear ordering, concept of, activities to develop, 243
Locke, J., 17, 171
Logical knowledge: activities to develop, 238–40; use of arts in gaining, 323
Low-income groups: family as agent for early education, 6; effect of early intervention on cognitive performance, 24–26; parent-teacher

Low-income groups (*cont'd.*)
interaction, 113–14; home-based programs, 125–35; training women to be parent educators (Parent Education Project), 127–29; teacher's challenge in dealing with children, 140; families headed by women, 140; perspectives of mothers, 158; study of academic performance, 162; the deficit model, 171–72; criticisms of schools for low achievement of children, 176; early education programs, 194–202; issues differentiating programs of early education, 202–13. *See also* Early education; Head Start
Lyford, J. P., 172, 179

Malnutrition: and physical and mental development, 18; and behavior, 173
Mansfield, R. G., 352
Mass media, 5–6
Matching quantities, testing of, 384
May, M. A., 265
Measles, 345
Median family income, for blacks and whites, 152
Medical crises: illness and injury, 342; eye, ear, nose, and throat infections, 342–45; reportable diseases, 345; immunizations, 345; broken bones and head injuries, 345–48; severe injuries, 348; minor injuries, 348–50; miscellaneous medical problems, 350–52
Melting pot concept, 148–49
Mental abilities, ranked within cultural groups, 162
Mexican-Americans: population, 57; First Texas Conference for, 141; prejudice and discrimination against, 148–49; Tucson Early Education Project, 194–95
Middle-income groups, parental attitudes and children's orientation for school, 126–27
Miller, J. O., 27
Miller, L. B., 26
Minor injuries: cuts, 349; scrapes, 349; burns, 349; sand-in-eye, 349; nose-bleed, 349; abdominal pain, 349; choking, 349–50
Minority groups: family as socializing agent, 6; population, 57; academic achievement, 162; criticisms of schools for low achievement of children, 176; cultural differences and poor achievement, 174–75. *See also* Blacks; Racial awareness; Racial discrimination

Miseducation model, and failure of poor children to achieve, 175–76

Modeling and imitation, and modifying behavior, 280–82

Montessori, M., 169, 192, 200

Moral development: dimensions of morality, 263; acquisition of morality, 263–66; limits of comprehension, 264–66

Mother-Child Home Program (New York), 131–32

Mothers, and evauation of teachers, 368

Mother's Knee, School of the, 171

Mothers' Training Program (University of Illinois), 129–31

Motivation: to teach young children, 1–4; as component of educability, 120–21; extrinsic versus intrinsic, 210–14

Motor development, and language development, 226

Music: internal responses to, 298–302; activities and goals, 306, 315; integrating power of, 325–26

Naming objects from memory, testing of, 380

National Association for the Education of Young Children, 53, 136

National Education Association, Educational Policies Commission: 1960 recommendation for expansion of public early education programs, 9

National Laboratory on Early Childhood Education, 27

National Nutrition Survey, 173

Negroes, see Blacks

New Hampshire, minority-group population, 57

New Mexico, minority-group population, 57

New York City, study on achievement, 162–64

Nichols, I. A., 226

Nimnicht, G., 196

Noise, and emotional climate of school, 65

Nonverbal communication, 219

Nonwhite women, employment patterns, 153

North Dakota, minority-group population, 57

Nosebleed, 349

Number concept, activities to develop, 240–43

Nursery schools: description, 11; college-trained teachers, 50; commercial, 54; physical environment and goals of program, 63–67; community control of, 77–81, 82; liability under the law, 352–55; need for adequate reporting and re-

Nursery schools (cont'd.)
cording, 356; need for comprehensive safety measures, 356–57; need for realistic insurance coverage, 356, 357; coping with crisis, 357–61. See also Early education; Preschool

Oakland Preschool Program, 132–34

Observation, as formal method of evaluation, 374

Office of Child Development (Department of Health, Education, and Welfare), 53, 126, 136

One-parent families: and interaction with teachers, 105; informal conferences, 115

Open Education Model, 198–99

Open house, to involve parents, 109, 111

Ordering-sequencing, testing of, 383

Ordinal numbers, recognition and testing of, 384

Ornati, O., 142

Orphanage children, 19; compared to infants raised in nursing home, 20–21; effect of transfer to institution for mentally retarded women, 20–21, 22

Owen, R., 17

Owners of nursery schools: functions of, 46–48; legal responsibilities of, 352–57

Parallel sentence production, testing of, 384

Parent-Child Centers, 183, 185

Parent-child system, teacher as part of, 86–91

Parent co-ops: description, 11; requirement of parent participation, 55; funding, 59; organizational structure, 60; rating scale of emphasis, 212

Parent Education Project (Florida), 127–29

Parents: relations to teachers, 76–81; and early education programs, 76–81, 181–82, 187; interaction with teachers, 81–85; peer and friendship roles, 82; boss and employee roles, 82; as staff members, 82, 85; as home-based teachers, 85; role in teacher-parent-child system, 88–89; subtle competition with teachers, 95–98; dependence on teachers, 98; training centers for, 100; as source of enrichment, 100–101; isolation and non-participation, 104–6; encouraging their participation in goals of school, 106–12; attitude toward home visits, 114; involvement of fathers in preschool programs, 116–20; and educability of children, 120–22; interaction about intellec-

Records: "most useful," 38; to reduce dimensions of legal crisis, 356
Reinforcement, 281–82
Relative size, developing concept of, 240
Research: university-affiliated nursery schools, 55; as evaluation, 389–94; interdependence of evaluation and research, 389–90; goals of, 390–91; ethics of, 391–93; using results, 393–94
Res ipsa loquitur, doctrine of, 355
Resnick, L. B., 198
Responsibility, structure of, 33–66
Responsive Model, 196–97
Retarded children, language learning in institutions, 225–26
Rewards, use of, 194, 196, 197, 201, 211, 212, 281–82
Riles, W., 386
Ringworm, 350
Ripple effect, and psychological crisis, 341, 359
Role definitions: staff conflicts over, 35-36; assistant teachers, 36–40; teachers, 39, 40–41; teachers' aides, 41–43; volunteers, 44–45; administrators, 46–48
Role-taking ability, and social development, 256–58
"Room mother" system, to involve parents, 112
Rosenberger, E. F., 226
Rosenzweig, M. R., 18
Rousseau, J. J., 16, 202-3, 208
Rule-learning, 262–63, 278–79

Safety rules and measures, 351, 356–57
Samuel, E. L., 18
Sand-in-eye, 349
School: as agent of socialization, 7–8; as principal instrument for change, 148
Schulz, C., 219
Schwartz, J. B., 303
Scrapes, 349
Self-concept: and cognitive activity, 251; major sources of, 253–56; development of, 261; testing for, 382
Self-discovery, versus planned instruction, 208–10
Self-esteem: among disadvantaged groups, 156; and failure, 195; and success, 196; programs to build, 207; relation to self-concept, 251; major sources of, 253–56; development of, 261

Self-evaluation: developing history of teaching experiences, 398–99; feedback from children, 400–402; feedback from colleagues, 402–4; feedback from parents, 404–6; methods of, 406–9; setting goals and assessing progress, 410–11, 416–18; summary of steps in self-change, 419–22
Self-knowledge, 251–56; growth of, 250–58; role-taking ability, 256–58
Self-reliance, parental encouragement of, 123–24
Seriation, development of, 239–40
Sesame Street, 127, 314, 387
Severe injuries, 348
Sex-related behavior, 275, 276–77
Sex roles, 89–90, 91, 276–77
Sex-typing, 89–90, 91
Shipman, V. C., 98, 121, 157, 158
Sibling rivalry, 269
Simultaneous voluntary movement, testing method, 380
Site selection, as school, 47
Situational setting, and language, 229–30
Skeels, H. M., 20, 21
Skill: affective versus cognitive, 207; as route to self-esteem, 255
Skin diseases, 350
Skinner, B. F., 209–210
Social behavior: social interaction, 267; territoriality, 268–69; approach and influence behavior, 269–70; alignment, 270–72; aggressive behaviors, 272–73; persuasive behaviors, 273–75; age- and sex-related behavior, 275–77
Social change, and role of education, 5–6, 7–8
Social-class awareness, development of, 260–61
Social-class level, and patterns of ability, 163
Social competence, development of, 283
Social crises, 339–41
Social development: and nursery school, 54; and role-taking ability, 256–58; relationship of arts to, 324, 325–26
Socialization, 5, 310–14
Social relevance, early education, 9–14
Social relationships, concepts of, 262–66, 383
Social responsibilities, of teaching, 422–24
Social Security Administration, definition of poverty, 140
Social smiling, in twins reared apart, 18
Society for Research in Child Development, 53

Tuberculosis, 345
Tucson Early Education Model, 194
Twentieth Century Fund, report on poverty, 142
Twins: social smiling in, 18; onset of speech, 220
Tyack, D., 149

United States: social cleavages and role of education, 5-6; number of children in preschool programs (1972), 10; children under age 5, 48; projected need for trained personnel in early education, 48; as melting pot of different peoples, 148-49; unequal distribution of privileges and resources, 147-48; poverty in, 140-42
Universities: establishment of child-care facilities, 12; training for nursery school teachers, 50
Unobtrusive measures, in evaluation, 374-75
Upward Bound, 164

Values, conflict in, as base of psychological crises, 341
Verbal facility, testing for, 384
Visual discrimination, testing of, 381
Visual perception, testing method for, 381
Vocabulary, teacher's provision of labels, 321-22
Volunteers, role description, 44-45

Wachowiak, F., 304
Weight gains, of orphanage children, 19
Weikart, D. P., 23, 24, 25, 26, 126, 134
Weinstein, G., 176
Welfare programs, parental view of teachers, 113-14
Westinghouse Learning Corporation study, 10, 26, 28, 186
White House Conference on Children (1950), 9
White House Conference on Children (1970), 9
Willingness to learn, and effectiveness of teacher's efforts, 4
Wittes, G., 281
Women: patterns of employment, 151-52; earnings and formal education, 153. *See also* One-parent families
Woodworking, 304
Word meaning, knowledge of, testing for, 385
Working mothers, 10
Workshop meetings, and parent participation, 111-12; successful and unsuccessful, 115-16

Ypsilanti-Perry Preschool Project, 23-24, 25, 26, 134-35